Eschatology at the Beginning of the Third Millennium

Theology at the Beginning of the Third Millennium

Series Preface

Theology at the Beginning of the Third Millennium is a new series of theological monographs which seek to examine the *status quaestionis* of various sub-disciplines within the field of theology in this second decade of the third millennium and some half a century after the conclusion of the Second Vatican Council. While the impetus for the series has come from scholars at the University of Notre Dame (Australia), the Catholic Institute of Sydney, and Campion College (Sydney), contributors to the volumes come from a diverse array of theological academies. A feature of the series is the fact that although the majority of the contributors are situated within the Catholic intellectual tradition, scholars from other traditions are also welcome.

The various sub-disciplines which form the subject of each volume are examined from the perspective of scripture scholarship, fundamental, systematic and dogmatic theology, spirituality, historical theology, ecumenical and pastoral theology and the theology of culture. This is consistent with the Balthasarian metaphor that "Truth is Symphonic" and thus created by an harmonious integration of different disciplines or "sections" of the theological orchestra. Consistent with the charism of St. James the contributors share a high degree of respect for the deposit of the faith, a Johannine interest in integrating spirituality and mystical theology with dogmatic and fundamental theology, a Pauline sensitivity to the influence of the Holy Spirit, a Petrine interest in official magisterial teaching and, above all, a Marian disposition of receptivity to the Divine *Logos*.

Eschatology at the Beginning of the Third Millennium

EDITED BY
Kevin Wagner,
Peter John McGregor
AND
Danijel Uremović

☙PICKWICK *Publications* · Eugene, Oregon

ESCHATOLOGY AT THE BEGINNING OF THE THIRD MILLENNIUM

Theology at the Beginning of the Third Millennium

Copyright © 2025 Wipf and Stock Publishers. All rights reserved. Except for brief quotations in critical publications or reviews, no part of this book may be reproduced in any manner without prior written permission from the publisher. Write: Permissions, Wipf and Stock Publishers, 199 W. 8th Ave., Suite 3, Eugene, OR 97401.

Pickwick Publications
An Imprint of Wipf and Stock Publishers
199 W. 8th Ave., Suite 3
Eugene, OR 97401

www.wipfandstock.com

PAPERBACK ISBN: 979-8-3852-3849-1
HARDCOVER ISBN: 979-8-3852-3850-7
EBOOK ISBN: 979-8-3852-3851-4

Cataloguing-in-Publication data:

Names: Wagner, Kevin [editor]. | McGregor, Peter John [editor]. | Uremović, Danijel [editor]. | Naumann, M. Isabell [series editor].

Title: Eschatology at the beginning of the third millennium / edited by Kevin Wagner, Peter John McGregor, and Danijel Uremović.

Description: Eugene, OR: Pickwick Publications, 2025 | Series: Theology at the Beginning of the Third Millennium | Includes bibliographical references and index.

Identifiers: ISBN 979-8-3852-3849-1 (paperback) | ISBN 979-8-3852-3850-7 (hardcover) | ISBN 979-8-3852-3851-4 (ebook)

Subjects: LCSH: Eschatology. | Eschatology—History of doctrines. | Philosophy and religion. | Catholic Church—Doctrines.

Classification: BT821.2 W346 2025 (paperback) | BT821.2 (ebook)

VERSION NUMBER 12/02/25

Emphasis added to Scripture quotations.

Scripture quotations marked DR are taken from the Douay-Rheims Bible, originally translated from the Latin Vulgate by the English College at Douay and Rheims, and revised by Bishop Richard Challoner between 1749 and 1752. The text is in the public domain.

Scripture quotations marked NIV are taken from the Holy Bible, New International Version®, NIV®. Copyright © 2011 by Biblica, Inc.™ Used by permission. All rights reserved worldwide.

Scripture quotations marked NRSV are from the New Revised Standard Version, copyright © 1989, Division of Christian Education of the National Council of the Churches of Christ in the United States of America. Used by permission. All rights reserved.

Scripture quotations marked NRSVCE are taken from the New Revised Standard Version Bible: Catholic Edition, copyright © 1989 National Council of the Churches of Christ in the United States of America. Used by permission. All rights reserved worldwide.

Scripture quotations marked RSV are taken from the Revised Standard Version of the Bible, copyright © 1971 National Council of the Churches of Christ in the United States of America. Used by permission. All rights reserved worldwide.

Scripture quotations marked RSVCE are taken from the Revised Standard Version of the Bible: Catholic Edition, copyright © 1966 by the Division of Christian Education of the National Council of the Churches of Christ in the United States of America. Used by permission. All rights reserved.

Contents

Contributors | ix

Abbreviations | xii

Preface—*Danijel Uremović* | xvii

1. Eschatology at the Beginning of the Third Millennium | 1
   —*Andrew T. J. Kaethler*

2. Technology and Eschatology | 27
   —*Paul Tyson*

3. The Temporality of Eschatology: A Philosophical Analysis | 49
   —*Angus Brook*

4. Eschatological Victory or *Apokatastasis* of the Universe? Versions of Salvation from the Apocalypse of Peter to Maximus the Confessor | 67
   —*Adam G. Cooper*

5. The End-Times Throughout History: The Problem of the Year 1000 | 90
   —*Mario Baghos*

6. "Purgatory": An Approach Through Syriac Typology | 106
   —*Joseph Azize*

7. Human Persons Defined by Their End: Eschatology and Anthropology Within the Thought of Romano Guardini | 126
   —*Paschal M. Corby OFM Conv.*

8. *Imago Dei* as an Eschatological Promise: Genesis 1:26–27 in Light of Ratzinger's Augustinianism | 144
—*Tegha A. Nji*

9. Punishment in the Eschaton: C. S. Lewis's Imagination at the Service of Aquinas's Theory | 167
—*Christian Stephens*

10. Cosmos and *Contrapasso*: Subject, Sin, and Suffering in Dante's *Inferno* | 191
—*Danijel Uremović*

11. Reading Backwards: The Senses of Scripture and Eschatological Exegesis | 211
—*Susanna Edmunds OP*

12. The Resurrection of the Body and the Future of Creation | 233
—*Alenka Arko*

Contributors

Alenka Arko was born in 1966 in Ljubljana, Slovenia. She studied Eastern theology at the Pontifical Oriental Institute and theology at the Pontifical Gregorian University, where she earned her PhD. She is Professor of Systematic Theology at the Faculty of Theology, University of Ljubljana. Since 2014 she is a member of the International Theological Commission. Her studies focus mainly on cosmology, anthropology, and eschatology, with special emphasis on the church fathers and various aspects of Eastern theology and spirituality.

Joseph Azize has published in law, ancient history, and religious studies. His latest book, *Gurdjieff: Mysticism, Contemplation, and Exercises* (2020), deals with Gurdjieff's adaptation of hesychast spiritual techniques for the modern world. He has also published in Maronite and Syriac studies, where he is rehabilitating the ancient Semitic wisdom we call "typology" (reasoning by analogy from the revelation of God, whether in Scripture or creation).

Mario Baghos is Senior Lecturer in the School of Philosophy and Theology at the University of Notre Dame Australia. From 2018 to 2023, he was Adjunct Lecturer in Theology in the Faculty of Arts and Education at Charles Sturt University. From 2010 to 2017 and 2020 to 2022, he taught patristics and church history at St Andrew's Greek Orthodox Theological College. He has also lectured and tutored in the discipline of studies in religion at the University of Sydney. He has published broadly in the areas of Byzantine studies, patristic theology, and religious studies.

Angus Brook is Lecturer in Philosophy at the University of Notre Dame Australia. His research interests are Aristotle, Thomas Aquinas, philosophy of technology, philosophy as a way of life, and metaphysics.

Adam G. Cooper taught theology and church history at Catholic Theological College, Melbourne. Prior to this, he taught Greek at the University of Durham, patristics at the Melbourne Institute of Orthodox Christian Studies, and theological anthropology, historical theology, and moral theology at John Paul II Institute for Marriage and Family. His books include *The Body in St Maximus the Confessor* (2005), *Life in the Flesh* (2008), *Naturally Human, Supernaturally God* (2014), and *Holy Eros: A Liturgical Theology of the Body* (2014).

Paschal M. Corby is a priest of the Order of Friars Minor Conventual. He is Lecturer in Moral Theology and Bioethics at the University of Notre Dame Australia (Sydney), with particular interest in areas of anthropology, moral conscience, and the thought of Joseph Ratzinger. He is the author of *The Hope and Despair of Human Bioenhancement: A Virtual Dialogue Between the Oxford Transhumanists and Joseph Ratzinger* (Pickwick, 2019).

Susanna Edmunds is a member of the Dominican Sisters of Saint Cecilia. Currently based in her home city of Sydney, she serves as the Dean of Studies at the Seminary of the Good Shepherd and teaches at a local Catholic high school. She holds an MPhil from the University of Notre Dame Australia with her thesis titled "Aquinas's Four-Fold Senses of Scripture: Harnessing Metaphysical Analogy for Theological Exegesis."

Andrew T. J. Kaethler is the Dean of Studies at the Buckfast Institute, Buckfast Abbey, Devon, United Kingdom. Kaethler specializes in theological anthropology, particularly in the work of Joseph Ratzinger and Alexander Schmemann. He has published in various journals, including *Modern Theology, New Blackfriars, Pontificia Academia Theologica*, and *Logos: A Journal of Catholic Thought and Culture*. With Sotiris Mitralexis he has co-edited two volumes, the latest titled *Mapping the Una Sancta: Eastern and Western Ecclesiology in the Twenty-First Century* (2023). His most recent monograph, *The Eschatological Person: Alexander Schmemann and Joseph Ratzinger in Dialogue*, was published with Cascade in 2022.

Tegha A. Nji is a priest of the Diocese of Buea, Cameroon. He recently completed his PhD in systematic theology at the University of Notre Dame, Indiana. He is now serving as Assistant Professor of Theology at the Graduate School of Theology of the Augustine Institute, Florissant, Missouri. Recent publications include "Odozor and Benedict XVI on the Question of Moral Objectivity: A Morality Truly Christian and Truly African?" in *Continuing the Quest for Morality Truly Christian, Truly African* (2025); and "Primacy of the Logos in the Formation of Missionary Disciples: Re-Centering Participation and Dialogue for Africa and the World," in *Journeying Together with God: Proposals for Implementation of the Final Document of the Synod on Synodality* (2025). He is now revising his dissertation, "The Burden of Election and Modern Individualism: Toward a Ratzingerian Critique," for publication as a monograph.

Christian Stephens is Lecturer in the School of Philosophy and Theology at the University of Notre Dame Australia. He is currently a doctoral candidate, exploring Aquinas's understanding of idolatry and its contemporary significance.

Paul Tyson is an Honorary Senior Fellow with Historical and Philosophical Inquiry at the University of Queensland. He works largely in applied metaphysical theology, recently centered around attempting to rethink what we mean by "science and religion."

Danijel Uremović studied philosophy and theology at the University of Notre Dame Australia. He is set to commence his doctoral studies at Saint Patrick's Pontifical University in Maynooth, Ireland. His interests include theology and culture, theology before and after Vatican II, liturgical theology, and metaphysics in the Scholastic tradition. He currently resides in Zagreb, Croatia.

Abbreviations

1 Sent.	*Commentarius in I Librum Sententiarum: De Dei Unitate et Trinitate*
2 Sent.	*Commentarius in II Librum Sententiarum: De Rerum Creatione et Formatione Corporalium et Spiritualium*
AB	Anchor Bible
ACCS	Ancient Christian Commentary on Scripture
ACW	Ancient Christian Writers
Amb.	*Ambigua*
ANF	*Ante-Nicene Fathers*
Ang	*Angelicum*
Apol.	*Apologeticus*
Aug	*Augustinianum*
b.	Babylonian Talmud
Bapt.	*De baptismo*
Ber.	Berakhot
BETL	Bibliotheca Ephemeridum Theologicarum Lovaniensium
CCC	*Catechism of the Catholic Church*. 2nd ed. Vatican City: Libreria Editrice Vaticana, 1997
Cels.	*Contra Celsum*
Civ.	*De civitate Dei*

Comm	*Communio*
Comm. Cant.	*Commentarius in Canticum*
Conf.	*Confessionum*
Crat.	*Cratylus*
CSEL	Corpus Scriptorum Ecclesiasticorum Latinorum
DH	Denzinger, Heinrich, et al., eds. *Compendium of Creeds, Definitions, and Declarations on Matters of Faith and Morals.* San Francisco: Ignatius, 2012
DivThom	*Divus Thomas*
Doctr. chr.	*De doctrina christiana*
Ep.	*Epistula; Epistulae*
Faust.	*Contra Faustum Manichaeum*
FOTC	The Fathers of the Church: A New Translation
Fug.	*De fuga in persecutione*
Gen. imp.	*De Genesi ad litteram imperfectus liber*
Gen. litt.	*De Genesi ad litteram*
Gorg.	*Gorgias*
Haer.	*Adversus haereses* (*Elenchos*)
Hist. eccl.	*Historia ecclesiastica*
Hom.	*Homilia; Homiliae*
Hom. 1 Reg.	*Homiliae in I Reges*
Hom. Lev.	*Homiliae in Leviticum*
HTR	*Harvard Theological Review*
Ign. Rom.	Ignatius, *To the Romans*
Inf.	*Inferno*
JTS	*Journal of Theological Studies*
LCL	Loeb Classical Library
Marc.	*Adversus Marcionem*
Menaḥ.	Menahot
NBf	*New Blackfriars*

NICNT	New International Commentary on the New Testament
NPNF¹	*Nicene and Post-Nicene Fathers*, 1st ser.
NV	*Nova et Vetera*
Or. Bas.	*Oratio in laudem Basilii*
OrChrAn	Orientalia Christiana Analecta
Or. Graec.	*Oratio ad Graecos (Pros Hellēnas)*
Paed.	*Pedagogus*
Par.	*Paradiso*
ParOr	*Parole de l'orient*
PATH	*Pontificia Academia Theologica*
PBC	Pontifical Biblical Commission
Pecc. merit.	*De peccatorum meritis et remissione*
PG	Patrologia Graeca [= *Patrologiae Cursus Completus: Series Graeca*]. Edited by Jacques-Paul Migne. 162 vols. Paris, 1857–86
PGL	*Patristic Greek Lexicon*. Edited by Geoffrey W. H. Lampe. Oxford: Clarendon, 1961
Phaed.	*Phaedo*
Phaedr.	*Phaedrus*
PL	Patrologia Latina [= *Patrologiae Cursus Completus: Series Latina*]. Edited by Jacques-Paul Migne. 217 vols. Paris, 1844–64
Princ.	*De principiis (Peri archōn)*
Purg.	*Purgatorio*
Res.	*De resurrectione; De resurrectione carnis*
Resp.	*Respublica*
Retract.	*Retractationum libri II*
RRRCT	Ressourcement: Retrieval and Renewal in Catholic Thought
SC	Sources chrétiennes
SCG	*Summa Contra Gentiles*

SP	*Sacra Pagina*
Spect.	*De spectaculis*
Spir. et litt.	*De spiritu et littera*
St	*Studium*
ST	*Summa Theologiae/Summa Theologica*
StPatr	*Studia Patristica*
t.	Tosefta
Theol	*Theologica*
Tim.	*Timaeus*
TLZ	*Theologische Literaturzeitung*
Tract. ep. Jo.	*In epistulam Johannis ad Parthos tractatus*
Tract. Ev. Jo.	*In Evangelium Johannis tractatus*
Trin.	*De Trinitate*
TS	*Theological Studies*
VC	*Vigiliae Christianae*
VCSup	Supplements to Vigiliae Christianae
WBC	Word Biblical Commentary

Preface

DANIJEL UREMOVIĆ

Perhaps no discipline within Catholic theology can appear as troublingly speculative as that of eschatology. The study of the "final things"—death, judgment, hell, (purgatory), and heaven—is, of its nature, a study of realities beyond the experience of those still living. Even where the biblical data is corroborated by private revelations or occurrences nearing death, the ultimate and definitive experience of these states belongs properly to those who have made the transition from this world to the next. Because of this, little, it would appear, can be fairly and fruitfully said concerning those things that are yet to come or be undergone.

The words of St. Paul, indeed, seem to affirm as much: these *novissima*, the apostle says, "no eye has seen, nor ear heard, nor the heart of man conceived" (1 Cor 2:9 RSV). The saint's words, insofar as they might serve an eschatological principle, appear to confine our reflection on the "final things" to mere speculation, if such does not itself overstep the boundary of epistemic humility.

At least this might seem the case, were these coming realities not "those which," St. Paul continues, "God has prepared for those who love him." Mystery necessarily marks the study of eschatology, for human concepts remain limited in their power to adequately explain realities divine. And yet, the apostle's truism serves as a reminder that the final things are not beyond the content of study, contemplation, and prayer, but remain bound up to both a divine plan ("what God has prepared") and a human response (by "those who love him"). Despite the limits of human language and intellection, the "final things" cannot be swept under the rug of guesswork, but must rather be appreciated according to their most radical meaning for man. A divine plan mindful of the human creature cannot be given over in toto to speculation.

Granting this, however, eschatology, not unlike various other fields of theological study, regularly enjoys an air of having been definitively laid out as far as the content of revelation permits. Between the above speculation and the limited "nonnegotiables" of doctrine, however, arise the deeper questions of what these fundamentals reveal about God and man. While the stage has, in this sense, been long ago readied by centuries of theological development, it is recalling the *dramatis personae*—God and man—that perhaps remains the central task of eschatology in the third millennium.

This collection of essays, the fifth installment in the Theology at the Beginning of the Third Millennium series, can perhaps be viewed as an example of a collective effort to trace matters seemingly speculative back to both their divine source and human site of meaning. Such a pursuit would appear to align well with the notion of theology (*sacra doctrina*) outlined by the Angelic Doctor when he states: "All things are treated in sacred doctrine under the aspect of God, either because they are God himself, or because they refer to him" (*ST* q.1, a.7, c.; author's translation). Despite the variety of themes and questions taken up in these chapters, their authors can be seen as concerned less with end-time datings, topographies of hell, or a metaphysics of resurrection than with the christological center of these realities, and the deepened eschatological awareness that this center opens up. Of particular concern throughout these chapters are the divergent paths that a deficient eschatological awareness has historically trod.

Andrew Kaethler's opening chapter introduces some of the contemporary concerns felt by an eschatology that is "no longer the storm center of theology." In his overview of postconciliar eschatology and its fascination with mortality, temporality, and universal salvation, Kaethler shows that what remains decisive is not the "shadow of death" but eschatology as the "shadow of Christ."

While the horrors of communism or the injustices addressed by liberation theology might seem distant concerns for younger readers or those within Anglophone settings, the technologically driven permutation of this same immanentism is surely familiar to them. **Paul Tyson**'s chapter alerts us to this pervasive (indeed, seemingly omnipresent and omniscient) force of technology that threatens to usurp the place of God, and even offers its own alternative vision of salvation.

The burning concerns noted by Kaethler find a focused treatment in the chapter by **Angus Brook** concerning the human experience of mortality and temporality. Beginning with the biblical categories of *chronos* and *kairos*, Brook explores how Aquinas's vision of God and creation better accounts for the experience of human finitude than Heidegger's distinction between authentic and inauthentic temporality. From here, the Liturgy of the Hours, as the particular example of this chapter, reveals how "living in the light," more than Dasein's "being towards death," opens up for man his true eschatological horizon.

Beyond the more contemporary themes of the above-mentioned chapters, **Adam Cooper** and **Mario Baghos** both highlight, with reference to patristic questions, eschatology's age-old need to be continually re-centered on Christ. Cooper's examination of the Apocalypse of Peter and the works of Maximus the Confessor shows how the millenarian and universalist interests in the former gave way to greater affirmations of the mercy of God and human dependence upon him in the latter. Similarly, Baghos's review of the millenarist question highlights the historical deviation away from the ancient awareness of God's eschatological presence within the liturgy, above and beyond concerns of calculating the end-time. While the flow of history had been the clearest answer to the controversy, popular fascination along similar lines can perhaps find a sobering freedom in the wisdom of the Fathers traced out by Baghos and Cooper.

Similar patristic notes resound in **Joseph Azize**'s study of purgatory in the Syriac typological tradition. Alongside the various differences identified by Fr. Azize between the Latin and Syriac styles, his suggestion that typological categories might supply for what is wanting in analytical ones is but another possible means by which eschatology in the third millennium might refocus its gaze upon its ultimate subject.

The words of St. Paul in 1 Corinthians, uniting divine plan and human purpose, take root particularly in the chapters by **Paschal Corby** and **Tegha Nji**. Father Corby's study of Romano Guardini identifies the *exitus-reditus* of the divine Logos as the same path taken by man as he moves towards his ultimate destiny. The Augustinian (and Bonaventurian) influences flow into Fr. Nji's treatment of the *imago Dei* in the thought of Ratzinger. Casting a similar eschatological light upon man, Fr. Nji shows how the person made in God's image and likeness is already shot through with the arrow of eschatological finality.

Beyond the more (markedly) philosophical or theological voices, however, **Christian Stephens**'s chapter on Lewis's *The Great Divorce*, and my own on Dante's *Commedia*, draw from the insights of two literary classics. Stephens's study exposes certain deviations within the modern understanding of the eschaton as something not arbitrarily determined, but undergone in proportion to the dispositions of the individual. My own chapter suggests a similar convergence of sin, subject, and suffering in hell, there against a backdrop of divine presence and order (rather than absence and chaos).

Turning to the sacred page, the presentation of eschatological exegesis by **Susanna Edmunds OP** seeks to recover the neglected role of anagoge, not only for such obvious (though, as she demonstrates, forgotten) beneficiaries as the book of Revelation, but for the entire biblical canon. By grounding exegesis in a metaphysics of analogy (with Christ as the prime analogate), Sr. Edmunds helps bring out the christological shape of anagoge.

Finally, **Alenka Arko**'s treatment of resurrection situates the human—and indeed, cosmic—longing for eternity within the singular resurrection of Christ. Against reductive views of the resurrection that place the accent on man's spiritual being, she demonstrates how the Risen Lord, who "became flesh" and "makes all things new" (John 1:14; Rev 21:5 RSV), has destined not only man in his corporeality but all creation to a share in eschatological fulfilment.

From Ephrem and Maximus to Heidegger and Marx, the eschatological question is evidently a "timeless" one, not simply on account of its otherworldly subject matter but by virtue of the most ancient longings in the heart of man that give rise to this question: longings for justice, truth, transformation, eternity. Even without the explicit rubric of a "convergence theology" in a call for papers, it can be easily ascertained where the key questions of eschatology in the third millennium are felt to lie. It is our sincere hope then, that the latest addition to this Third Millennium series might prove a meaningful aid and contribution to this task of presenting anew both eschatology's christological center and the radical meaning it has for man.

1

Eschatology at the Beginning of the Third Millennium

Andrew T. J. Kaethler

Make strong my tongue that in its words may burn
One single spark of all Thy glory's light
For future generations to discern.[1]

It could be said that the twentieth century is theologically the century of eschatology. Figures such as Albert Schweitzer, C. H. Dodd, Rudolf Bultmann, Oscar Cullmann, and Karl Barth loom large. "Balthasar described eschatology as the 'storm center of the theology of our times.'"[2] The famous line from Barth's *Epistle to the Romans* summarizes this eschatological focus: "Christianity that is not irreducibly eschatological has entirely and altogether nothing to do with Christ."[3] While Barth, Bultmann, Cullmann, and Schweitzer are not Catholic theologians, their work and focus affected theology in toto.

In contemporary Catholic theology eschatology is no longer the "storm center," but there are three aspects of eschatology that are receiving significant attention, namely, death, temporality, and *apokatastasis* (universal salvation). In what follows I will explore current theological engagements with these three aspects and examine the various positions

---

1. Dante, *Par.* 33:70–72.
2. Müller, *Doctrine of Creation, Eschatology*, 128; quoting Balthasar, *Word Made Flesh*.
3. Barth, *Epistle to the Romans*, 314.

through a broadly Ratzingerian/*ressourcement* christological lens, in which "eschatology is the shadow cast by Christ."[4]

DEATH

> Death is swallowed up in victory.
> O death, where is thy Victory?
> O death, where is thy sting? (1 Cor 15:55)[5]

The great continental philosophers made death a cornerstone of their work. Fittingly, the philosophers were working within a philosophical eschatology, an eschatology "in which the eschaton is postulated or posited from within a system; its warrant is the logical structure of that system, and it is related to present life and history as the 'end' that ensures their shape. This is the characteristic form of post-Enlightenment eschatology."[6] The eschatological context is where these philosophers fleshed out and developed their theories of freedom. Closely wed to philosophy, it is no surprise that twenty-first-century theology continues to wrestle with questions of death, history, and freedom. Philosophy is not the only impetus. The natural sciences have also pushed theologians to think through the meaning of death. If death is at the heart of the cosmos, astronomically with the connection of birth and death of stars and the development of the solar system,[7] and evolutionarily with the necessity of death for the development of species,[8] is there a theological approach that resonates with an affirmative outlook on death?

Memento mori (remember that you must die) can have a morbid tenor, and its association with medieval Christianity does not always help. In this context it is linked to the four last things—death, judgment, heaven, and hell—three of which are seemingly ominous. Existentially, the gravitas of *memento mori* is experienced at the Ash Wednesday liturgy: "Remember that you are dust and to dust you shall return." Yet, our finitude and our ever-progressing movement toward death is not without hope. Within theology hope is always related to death because hope arises from the other side of the coin, namely, life. As historical creatures our existence is marked by both sides of the coin. Death is part

---

4. Kaethler, *Eschatological Person*, 137.
5. All Scripture passages in this chapter are from the RSVCE.
6. Wolfe, "Eschatological Turn," 57.
7. Filippenko, "Made of Star-Stuff."
8. Jaeger, "Biochemical Perspective."

of life and death points to life. In this sense death is a positive reality. Writing about Michel Henry's phenomenology of life, Christina M. Gschwandtner highlights that death, as a subject, can act productively by weaning us from "a definition of the human in terms of powers and capabilities. Realizing the 'pathos' of life also means to recover its connotations of *passivity*: we receive life, we do not give it to ourselves."[9] All our powers and capabilities are "rooted in our condition as sons of Life."[10] While we are certain that each one of us will die, we are also certain that we were born. Life must precede death.

Understood aright, *memento mori* should be anything but morbid, for it is death that reawakens us to life, and we need to be awoken because the modern person goes through life as a somnambulist. We work and play and are caught up in the hustle and bustle of life; yet life and death are not contemplated and thus do not shape our living. The killing of the unborn is one such example. Secular societies have sanitized abortion by reshaping the narrative. Abortion is no longer coupled with a sense of death. Rather, the narrative is that abortion concerns women's health and is essential healthcare. Have we forgotten that we too were once born, that we too passively received life from our mothers? How do we awaken to life? Jesus paradoxically says, "Truly, truly, I say to you, unless a grain of wheat falls into the earth and dies, it remains alone; but if it dies, it bears much fruit" (John 12:24). If one wants to live, one must first die. This is the sacramental logic highlighted in baptism—death leads unto life.[11]

On the surface life and death seem to be most obviously a biological reality, in which "from a biochemical perspective, the process of life cannot be separated from the notion of death."[12] Nevertheless, it is difficult for the empirical sciences to define life and death. For example, medical science only understands life through death because its starting point is death: "the epistemologically normative body for modern medicine is the dead body."[13] According to Jeffrey P. Bishop, modern medicine can only give a

---

9. Gschwandtner, "How Become Fully Alive?," 63; emphasis in original.

10. Gschwandtner, "How Become Fully Alive?," 64.

11. Noting how Ratzinger takes up St. Augustine's conception of sacrifice, Uwe Michael Lang writes that sacrifice "can refer not only to objects but also to persons; hence a consecrated person who dies to the world in order to live for God alone can be considered a sacrifice" ("Transforming the World," 666–67). With an understanding of sacrifice being related to death we can see that death leading to life is a sacramental logic that can be applied to all the sacraments.

12. Jaeger, "Biochemical Perspective," 14.

13. Bishop, "On Medical Corpses," 166. Luc Jaeger highlights the challenge of

wanting definition of life as mechanical function.[14] Conor Cunningham paints a bleaker picture, arguing that from a materialist's position there is no difference between death and life. In fact, from a materialist approach death is impossible; death is merely the relocation of matter. A metaphysical approach that recognizes transcendence is necessary in order to speak about death and life.[15] "Pure matter," writes Cunningham, "is radically dependent, fully inherent, and it is only through the priority of *ipsum esse* that we understand the profound concert between matter and form, indeed portions of matter, so to speak, are mere 'stuff,' but as Hegel rightly said, who can find such stuff: no form, no matter."[16]

Matter needs form; the two are intimately intertwined. The metaphysical or spiritual element of life and death cannot be compartmentalized without eroding the natural sciences. If we are to conceptually think or speak of reality, or, for that matter, be persons, we need the language of the soul. Life concerns the soul, for the soul is that which gives form to matter, making it a living reality. If life in this deepest of senses is beyond matter, then biology does not have the ultimate word on the subject. Hence, Bishop appropriately writes that "for the Christian, the resurrected body is not only epistemologically normative, it is also the formal and final cause of our material bodies."[17] Here we can see how eschatological 'elements'— (immortal) soul, death, and resurrection—concern the present and are necessary for the concept of life and death. Death is key to life, to *living*. It "attests to the transformation of finitude (resurrection of the body)."[18]

Death surrounds us but in an extrinsic manner. Our only experience of death is in the third person: she dies, not me. Thus, death is a detached experience, but it does not need to be. Through love we can cross the third person barrier and have a real experience of death. By opening us to the other, love enables us to experience mortality. To be aloof from death, then, is to cheat oneself of one of the profoundest insights of personal reality, or, to put it more starkly, it is to deny the other. Death is connected to love, and the person who loves experiences deep and

---

biologically defining living and nonliving matter: "A clear distinction between living and non-living matter becomes more and more elusive as researchers investigate the possible bridges that link chemistry to biology.... One aspect that contributes to the difficulty in defining life at an organic level is that it is a process rather than a pure substance" ("Biochemical Perspective," 16).

14. Bishop, "On Medical Corpses," 167.
15. Cunningham, "Life Before Death?," 122–23.
16. Cunningham, "Life Before Death?," 132–33.
17. Bishop, "On Medical Corpses," 178.
18. Falque, "Suffering Death," 46.

awful loss in death.[19] Ways of remaining aloof, however, have developed over the centuries with the commercialization of the funeral home.[20] A concomitant of this is the increase of people choosing cremation over burial.

Since 1963 the church has released four key documents on the topic of burial and cremation.

> Each of these documents urges, strongly prefers, and earnestly recommends that Catholics continue the reverent and unbroken (*piam et constatem*) practice of burying the bodies of the faithful dead. The documents allow for cremation, but in language that is guarded and implicitly censorious: the Church does not forbid cremation; she does not object to it where there is an upright motive, based on serious reasons; she makes allowance for it in cases of necessity, and so on.[21]

Unfortunately, argues Patricia Snow, this led to an almost all-out acceptance of cremation, which undermines one of the key markers of Christianity: the unity of body and soul. This unity is based on the central tenant of Christ's bodily resurrection from which our understanding of the body derives.

With the crucified body of Jesus stretched out upon the cross, the entombment of saints, and open caskets at funerals, Catholicism bears witness to the wholeness of bodily existence. The bodies of the incorruptibles confirm the intimate union of body and soul and that eternal life begins here and now. The open casket bears witness that we no longer live in fear of death. Whereas cremation hides death and decay. "If God has not come in the flesh, then the flesh can be thrown away. If the flesh can be thrown away, then God has not come in the flesh. The attack can come from either direction, but the goal is the same: uncreation."[22] Those in favor of cremation emphasize that God is omnipotent and can put us back together at the resurrection of the dead. But omnipotence is not under question. The question is, will we align ourselves with God and with how he created us, or will we test God's power? Burying the dead is a testimony to the resurrection. How we treat the bodies of the deceased reveals our beliefs about Christ.

In "Life and Death in the Age of Martyrdom" John Behr sees martyrdom as a clue for making sense of the significance of death. The

19. Pieper, *Death and Immortality*, 12.
20. See Delorenzo, *Work of Love*, 24–32.
21. Snow, "Body and Christian Burial," 399.
22. Snow, "Body and Christian Burial," 407.

martyr Ignatius of Antioch reverses our usual ways of speaking of death: "'Hinder me not from living,' by seeking to stop my martyrdom; 'do not wish me to die' by trying to keep me 'alive'!"[23] In martyrdom one enters into Christ and the *via dolorosa*, and if Christ is the perfect human—*ecce homo*—the man fully alive, then to enter into Christ's way of suffering and death is to be fully alive. The paradigm of the living human being is the martyr. It is the martyr who is most free, for he has freely chosen to enter into the life of Christ. In this free act the martyr matures and becomes fully human. "In this way, then, the desired intention of God expressed in Genesis, to make a human being, is realized, when the creature brought into existence gives his or her own 'fiat'—'Let it be!' For every other aspect of creation, all that was needed was a simple divine 'fiat'—'Let it be!' But for the human being to come into existence, required a creature able to give their own 'fiat!'"[24] Behr points out that martyrdom fits within the original pattern of creation, which always included salvation within itself. "Jesus Christ is not plan B."[25] It was always intended that the human person would offer himself as a living sacrifice, to find his life in another. God "uses our mortality to educate us of our finitude, our embodiedness, and our earthiness, and so enables us, finally, to receive that which we don't have in or from ourselves, that is, life."[26]

Concluding Thoughts on Death

I have described how contemporary scholars have thought through the various modes of death in a positive manner. By affirming life through death, they highlight the goodness of embodied existence. Death is not set out as escapism. At the outset of this section, I mentioned the importance of death for astronomy and other natural sciences: "Without death the world would be a static world with no development, there would be no emergence of new forms of life."[27] In a broad manner what I have presented here fits with this approach to death. However, death takes on different connotations with the human person than it does with the rest of creation.

The human person certainly exists together *with* the rest of creation, but he is distinct, for his life also exists within a moral fabric. It is

23. Behr, "Age of Martyrdom," 80.
24. Behr, "Age of Martyrdom," 91.
25. Behr, "Age of Martyrdom," 93.
26. Behr, "Age of Martyrdom," 95.
27. Novello, "Life Out of Death," 116.

because we are moral creatures that St. Paul asserts, "For the wages of sin is death, but the free gift of God is eternal life in Christ Jesus our Lord" (Rom 6:23). The moral element—death as a punishment (Gen 3:19)—in contemporary theology has been pushed to the periphery. The importance of death for our development as human creatures who are on the way to becoming little christs should not be downplayed. At the same time, death should not be naturalized as this would elide St. Paul's claim concerning the wages of sin. Death is not merely a natural event but is experienced as a violence, which goes against all our impulses. *Natural* means fitting. Is it fitting that man dies and his soul is torn apart from the body? Death is unnatural in this sense, and yet it is indispensable for concrete existence because it is punishment for something that I deserve, i.e., the consequence of my sin. What is sin? Josef Pieper writes,

> We have the capacity to turn away, in clear consciousness and on the basis of a free decision, from what we know to be the true meaning of our life—this is an inescapable fact about ourselves. "Sin" is just that, that alone. "Sin" in the strict sense is not any kind of misdemeanor, violation, infraction of rules; it is deliberate turning away from God, although it may manifest itself in a thousand concrete forms.[28]

Where does man go, if he turns away from God? God *is*; all creation exists in and through him. Therefore, he absurdly goes toward incomprehensible nothingness—the mystery of iniquity. Death is God's means of startling fallen humankind from such an absurdity. So too are all the little "deaths"—illness, failure, loss, etc.—preceding bodily death. These little deaths or breakdowns that "together make up our one death, are, therefore, not just random annoyances and not just blind biological occurrences; rather, they are ultimately God's action upon us, through which he tears away from us our selfish, self-seeking, egotistical existence so as to reshape us according to his image."[29] This is what Pieper means by punishment. Punishment is always just, otherwise it is not punishment. It is always for our good, for breaking us away from our egotism so that we can find life in God. Divine punishment is not juridical but ontological.

In the moral sense death is unnatural, but ontologically it is natural. The human person does not have life within herself but receives it. If she possessed it within her own nature, she could never lose it without losing her own self. Prior to the fall, immortality was to be a gift that would have enabled the spiritual soul to be so infused with the body that

28. Pieper, *Death and Immortality*, 57.
29. Ratzinger, *Dogma and Preaching*, 250.

the body could not dissolve against man's will. Since it was to be a gift it would not have been *natural*; however, the gift would have been fitting to man's being. With this in mind, Pieper maintains that the only way to face death or to avoid falling into a state of revolt against creation because of death is to accept death as punishment; death is a moral reality. Only this acceptance can make death meaningful.

Pieper's conception of punishment fits with the other approaches that have been set out without overlooking or underplaying God's part or our part and the role of sin in death. Together with the other formulations we are given a full picture of death, both its horror and its glorious transformation in Christ. Such a picture can provide a robust response to current ethical questions regarding transhumanist desires to circumvent death.

TEMPORALITY

And so my mind, bedazzled and amazed,
Stood fixed in wonder, motionless, intent,
And still my wonder kindled as I gazed.[30]

Writing about the Second Vatican constitution *Dei Verbum*, Brian E. Daley notes that "it is an acknowledgement of the legitimacy of the more historically conscious, spiritually and liturgically oriented, and existentially focused style of thought, marked by the call to 'return to the sources' in the scriptures and the Fathers, which in the 1940s and 1950s had been pejoratively branded as 'the new theology'—*la nouvelle théologie*."[31] The elements of *nouvelle théologie* (*ressourcement* theology) that Daley describes mark the twenty-first century, in toto. Hence, the historically conscious approach set out by *ressourcement* theologians, a clear change from the Baroque and manualist tradition that dominated the nineteenth and early twentieth century, marks current eschatological thought.[32] Articulating the historical approach, Marie-Dominique Chenu posits that "the theologian works with a history. His 'data' are not the nature of things, or the timeless forms; they are events, corresponding to an *economy*, whose realization is bound to time.... The *real* world

---

30. Dante, *Par.* 33:97–99.
31. Daley, "Knowing God in History," 334.
32. Ruddy, "*Ressourcement* and *Enduring* Legacy," 186.

is this one, not the abstraction of the philosopher."[33] With an emphasis on history it is only natural that theologians have taken a conceptual step backward and developed a theological sense of temporality itself, including time and history.

Questions of temporality belong under the umbrella of eschatology. Temporality finds meaning in history, and for history to be history there must be an end (eschaton). Without an end there is just endless flux and no narrative. Eschatology infuses temporality with meaning. Furthermore, if eschatology is seen as the shadow of Christ (Christ is the kingdom), then the incarnation, which is eschatological, is at the heart of temporality.[34] Reflecting on Balthasar's *Theology of History*, Ratzinger writes,

> The humanity of Jesus, which placed him in the midst of that age, is presented to us in every line of the Gospels; and we have, in many respects, a clearer and more living picture of him than was vouchsafed to earlier periods. But this "standing in time" is not just an outward cultural and historical framework, behind which could be found somewhere or other, untouched by it, the supra temporal essence of his real being; it is much rather an anthropological state of affairs, which profoundly affects the form of human existence itself. Jesus has time and does not anticipate in sinful impatience the will of the Father. "Hence the Son, who has time, in the world, for God, is the point at which God has time for the world. Apart from the Son, God has no time for the world, but in him he has all time." God is not the prisoner of his eternity: in Jesus he has time—for us, and Jesus is thus in fact "the throne of grace" to which at any time we can "with confidence draw near" (Heb 4:16).[35]

Ratzinger presses the point that our temporality is not a barrier to God. Without denying the Creator-creature distinction, Ratzinger contends that by its nature finiteness is in relation to the Infinite One. It is not because of who the human person *is* but because of who the human person is *in relation to* that gives to the person her very being. Jesus has time for us because he *is* near to us. The "*is*-ness" of this statement is Trinitarian. God is a relation of persons and because of this the Son's time for us is who he *is*. In Balthasar's words, "It is therefore vain to look for a

---

33. Marie-Dominique Chenu, "Position de la théologie," in Daley, "Knowing God in History," 337.

34. Ratzinger, *Eschatology*, 32–35.

35. Ratzinger, *Introduction to Christianity*, 317–18.

contradiction between the Son's temporal and eternal form of existence or to seek within his creatureliness for any opposition between a lower sphere within time in which he receives and acts and a supreme 'eternal' sphere in which he enjoys calm, self-sufficient possession of himself."[36] Any philosophy that argues that time is a mere "mode of perception" to be explained away in light of a "supratemporal sphere" must be rejected.[37]

Following Ratzinger and Balthasar, temporality should be understood through relation and not the inverse. The ground of all reality is not time but relation, i.e., the Trinity.[38] Temporality is understandable only in Christ. John P. Manoussakis posits that "without him who comes there is neither coming nor becoming, neither advent nor adventure, there is no event (in its etymological sense as that which has come, the outcome). He doesn't come, therefore, because there is time, rather, if time exists it only exists because he who comes is coming."[39] Time exists within the Son; time exists within relationality and not the inverse. José Granados words this well: "Time obliges us to understand life as something open, as something relational. In such a horizon we can see time as an opening to others, as a form of personal existence that is open to communion, and that in this way rises above itself."[40] Too often time is construed as if it is its own thing, and the result is that God is imprisoned by his eternity.

Time is sacramental. Time connects us with God. Easter reveals that all time "leads from the Father's love to his final embrace."[41] Time is good. Balthasar notes that "God intended man to have *all* good, but in his, God's time; and therefore, all disobedience, all sin, consists essentially in breaking out of time."[42] The most recent book that takes Balthasar's claim seriously is John E. Thiel's *Now and Forever: A Theological Aesthetics of Time*. Thiel maintains that time is a crucial dimension of creation and thereby a medium of God's grace. Taking this into account, he sets out a speculative theology of time, suggesting that time continues in heaven. While this is a vision that differs from St. Thomas's beatific vision, it is not without theological support.[43] Thiel points out that Ratzinger sets

---

36. Balthasar, *Theology of History*, 34.
37. Balthasar, *Theology of History*, 34–35.
38. Kaethler, *Eschatological Person*, 116–34.
39. Manoussakis, "Cup of Time," 457.
40. Granados, "First Fruits," 18.
41. Granados, "Risen Time," 13.
42. Balthasar, *Theology of History*, 36–37.
43. See Steinkerchner, "Time in Heaven." Steinkerchner argues that time will

out his own vision of this in *Eschatology: Death and Eternal Life*.[44] In a christological tenor, Ratzinger argues that death does not separate us from history. Ratzinger writes, "This truth consists, first and foremost, in the indestructible relation which it posits between human life and history. The incarnation of God brings this truth onto a deeper plan where it becomes the theological assertion that in the man Jesus God has bound himself permanently to human history."[45] In addition, in 1992 the International Theological Commission followed a similar path:

> If time should have no meaning after death, not even in some way merely analogous with its terrestrial meaning, it would be difficult to understand why Paul used formulas referring to the future (*anastesontai*) in speaking about their resurrection, when responding to the Thessalonians who were asking about the fate of the dead (cf., 1 Thess 4:13–18). Moreover, a radical denial of any meaning for time in those resurrections, deemed both simultaneous and taking place in the moment of death, does not seem to take sufficiently into account the truly corporeal nature of the resurrection; for a true body cannot be said to exist devoid of all notion of temporality. Even the souls of the blessed, since they are in communion with the Christ who has been raised in a bodily way, cannot be thought of without any connection with time.[46]

Heaven is not a "place" for angels. Death does not strip us of our humanity. We remain creatures. Christ himself did not shed his humanity in the ascension but brought it, and thereby us, into the Trinitarian relation. "The flesh of Jesus, therefore, is never his alone, but rather bears in itself a bond to all of humanity and all of creation. The absolute plenitude of his flesh, a glory that admits of no further increase, would only be accomplished when the body of Jesus, in its glory, would have assumed the body of the Church, and, in this body, the entire cosmos."[47] The resurrection of the body affirms our embodied creaturely existence. Certainly "redemption is not incompatible with the condition of creatureliness."[48]

---

manifest differently in the eschaton in that we may be able to move back and forth within time.

44. Thiel, *Now and Forever*, 18.
45. Ratzinger, *Eschatology*, 187.
46. International Theological Commission, "Current Questions in Eschatology."
47. Granados, "First Fruits," 26.
48. Thiel, *Now and Forever*, 20.

Thiel pushes his speculation in a direction that is shaped by a universalist vision. He writes,

> The beauty of eschatological time lies in its capacity to offer an infinite horizon for resurrected persons to act in order to negotiate morally the sin they have committed and the sin they have suffered, and to do so in the vast proportions of the communion of the saints before and after the Last Judgement . . . heavenly time opens a graceful duration of endless proportions within which to imagine the workings of heavenly virtue capable of reconciling the eschatological heritage of sin.[49]

Commendably, Thiel argues that time is not a metaphysical lack but gracious plenitude. Time should not be seen in a dialectic relation to eternity but should be understood analogically. "Time is a creaturely measure of eternal movement that shapes the bonds of divine love—the mutual love of the Trinitarian persons and the love of God for the world."[50] In heaven time will remain as a created good and will be continuous with the present eschatological now. Yet, it would be time that is void of death; "dead time has passed away";[51] therefore, there would no longer be boredom, nor would there be any correlation to loneliness or trauma.

There is a profundity to Thiel's vision, but it loses balance and topples over. He argues that the effects of sin continue in the eschaton.[52] After all, the Resurrected Christ continues to bear the scars of his crucifixion (John 20:24–29). Heaven is a place where everyone is given an infinite amount of time to redress wrongs of these lingering wounds. While ongoing redemption and virtue formation are appealing, Thiel's vision is too circumscribed by our present existence.[53] Undoubtedly Christ's "wounds share in his glory," but does that mean that we will all be infinitely marked by our wounds?[54] Will John the Baptist embody his icon and walk around

---

49. Thiel, *Now and Forever*, 23.
50. Thiel, *Now and Forever*, 79.
51. Thiel, *Now and Forever*, 165.
52. Thiel, *Now and Forever*, 169.
53. Imaginative thinking is important for eschatology. "When the afterlife is no longer strained to be imagined, fleshed out in our longings, envisioned as a dramatic commingling of *philia*, *eros* and *agape*, its architecture recedes only to the depository of thoughtlessness, the unthought festivity that secretly begins the turn away from God more primordially than any atheistic philosophical system. All atheisms begin in a misunderstood human nature, and that error of all errors originates in the loss of Heaven, for our human nature is realized only in our permanent home" (Gilson, "Heaven and Transcendental Meaning," s.vv. "Death and Grief: Unexpiated Tears").
54. Thiel, *Now and Forever*, 170.

in heaven carrying his own head? Will Maximus the Confessor be lacking his tongue (and his right hand), a heavenly mute who forever is incapable of verbally communicating? Can we not imagine heavenly time but without the lingering effects of sin?

Regardless of Thiel's shortcomings, I agree that a depiction of heaven as static is not fitting for us as creatures. It does not preserve the Creator-creature distinction, and it does not maintain a consistent sacramental or relational logic. Alexander Schmemann put it well, "God revealed and offers us eternal Life and not eternal rest. And God revealed this eternal Life in the midst of time—and of its rush—as its secret meaning and goal. And thus he made time, and work in it, into the sacrament of the world to come, the liturgy of fulfillment and ascension."[55]

Concluding Thoughts on Temporality

Robert Barron notes, "At the Second Vatican Council, the ressourcement movement won the day. Many ressourcement theologians were *periti* at the council, shaping both the substance and style of the documents, all of which were approved with overwhelming support."[56] Working out the vast implications of the *ressourcement*-shaped council, twenty-first-century theologians are thinking with a refined sense of temporality. This has implications for how we understand salvation history, everyday life, and even the eschaton itself. Rethinking time in light of Christology, so that it sits within the framework of relation, also has implications for how we commune with our fellow Christians and the communion of saints.[57] Similar to the topic of death, much of twenty-first-century eschatological reflection on temporality is oriented toward theological anthropology and works broadly within a relational ontology.[58] These conceptions and the concomitant questions bleed into other areas. One of these is authority. St. John Henry Newman awoke the church to the relationship between history and doctrine with his notion of doctrinal development, and this needs to be further expanded, particularly in regard to the authority of church documents.[59] Authority can no longer be thought of in an extrinsic and atemporal manner. Arguably it needs to be conceived

---

55. Schmemann, *For the Life*, 65.
56. Barron, "'New Ressourcement'?," 2.
57. See Delorenzo, *Work of Love*.
58. By relational ontology I mean a Trinitarian ontology in which person is understood in terms of relation and not simply substance.
59. An example of this is Levering, *Newman on Doctrinal Corruption*.

of in a manner that resonates with a relational ontological approach that is grounded in an eschatological understanding of temporality. A proper approach needs to sail between Scylla's historicism and Charybdis's unchanging eternity.

UNIVERSAL SALVATION

"I began to think and to think is one real advance from hell to Heaven."[60]

"O Beautiful angel! Lay down your sword.
It is not for you to judge
The nature that I raise up
And have desired to redeem.
It is I, named Jesus,
Who will judge the world!"[61]

In 2019 David Bentley Hart published *That All Shall Be Saved: Heaven, Hell, and Universal Salvation*, and the effects of this book are ongoing.[62] The book is filled with invective; straw man, false dilemmas, and ad hominem arguments abound alongside personal pathos. Although backed by almost no sources, Hart's standing as a brilliant academic means that the book cannot be ignored. That said, Hart's claims are not unique. He heavily depends on Gregory of Nyssa and tips his hat to the Scottish writer George MacDonald. In many ways, Hart's book is simply an extended version of MacDonald's argument for universal salvation.[63]

The core of Hart's argument is summarized by the following rhetorical question: Could we freely and justly love an omnipotent and omniscient God who created a world in which a rational soul could condemn itself to everlasting torture?[64] Hart answers, if Christianity demanded adherence

---

60. Defoe, *Moll Flanders*, 265.

61. St. Thérèse of Lisieux, *Pious Recreations*; quoted in Balthasar, *Dare We Hope*, 81.

62. Roberto J. De La Noval suggests that today universalism "has ceased to be merely the opinion of an eccentric minority and has acquired more mainstream legitimacy, not only among many Christian academics and swaths of the laity who often hold an implicit universalist faith, but even among prominent church authorities" ("Divine Drama," 201).

63. See "Justice" in MacDonald, "Unspoken Sermons."

64. Hart, *All Shall Be Saved*, 13.

to belief in a God so described, he would conclusively have nothing to do with it.[65]

Hart hangs his hat on a particular philosophical peg and has created a system in which everything must hang on this peg or be rejected. Part and parcel of this is his conception of God. Hart posits that

> God is not an "entity." Neither, for that reason, is he some sort of particular object that one could choose or reject in the same way that one might elect to drink a glass of wine or to put it out in the dust. He is, rather, the fullness of Being and the transcendental horizon of reality that animates every single stirring of reason and desire, the always more remote end present within every more immediate end.[66]

To add to this, "God is not only the ultimate reality that the intellect and the will seek but is also the primordial reality with which all of us are always engaged in every moment of existence and consciousness, apart from which we have no experience of anything whatsoever."[67] In view of this, Hart argues that if God is everything and all rational thought finds itself in God alone, how can we miss our end, which is the only end. As the fullness of being, God is not one option among many. Rationally speaking, there is nothing else to choose. Any rejection of God on the part of the human creature must come down to gross ignorance. Divine permission of a self-damning ignorance is absurd. Would God who is all good and loving allow a finite creature to ignorantly make an irrational decision that would condemn him forever to the fiery abyss of hell?

God is the fullness of being and the end toward which our freedom moves. We are only free when we move toward God. Furthermore, we are created in such a manner that we are necessarily inclined to seek happiness. If this is the case, is it not "natural" that we should necessarily attain happiness? Could a God of love and mercy hold us accountable for our inherited limitations? Would not an omnibenevolent, omnipotent, and omniscient God order reality so that all shall be saved?

Hart has a deterministic intellectualist view of freedom.[68] "For Hart, compatibilism and a rejection of the free will defense necessitate universal salvation. Since all men are oriented by nature to the Good and would infallibly choose the Good if they were presented with it, it is impossible

---

65. Hart, *All Shall Be Saved*, 208.
66. Hart, *All Shall Be Saved*, 183.
67. Hart, *Experience of God*, 10.
68. Brotherton, review of *All Shall Be Saved*, 1051.

for any truly free and rational creature ultimately to reject God."[69] This raises an even greater problem. On one hand Hart's universalism is a solution to the problem of evil because everything ends well. On the other hand, he has removed the importance of history[70] and exacerbated the problem of evil:

> Why doesn't God save us all at the beginning? Why didn't he confer upon us whatever perfection eschatological salvation implies when he created us? Why the wait, God? . . . If he could, and he is not impeded by anything—for what could impede an omnipotent God?—he ought to have already done so, that is, he ought to have directed my will and my actions in such a way so that there would be no sin and no evil, no pain that I suffer or cause others to suffer, if this is his will.[71]

As previously set out, Hart is overly committed to a system of thought of his own making, a perennial danger for theologians who have a capacious intellect.[72] Karl Rahner's succumbs to the same thing with his endeavor to reconcile ontology and history. Ratzinger argues that Rahner's

> attempt fails because he tries to create an airtight system that explains the whole. Any such explanatory system pushes freedom out of the picture. Since there is, and should be, a spiritual tension between history and being, and because Christianity is grounded in freedom, there can be no all-embracing Christian synthesis. Ratzinger writes, "The key thought of a Christian philosophy and theology would, therefore, have to be freedom—that true freedom that includes also the nondeducible and hence excludes perfect conceptual cohesion."[73]

The parallels with Rahner and Hart are obvious. Hart's rationalism erases "the spiritual tension between history and being." To put it differently, "as with many arguments within this text [*That All Shall Be Saved*], one has

---

69. O'Neill, review of *All Shall Be Saved*, 1059.

70. "And, frankly, I have no great interest in waiting upon God, to see if in the end he will prove to be better or worse than I might have hoped" (Hart, *All Shall Be Saved*, 103). Manoussakis points out that waiting is nothing less than history itself ("Salvation à la Hart").

71. Manoussakis, "Salvation à la Hart," 8–9.

72. See Manoussakis, "Salvation à la Hart," 4.

73. Kaethler, *Eschatological Person*, 100–101; quotation from Ratzinger, *Principles of Catholic Theology*, 170.

the feeling that Hart is pushing the *analogia entis* to its breaking point. At times, he seems to push it straight into univocity."[74]

Hart's description of God is beautiful, but it is one sided and incomplete. Essentially, he defines God as *Logos* but without a robust Christology. The church fathers used the philosophical language of *logos* but transformed and extended it. For example, in the story of the burning bush they saw that God is the God of the philosophers. God is being himself—YHWH, I am who I am (Exod 3:14–15). Yet God is personal. He is the God of Abraham, Isaac, and Jacob. This is not Aristotle's God, the unmoved mover. God *personally* sends Moses. The personal is amplified in the ultimate revelation, Jesus Christ. Christ is the *Logos* who reaches out to us as a person (John 1:1–4). Jesus Christ is the fullness of being who loves, *as* a person, *us* who are persons. Because Jesus Christ is the *Logos*, for Christians

> the aim is different from that of the philosopher seeking the concept of the highest Being. The concept is a product of thinking that wants to know what that highest Being is like in itself. Not so the name. When God names himself after the self-understanding of faith, he is not so much expressing his inner nature as making himself nameable; he is handing himself over to men in such a way that he can be called upon by them. And by doing this he enters into coexistence with them; he puts himself within their reach; he is "there" for them.[75]

Hart does not include this "handing himself over" in the conception of God that he gives us in the book. Hart's philosophical approach overshadows the christological paradox: fully God and fully man; fully *Logos* and fully personal. Mats Wahlsberg writes,

> The question is, however, why could God not be both an object of potential choice or rejection, and the fullness of Being? This, of course, is a very paradoxical idea, and it would be appropriate to follow Hart in pouring scorn on it, were it not for the fact that divine revelation tells us that it is true. Through the Incarnation, which is the paradox at the heart of Christianity, God clearly showed that he wishes to relate to us in accordance with the logic of personal relations. In Bethlehem, he made himself an object of potential choice or rejection. Apparently, then, God wants us to reach our telos—to come to Him who is the fullness

---

74. O'Neill, review of *All Shall Be Saved*, 1058.
75. Ratzinger, *Introduction to Christianity*, 134.

of Being and the transcendental horizon of reality—by freely choosing to become friends with Christ.[76]

The last critique is that the premise of Hart's argument is based on a false dilemma. One is either an infernalist or a universalist. The either-or glosses over the nuances and misrepresents the position of many theologians and philosophers. For example, Eleonore Stump argues that

> as Dante presents Aquinas's understanding of the Christian doctrine of hell, hell is founded on God's love. It is not a place where God exacts endless retributive punishment from those whose sins do not merit what they receive there. It is the condition of those who reject the love that God bathes them in—to the extent to which they will allow it. The offer of God's love is there for every human person always, but the joy of union between God and those who are open to that love cannot be undermined by someone else's self-exclusion from that love and joy.[77]

God cannot be held captive to an unrequited love, nor does an unrequited love change God. He remains love and can do nothing other than love. Thus, hell is that state of existence in which one is loved by God but refuses to love him in return. Indisputably this is not an infernalist position.

I have critiqued Hart's universalist claims, but he is not without his defenders, theologians who are faithfully seeking to wrestle with the question of universalism in relation to the living tradition of the church. There is a certain irony in this because Hart claims "for himself that extraordinary authority (historically restricted only to synodal proclamations of the Church) of knowing the proper and improper readings of the Scriptures and so to be able to judge which of the Church Fathers read it faithfully or not?"[78] Unlike Hart, these Catholic authors do not position themselves as ultimate arbiters of the tradition. For example, R. Trent Pomplun highlights the ambiguity that marks specific Latin words used in the magisterial documents. By way of illustration, he argues that apart from "later theological accretions, the term *damnatio* refers strictly to the sentencing, not the sentence itself. . . . *Supplicum*, another term for punishment . . . refers to the act of kneeling, often to receive punishment, but just as often to beg for mercy. . . . Even *poena*, which is everywhere rendered 'pain' or 'punishment,' can mean 'price,'

---

76. Wahlsberg, "Problem of Hell," 67.
77. Stump, "God of Love," final para.
78. Manoussakis, "Salvation à la Hart," 4.

'payment,' or 'recompense.'"⁷⁹ Yet, the punishment following judgment is characterized by magisterial documents in terms of *aeternitas* and *perpetuitas*, which seem to clearly remove the possibility of holding to the eventual redemption of all souls. Again, Pomplun demonstrates that there is no univocal definition of such terms. Albert the Great, Duns Scotus, and Bonaventure use these terms in a variety of ways:

> It is perfectly in keeping with the Latin to say that hell's *poenae aeternae* last an *aevum*—or in Greek an *aiōn*—that is to say, they last a finite eschatological measure that we cannot calculate ourselves. We may rest assured—and tremble—that God, being infinitely just, has determined their duration accordingly. We may also pray that in dying to sin in faith, we may be saved from this terrifying eschatological trial.⁸⁰

Like words, documents and doctrinal statements need to be (re)interpreted. Justin Shaun Coyle thoughtfully lays out the challenge of interpretation that theologians must confront. He admits that there are doctrinal statements that unambiguously articulate eternal punishment. Nevertheless, the question persists, should these statements be redefined or reinterpreted? After all, there is historical precedence for doing this, and in regard to fundamental doctrinal issues. "Take, for example, the anathema which closes the Nicene Symbol. It anathematizes whoever confesses that the Son differs from the Father by either *hypostasis* or essence (ἢ ἐξ ἑτέρας ὑποστάσεως ἢ οὐσίας). Here Nicaea's original historical meaning—trading as it does on a middle and neoplatonic conflation between *ousia* and *hypostasis*—just obviously isn't Chalcedon's (to say nothing of Constantinople II or III)."⁸¹ Universalism is not in the church's teachings, but perhaps it should be reintroduced. Since there is "no clear teaching against interpreting *de fide* doctrine to support universalism," the Catholic theologian is left to his work. "Our task as Catholic theologians is not first and last 'getting it right.' No, our task is to submit what we *take* to be right to the magisterium's scrutiny. Most will, as a result, sink Peter-like into the waves as they disembark to follow the Lord's call. But who wouldn't judge the risk worth the attempt to take his hand?"⁸² This segues into Balthasar's *Dare We Hope "That All Men Be Saved"?*, a book that precedes Hart and his followers.

---

79. Pomplun, "Heat and Light," 528.
80. Pomplun, "Heat and Light," 529.
81. Coyle, "May Catholics Endorse Universalism?," sect. 3.
82. Coyle, "May Catholics Endorse Universalism?," final para.; emphasis in original.

Balthasar's engagement with the question of eternal perdition raises similar questions to Hart. Like Coyle, he is creative and takes a theological risk. Unlike Hart, Balthasar's position remains agnostic; he rests in the incomprehensible mystery of God. Balthasar argues that the church has been led by the nose by St. Augustine who, unlike fathers such as Clement of Alexandria, Gregory of Nyssa, Didymus the Blind, Gregory Nazianzen, and Maximus the Confessor, held with absolute certainty not only the reality of hell but also of its numerous inhabitants. "His [St. Augustine's] campaign was directed not only against the presumptuous hope of the great Church Fathers mentioned above that Christians, even when they were grievous sinners, would not need to have any fear of final condemnation. This had to be corrected. It is only regrettable that the great man, to whom posterity owes so much, did not do that with the limits laid down by the Gospel."[83] In short, Saint Augustine "throws sacred history out of balance by centering it on Adam instead of Christ."[84]

The difference of opinion among the fathers reflects the variance within the New Testament itself. Balthasar lets Scripture speak for itself rather than synthesize it to fit his preferences. He writes, "it is generally known that, in the New Testament, two series of statements run along side by side in such a way that a synthesis of both is neither permissible nor achievable: the first series speaks of being lost for all eternity; the second, of God's will, and ability, to save all men."[85] Jesus gives images of separation, the "worm that shall not die," "outer darkness," "the gnashing of teeth," and "the fire of hell." Be that as it may, these either-or images are not a preview of what is to come. They are a disclosure of the present situation to whom Jesus is addressing. Jesus is challenging his listeners to make an irrevocable decision.[86]

Saint Paul writes that God "consigned all men to disobedience, that he may have mercy upon *all*" (Rom 11:32). "All" is repeated throughout Paul's writings: "God our saviour . . . desires *all* men to be saved and to come to the knowledge of the truth. . . . For there is one God, and there is one mediator between God and men, the man Christ Jesus, who gave himself as a ransom for *all*" (1 Tim 2:4–5). Paul tells the church to pray for *all* men (1 Tim 2:1), which, Balthasar points out, "could not be asked of her if she were not allowed to have at least the hope that prayers

---

83. Balthasar, *Dare We Hope*, 52–53.

84. Andrê Manarche, *Le monothéisme chrétien*; quoted in Balthasar, *Dare We Hope*, 52n55.

85. Balthasar, *Dare We Hope*, 18.

86. Balthasar, *Dare We Hope*, 20.

as widely directed as these are sensible and might be heard."[87] This "all" fits with the movement of Paul's theology in which God will be all in all (1 Cor 15:28).

Hope is the key word for Balthasar. Hope extends beyond us and beyond what we can achieve on our own. It requires trust and it looks forward, resting in the love who is God and in the mercy of the Judge, who is also our redeemer. He writes, "One ought to stay well away from so systematic a statement [*apokatastasis*] and limit oneself to that Christian hope that does not mask a concealed knowing but rests essentially content with the Church's prayer, as called for in 1 Timothy 2:4, that God wills that all men be saved."[88] We are to condemn no one. Rather, we are to have hope for all. Hell is a personal matter; the possibility of *my* damnation should push *me* to probe deep into *my* conscience—am I damning myself? This existential probing should propel me ever closer to God.[89] In short, Balthasar is hopeful that God's mercy will overcome man's rejection; "we are permitted to hope that hell might be empty of men."[90]

Concluding Thoughts on Universal Salvation

Ratzinger begins *Eschatology: Death and Eternal Life* by asking why eschatology in the twentieth century came to dominate the theological landscape. He concludes that it is not the result of new exegetical discoveries but a change in historical consciousness. A similar question should be raised in terms of *apokatastasis*. Why is there so much interest in universal salvation, and how does it reflect our contemporary historical consciousness? Is it because of the Western theological retrieval of the Eastern fathers who held to universal reconciliation? Has greater understanding and appreciation of major world religions led to greater openness? Or does the interest arise in contrast to the fire and brimstone,

---

87. Balthasar, *Dare We Hope*, 23.

88. Balthasar, *Dare We Hope*, 30–31.

89. Ratzinger follows Balthasar in this regard. See Ratzinger, *Eschatology*, 217–18.

90. Balthasar, *Dare We Hope*, ix. Hart dismisses Balthasar's position: "I see no great virtue in vacillation, especially when it seems like a strategy for crediting oneself with a tender heartedness that one might nevertheless be willing to doubt in God" (*All Shall Be Saved*, 103). Jordan Daniel Wood, a Catholic universalist, levels a similar accusation against Balthasar ("George Macdonald Against Balthasar"). Whereas, coming at Balthasar from a non-universalist position, Catholic theologian Joshua R. Brotherton argues that Balthasar does not adequately take into account the persistence of evil ("Universalism and Predestinarianism," 624).

infernalist either-or theology that is especially strident in America, a theology deeply embedded in a deeply divided political landscape?[91]

Joshua R. Brotherton makes an interesting point: "Certainly, emphasis on the universal salvific will of God is truly necessary at a time when divine mercy is in such demand. But no less is there a need for a robust theological vision of the human being as *imago Dei*, that is, as endowed with a radical freedom for which he must be fully responsible."[92] Brotherton's emphasis on radical freedom brings us back to the section on death. Perhaps the influence of philosophical eschatology, which was deeply concerned with human freedom, has reached its zenith. Likewise, maybe the Lockean notion of freedom that profoundly marks American thought is also reaching its apogee and therefore garnering attention. John Paul II notes something similar: "The human issues most frequently debated and differently resolved in contemporary moral reflection are all closely related, albeit in various ways, to a crucial issue: human freedom."[93] Incontrovertibly, freedom looms large in the debate surrounding *apokatastasis*. The question of salvation intensifies the question of freedom. In this sense, the theological conflict over *apokatastasis* is a needful reminder of the exigency to further develop a theological conception of human freedom. The challenge for theologians concerning *apokatastasis* is to take up a theological position that is neither ossified by the past nor blinded by the Zeitgeist.[94]

CONCLUSION

Eternity is the centre of all things. From it all things proceed, to it all things return.[95]

In the twenty-first century eschatology plays a key role in Catholic theology. Death, temporality, and universal salvation are of particular concern, but these do not stand alone. They relate to other aspects of eschatology as seen in the other chapters of this book. One of the common threads that is informing and being informed by eschatology

---

91. N. T. Wright finds himself disturbed by how Americans are so fixated on hell (Nick, "N. T. Wright").

92. Brotherton, "Universalism and Predestinarianism," 624.

93. John Paul II, *Veritatis Splendor* §31.

94. Benedict XVI, "Christian Universalism," 139.

95. Guardini, *Last Things*, 111.

is theological anthropology. Personalism, or what we could refer to as relation ontology, raises various questions about death, time, and salvation, and helps us see unique ways to come at these eschatological concerns.[96] John Paul II writes, "Eschatology . . . is *profoundly anthropological*, but in light of the New Testament, it is above all centered on Christ and the Holy Spirit, and it is also, in a certain sense, *cosmic*."[97] Eschatology should be seen as the shadow cast by Christ. In this way the perennial relevance of eschatology is secured. "Every Christian discussion of the last things, called eschatology, always starts with the event of the Resurrection; in this event the last things have already begun and, in a certain sense, are already present. . . . Our future is 'to be with the Lord.' As believers, we are already with the Lord in our lifetime; our future, eternal life, has already begun."[98] The last word *is* the Word, he who *is* Eucharist (thanksgiving), *is* the kingdom, and *is* the great mystery of love.

> High phantasy lost power and here broke off;
> Yet, as a wheel moves smoothly, free from jars,
> My will and my desire were turned by love,
> The love that moves the sun and the other stars.[99]

BIBLIOGRAPHY

Balthasar, Hans Urs von. *Dare We Hope "That All Men Be Saved"? With a Short Discourse on Hell*. Translated by David Kipp and Lothar Krauth. 2nd ed. San Francisco: Ignatius, 2014.

———. *A Theology of History*. San Francisco: Ignatius, 1994.

Barron, Robert. "What's New About the 'New Ressourcement'? The Changed Circumstances of a Perennial Project of Retrieval." *New Ressourcement* 1 (2024) 1–20.

Barth, Karl. *The Epistle to the Romans*. Translated by Edwyn C. Hoskyns. Oxford: Oxford University Press, 1933.

Behr, John. "Life and Death in an Age of Martyrdom." In *The Role of Death in Life: A Multidisciplinary Examination of the Relationship Between Life and Death*, edited by John Behr and Conor Cunningham, 79–95. Veritas. Eugene, OR: Cascade, 2015.

---

96. This is fitting for a christologically focused eschatology. Christ is the eschaton, and he is eternity. Thus, eschatology concerns, as Guardini puts it, "a relation between persons" (*Last Things*, 108).

97. John Paul II, "Does 'Eternal Life' Exist?," para. 11; emphasis in original.

98. Benedict XVI, "General Audience," paras. 1–2.

99. Dante, *Par.* 33:142–45.

Benedict XVI. "Christian Universalism: On Two Collections of Papers by Hans Urs von Balthasar." In *The Unity of the Church*, edited by David L. Schindler, 131–43. Vol. 1 of *Joseph Ratzinger in* Communio. RRRCT. Grand Rapids: Eerdmans, 2010.

———. "General Audience." Vatican, Nov. 12, 2008. https://www.vatican.va/content/benedict-xvi/en/audiences/2008/documents/hf_ben-xvi_aud_20081112.html.

———. *See also* Ratzinger, Joseph.

Bishop, Jeffrey P. "On Medical Corpses and Resurrected Bodies." In *The Role of Death in Life: A Multidisciplinary Examination of the Relationship Between Life and Death*, edited by John Behr and Conor Cunningham, 164–78. Veritas. Eugene, OR: Cascade, 2015.

Brotherton, Joshua R. Review of *That All Shall Be Saved: Heaven, Hell, and Universal Salvation*, by David Bentley Hart. *NV* 18 (2020) 1050–55.

———. "Universalism and Predestinarianism: A Critique of the Theological Anthropology That Undergirds Catholic Universalist Eschatology." *TS* 77 (2016) 603–26.

Coyle, Justin Shawn. "May Catholics Endorse Universalism?" *Eclectic Orthodoxy*, Sept. 22, 2019. https://afkimel.wordpress.com/2019/09/22/may-catholics-endorse-universalism/.

Cunningham, Conor. "Is There Life Before Death?" In *The Role of Death in Life: A Multidisciplinary Examination of the Relationship Between Life and Death*, edited by John Behr and Conor Cunningham, 120–51. Veritas. Eugene, OR: Cascade, 2015.

Daley, Brian E. "Knowing God in History and in the Church: *Dei Verbum* and 'Nouvelle Théologie.'" In *Ressourcement: A Movement for Renewal in Twentieth-Century Catholic Theology*, edited by Gabriel Flynn and Paul D. Murray with Patricia Kelly, 333–51. Oxford: Oxford University Press, 2012.

Dante Alighieri. *Paradise*. Translated by Dorothy L. Sayers and Barbara Reynolds. Vol. 3 of the *Divine Comedy*. Penguin Classics. London: Penguin, 2004.

Defoe, Daniel. *Moll Flanders*. Penguin Classics. New York: Penguin, 1978.

De La Noval, Roberto J. "Divine Drama or Divine Disclosure? Hell, Universalism, and a Parting of the Ways." *Modern Theology* 36 (2020) 201–10.

Delorenzo, Leonard J. *Work of Love: A Theological Reconstruction of the Communion of Saints*. Notre Dame, IN: University of Notre Dame Press, 2017.

Falque, Emmanuel. "Suffering Death." In *The Role of Death in Life: A Multidisciplinary Examination of the Relationship Between Life and Death*, edited by John Behr and Conor Cunningham, 45–55. Veritas. Eugene, OR: Cascade, 2015.

Filippenko, Alexei V. "Made of Star-Stuff: The Origin of the Chemical Elements in Life." In *The Role of Death in Life: A Multidisciplinary Examination of the Relationship Between Life and Death*, edited by John Behr and Conor Cunningham, 3–13. Veritas. Eugene, OR: Cascade, 2015.

Gilson, Caitlin Smith. "Heaven and the Transcendental Meaning of Death." *Church Life Journal*, Dec. 12, 2022. https://churchlifejournal.nd.edu/articles/heaven-and-the-transcendental-meaning-of-death/.

Granados, José. "The First Fruits of the Flesh and the First Fruits of the Spirit: The Mystery of the Ascension." *Comm* 38 (2011) 6–38.

———. "Risen Time: Easter as the Source of History." *Comm* 37 (2010) 6–33.

Gschwandtner, Christina M. "How Do We Become Fully Alive? The Role of Death in Henry's Phenomenology of Life." In *The Role of Death in Life: A Multidisciplinary*

Examination of the Relationship Between Life and Death, edited by John Behr and Conor Cunningham, 56–75. Veritas. Eugene, OR: Cascade, 2015.

Guardini, Romano. *The Last Things: Concerning Death, Purification After Death, Resurrection, Judgment, and Eternity*. Translated by Charlotte E. Forsyth and Grace B. Branham. Notre Dame, IN: University of Notre Dame Press, 1965.

Hart, David Bentley. *The Experience of God: Being, Consciousness, Bliss*. New Haven, CT: Yale University Press, 2013.

———. *That All Shall Be Saved: Heaven, Hell and Universal Salvation*. London: Yale University Press, 2019.

International Theological Commission. "Some Current Questions in Eschatology." Vatican, 1992. https://www.vatican.va/roman_curia/congregations/cfaith/cti_documents/rc_cti_1990_problemi-attuali-escatologia_en.html.

Jaeger, Luc. "A Biochemical Perspective on the Origin of Life and Death." In *The Role of Death in Life: A Multidisciplinary Examination of the Relationship Between Life and Death*, edited by John Behr and Conor Cunningham, 14–28. Veritas. Eugene, OR: Cascade, 2015.

John Paul II. "Does 'Eternal Life' Exist?" Vatican, n.d. https://www.vatican.va/archive/books/threshold_hope/documents/chap28.html.

———. *Veritatis Splendor*. Vatican, Aug. 6, 1993. https://www.vatican.va/content/john-paul-ii/en/encyclicals/documents/hf_jp-ii_enc_06081993_veritatis-splendor.html.

Kaethler, Andrew T. J. *The Eschatological Person: Alexander Schmemann and Joseph Ratzinger in Dialogue*. Veritas. Eugene, OR: Cascade, 2022.

Lang, Uwe Michael. "Transforming the World into Communion with God: The Sacred Liturgy in the Thought of Joseph Ratzinger." *Comm* (2023) 657–84.

Levering, Matthew. *Newman on Doctrinal Corruption*. Park Ridge, IL: Word on Fire Academic, 2022.

MacDonald, George. "Unspoken Sermons: Third Series." Christian Classic Ethereal Library, n.d. https://www.ccel.org/ccel/macdonald/unspoken3.html.

Manoussakis, J. P. "The Cup of Time: Christology and Eschatology." *PATH* 18 (2019) 445–59.

———. "Salvation à la Hart." Academia, 2019. https://www.academia.edu/40052533/SALVATION_à_la_HART.

Müller, Gerhard. *Doctrine of Creation, Eschatology*. Translated by William Hadfield-Burkardt. Vol. 1 of *Catholic Dogmatics: For the Study and Practice of Theology*. New York: Crossroad, 2017.

Nick. "N. T. Wright Reflects on Rob Bell and Hell." *Reading Theology*, May 29, 2011. https://readingtheology.com/n-t-wright-reflects-on-rob-bell-and-hell.

Novello, Henry L. "New Life as Life Out of Death: Sharing in the 'Exchange of Natures' in the Person of Christ." In *The Role of Death in Life: A Multidisciplinary Examination of the Relationship Between Life and Death*, edited by John Behr and Conor Cunningham, 96–119. Veritas. Eugene, OR: Cascade, 2015.

O'Neill, Taylor Patrick. Review of *That All Shall Be Saved: Heaven, Hell, and Universal Salvation*, by David Bentley Hart. *NV* 18 (2020) 1055–59.

Pieper, Josef. *Death and Immortality*. Translated by Richard Winston and Clara Winston. South Bend, IN: St. Augustine's, 2000.

Pomplun, R. Trent. "Heat and Light: David Bentley Hart on the Fires of Hell." *Modern Theology* 37 (2020) 523–30.

Ratzinger, Joseph. *Dogma and Preaching: Applying Christian Doctrine to Daily Life.* Translated by Michael J. Miller and Matthew J. O'Connell. San Francisco: Ignatius, 2011.

———. *Eschatology: Death and Eternal Life.* Translated by Michael Waldstein. Dogmatic Theology 9. Washington, DC: Catholic University of America Press, 1988.

———. *Introduction to Christianity.* Translated by J. R. Foster. Rev. ed. Communio. San Francisco: Ignatius, 2004.

———. *Principles of Catholic Theology: Building Stones for a Fundamental Theology.* Translated by Mary Frances McCarthy. San Francisco: Ignatius, 1987.

———. *See also* Benedict XVI.

Ruddy, Christopher. "*Ressourcement* and the *Enduring* Legacy of Post-Tridentine Theology." In *Ressourcement: A Movement for Renewal in Twentieth-Century Catholic Theology*, edited by Gabriel Flynn and Paul D. Murray with Patricia Kelly, 185–201. Oxford: Oxford University Press, 2012.

Schmemann, Alexander. *For the Life of the World: Sacraments and Orthodoxy.* Crestwood, NY: St. Vladimir's Seminary Press, 1973.

Snow, Patricia. "The Body and Christian Burial: The Question of Cremation." *Comm* (2012) 399–412.

Steinkerchner, Scott. "Time in Heaven: From Glory to Glory." *NBf* 100 (2019) 264–83.

Stump, Eleonore. "The God of Love." *Church Life Journal*, Apr. 13, 2023. https://churchlifejournal.nd.edu/articles/can-hell-and-the-god-of-love-coexist/.

Thiel, John E. *Now and Forever: A Theological Aesthetics of Time.* Notre Dame, IN: University of Notre Dame Press, 2023.

Wahlsberg, Mats. "The Problem of Hell: A Thomistic Critique of David Bentley Hart's Necessitarian Universalism." *Modern Theology* 39 (2023) 47–67.

Wolfe, Judith. "The Eschatological Turn in German Philosophy." *Modern Theology* 35 (2019) 55–70.

Wood, Jordan Daniel. "George Macdonald Against Hans Urs von Balthasar on Universal Salvation." *Eclectic Orthodoxy*, Apr. 26, 2020. https://afkimel.wordpress.com/2020/04/26/george-macdonald-against-hans-urs-von-balthasar-on-universal-salvation/.

2

Technology and Eschatology

Paul Tyson

Given the profound religious and political turmoil in Western Europe in the sixteenth and seventeenth centuries, the intimate connections between the birth of modern science and fears regarding the end of the world are well understood by historians.[1] But it was also a time of apocalyptic optimism. The frontispiece of Francis Bacon's 1620 publication *The Great Instauration* shows a ship sailing through the pillars of Hercules out into the Atlantic Ocean, bearing this eschatological quotation from the prophet Daniel: "Many shall go to and fro, and science shall be increased."[2]

Bacon saw science's mastery over nature as not simply a means of advancing human utility, but as a redemptive response to the fall of man.[3] Our rightful dominion over the earth could be reclaimed via science and technology, and this would usher in the end of the age and welcome in the kingdom of God on earth.[4] The idea of civilizational progress being a function of scientific advance, and the aspiration for a realized eschatology of scientific progress, have clear Christian theological roots in Western modernity. These roots remain implicit even when taken up

---

1. See Webster, *Paracelsus*; Henry, *Knowledge Is Power*.

2. This frontispiece is reproduced in Shapin, *Scientific Revolution*, 21, and the above-quoted translation of Bacon's text is on page 20. On the actual frontispiece, Bacon's excerpt from Dan 12:4 reads: "Multi pertransibunt & augebitur scientia." The 1611 King James Bible translates Dan 12:4 thus: "But thou, O Daniel, shut vp the words, and seale the booke euen to the time of the ende: many shall runne to and fro, and knowledge shall bee increased."

3. Harrison, *Fall of Man*, 186–244.

4. For why I think Bacon's dominion theology is profoundly problematic, see Tyson, *Theology and Climate Change*, 51–75.

by explicitly atheist eschatological enterprises such as Marxism. Though the West has been deeply secularized, and God has been replaced by humanity or perhaps AI created in our super image, technology remains a profoundly eschatological enterprise in the West to this day.

Taking the intimate relationship between technology and a now secularized eschatology (marked either by the fear of apocalyptic destruction or the hope of utopian transformation) as given, this chapter will reflect on technology and eschatology in two registers. First, three contexts in which technological eschatology is presently at play—AI, climate change, and the cloud—will be described and briefly analyzed. Second, a Christian response to secular apocalyptic fears and the naturalistic hope of technological salvation will be attempted. A Christian response to technological eschatology is a more difficult challenge than may be initially apparent, but drawing on Josef Pieper's theological philosophy of history, Peter Harrison's analysis of anti-supernatural naturalism, and Ian Hunt's understanding of secularization as a combat concept, a possible way forward will be suggested.

AI AS A POST-HUMAN ESCHATOLOGICAL HOPE

Any exploration of consciousness that does not recognize a fundamental distinction between a very convincing replica of what consciousness can *do*, and the ontology of what consciousness *is*, is operating within a reductively physicalist ontology that cannot possibly be true. David Bentley Hart's book on the philosophy of mind demonstrates this so effectively that I will not take up space in this chapter justifying the above observation.[5] Yet, it is a sign of the functionally materialist ontology assumed in our times that our technological, academic, and commercial cultures cannot tell the difference between quantity and quality, between thought and computer operations, between a person and a nonperson, between the living and the nonliving, between data and information versus meaning and significance. But because we cannot discern these basic differences of ontological order, brilliant computerized replications of human communications make it appear to us as if we are creating consciousness via AI. This is not true, but our dominant culture cannot see why it is not true because, effectively, it believes that human consciousness as a genuinely spiritual and intellective reality does not exist. Because we assume that our minds are emergent epiphenomena of

---

5. Hart, *Full of Gods*. For a brief account of Hart's powerful reasoning in this domain, see Hart, "Myth of Machine Consciousness."

merely material and unthinking physical reality, our minds are thought of as computers. To emphasize again, this is false, but the fact that we believe it is very worrying when we are computationally engineering such powerful replicas of human communication and reasoning. The actual effect of this is not that we will create artificial consciousness, but that we will functionally so downgrade our understanding of human consciousness to the level of a computer that we will come to treat humans as machines. This, effectively, is what twenty-first-century developments in social media, algorithmic online surveillance, and continuous internet connectivity—all for the instrumental purpose of commercial harvesting—have already achieved.

Paul Kingsnorth's essay "The Universal" looks at the secular eschatological implications of contemporary AI developments and brings Christian eschatological thinking to bear on this topic.[6] Kingsnorth notes the shocking hubris and blasphemous impiety that transhumanists have when they speak theologically about AI development:

> Martine Rothblatt says that by building AI systems "we are making God." . . . Elise Bohan says "we are building God." Kevin Kelly believes that "we can see more of God in a cell phone than in a tree frog." "Does God exist?" asks transhumanist . . . Ray Kurzweil. "I will say, 'Not yet.'"[7]

Drawing on the non-Christian yet remarkably astute observations of René Guénon and Rudolf Steiner, Kingsnorth unpacks how the concept of the spiritual principal of Ahriman speaks to the type of god-building games we are presently playing with AI. The idea here is that Ahriman is a powerful spiritual delusion that operates in our culture as the Reign of Quantity. That is, this is a spiritual principality that poses as an entirely material power. Appealing to the Russian Orthodox Saint Ignatius Brianchaninov, Kingsnorth links this materialist principality with the Christian understanding of the antichrist.

The secular eschatological prophecies of the transhumanist Ray Kurzweil predict that machines will achieve equality with human intelligence by 2029, which will start a merging of humans with machines to create a giant superintelligence by 2045, ushering in a new age of spiritual machines.[8] But at that point humans will be neither the most intelligent nor the dominant species on the planet. We will realize both

---

6. Kingsnorth, "Universal"; "Neon God."
7. Kingsnorth, "Universal."
8. Kurzweil, *Age of Spiritual Machines.*

the creation of god on earth, and the kingdom of heaven on earth, thanks to the emergence of a new superintelligence through the computerized images of human consciousness that we ourselves make. We will then bow down and worship these images and they will rule over us.[9]

Let us leave this technological eschatology of secular hope hanging in the air for the present and turn our attention to the apocalyptic fear of technologically produced climate change.

CLIMATE CHANGE

One of the premier eco-theologians writing today is Michael Northcott.[10] He has recently reevaluated his understanding of the politics and science of climate change in ways that I at first found perplexing, but which now strike me as warranting very close attention.

Northcott has become very wary of environmental apocalypticism. Climate destabilization and radical habitat change is certainly going on at a phenomenal pace, and yet the astonishing rebalancing powers of nature on the one hand, and what Northcott sees as the sinister powers of environmental activism and state/corporate integration on the other hand, have led Northcott to think of environmental apocalypticism as a dangerous false consciousness.

The climate apocalypse narrative goes like this. The end of the world as we know it is coming. As we pass one tipping point after another without effectively slowing down—let alone stopping or reversing—the increase of the concentration of carbon dioxide particles in the atmosphere, irreversible global warming is upon us. The consequences of global warming are more extreme weather events, rising sea temperatures and levels, less water in the soil, stronger and more prevalent fires and

---

9. C. S. Lewis observes that those who do not believe in the gods, and yet call on the gods, are very unwise, for the gods may well come when called. "There goes one . . . who has called on gods he does not believe in. How will it be with him if they have really come?" (*Last Battle*, 106).

10. For what I have found to be the most penetrating and thought-provoking book in this arena, see Northcott, *Theology of Climate Change*. Recently (alas) Northcott has moved away from what I understand to be an orthodox theology of God. Northcott's *God and Gaia* is a very interesting book, and I had long discussions with Northcott about its theology of God when it was in its manuscript stage. Northcott is a very powerful and well-informed thinker and a man of astonishing moral commitment and activism, whom I respect enormously, but I believe he is merging a Lovelock-framed earth systems science with his Christian theology, which makes any real distinction between a pagan concept of Gaia as a living spiritual entity upon which we all depend and the transcendent Creator God of Christian orthodoxy hard to find.

so forth, which will reduce global food supplies leading to war, and the destruction of irreplaceable natural habitats and species. Doom is coming to energy hungry, polluting, nature-despoiling, technological Man.

The consequence of this message of doom is twofold. On the one hand, the young and the environmentally educated are filled with despair. On the other hand, globally powerful commercial interests can harness this despair to gain unprecedented political and commercial control over the resources and inhabitants of the earth.[11] The manner in which the nation state and the international corporation increasingly bypass the normal political process in various states of emergency requires and feeds an administration of fear.[12] What bigger cause for fear can one want to drive this process than the end of the world? And, of course, the only answer we can think of to this apocalypse is to apply more of what caused it: nature-exploiting technology in the hands of for-profit global corporations.[13]

None of this is to say that we do not have a serious problem embedded in the very fabric of our modern technological relationship with creation; that there really are terrible natural depletions and imbalances going on around us at a frightening and increasing speed, and our political dynamics really do seem incapable of responding adequately. But Northcott sees debilitating fear and paralysis due to a despairing

---

11. Estes, "Bill Gates." On how all disasters tend to be harnessed for commercial profit and greater political control, see Klein, *Shock Doctrine*.

12. See Virilio, *Administration of Fear*. Virilio notes that as our technologies get faster and faster, we must keep accelerating every aspect of our way of life just to keep up with the new developments. The driver of ever-accelerating speed is commercial surveillance and advantage and also governmental surveillance and advantage; commerce and governance are now intimately related. At some point the speed of our way of life is going to produce a catastrophic high-speed accident, such as the 2008 global financial crisis. A sense of being out of control, of buckling down and just pedaling harder is now a pervasive background feature of our way of life. This fear and unease must be harnessed and redirected away from its ever-accelerating technological commercial and governmental causes by those who govern our way of life. This is why our lives are now embedded in carefully produced manufactured fears that are not the real source of our sense of being out of control: illegal immigrants, disinformation conspirators, religious terrorists around every corner, and so forth.

13. Gates, *Avoid Climate Disaster*. The manner in which environmental activists like Naomi Klein and George Monbiot have snuggled up to corporate global power figures, such as Bill Gates, speaks of the arrival of a potent instrumental pragmatism in Green circles. Corporations seem able to achieve what governments cannot (though corporations are profit driven, and governments are meant to work for the common good of their citizens), so Green politicians are making corporate power alliances that give whole new layers of complexity to greenwashing, carbon trading, and commercially interested legislation.

environmental apocalypticism as easily politically and commercially exploited by corporate superpowers in league with national security states. This alliance will not only fail to respect the integrity of creation but will increasingly oppress and exploit the governed and the commercially controlled. Again, it is the Reign of Quantity and Max Weber's "iron cage" of instrumental bureaucratic governance that form the spiritual principality controlling the pragmatics of environmental and political power—a principality blind to sacred and moral truth. We are entering a frightening age of the technologically enabled spiritual oppression of both nature and humanity, and secular environmental apocalypticism is a powerful force propelling us there.

THE CLOUD

The third area of eschatological transition that I wish to briefly explore is the cloud. This ties in with the section on AI in that our complete embedding in an online lifeworld is shaping who we are in very far-reaching ways.

The Greek economist Yanis Varoufakis has recently published a fascinating book titled *Technofeudalism*. In this book Varoufakis persuasively argues that we no longer have capitalism where the wealthy owners of the means of production, spurred into astonishing activity by the profit motive, invest in employing people and making things, which they then supply to sellers who trade on markets that are in some sense free. Instead, we are now all hooked into online commercial spaces which are rentier economies. Thanks to the iPhone and Google's algorithms and supercomputer analysis and manipulation of user attention, platforms like Amazon are fiefdoms that connect sellers to buyers, at rental cost to the seller and free labor to the buyer. That is, we all work for free (as cloud serfs) telling Google and Amazon what our commercially exploitable interests, fears, desires, and tastes are, and then our cloud masters can use this detailed and individually specific commercial information by asking buyers to pay 40 percent of their sale price to Amazon for anything sold on their platform. This bypasses normal marketplace dynamics and makes investment in production a secondary feature of the most serious forms of economic activity. Real power is concentrated in the owners of cloud real estate: here cloud serfs work for free, while cloud sellers pay rent to the real estate's owners for access. Technofeudalism is thus a new type of global economic power system.

Varoufakis, as a libertarian Marxist, is horrified by how capitalism has died and we have all become techno serfs, without our even noticing it. His interest is not in undoing the technological cloud, but in trying to work out how to live in the cloud without being a serf. To Varoufakis, the central matter at issue is the ownership of the means of cloud communication and marketing, and ownership of one's own data. The system is set up to deprive us ordinary cloud plebeians of any real ownership in the economic and governance structures in which we are now so deeply embedded. This can only result in the continuous removal of agency and freedom for us cloud serfs, and the enhancement of power for the interests and privilege preservation of our cloud masters. This is hardly the day of judgment for capitalism that Marxists had eschatologically dreamed of.

While I feel a sympathetic sense of dismay for Marxists who were looking for the kingdom of heaven on earth after the inevitable demise of capitalism, there are bigger spiritual fish I wish to fry.

FROM BABEL TO THE CLOUD, AND ON TO HEIDEGGER

In classical Greco-Roman thinking, the daemonic was the heavenly domain of the immortal gods as situated between mortal humanity and high deity. The daemonic pagan gods of old liked to play with the fate of mortals and found the tragicomic struggles of humanity rather amusing. When you go to an arena, you are situated above the life and death struggles down there on the ground, and you are elevated into a semi-daemonic space, and can—for a time—enjoy the vantage of the gods. The spectacle was understood as a spiritual theatre, and Christians of late antiquity did not participate in this spectacle—other than as occasional objects of slaughter—because it was consorting with demons.[14]

The aim of getting up off the earth and into the heavenly domain of the gods is an old idea, intimately linked with the building of ziggurats and the biblical narrative of the tower of Babel. Today, we now all dwell in the electromagnetic clouds, and all feel the sense of being somehow super mortal, for we are no longer limited by place, we have all knowledge at our fingertips, we can buy and sell anything, anywhere, and we can indulge forms of imaginative self-construction online that were impossible before the internet. This is profoundly changing how we communicate, do business, live, and even how we think, feel, and believe. And, as

14. Ross, *Gifts Glittering and Poisoned*.

Varoufakis points out, we are now serfs in this new domain, embracing our chains with joy.

This is not an apocalyptic change that is going to happen—it has happened. And could it be that it is in this new cloud domain that the AI gods of the Reign of Quantity are coming down to meet us? For while the ancient Mesopotamian ziggurat was indeed a hubristic human enterprise in building a platform up into the domain of the gods, the purpose of this platform was as a landing place to enable the gods to come down to us. This is a hubristic revolt against mortal creatureliness, a taking of heaven by force, but it is also the desire to serve the daemonic gods in exchange for participation in their divine power. But what if the daemonic gods actually come to us via the digital platform we have made for them?

Can technology be a platform for the demonic? Is the current place of our technology of eschatological significance? Let us touch on these questions, initially, via Heidegger.

HEIDEGGER ON THE ESSENCE OF TECHNOLOGY AND ON THE COMING OF A GOD

Heidegger maintains a contemplative quietism in the face of our technological alienation from nature and our fellow man such that we are neither compelled to "push on blindly with technology" as its slaves, nor "rebel helplessly against it and curse it as the work of the devil."[15] How we are to actually respond to technology is something beneath Heidegger's elevated mind. Yet, Heidegger is waiting for a god to appear, or—as the onto-theological nihilist that he is—for this god to not appear,[16] to save us from the forces of technicity and from a cybernetics which is totally changing our relation to nature and our own and other people's humanity.[17]

As I read Heidegger, he is sensing that the essence of technology is not this or that invention, and not even the power over nature that turns everything into a standing reserve for our use (technicity), but its essence is revealing. In making things we exercise the power to uncover things that are hidden and bring them into the domain of the tangible and the intelligible. But what concealed thing or person is technology revealing? As beings who must poetically reveal meaning, who are yet inexorably thrust towards Nothing, it seems that the god that Heidegger

---

15. Heidegger, "*Question Concerning Technology*," 25–26.
16. Heidegger, "Only a God Can Save," 57.
17. Heidegger, "Only a God Can Save," 59.

thinks we are looking for to save us from technicity (via the poetry of art) is Nothing.

Putting Heidegger and Kingsnorth together, it seems like the Reign of Quantity and a metaphysics of Nothing is producing the technologically enabled false eschatologies of our times. A return to real qualities, gifted to creation from the source of all being, and a metaphysics of a real divine Creator, rather than a dark Nothing that falsely promises our own self-creation as gods, seems the only appropriate Christian response to the false techno-eschatologies of our times. And if the ground of being is not Nothing, but God, then belief in a metaphysics of nothing enables a "powerful delusion" (2 Thess 2:11), which makes us slaves to "principalities and powers in high places of great wickedness" (Eph 6:12).

A CHRISTIAN RESPONSE TO SECULAR ESCHATOLOGY

As I read Christian eschatology, the Christian is to be unconcerned about the terrors of the future. God is present in the *now* and the future is in his hands. We can meet God now, obey him now, and thus act in hope for the future, whether our acts prove instrumentally effective or futile. For we are to be faithful witnesses and faithful servants, without neglecting what good we can do. The forward-looking justice that combats the evils of our age, we ought to pursue, whether or not we succeed. For the great message of the Apocalypse of John is that the Lord will return, the Lord will judge the peoples of the earth, and the Lord will judge the wicked heavenly principalities which we have actualized by our idolatrous poesis and hubristic technicity. The redemption of all things will come (Col 1:15–20; Rev 21:1–4). Maranatha![18]

But . . . the challenge of living by active faith under a Christian eschatological horizon is not as simple as just getting one's theology straight. We live within a lifeworld that is deeply shaped by a commonly assumed secular and immanent frame, where the horizon of faith has now faded from public view. Sociologically, this common lived reality shapes the Christian as much as it shapes the non-Christian. Yet, it is most effective in shaping us when we are unaware of it, when, like fish, it is simply the water in which we live. The rest of this chapter will seek to make three aspects of our lifeworld's secular eschatology visible enough to at least show us what the challenge we face in not being defined by

---

18. See 1 Cor 16:22. This is an Aramaic expression, *marana tha*, written in Greek in this passage as μαράνα θα, translated as "Come, O Lord." See also (just in Greek) Rev 22:20.

the spirit of our times entails. To that end we shall briefly unpack historiography, secularization, and naturalism as the non-eschatological premises that embed our very lifeworld in the profoundly anti-Christian and inherently delusional eschatological consciousness of our times.

ANTI-THEOLOGICAL HISTORIOGRAPHY

In his astonishing text on the philosophy of history Josef Pieper points out that for history to have an overarching meaning, a purpose, a direction, it requires both a revealed origin that does not arise from within the temporal contingency and flux of historical existence itself, and a revealed destiny, which is likewise not within history.[19] Even so, creation and eschaton as superhistorical realities are the grounds of history. Equally, Christ is the alpha and omega of redemption history, who must come into historical time, but does not himself arise from the contingent and linear categories of historical time as such. This traditional way of understanding how time and eternity relate to each other is now perhaps impossible for the mindset of our times to grasp. For our culture at large can no longer draw on the metaphysical theology that previously provided the West with a common framework of higher truth to temporal events than what can be discerned only in the immanent and phenomenological frames of observation and logic. Even so, the meaning of history remains—for the Christian—always situated within the revealing work of the Holy Spirit through the Scriptures and the orthodox interpretive traditions of the church, and through the metaphysical categories of the metaxological,[20] the analogical,[21] and the apophatic.[22] Reading the meaning of history has always been a complex matter, and was never like a mass spectrometer reading or a news report.

Thanks to the Enlightenment invention of modern historiography, the positive science of historical events denies any meaningful perspective on history itself that is outside of contingent, always situated, and entirely

---

19. Pieper, *End of Time*. For a Protestant presentation of a similar stance to Pieper's, see Löwith, *Meaning in History*.

20. See Desmond's "between" books, where the immanent is porous to the transcendent, but our actual experience of reality is always situated between a pure immanence (which is beneath our knowing) and a pure transcendence (which is above our knowing). See, for example, Desmond, *Being and the Between*.

21. Erich Przywara's *Analogia Entis* has been very significant in reviving analogical metaphysical theology. For a fine essay on the significance of Thomistic analogical metaphysics, see Betz, translator's introduction.

22. Nicholas of Cusa, *Of Learned Ignorance*; Pieper, *Silence of Saint Thomas*.

immanent and phenomenological frames of reference. Rejecting the God's eye view of the meaning of history, we have effectively cut historical reflection and interpretation off from revelation and from transcendence. And it is perhaps no surprise to discover that the first location where this modern historiography really gets into the air is the late eighteenth-century-Enlightenment-influenced textual analysis of the Bible by liberal Germanic Protestants. As Lynn White Jr. correctly discerned, this development produces a profound crisis for Christian theology; the crisis of the separation of myth (higher and timeless meaning) from history (contingent temporal events).[23] Following Pieper, Christians cannot accept the modern flatly immanent view of history itself if we are to be faithful to both sacred doctrine and to history itself having a real meaning. The context of information and mass communications in which we live means that we are almost unavoidably drawn into the total constructivism, the reductive immanence, and the always interested and instrumental nature of contemporary meaning—both in academia and in online environments—such that we are drawn into doomscrolling and the perpetual priming of anxiety and inchoate dread,[24] and a fixation with the news as if knowing what is going on (as fed to us)[25] is somehow empowering. This must be resisted by the Christian.

The loss of a shared theological horizon giving history and meaning itself its superhuman source is profoundly distorting of our perspective on temporal reality. And it is the assumed concept of nature, as flatly immanent, as non-metaphysically situated, as tacitly anti-supernatural, that shapes our entire intellectual culture now. This also needs to be understood and rejected by Christians.

ANTI-SUPERNATURAL NATURALISM

Peter Harrison's most recent book is a genealogy of how naturalism became anti-supernatural.[26] The trajectory that produced this novel nineteenth-century vision of nature as—functionally—not creation, but as just meaninglessly and materially "there," has a complex theological

---

23. White, "Christian Myth and History."

24. See again Virilio, *Administration of Fear*.

25. See Ellul, *Propaganda*. This is a fascinating sociologically and theologically framed exploration of modern mass media. The texture of the dynamics Ellul outlines has advanced in very much the trajectory Ellul described sixty years ago; this book is in no sense out of date.

26. Harrison, *Some New World*.

back story, well worth exploring. The manner in which the natural now excludes the supernatural has a very colorful history, particularly if one recalls that once—to paraphrase John Milbank—there was no "supernatural."[27] The supernatural only becomes a live idea—and then with a very different meaning to its present expression—in the thirteenth century. For in its premodern Christian context, the natural was nested in, and dependent on, yet not reducible to, the supernatural.[28] In this complex environment the regularities of natural phenomena and our own epistemic powers to grasp natural reality in some measure were upheld and guaranteed by God. Things develop in complex ways as a result of fourteenth-century nominalism and voluntarism, and dramatically, as a result of the Reformation, and then reactively with the Counter-Reformation invention of *natura pura*, until the high point of the career of the Western idea of the supernatural can be found in the occasionalism often assumed in the new natural philosophy of early modernity. Here—pace Newton—gravity and the laws of nature are the finger of God directly governing the regularities of nature. Here nature—unlike in the ontologically multilayered and multi-agential Middle Ages—is reductively subsumed into a monolithic supernature. But, as Harrison puts it,

> [early modernity's] scientific supernaturalism . . . was susceptible to a hostile takeover in which God's immediate action could be simply redescribed in purely naturalistic terms. All that was required was for God's ongoing but immutable activity to be given a new label: "nature." This option was not realized until the nineteenth century when habituation to the notion of laws of nature led to an amnesia regarding its theological origins.[29]

Come the late nineteenth century and Thomas Huxley[30] is implementing this hostile takeover by, among other things, polemically retrofitting history with the shamelessly false assertion that scientific naturalism has always been at war with religious supernaturalism. And—as we shall explore when we look at secularism below—Huxley's entirely fabricated polemic worked. As a result, the West is now post-Christian. What we now think of as naturalism is functionally anti-theological,

---

27. See the opening sentence of Milbank, *Theology and Social Theory*: "Once, there was no 'secular'" (9).

28. See Betz, *Christ the Logos of Creation*, for an excellent restating of this traditional stance in our contemporary context.

29. Harrison, *Some New World*, 238.

30. See Stanley, *Huxley's Church*.

and it has infected all academic knowledge and all categories of public meaning.

Our naturalistic knowledge culture has rejected any genuinely theological eschatology, and this rejection, on the one hand, makes history meaningless, but on the other hand, gives us an impossibly naïve and fundamentally idolatrous technological utopianism. It is naïve to think that there can be a meaningful eschatology without a divine source to the intelligible order of both nature and human history, and it is idolatrous to think that we can bring about the fulfillment of all human hopes and perfections by merely human means—as if we are our own Creator.[31] And as a marker of how inherently impossible this secular technological redemption myth is, it is our man-made technological society[32] itself that has summoned a frightening array of potential dooms to the horizon of our very existence—climate change, AI, species and natural habitat destruction, nuclear war, biological warfare, microplastics making us infertile, total surveillance, global travel–assisted pandemics, and so on—and yet technology is the only publicly acceptable and fittingly secular (i.e., anti-theological) site of hope for a viable future. Most seriously, this secularized eschatology is not so much something that one personally believes or disbelieves, this is a lifeworld, a common consciousness that we all share.

The above sentence may seem controversial, for we tend to assume that in liberal democracies we all have freedom of conscience and freedom of religion and can believe or not believe whatever we like. But this is false. William Cavanaugh points out that the very idea of modern liberalism replaces *every* substantive common good with a functional materialism where the *only* common goods are anti-theologically naturalistic.[33] A. J. Conyers points out that the real achievement of modern liberalism is not so much individual personal freedom; it is the morally and collectively unaccountable freedom forever consolidating

---

31. For very clear example of both of these impossibilities, see Harari, *Homo Deus*.

32. See Ellul, *Technological Society*, for a close analysis of the role technology plays in shaping and defining our contemporary lifeworld. As Ellul explains, the only value of the technological society is efficiency—faster, cheaper, more profit, more power, more instrumentally effective—but this is no value at all; it is the reduction of value and meaningful purpose to power. Our way of life is actually bereft of any commonly understood real values and purposes. And it is only real values and purposes held in common that make human society genuinely human. Our technological society thus powerfully erodes our humanity. Post-humanism is the literal aim of the technological society.

33. Cavanaugh, *Being Consumed*, 1–32.

power blocks to accumulate more profit and power.[34] Zygmunt Bauman notices that individual freedom is what is sold to us, but what we in fact buy is alienation and atomization.[35] As atomized and financialized units, we become alienated from the human bonds of close and extended family ties, from long association with a particular place and community, from middle-order social institutions like functional neighborhoods, local parishes, local schools, local community associations. Thus alienated, there are now only two orders of human arrangement, the individual and entirely impersonal massive power organizations that go by the labels of the state and the corporation. And so, the pipes of fear and desire are engineered for us, and the currents of atomized individuals flow in those pipes as the central pumps of corporate, techno-financial, and state power determine that they will flow, and we are told we are free. But this is an ersatz personal freedom where we consume and are in various ways consumed, only in the manner in which the ever-power-concentrating forces of the culture industry in cahoots with financial and technological power, and the modern security state, determine.[36]

As a result of the deep-laid social power structures in which we live, we may think and personally believe that theological frames of Christian eschatology are true, but for all practical purposes, we are just as eschatologically secularized and just as technologically utopian as the most overtly materialist and post-human advocates among us. If the church is to show a properly Christian alternative to the false and vain secularized eschatology of our times, and the technological utopian assumptions of our lifeworld, we must better understand how deeply

---

34. Conyers, *Long Truce*.

35. Bauman, *Liquid Modernity*.

36. There are a range of relevant literatures here. I offer here a small sample. For the manner in which the mass media age has co-opted the arts of culture for the purpose of forming individuals so as to facilitate the power arrangements of the modern mass society, see Adorno, *Culture Industry*. On the manner in which politics is being increasingly reduced to the sub-political safety management of bare bodies such that the security state in the state of emergency renders politics itself obsolete, see Agamben, *Where Are We Now?* On the seamless integration of transnational corporate power—in the high-tech sector in particular—with the administrative machinery and ever-expanding surveillance powers of the state and the corporation, see Zuboff, *Age of Surveillance Capitalism*. For the very large field of the relations between high finance, offshore tax havens, and the logic whereby national governments facilitate this wealth-transfer game from the poor and the local to the rich and the transnational, see Shaxson, *Treasure Islands*; *Finance Curse*. For how our very minds are being changed in order to make us happy appendages to online forms of virtualized reality to keep the wheels of attention and financial harvesting rolling, see Greenfield, *Mind Change*.

entangled we are in the lifeworld of our times. To do so we must better understand secularization.

SECULARIZATION

Contrary to the normal story equating secularization with either the Protestant Reformation or the seventeenth-century Scientific Revolution,[37] Ian Hunter notes: "Prior to the early 1800s nobody used the term 'secularization' to refer to an epochal transition from a culture of religious belief to one of rational autonomy."[38] Until the nineteenth century, the word "secular"—which means "age"—was used to distinguish between parish priests as distinct from cloistered nuns and monks, and also applied to the handing over of church property for nonliturgical use.[39] In the traditional Western Christian meaning of *saecula*, Christ, who is Lord of all ages—*Dominus in saecula saeculorum*[40]—is served by two types of specially set-aside ministers in the church. There are the *secular* priests who minister to believers in this present age (the church age), and the elites of the *religious* orders who devote themselves to prayer and look forward to the age to come after the eschaton (the kingdom of heaven on earth). In christological theology it has never been the view that there is a discrete domain of Christian life—private or public—that is *not* under the lordship of Christ. But the idea of a "secular" domain, where the church had no authority at all, is a combat concept which

---

37. "The Scientific Revolution" is a very recent invention. "The phrase 'the Scientific Revolution' was not in common use before Alexandre Koyré gave it wider currency in 1939" (Shapin, *Scientific Revolution*, 2).

38. Hunter, "Secularization," 2.

39. Hunter notes that the 1646 Treaty of Münster, leading up to the peace of Westphalia in 1648 does use the term *saecularisazio/Säkularisierung* as its first recorded use as a term of public law. This is not, however the nineteenth-century notion of a religion-free domain, as it was used by the French ambassador "simply to refer to the transfer of ecclesiastical property and territory into civil jurisdiction and control" ("Secularization," 5).

40. Note this traditional Roman Catholic formulation for the closing of prayer: "Per Dominum nostrum Jesus Christum Filium tuum: Qui tecum vivit et regnat in unitate Spiritus Sancti Deus, per omnia saecula saeculorum" ("Through our Lord Jesus Christ, your Son, who lives and reigns with you in the unity of the Holy Spirit, God, for ever and ever"). The Anglican Book of Common Prayer translates "in saecula saeculorum" as "world without end." The Lord's Prayer (*Pater Noster*) likewise typically has this inserted ending: "Quia tuum est regnum, et potestas, et gloria, in saecula. Amen" ("For thine is the kingdom and the power and the glory, forever and ever, Amen").

gets released into action in the 1848 *Vormärz* turmoil in the German Confederation.[41] Hunter notes:

> It was here, in the aftermath of Napoleon's dissolution of the empire's multi-confessional structure and the suspension of Brandenburg-Prussia's tolerationist constitution—the latter serving to maintain a plurality of confessional religions and defend them against the solvent of Protestant rationalism—that a plethora of secularist and anti-secularist factions could seek to imprint their programs on the future religious and political order of Germany. . . . It was in the [nonfactual] philosophical histories attached to these politicized philosophies that the [Enlightenment] concept of secularization as an epochal transition to rational autonomy first appeared, whether this was conceived in terms of the elimination of religion through philosophy and science, in terms of the transformation of religion into a moral philosophy that preserves religious norms, or in terms of the sublimation of religion into secular social institutions or its atheistic de-sublimation into anthropology or sociology.[42]

Towards the end of the nineteenth century, Anglophone movers and shakers like Thomas Huxley were assuming a sharp divide between a discretely religious and private domain of ecclesial authority and a secular public domain in which science and reason were entirely autonomous from faith and the authority of the church.[43] By the early twentieth century, secularization begins to really take off in the Anglophone world among the progressive elites of the Huxley influenced academy. This breaks out of the academy only in the 1960s, and then secularization—as the de-Christianization of Western public meaning and common morality categories—really does happen.

It is important to understand that the post-Christianization of Western culture has happened over only the past fifty years—this is no intrinsically modern phenomenon. Let us take Australia as a case study.

THE POST-CHRISTIANIZATION OF AUSTRALIA

At the birth of the federation of Australia in 1901, nearly all Australians identified as Christian. Australia was very much a part of the British Empire at that time, with Anglican and Catholic Church demographics

---

41. Hunter, "Secularization," 1.
42. Hunter, "Secularization," 4.
43. Stanley, *Huxley's Church*.

being dominant, and religion being integral with public laws, moral norms, and commonly assumed high meaning categories.

The Australian Bureau of Statistics paints a very clear macro trend as regards religious affiliation through the twentieth century.[44] In 1901 Christian affiliation was 96.1 percent, 1.4 percent non-Christian religion, 2.4 percent no religion or not stated. In 1911, Christian affiliation drops slightly to 95.9 percent but then goes up to its highest point on record, being 96.9 percent in 1921. There is a big drop during the Great Depression, and in 1933 Christian affiliation is down to 86.4 percent. After World War Two in 1947 Christian affiliation is slowly rising at 88 percent, rising further to 89.4 percent in 1954. But from here it slides downward only. In 1966 it is 88.2 percent, with no religion or not stated at 11.1 percent. In 1976 there is a substantial drop to 78.6 percent Christian affiliation and no religion/not stated up to 19.7 percent. This is the departure from the church of the progressive secularists among the young and hedonic postwar boomer generation. In 1986 Christian affiliation continues to fall to 73 percent, no religion/not stated climbs to 25.1 percent, and for the first time non-Christian religious affiliation rises to higher than 1901 levels to 2 percent. In 1996, Christian affiliation is at 70.9 percent, no religion/not stated at 25.6 percent, non-Christian religion at 3.5 percent. In 2006 there is a big drop as intergenerational post-Christian demographics kick in with 63.9 percent Christian, 30.6 percent no religion/not stated, and 5.6 percent non-Christian. The Australian Bureau of Statistics notes: "In 2006, 80% of persons aged 65 years and over [born on or before 1941] identified themselves as Christian, compared with 55% of 18–24 year olds [born between 1982 and 1988]."[45] That is, the Christian demographic is firmly aging, and Christianity in Australia is rapidly losing intergenerational replicability. This trend in decline continues strongly through the first quarter of the twenty-first century, indication that a broad-based post-Christian cultural trend is now fully entrenched. National Church Life Survey Research notes that "around 1.6 million or 7% of Australians attend church in an average week, in 2016."[46] In 2021 Christian affiliation is 43.9 percent, no religion is 38.9 percent, and non-Christian religious affiliation is 8.3 percent. So, the twenty-first-century decline in Christian affiliation is now consistent and steep, at 10 percent per decade. Christian affiliation goes from 63.9 percent in 2006, to 52.1 percent in 2016, and

---

44. See the twentieth-century overview of religious affiliation statistics in Australia (Australian Bureau of Statistics, *Year Book Australia, 2008*).

45. Australian Bureau of Statistics, *Year Book Australia, 2008*, s.vv. "14.39 Religious Affiliation."

46. Jacka and Powell, "Changes in Church Attendance," para. 1.

to 43.9 percent in 2021.[47] This is clear evidence of Australia having entered a post-Christian cultural domain, with the clear origins of the trend in non-rebounding decline being in the 1970s. Should this trend continue, within three decades non-Christian religions will collectively have stronger population affiliations than all Christian communities combined. Perhaps we are in the last days (at least for Christianity in Australia). Did not Christ wonder, "When the Son of Man comes, will he find faith on earth?" (Luke 18:8).[48]

The point of locating secularization as a nineteenth-century combat concept that is advanced through Enlightenment-framed progressive legal and academic reform movements, and eventually produces the post-Christianization of Western culture as recently as the 1970s, is that contemporary Australian Christians largely take our secular age for granted and do not even notice how incompatible it is with orthodox christological theology.[49] We have largely accepted Huxley's territorialization of the public zone of scientific facts from the private zone of religious faith.[50] Here faith and religion are firmly removed from the public domain, and the only public categories we have to address the rising sense of fear and insecurity produced by our technological age are inherently unworkable secular categories trying to perform theological functions. Faith is here rendered inherently quietist, and in order to be good citizens of our secular age, we only pray, worship, and *personally* (i.e., privately, individually) believe in Christian eschatological categories, which may indeed remain orthodox but are of no public and

---

47. Australian Bureau of Statistics, "Religious Affiliation in Australia."

48. Josef Pieper notes that the Scriptures predict the decline of faith, the rise of the antichrist, and the catastrophic destruction of culture and the earth at the end of the age, precisely to show that the end does not arise from *within* history but comes from outside of history (*End of Time*, 32). This is in direct contrast to the "unrestrained proliferation of utopian-millenarian expectations of intra-historical salvation" (28). Effectively, Scripture declares that technological realized and secularized eschatologies of progress will prove to be tragic and hubristic delusions.

49. This, of course, is an allusion to Charles Taylor's fabulously interesting book *A Secular Age*. Taylor describes in his rich mosaic manner how we came to think of ourselves as living in an exclusively immanent frame. Taylor himself is ever optimistic about the work of divine pedagogy through all ages, even our secular age, but I cannot see how Christians can accept the metaphysical heresy of the immanent frame, let alone the christological heresy of the notion of discrete domains of reality where the lordship of Christ is simply excluded.

50. See Harrison, *Territories*. The successful polemic isolation of public knowledge categories in secular naturalist and scientific terms from the freedom of private religious faith commitments is clearly described by Harrison as a late nineteenth-century achievement.

practical significance to our lifeworld at all. Unless Christians stop meekly submitting to the christological heresy of secularization, we might as well smoke our eschatological hope.

A CONCLUDING THOUGHT ON A VIABLE CHRISTIAN ESCHATOLOGICAL LIFEWORLD ALTERNATIVE TO SECULAR ESCHATOLOGIES THAT MUST FAIL

In the first half of this chapter, we identified three arenas—AI, climate disaster, the cloud—where technology performs a tower of Babel-like function in both replacing faith and in promising to carry us over a crisis threshold into a new utopian solution to catastrophic problems which technological power has itself facilitated. If, contrary to the line of my argument, technology *does* save us, without our turning to God, then—as Micaiah said—"the Lord has not spoken through me" (1 Kgs 22:28). But it is one thing to disbelieve that we can haul ourselves out of the problems our anti-supernatural technological secularism is bringing back onto our own heads, and it is another thing to work for a good future with all the energy and determination we can find, while not tacitly leaning into the naturalistic, secular, and techno-salvific hopes of our times. And on this point, I think we can learn something from the Anabaptists and Stanley Hauerwas.

I recall a very memorable conversation I had some time ago with Ray Gingerich, an Anabaptist theologian from EMU (Eastern Mennonite University) in Virginia, USA.[51] Being committed to nonviolence in the most gun-loving culture in the known universe, where almost every action movie revels in the theme of redemptive violence, Ray said of his Mennonite community, "we live in the belly of the beast." But they *could* live, and they *could* witness against the violence of their culture, because they were different enough to cling together and to offer the church as an alternative polity to the world. This alternative polity was offered as an eschatological sign of the kingdom to come, a kingdom that only God can bring about. Stanley Hauerwas has been deeply influenced by Anabaptist theology and ecclesial practice, and the notion of the church as an alternative polity—the city of God—bearing witness to the city of man is a key theme in Hauerwas's work.[52]

---

51. See Gingerich and Grimsrud, *Transforming the Powers*.

52. See, for example, Hauerwas and Willimon, *Resident Aliens*; Hauerwas, *After Christendom*.

Should there be a great spiritual renewal—it has happened before—we might, at this time, be spared going the way of all hubristic, idolatrous, and morally collapsing empires of the past. But if not, if the church continues to dwindle in size and influence, and the culture continues to denounce its Christian roots and celebrate all things post-Christian, then perhaps we will need to follow the Anabaptist lead and learn how to be an alternative polity, an eschatological sign of hope, living within the belly of the beast. We may need to develop distinctive attitudes to technology that explicitly do not reinforce a naturalistic and secular form of life, that do not reduce us and our children to stimulus and response behaviors brilliantly controlled by our algorithmic masters. We may need to develop approaches to technology that are not false tools of salvation, that do not crowd out the divine realities of real relationships, natural realities, and real communities of worship with virtual fakes. For technology will not save us, and Christians at least should know this.

However it is done, the church must not make peace with technological eschatology. To do this, we need to intelligently and collectively develop ways of being the people of God that bears witness to the true eschatological hope of humanity: the radical work of God from beyond history that gives us the light of hope and energizes us in the good works ordained for us to do, no matter how dark human sin and demonic evil may make the world.

BIBLIOGRAPHY

Adorno, Theodor W. *The Culture Industry: Selected Essays on Mass Culture*. Edited by J. M. Bernstein 2nd ed. Routledge Classics. London: Routledge, 2001.

Agamben, Giorgio. *Where Are We Now? The Epidemic of Politics*. Translated by Valeria Dani. London: Eris, 2021.

Australian Bureau of Statistics. *1301.0—Year Book Australia, 2008*. Australian Bureau of Statistics, Feb. 7, 2008. https://www.abs.gov.au/ausstats/abs@.nsf/7d12bof676 3c78caca257061001cc588/636F496B2B943F12CA2573D200109DA9?opendocument.

———. "Religious Affiliation in Australia: Exploration of the Changes in Reported Religion in the 2021 Census." Australian Bureau of Statistics, July 4, 2022. https://www.abs.gov.au/articles/religious-affiliation-australia.

Bauman, Zygmunt. *Liquid Modernity*. Cambridge: Polity, 2000.

Betz, John R. *Christ the Logos of Creation: An Essay in Analogical Metaphysics*. Renewal Within Tradition. Steubenville, OH: Emmaus Academic, 2023.

———. Translator's introduction to *Analogia Entis: Metaphysics: Original Structure and Universal Rhythm*, by Erich Przywara, translated by John R. Betz and David Bentley Hart, 1–115. RRRCT. Grand Rapids: Eerdmans, 2014.

Cavanaugh, William. *Being Consumed: Economics and Christian Desire*. Grand Rapids: Eerdmans, 2008.

Conyers, A. J. *The Long Truce: How Toleration Made the World Safe for Power and Profit*. Waco, TX: Baylor University Press, 2009.

Desmond, William. *Being and the Between*. New York: State University of New York Press, 1995.

Ellul, Jacques. *Propaganda: The Formation of Men's Attitudes*. Translated by Konrad Kellen and Jean Lerner. New York: Vintage, 1965.

———. *The Technological Society*. Translated by John Wilkinson. New York: Vintage, 1964.

Estes, Nick. "Bill Gates Is the Biggest Private Owner of Farmland in the United States. Why?" *Guardian*, Apr. 5, 2021. https://www.theguardian.com/commentisfree/2021/apr/05/bill-gates-climate-crisis-farmland.

Gates, Bill. *How to Avoid a Climate Disaster*. London: Lane, 2021.

Gingerich, Ray C., and Theodore C. Grimsrud, eds. *Transforming the Powers: Peace, Justice, and the Domination System*. Minneapolis: Fortress, 2006.

Greenfield, Susan. *Mind Change*. London: Random House, 2014.

Harari, Yuval. *Homo Deus: A Brief History of Tomorrow*. London: Vintage, 2016.

Harrison, Peter. *The Fall of Man and the Foundations of Science*. Cambridge: Cambridge University Press, 2007.

———. *Some New World: Myths of Supernatural Belief in a Secular Age*. Cambridge: Cambridge University Press, 2024.

———. *The Territories of Science and Religion*. Chicago: Chicago University Press, 2015.

Hart, David Bentley. *All Things Are Full of Gods: The Mysteries of Mind and Life*. New Haven, CT: Yale University Press, 2024.

———. "The Myth of Machine Consciousness Makes Narcissus of Us All." *Psyche*, May 22, 2023. https://psyche.co/ideas/the-myth-of-machine-consciousness-makes-narcissus-of-us-all.

Hauerwas, Stanley. *After Christendom*. Nashville: Abingdon, 1999.

Hauerwas, Stanley, and William H. Willimon. *Resident Aliens: A Provocative Christian Assessment of Culture and Ministry for People Who Know That Something Is Wrong*. Nashville: Abingdon, 1989.

Heidegger, Martin. "'Only a God Can Save Us': The Speigel Interview (1966)." Translated by William J. Richardson. In *Heidegger: The Man and the Thinker*, edited by Thomas Sheehan, 45–67. London: Routledge, 2009.

———. *"The Question Concerning Technology" and Other Essays*. Translated by William Lovitt. New York: Garland, 1977.

Henry, John. *Knowledge Is Power: How Magic, the Government and an Apocalyptic Vision Helped Francis Bacon to Create Modern Science*. London: Icon, 2017.

Hunter, Ian. "Secularization: The Birth of a Modern Combat Concept." *Modern Intellectual History* 12 (2015) 1–32.

Jacka, Kathy, and Ruth Powell. "Changes in Church Attendance in Australia." NCLS Research, 2020. https://www.ncls.org.au/articles/changes-in-church-attendance-in-australia/.

Kingsnorth, Paul. "The Neon God: Four Questions Concerning the Internet, Part Two." *Abbey of Misrule*, Apr. 26, 2023. https://paulkingsnorth.substack.com/p/the-neon-god.

———. "The Universal: Four Questions Concerning the Internet, Part One." *Abbey of Misrule*, Apr. 14, 2023. https://paulkingsnorth.substack.com/p/the-universal.
Klein, Naomi. *The Shock Doctrine*. London: Penguin, 2007.
Kurzweil, Ray. *The Age of Spiritual Machines*. New York: Penguin, 1999.
Lewis, C. S. *The Last Battle*. London: Penguin, 1973.
Löwith, Karl. *Meaning in History*. Chicago: Chicago University Press, 1949.
Milbank, John. *Theology and Social Theory: Beyond Secular Reason*. 2nd ed. Oxford: Blackwell, 2006.
Nicholas of Cusa. *Of Learned Ignorance*. Translated by Germaine Heron. New Haven, CT: Yale University Press, 1954.
Northcott, Michael S. *God and Gaia: Science, Religion and Ethics on a Living Planet*. Routledge Environmental Humanities. New York: Routledge, 2023.
———. *A Political Theology of Climate Change*. London: SPCK, 2013.
Pieper, Josef. *The End of Time: A Meditation on the Philosophy of History*. San Francisco: Ignatius, 1999.
———. *The Silence of Saint Thomas*. South Bend, IN: Saint Augustine's, 1999.
Ross, Chanon. *Gifts Glittering and Poisoned: Spectacle, Empire, and Metaphysics*. Kalos. Eugene, OR: Cascade, 2014.
Shapin, Steven. *The Scientific Revolution*. 2nd ed. Chicago: University of Chicago Press, 2018.
Shaxson, Nicholas. *The Finance Curse*. London: Vintage, 2018.
———. *Treasure Islands*. London: Vintage, 2012.
Stanley, Matthew. *Huxley's Church and Maxwell's Demon: From Theistic Science to Naturalistic Science*. Chicago: Chicago University Press, 2015.
Taylor, Charles. *A Secular Age*. Cambridge, MA: Harvard University Press, 2007.
Tyson, Paul. *Theology and Climate Change*. Routledge Focus on Religion. London: Routledge, 2021.
Varoufakis, Yanis. *Technofeudalism: What Killed Capitalism*. London: Bodley Head, 2023.
Virilio, Paul. *The Administration of Fear*. Los Angeles: Semiotext(e), 2012.
Webster, Charles. *Paracelsus: Medicine, Magic and Mission at the End of Time*. New Haven, CT: Yale University Press, 2008.
White, Lynn, Jr. "Christian Myth and Christian History." *Journal of the History of Ideas* 3 (1942) 145–58.
Zuboff, Shoshana. *The Age of Surveillance Capitalism: The Fight for a Human Future at the New Frontier of Power*. London: Profile, 2019.

3

The Temporality of Eschatology
A Philosophical Analysis

Angus Brook

INTRODUCTION

In *Being and Time*, Martin Heidegger proposed that Dasein's sense of being, our sense of being, is grounded in temporality; an experience of time that is rooted in our relation to our own being. Heidegger argues that we can experience time in two distinct ways: an inauthentic temporality wherein we ground our sense of time on the cosmos, or an authentic temporality wherein we ground our sense of time on the finitude of our own being.[1] Thus, authentic temporality is constituted as a being resolute towards our own potentiality for death; for being or not being. This argument about time can be traced back to one of Heidegger's earliest lectures on the phenomenology of religious life: a lecture series in which Heidegger takes his notion of time from the everyday eschatology expressed in St. Paul's First Letter to the Thessalonians.[2] Heidegger, in reading First Thessalonians, takes St. Paul's use of the terms *chronos* and *kairos* to signify the distinction between inauthentic and authentic temporality. The passage Heidegger focuses on is 1 Thess 5:1–2 RSV:

> Now concerning the times [*cronōn*] and the seasons [*kairōn*], brothers and sisters, you do not need to have anything written to

---

1. Heidegger, *Being and Time*, 304–8, 349–52.
2. Heidegger, *Phenomenology of Religious Life*, 71–74.

you. For you yourselves know very well that the day of the Lord will come like a thief in the night.

However, Heidegger also flips the meaning of *kairos* on its head such that *kairos* no longer signifies the expectation of Jesus Christ's return, but rather the expectation of our own end, viz., death. The disagreement between St. Paul and Heidegger over the nature of temporality, if we can call it such, is a disagreement about what it is to be human, what our proper end is, i.e., what our purpose is, and in this, what the proper temporality of the everyday human experience of eschatology ought to be. In this chapter, I plan, with a bit of help from Thomas Aquinas, to develop an alternative philosophical analysis of the temporality of everyday eschatology found in the Letter to the Thessalonians. In doing so, the chapter will look to eschatology as it is found in liturgy, particularly the Liturgy of the Hours, to illustrate its arguments.

In order to achieve this, the chapter will be divided into three main sections. First, I will tackle Martin Heidegger's and Thomas Aquinas's reading of First Thessalonians, particularly with an eye to the account of eschatology and temporality they give in their interpretations. Following this, the chapter will focus on the work done by Pierre Hadot, Richard Sorabji, and Eamon Duffy to trace the origin of the Liturgy of the Hours in classical philosophy and its development in early Christian practices through to the breviary in the medieval period. This discussion will serve as a case study in the practical and experiential conditions of the temporality of everyday eschatology. On this basis, the chapter will then provide a general philosophical examination of the eschatological temporality found in First Thessalonians and an alternative account of everyday temporality grounded in Thomas Aquinas's account of time and eschatology.

But first a note on the way that I will be using the terms "temporality" and "time" in this chapter. It is worth noting that both Heidegger and Thomas Aquinas in their own way depend on Aristotle's account of time and in this sense are in rough agreement on the following: that time is the measurement of motion or becoming; that time is a measurement of a relation, that time is accordingly a feature of logical being (the being of thinking), and thus that there are various senses of time.[3] For the purpose of this chapter, I will be taking temporality to signify a species of time wherein humans measure our own becoming: our own internal sense of motion in experience and thought in relation to some final end. I take

---

3. Aristotle, *Physics*, 223a30–35. See also Brook, "Aristotelian Conception of Time(s)."

temporality in this sense to be something common to both Heidegger's and Thomas Aquinas's account of eschatology.

A second point to note here at the outset pertains to the matter of dispute and debate: What is the proper and true object of our final end? There are a variety of ways of talking about eschatology or final things in this context: the first is to think of the end of the world or the historical moment that Jesus returns in judgment; a second is to think about the final end of each human person and our personal relationship with our own end. The subject of this chapter, and the matter of dispute and debate between Heidegger and Thomas Aquinas, is this latter sense of eschatology: our relationship with our own final end and our experience of this relationship in our everyday living. It is in this context that temporality emerges as a theme for analysis. In this, I would argue, both Heidegger and Thomas Aquinas implicitly agree; temporality is grounded in an ordinary lived experience of eschatology, a measurement of our own relationship and dispositions towards the expectation of obtaining our own final end. The nub of their disagreement, likewise, is found in what our final end consists in. For Heidegger, our final end is death; for Thomas, our final end is beatitude. The task of this chapter is largely to unpack and explain in outline how, for Thomas Aquinas, our final end of beatitude may generate a certain everyday eschatological temporality.

There is a third way of thinking about eschatology that will necessarily inform this chapter, viz., the presence of God in any age or community, and particularly the eschatological age of the kingdom of God inaugurated by the birth, life, death, and resurrection of Jesus. This is the eschatological age present in and through the church via the Holy Spirit, as Matthew Levering remarks.[4] This third way of thinking about eschatology will serve as the horizon of Thomas's reading of First Thessalonians and therefore the context of the extraction of an everyday eschatological temporality in this chapter.

HEIDEGGER'S AND THOMAS AQUINAS'S READING OF ESCHATOLOGY IN FIRST THESSALONIANS

I do not plan to treat Martin Heidegger's notion of temporality or eschatology in any depth, but it is very difficult—if not impossible—to avoid Heidegger on this topic given his place in twentieth-century philosophical arguments about time, and particularly an eschatological notion of temporality. For those hoping for more depth, there is already

---

4. Levering, *Aquinas' Eschatological Ethics*, 18–19.

a great deal of excellent research in this area, starting with John van Buren's chapter "Martin Heidegger, Martin Luther," which traces Heidegger's intellectual development and his engagement with the theology of Martin Luther, and Kisiel's chapter "Heidegger (1920–21) on Becoming a Christian," an analysis of Heidegger's relationship with Christian theology.[5] This chapter will take Heidegger's arguments about temporality and eschatology more as a foil against which an alternative, Thomist everyday temporality of eschatology might be developed. As such, I will briefly outline the general horizon and structure of Heidegger's reading of First Thessalonians, drawing out some of the key concepts and arguments upon which we can then see the significant disagreements between Heidegger and Aquinas on how to live out an everyday eschatological temporality.

Heidegger's Reading of First Thessalonians

Martin Heidegger's philosophical writing style in German (let alone the English translation) is notoriously difficult and his philosophical position is even more so. As such, I cannot hope to do justice to all the nuances of Heidegger's reading of First Thessalonians or his way of extracting a notion of authentic temporality from it. What I will do instead is provide a rough and broad-brush overview of the approach Heidegger takes to reading St. Paul's epistles and the conceptual process by which his account of authentic and inauthentic temporality emerges. The first point to note, in this context, is that although Heidegger had grown up Catholic, and in fact had been a Jesuit seminarian, by the time he landed his first lecturing job he had become a convert to Lutheran Protestantism and had begun to engage in extensive reading and study of the theological writings of Martin Luther and other Protestant writers. On this basis, Heidegger approaches interpreting Paul's epistles already assuming that: (1) God is known to humans only via Christ crucified; (2) God is not known through the created order; and (3) the primary feature of God, for Christians, is distress and insecurity in the face of God's hiddenness and absence from everyday living.[6] It is not entirely clear, but it is also fairly certain, that Heidegger had taken on a certain reading of the effects of original sin closer to the "total depravity" end of the spectrum, viz., that original sin brought about a general "fallenness" or "absence of goodness" of nature.

5. Van Buren, "Martin Heidegger, Martin Luther"; Kisiel, "Heidegger (1920–21)."
6. Heidegger, *Phenomenology of Religious Life*, 67–69, 73.

According to Van Buren, Heidegger turned to reading Martin Luther after World War I with an assumption that early Christianity had been distorted and covered over by the infiltration of Hellenistic thought, particularly ancient Greek natural philosophy.[7] What Heidegger apparently admired most about Luther was his efforts to destroy or remove the influence of Aristotle and Neoplatonic thought in reading Scripture. In this context, the main target of Heidegger's initial destructive endeavors in reading First Thessalonians was the removal of natural theological assumptions, particularly the notion that God can be known via creation in conjunction with reason and a corresponding assertion that God is hidden and thus knowledge of God is restricted to Christ crucified.[8] In this way, Heidegger also implicitly rejects the notion of the goodness of the created order, collapses the Aristotelian distinction between nature and art, and assumes that human nature is sinful or at least fallen. In this case, eschatology, from the primordial Christian point of view according to Heidegger, must be understood as a relationship with a God who is absent and a temporality of living an authentic human life: living in the moment of our possibilities for being, obstinately expecting death.[9]

When we turn specifically to Heidegger's reading of Paul's letters, it is important to note that Heidegger's main agenda is not a theological exegesis, nor even a phenomenological interpretation of early Christian experience of temporality. Rather, to put it bluntly, what Heidegger is looking for is a way to extract a general phenomenological analysis of temporality, both authentic and inauthentic, from the text. In this way, God's almost immediate disappearance from Heidegger's interpretation of temporality in Paul's epistles merely reflects Heidegger's theological precommitment to a hidden God (not accessible to human experience) and his clear intention to extract a purely philosophical—rather than theological—analysis of temporality from them.

Heidegger reads First Thessalonians, broadly speaking, to reflect Paul's own sense of being a Christian and in this sense, his "having become" turned around by God.[10] This "having become" according to Heidegger is marked by two features: the first is a joy bound up with the knowledge of God through the Holy Spirit, the second a despair and distress in awaiting the end of time and the second coming of Jesus.[11]

---

7. Van Buren, "Martin Heidegger, Martin Luther," 160.
8. Van Buren, "Martin Heidegger, Martin Luther," 161.
9. Heidegger, *Phenomenology of Religious Life*, 66, 73.
10. Heidegger, *Phenomenology of Religious Life*, 66.
11. Heidegger, *Phenomenology of Religious Life*, 67.

Paul and all of the early Christians, according to Heidegger, are constantly beset both by joy in the Holy Spirit and suffering/distress in expecting the calling in of the end of time and the presence of the hidden God.[12] For Heidegger, this end of time is no end of history, but rather, a personal and individual end, a personal attitude towards time itself and how to measure and interpret one's own existence.[13] The whole temporality of eschatology, for Heidegger, is thus summed up as an "obstinate waiting" for the day of the Lord, viz., our own death.[14]

In an implicit shift from what he calls primordial Christian experience, Heidegger uses Paul's First Letter to the Thessalonians as a basis for extracting what he takes to be a proper phenomenological understanding of human temporality, which can be either authentic or inauthentic. Authentic temporality, as we see more fully developed in *Being and Time*, is a living resolutely in the face of and towards our own end in death.[15] Inauthentic temporality, as such, is to flee our eschaton, to flee death, into the world of chronological time where we measure our lives by the motion of things in the world, pretending to ourselves in everyday life that we will never die.

It is important to note that authentic temporality for Heidegger is fundamentally and always eschatological, but it is an eschatology of the individualized human stripped of relations and stripped of God's presence in nature, and perhaps even stripped of the hope of God's presence after death. The choice we have from Heidegger is an eschatological temporality in which we either orient ourselves towards our own death, our own temporal end, and resolutely live in the face of death, or we flee into the world and measure our own lives in relation to the regular countable motions of the world. Heidegger's everyday eschatological temporality is one in which humans are left in a relation to their own possibilities for being towards death and an absent God.

Thomas Aquinas's Reading of the Temporality of Eschatology in First Thessalonians

For Heidegger, the primary focus of temporality in First Thessalonians is an eschatological future. However, Thomas Aquinas reads in First Thessalonians a full spectrum of eschatological temporality, for wherever

12. Heidegger, *Phenomenology of Religious Life*, 68–69.
13. Heidegger, *Phenomenology of Religious Life*, 70–72.
14. Heidegger, *Phenomenology of Religious Life*, 79.
15. Heidegger, *Being and Time*, 304–11, 349–58.

and whenever God is present, so too in some way is the eschaton: past, present, and future. Thomas's prologue to the First Letter to the Thessalonians connects the church to the ark, the present to the past, considering Gen 7:17—the story of the flood. Here, the church of the Thessalonians is connected to the past trials and tribulations of Noah, his family, and all the animals on the ark. The church, as such, is referred back to the past and the past anticipates both the present and the future insofar as the ark symbolically anticipates the church—particularly the way that the church suffers tribulations in the hope of salvation and in the presence of God.[16] According to Thomas, as such, the whole orientation of First Thessalonians at the outset is the way that the past, which is no longer, nonetheless anticipates and is carried into the present reality of the Christian life experience of the Thessalonian church.

The opening line of Aquinas's lecture on chapter 5 of First Thessalonians refers the reader immediately to time, asserting that the preceding chapters ordered the Thessalonians to the past and the present, but now chapter 5 refers them to the future. In this context, Thomas comments that the future can be understood in two ways. The first concerns the times of nature, which no one but God the Father can know and of which no one but God the Father is in control.[17] The only thing we know about this kind of future time is that every day depends on God's creative and sustaining act, i.e., on God's providence. This time, the Thessalonians do not need to be written to about, because they already know that no one but God the Father knows the when. The second sense of the future, however, does need to be written about, because this sense of the future is something that the Thessalonians can and must prepare for. This second sense of the future, according to Thomas, is the day of the Lord, the day of salvation, the universal final end of human existence, viz., the presence of God.[18]

According to Thomas, the second sense of the future, the day of the Lord, is experienced in two ways, depending upon the preparations made: for the good and the saved (which is the same thing for Aquinas) the day of the Lord will be experienced as a wedding feast ("behold, the bridegroom"); for the evil, they will be met with sudden destruction.[19] There are two metaphors used here to contrast these ways of experiencing the day of the Lord: awake and asleep; light and darkness. Those who

---

16. Aquinas, *Commentary on First Thessalonians*, 149.
17. Aquinas, *Commentary on First Thessalonians*, 190.
18. Aquinas, *Commentary on First Thessalonians*, 192.
19. Aquinas, *Commentary on First Thessalonians*, 191.

are good (virtuous) are both awake and in the light; those who are evil (vicious) are both asleep and in darkness. According to Thomas, both these metaphors tell us something important about the relationship of humans to the day of the Lord, our final end, both our preparations for it and our future experience of it.[20]

Thomas argues that Paul should be read as informing us of two primary ways to prepare for the day of the Lord. The first, he argues, is to remain awake and live in the light by avoiding vice and pursuing virtue; the second—he writes—is to pray without ceasing.[21] Thomas, I think, takes these two ways of preparing for the presence of God to be intrinsically connected for the Christian. Indeed, in the lived Christian experience that Thomas is leaning on in his commentary, the formation of virtue and the pursuit of natural happiness is integrated with the sense of God's presence through the everyday prayer and liturgical life of the church community in an inextricable way.

What then, in brief, does Thomas's interpretation of the First Letter to the Thessalonians have to teach us about a temporality of everyday eschatology? There are a few points worth briefly making here. First, it is worth noting that Aquinas prioritizes the reality of the present and, like both Augustine and Aristotle, would claim that the past no longer exists, and the future does not yet exist. Further, as with Aristotle and Augustine, Aquinas is of the view that the present, the now, is not temporal (it is not a measurable motion).[22] We can see this play out in a number of ways: to begin with, Thomas is concerned with the past as something that remains in the present, particularly the constant experience of tribulation and the need to endure it with the help of God's grace. Equally, Thomas's reading of the fifth chapter of the First Letter to the Thessalonians is concerned with the orientation of the Christian, in everyday life, to the presence of the eschaton in the present as a way of life (living in the light and remaining awake). Finally, the future is something anticipated in and by the way we live now, i.e., the future is a matter of our preparations now.

Second, it is also worth noting that Aquinas generally follows Aristotle in arguing that time is the measurement of two kinds of motion in relation to each other, and thus time in general as a measurement is largely—but not entirely—circular because the most perfect natural motions are circular and continuous.[23] Think by way of example: we

20. Aquinas, *Commentary on First Thessalonians*, 192–93.
21. Aquinas, *Commentary on First Thessalonians*, 192.
22. Aquinas, *Commentary on Aristotle's "Physics,"* 287.
23. We see this in Aquinas, *Exposition of Aristotle's Treatise*. It is interesting to note

measure our own actions by the rotation of the earth on its axis (days) or the regular motion of the earth around the sun (years). Time, in these examples, always reflects a measurement of what happens, or what we do, or what changes occur, in relation to another motion, i.e., the motion of the earth. This way of thinking about time as circular, or at least grounded in circular motion, is crucial to Thomas's teleological understanding of the created order. Circular motion according to Thomas, following Aristotle, is teleological precisely because circular motion expresses a motion out of desire (or attraction) for completion and/or perfection. In particular, circular motion expresses motion grounded in desire for an external subject, i.e., a desire for the completion of a certain kind of relation.

I would suggest that, in this context, the circularity of time can be thought of in two ways. The first is what we might call chronological time, the measured time of days, seasons, and years. The Christian takes this kind of time to reflect God's creative act and God's providential relation to the created order. In this, the Christian experiences chronological time as a way in which God's goodness and providence operates in creation, and further, the way in which the eternal touches the finite, i.e., the created order revolves around eternity out of desire for completion, rest, and perfection. Additionally, we can think of circular time in a second (teleological) way inasmuch as we can take each day (or each moment) to be the reality from which and upon which we are ordered towards our end. In this respect, the circularity of time, or the grounding of time in circular motion, enables us to experience time as an orientation towards our own perfection via virtue, or towards our own destruction via vice. This is precisely the sense in which I think Thomas talks of living in the light and remaining awake in opposition to living in the darkness and falling asleep.

A third point worth making is that for Aquinas, contra Heidegger, the distinction between authentic and inauthentic time, if there is such a line to be drawn, will be reversed. It is hard to think that Thomas would accept a division between authentic and inauthentic time because he is committed to the truth (and reality) of both forms of temporality, i.e., both chronological and eschatological time are expressions of the reality of our experience of motion and change and both express the reality of God's presence in the created order. On the other hand, there is a similar division in Aquinas's thought between virtue (living in the light) and vice

---

here that it would appear that—for Thomas—the closest way that the created order imitates the eternity of God the Father is through a potentially eternal cyclical motion.

(living in a self-destructive way in the dark), but this division in Thomas's thought is the inverse of that made by Heidegger, i.e., for Thomas it is only in loving and pursuing God as our natural final end that being human is perfected. Thomas will think of our awareness (or lack of awareness) of God's presence in the created order and in our day to day lives as the cause of motion is the crucial feature of how we experience time. In this case, the awareness of God the Father (the Creator) and God the Son (the Logos of creation), would form our experience of the temporality of the created order: years, seasons, weeks, and days. Likewise, any division of the motions of the day, for a Christian, will be marked out by an experience of the presence of God with us through the Holy Spirit. For Thomas, however, whether we experience the presence of God in the created order or not, whether we are virtuous or vicious, will not change the real temporal order of God and creation.

A fourth, and final, point of comparison between Aquinas and Heidegger is their distinctly inverted sense of the relationship that constitutes the ground of temporality. For Heidegger, temporality is ultimately based on an individuating relationship, an interior relationship of the human person to their own end in death. By contrast, implicit in Thomas's account is an assertion of the reality and priority of external relationships. Aquinas, following Aristotle, is firmly of the view that time is the measure of motion that involves a relation of regular motion (like the revolution of the earth on its axis) and the motion of the substance (in this case, the human person), qua moved. This external relation of living in the light and staying awake is in the first instance communal; it is to do with the pursuit of virtue through actions in relation to others in community. The external relationship is also a relationship with God, and in particular, one grounded in a relationship with Jesus Christ, who has already been born, lived, died, and was resurrected from the dead; it is a relationship with Jesus who the Christian in the church expects to return again at the day of the Lord. In sum, Thomas's eschatological temporality is fundamentally communal and grounded in the reality of external relations.

I do not have room in this chapter to explore this further, but it seems to me that for Aquinas, temporality (in the sense Heidegger formulates as an everyday experience of time) will be Trinitarian; it will be measured out by the various ways that God is present in the life of the Christian and the church, and this in a circular way that connects the finite and eternal in a teleological relation by which and through which we are moved towards our final end; our capacity for goodness in its connection to experiencing the presence of God. I think, and in fact the argument of this chapter is, that we can see this sense of temporality playing out in the Liturgy of the Hours.

Case Study: The Temporality of Eschatology in the Liturgy

My interest in the Liturgy of the Hours began more than a decade ago, and largely through engaging in scholarship to improve the ancient philosophy course I regularly teach. In my scholarly investigation of the relationship between Hellenistic philosophical thought and practices and early Christian thought I became more and more interested in the arguments that philosophy was, in the ancient world, a way of life that intended to fulfill human nature and thus enable *eudaimonia*.[24] In the midst of all of this reading, I stumbled across Hadot's argument, hidden away in various texts, that the early Christian cycle of daily prayer not only imitated its Hebrew precedents, and did not merely take seriously the command to prayer at regular times of the day such that the Christian in prayer followed the birth, life, teaching, passion, death, descent into hell, and resurrection of Jesus each day. Additionally, according to Hadot, early Christians also integrated elements of Stoic and Cynic meditative techniques in order to enable Christians to live well and become virtuous.[25]

Hadot argues that early Christians often saw themselves, and their way of life, as a distinctive philosophical way of life; in fact, the only true philosophical way of life.[26] In particular, he focuses on the way that Stoic meditative practices would go on to inform Christian prayer and meditative practices. In this, Hadot identifies core ingredients of this influence: attention to oneself, constant vigilance, with the aim of developing a self-consciousness that is a thoroughly moral consciousness ordered towards human flourishing.[27] A central example of how Stoic practices may have influenced early Christian thought and practice can be found in Marcus Aurelius's *Meditations*. We find Marcus Aurelius starting his day with thankfulness for all that he has been given from those who have loved and taught him, and all that he learned about the good from them.[28] This is then followed by a meditation that allows one

---

24. See for example: Annas, *Morality of Happiness*; Nussbaum, *Therapy of Desire*; Reeve, *Action, Contemplation, and Happiness*; Hadot, *What Is Ancient Philosophy?*
25. See, for example, Hadot, *Philosophy*.
26. Hadot, *Philosophy*, 127–30.
27. Hadot, *Philosophy*, 130.
28. Marcus Aurelius, *Meditations*, bk. 1.

to prepare for the day, particularly preparing for humans to act in ways that appear to be bad and: (1) remind oneself of our common humanity and our communal nature, that we are made for cooperation, (2) remind oneself that others are acting for the sake of ends they believe good, and (3) plan for the day by working through what might go wrong and how one might respond in a virtuous way. Marcus Aurelius reminds himself to stop and meditate "every hour":

> Every hour make up thy mind sturdily as a Roman and a man to do what thou hast in hand with scrupulous and unaffected dignity and love of thy kind and independence and justice; and to give thyself rest from all other impressions. And thou wilt give thyself this, if thou dost execute every act of thy life as though it were thy last, divesting thyself of all aimlessness and all passionate antipathy to the convictions of reason, and all hypocrisy and self-love and dissatisfaction with thy allotted share. Thou seest how few are the things, by mastering which a man may lead a life of tranquillity and godlikeness; for the Gods also will ask no more from him who keeps these precepts.[29]

We see, then, a pattern emerges in Marcus Aurelius's *Meditations* that supports Hadot's claim that we find in Stoic meditative practices a model for breaking down the day into moments of prayer, and further, that each of these moments of meditation orders the person away from vice, towards virtue, in a life of human flourishing that is inherently communal. We find then in both Hadot's arguments and Marcus Aurelius's *Meditations* evidence of a central line of influence from Stoic practices into the prayer life of Christians, viz., that in breaking up the day into regular hours of meditation and reflection, each with its own key theme and subject, the human person undertaking those meditations is oriented towards virtue and goodness, and therein human flourishing.

What I find particularly interesting here, both in Hadot's arguments and in Marcus Aurelius's *Meditations*, is the sense in which living the good human life appears to involve a certain way of ordering one's day and thus experiencing time. Each day, it seems, is taken to be a now or present that is equivalent to a whole human life. The day, as it is a life lived (perhaps even the last day of life lived), is then divided into hours by which the person orders themselves towards virtue, and particularly virtues needed at specific hours of the day or moments of life. For the Stoic, the day ends, it seems, with a preparation for death and a reminder of what constitutes a good life and human flourishing. This, I think, is an

29. Marcus Aurelius, *Meditations*, 15.

experience of time that is eschatological in the sense we are focused on in this chapter, and an eschatological sense of time ordered towards the good, virtue, and human flourishing in relation to other humans, nature, and the divine. In sum, we find in Hadot's arguments about the influence of Stoic meditative practice on Christian asceticism and the Christian prayer life, precisely what Thomas suggests when he discusses living in the light and staying awake: a life of constant prayer oriented towards virtue.

Richard Sorabji's work *Emotion and Peace of Mind* adds another interesting layer to the connection between Hellenistic thought, early Christian thought, and the Liturgy of the Hours. In this work, Sorabji carefully justifies his argument that at least in part the Liturgy of the Hours developed in the desert fathers, and in the early monastic movement, as a means to ward off the seven deadly sins.[30] There are two key arguments in this work worth drawing briefly to your attention. The first is that the early church fathers clearly connected certain hours, or periods, of the day with temptation, especially the seven deadly sins.[31] Second, Sorabji argues that prayer was seen as a way to combat these temporal temptations as a point of origin for the proper Christian life of virtue and contemplation.[32] The Liturgy of the Hours, in this sense, illustrates a second feature of Thomas's reading of First Thessalonians, viz., that particular moments of the day tempt humans to live in the dark or perform actions that they will then want to hide from others, and that praying without ceasing is the appropriate Christian response to our temptation to fall asleep or live in the dark. The temporality of the Liturgy of the Hours, in this sense, then, recognizes the experience of temptations in the regular temporal rhythm of daily life towards living in the dark through vice, which then causes us to fall asleep and makes us blind to the presence of Christ.

There are two general features of the Liturgy of the Hours that I think are important to draw attention to before I move on to briefly outlining the temporality implicit in First Thessalonians as illustrated in the Liturgy of the Hours. The first is this: that there is clearly a general teleological structure to be found in the Liturgy of the Hours that illustrates the teleology that is implicit in First Thessalonians, viz., to fulfill our nature we need to engage in prayer and meditation as a means to avoid vice and form virtue. This, in one sense, is precisely what it means to live in the light and to stay awake, because it is through prayer that we

---

30. Sorabji, *Emotion and Peace*, 357–68.
31. Sorabji, *Emotion and Peace*, 364–65.
32. Sorabji, *Emotion and Peace*, 360–61.

experience our daily temporal life as illuminated by a light that is not our own and moved by the gifts of a Creator who transcends our powers. The second point is this: there is also an eschatological structure to be found in the Liturgy of the Hours; through the Holy Spirit the Christian community may experience and follow the life of Christ each day from conception through to death and resurrection; and further, the Christian community is expected to experience their own daily life, a temporality if you will, of the presence of Christ and the kingdom of God now. Teleology and eschatology are brought together inasmuch as there is a deep and strong analogy between God as Trinity and the created order such that the attainment of the teleological is perfected or completed by the eschatological. There is no teleology without eschatology, but also no eschatology without teleology.

It is certainly clear in Eamon Duffy's work on *Marking the Hours* that by the time we reach the high medieval period the connection between the daily reading, praying, and contemplation through the book of hours and the development of virtue was thought to be fairly self-evident. The day for many if not most medieval people was temporally marked out by reliving the presence of Jesus through the Holy Spirit in prayer. For many medieval women, they not only experienced the presence of Christ through the hours, but they followed Christ through the example of the Virgin Mary, complete with vivid images to focus their prayers and meditations on the hours of the day.[33] These prayers and meditations were thought, and perhaps should still be thought, to foster the development and further formation of seven virtues: the four cardinal and the three theological virtues. So, our first interesting connection here between the Liturgy of the Hours and temporality is just as Thomas Aquinas indicated in his interpretation of First Thessalonians; each day should entail following Christ and being aware of Christ's presence in daily life in such a way that the Christian lives in the light, and remains awake, by living virtuously, and thus fulfilling our ultimate end.

The eschatological temporality that we find illustrated in the medieval breviary exemplifies Aquinas's reading of First Thessalonians that is worth drawing out in a little more depth. The breviary exemplifies in quite a beautiful way the sense in which, both through the created order and the Holy Spirit, Jesus is thought to be (and perhaps experienced as being) actually present, or truly present in activity, in the daily lives of those praying the Liturgy of the Hours. The first hour of the breviary (Prime) celebrates the presence of Jesus as the Logos (the spiritual and

---

33. Duffy, *Marking the Hours*, 11–13.

intellectual light of the world) and Jesus' incarnation, as well as the resurrection. Throughout the hours of the day (Terce, Sext, and None), the Liturgy of the Hours engages with Jesus' life, passion, and death. The hours of the day also celebrate Pentecost and God's providential presence in the created order and human life. The final hour of the day in the breviary (Compline) then celebrates Jesus' descent, his defeat of death, and asks of the Christian that they remain awake and in the light through reflection on Jesus' midnight prayer (the Vigil or Matins). Through the breviary, the Christian literally relives Jesus' life, and in that, celebrates Jesus' presence. In this way, every day the prayer life of the church community lives out an eschatological temporality of the presence of Jesus Christ and the kingdom of God.[34]

In the breviary, we also find the exemplar of the daily life (and life as a whole) of the perfect human, Jesus, upon which we can model our actions in the quest for virtue, goodness, and beatitude. We also find the exemplar of the daily life of the church, through the life of Mary, upon which we can model our faith. Through the Liturgy of the Hours, we can be aware of the presence of the kingdom of God in our daily life. Aquinas writes of praying "thy kingdom come," we pray: first, that we will be entirely subject to God's will and thus achieve virtue; second, that we avoid wickedness and vice that deserves punishment; and third, in the hope for the presence of Christ (who is life) will destroy death.[35]

Extracting a Temporality of "Living in the Light" or a "Temporality of Life"

The final task of this chapter is to sketch out what a philosophical account of the temporality found in the Liturgy of the Hours and First Thessalonians might look like. In this respect, it might be helpful to go back to the start and compare Heidegger's account of temporality to the one we find in the Christian tradition. Heidegger's notion of temporality is something like this: each day one must experience oneself as having an almost infinite range of possible ways of being, or ways of acting, or ways of interpreting the world, but all of these possibly infinite ways of being are placed within a final limit that is death. For this reason, Heidegger's notion of temporality is much more existentialist than he ever liked to admit, for his account of temporality boils down to something like this:

---

34. Rausch, *Eschatology, Liturgy, and Christology*, 125. Rausch's focus is on the Eucharist, but I would suggest that an analogous sense of eschatological temporality is found in the Liturgy of the Hours.

35. Aquinas, *Aquinas Catechism*, 124–25.

today, knowing that I am going to die at some point—perhaps even soon—I will assert myself and my possibilities for being resolutely; I will be a light to myself in the universal darkness I find myself fallen into. Through my sense of time, I will assert my individual human freedom in the face of death. In my view, this account of temporality is best called an *a*-theistic temporality of possibility and death.

The sense of temporality I have extracted from the Liturgy of the Hours, with some guidance from Aquinas, is quite to the contrary. As Thomas argues, in a sense, death is unnatural for humans and thus death is not our end, either teleological or eschatological. So, what we find in the Liturgy of the Hours is a temporality that is cyclical and ordered towards an extended now: every day we follow Christ, every day we live illuminated both perceptually and intellectually by a light that is not our own, and every day we go to sleep in the hope of new life (and eternal life); waking up to a new day, a new creation, the resurrection of Christ.[36] In sum then, the temporality we find here is a temporality of light and life; that in living each present day in the light that is not our own, we live each day a specifically human life, and in the hope of eternal life. If I were to put this in more philosophical terms, albeit still explicitly Christian, I suspect that the temporality we can extract from First Thessalonians will be Trinitarian:

1. We will first have an everyday temporality of the presence and goodness of God in the regular motions of the created order: the days, the seasons, the year, etc. In this way, we have an everyday temporality by and through which the present is connected to eternity through the cyclical teleological motions of the cosmological order in which motion occurs out of a desire for goodness.

2. We will also have an everyday temporality of our daily moral order following Christ the perfect human; our efforts to remain awake and live in the light, to avoid vice and to practice virtue, and therein to fulfill our own nature. Shadowing this is an everyday temporality of our daily life of faith, following Mary as the exemplar of the life of the church.

3. We will finally have an everyday temporality of the presence of the Logos as our final end, and this more so in our intellectual or contemplative awareness of the analogy between the motion of the created order and the transcendent. In this, I think we find a temporality of the finite measured in relation to the eternal:

---

36. Roguet, *Liturgy of the Hours*, 30.

an expectation of the presence of God that plays out in how we experience everything we do, and a temporality completed in prayer and contemplation.

BIBLIOGRAPHY

Annas, Julia. *The Morality of Happiness*. Oxford: Oxford University Press, 1993.
Aquinas, Thomas. *The Aquinas Catechism: A Simple Explanation of the Catholic Faith by the Church's Greatest Theologian*. Manchester, NH: Sophia Institute, 2000.
———. *Aquinas' Exposition of Aristotle's Treatise on the Heavens*. Translated by Pierre Conway and Fabian R. Larcher. Past Masters. Charlottesville, VA: InteLex, 1993. Ebook.
———. *Commentary on Aristotle's "Metaphysics."* Translated by John P. Rowan. Notre Dame, IN: Dumb Ox, 1995.
———. *Commentary on Aristotle's "Physics."* Translated by Richard J. Blackwell. Notre Dame, IN: Dumb Ox, 1995.
———. *Commentary on the First Letter of Saint Paul to the Thessalonians*. Translated by F. R. Larcher. Lander, WY: Aquinas Institute for the Study of Sacred Doctrine, 2012.
Aristotle. *Physics*. Translated by P. H. Wicksteed and F. M. Cornford. London: Harvard University Press, 1957.
Brook, Angus. "An Aristotelian Conception of Time(s)." *Metaphysica* 24 (2023) 129–45.
Duffy, Eamon. *Marking the Hours: English People and Their Prayers*. New Haven, CT: Yale University Press, 2011.
Hadot, Pierre. *Philosophy as a Way of Life*. Translated by Michael Chase. Oxford: Blackwell, 1995.
———. *What Is Ancient Philosophy?* Translated by Michael Chase. Cambridge, MA: Harvard University Press, 2004.
Heidegger, Martin. *Being and Time*. Translated by John Macquarrie and Edward Robinson. New York: Harper & Row, 1962.
———. *The Phenomenology of Religious Life*. Translated by Matthias Fritsch and Jennifer Gosetti-Freencei. Bloomington: Indiana University Press, 2004.
Kisiel, Theodore. "Heidegger (1920–21) on Becoming a Christian: A Conceptual Picture Show." In *Reading Heidegger from the Start: Essays in His Earliest Thought*, edited by Theodore Kisiel and John van Buren, 175–92. New York: State University of New York Press, 1994.
Levering, Matthew. *Aquinas' Eschatological Ethics and the Virtue of Temperance*. South Bend, IN: University of Notre Dame Press, 2019.
Marcus Aurelius. *Meditations*. Translated by Martin Hammond. Milton Keynes, UK: Penguin Classics, 2008.
Nussbaum, Martha. *The Therapy of Desire: Theory and Practice in Hellenistic Ethics*. Princeton, NJ: Princeton University Press, 1996.
Rausch, Thomas P. *Eschatology, Liturgy, and Christology: Toward Recovering an Eschatological Imagination*. Collegeville, MN: Liturgical, 2012.
Reeve, C. D. C. *Action, Contemplation, and Happiness*. Cambridge, MA: Harvard University Press, 2012.
Roguet, A. M. *The Liturgy of the Hours*. Translated by Peter Coughlan and Peter Purdue. London: Chapman, 1974.

Sorabji, Richard. *Emotion and Peace of Mind: From Stoic Agitation to Christian Temptation*. Oxford: Oxford University Press, 2000.

Van Buren, John. "Martin Heidegger, Martin Luther." In *Reading Heidegger from the Start: Essays in His Earliest Thought*, edited by Theodore Kisiel and John van Buren, 159–74. New York: State University of New York Press, 1994.

4

Eschatological Victory or *Apokatastasis* of the Universe?
Versions of Salvation from the Apocalypse of Peter to Maximus the Confessor

ADAM G. COOPER

Early Christian versions of salvation emerged and developed through a dynamic and interactive process involving ritual experience, liturgical instruction, social conflict, intellectual reflection, and polemical argument. Already from the first century three analogies of salvation had emerged as categorically dominant themes: physical healing, spiritual redemption, and eschatological victory. Each of these themes, in turn, found a common site of cultivation in the initiatory practices of baptism, by which Christians believed they were joined to the world-changing death of Jesus and raised to heavenly life in his church, a kind of earthly anticipation of heavenly paradise.

This chapter focuses first on the analogy of salvation as physical healing. In this well-known model, Christ is envisioned as the paradigmatic doctor, and the human malady a sickness that requires healing by his hand. Next it turns to study the vision of heavenly salvation through Christ as spiritual redemption and a victory over hostile cosmic powers. Here is explored the controversial question of a universal *apokatastasis*, and the merit and fate of Origen's infamous proposals on the topic. Finally, the chapter turns to more apocalyptically styled proposals of Christ's victorious reign, which were found widely in both staunchly orthodox and more marginal Christian texts. Starting from the Apocalypse of Peter and moving through to the seventh-century theology of Maximus the

Confessor, we discover how more spectacular descriptions of heaven and hell, including various millenarian and universalist versions, give way to more guarded affirmations of final stability in God and of the abiding vulnerability of the Christian disciple.

SALVATION AS PHYSICAL HEALING

In a pioneering and detailed historical study on the subject, Adolph von Harnack argued that early Christianity was above all a religion of healing.[1] There is much in the New Testament writings that seems to support this view. Healing was not peripheral to Jesus' ministry, but formed an essential component of his redemptive mission and of the dominically mandated activity of the nascent apostolic church (Isa 53:5; Matt 8:16–17; 10:8; 25:36; Jas 5:14). Jesus' healing ministry was understood as a sign confirming the advent of the messianic kingdom (Isa 58:8; Jer 33:6; Mal 4:2; Matt 4:23–25; Mark 1:34; Acts 10:38). His acts of healing commonly had a holistic impact—anthropologically, socially, and theologically—being more or less explicitly or implicitly linked to faith and forgiveness, restoration and salvation (Matt 9:22; Luke 8:48; 13:14–17; 18:42; 1 Pet 2:24; John 7:23). Through the healing ministry of Jesus we learn that the sick are objects of especial divine solicitude: "It is not the healthy who need a doctor, but the sick" (Luke 5:31; see also Matt 8:3). The formula "the sick" (*hoi kakōs echontes*), however, must be interpreted to include more than just the demographic of the physically afflicted. As Jesus goes on to explain: "I have come to call not the righteous, but sinners to repentance" (Luke 5:32).

Already by the time of Ignatius of Antioch (d. ca. 115), the belief that Jesus is the true physician appears to be a crucial christological motif, very likely set in opposition to the rival healing cult of Asclepius.[2] The simultaneously chiastic and parallelistic structure of the famous christological confession of Ignatius's *Letter to the Ephesians* 7.2 artfully underscores this claim:

---

1. Harnack, *Mission and Expansion*. See also Dumeige, "(Christ) médecin"; Larchet, "Christ médecin."

2. Scholarship is divided on the extent to which there existed a Christ-Asclepius rivalry in early Christianity. See inter alia Heyne, "Healing and Asclepian Cult"; Porterfield, *Healing in Christianity*; Dinkler, *Christus und Asklepios*.

A	There is one physician ...	
B	of flesh	of Spirit
C	generate	ingenerate
D	in a man	God
D'	in death	true life
C'	from Mary	from God
B'	first passible	then impassible
A'	... Jesus Christ our Lord.	

According to Harnack, although this theme was taken up by numerous writers, including Clement of Alexandria, for whom Christ stands in contrast to the "invented savior" and healer Asclepius,[3] it was Origen of Alexandria who depicted Jesus' function as physician "more frequently and fully than anyone else."[4] Many of Origen's statements on the theme were elaborated in his treatise against Celsus. Celsus had criticized Christianity for what seemed to him to be its ostensible interest in offering refuge to morally dubious types. "Let us hear what sort of people these Christians invite. Everyone, they say, who is a sinner, who is devoid of understanding, who is a child, and, to speak generally, whoever is unfortunate, him will the kingdom of God receive."[5] In answer, Origen affirmed Christianity's welcome extended especially to sinners, but pointed out that it is with a view towards their healing and restoration that the invitation is given. A thief invites other thieves into his fellowship in order to help him steal. A Christian, on the other hand,

> even though he invites those whom the robber invites, invites them to a very different vocation, namely, to bind up his wounds by the word [of Christ], and to apply to his soul, festering amid evils, the medicines obtained from the word, and which are

---

3. Clement of Alexandria, *Exhortation to the Greeks* 2.23; see also *Paed.* 1.2.
4. Harnack, *Mission and Expansion*, 98n37.
5. Origen, *Cels.* 3.59 (Borret, 136–38).

analogous to the wine and oil, and bandages, and other healing applications which belong to the art of medicine.[6]

The analogy between the art of medicine and the ministry of Christian healing only goes so far, however, for Christ the Savior is the "true physician" not just of bodies, but also of souls.[7] Indeed, Origen calls Jesus not just *iatros*, a doctor, but the *archiatros* or chief physician.[8] Probably the only other patristic author who comes close to Origen's enthusiasm in exploiting the *Christus medicus* motif to this extent is Augustine, who, echoing Origen, calls Christ the "complete physician" (*totus medicus*),[9] the "doctor of all" (*medicus omnium*),[10] the only one able to heal all our wounds of body and soul. Indeed, he is both the doctor and the medicine itself (*ipsa medicus, ipsa medicina*).[11]

SALVATION AS SPIRITUAL REDEMPTION

The redemption of all creation is envisioned in early Christian teaching as both a fruit of Christ's incarnate and redemptive economy and the original goal of God's initial creative acts. The idea that creation exists for the sake of the incarnation, expressed in the New Testament proposal of Christ as the archetypal image of God and creation's original agent, goal, and binding force (Col 1:15–17; Eph 1:1–10; 2 Tim 1:9–10; Heb 1:3), along with the vision of creation's end in God's being "all in all" (1 Cor 15:28), impelled Christian thinkers to try and relate protology to eschatology, via the incarnation, in a harmonious and purposeful trajectory. Few gave this challenge as much intellectual energy as Origen. His basic working principle was simple: the end is like the beginning. The one end, asserted by the apostle in 1 Cor 15:28 to consist in the subjection of all things to the Father through Christ, indicates one beginning.[12] Its accomplishment signals the total actualization of the rational creature's potential for likeness to God achieved by free will (and not necessity) and divine training. Purified from all wickedness and all desire for sin, fully

---

6. Origen, *Cels.* 3.61 (Borret, 142).
7. Origen, *Hom. Lev.* 7.1 (PG 12:476B).
8. Origen, *Hom. 1 Reg.* (PG 12:1021).
9. Augustine, *Tract. Ev. Jo.* 3.2f (PL 35:1396f).
10. Augustine, *Tract. ep. Jo.* 2.1 (PL 35:1989).
11. Augustine, *De doctrina Christiana* 1.14.13 (PL 34:24). This theme is found also in Jerome and Ephrem. See Arbesmann, "Concept of *Christus Medicus*."
12. Origen, *Princ.* 1.6.2 (Behr, 54–56).

and permanently possessed of the good, reestablished in its original unity and perfection, the rational being is so filled with God that nothing else can be desired beside him. Between God and the soul no difference can be discerned, for God has truly become "the mode and measure" of all the soul's movements.[13]

Origen importantly regarded this subjection, which equates to the fullness of salvation, as voluntary, not forced. This suggests that all rational beings, even God's enemies, will somehow come to consent to final salvation: "Divine providence will never abandon the universe. For even if some part of it becomes very bad because the rational being sins, God arranges to purify it, and after a time to turn the whole world back to Himself."[14] Within such a framework, Origen could not avoid considering the demons and even Satan himself as objects of divine solicitude; indeed, the final integrity of the whole depends also on them. It is possible he later withdrew this opinion, as Rufinus and Jerome suggested on the basis of a now lost letter.[15] But the realization of God's being "all in all" in a final *apokatastasis*, or redemptive restoration of all creation, remained the determinative principle of his eschatology.

It took some time for thinkers in the Alexandrian intellectual tradition to realize that such a strict correlation of beginning and end made it difficult to offer any positive account of the motion and material multiplicity that mark creaturely history. It also made it difficult to reconcile the final unity of things in God with a decisive and eternally irreconcilable difference between the saved and the damned. Origen had faced this question squarely, but had prudently left judgment on it to his readers.[16]

What was less open to question was the determinative status and destiny of the body in human salvation. Interestingly, nowhere does the New Testament use the phrase "resurrection of the flesh"; it speaks instead of resurrection "from the dead" (*ek nekron*).[17] The modification, which also found its way into the early baptismal creeds, seems to have been specifically precipitated by the second- and third-century polemical contests with heretical Christian teachers who denied salvation to the

---

13. Origen, *Princ.* 3.6.3 (Behr, 225).
14. Origen, *Cels.* 4.99 (Chadwick, 263). See also Origen, *Princ.* 1.6.1 (Behr, 53–54).
15. Stephen Colquitt Thomas, "Demonology," in McGuckin, *A–Z of Origen*, 85–86.
16. Origen, *Princ.* 1.6.3.
17. Eg., Matt 17:9; Mark 6:14; Luke 16:31; John 21:14.

physical body and interpreted scriptural references to resurrection in a purely symbolic way.[18]

In his influential treatise *On the Resurrection of the Dead*, Tertullian turned his oratorial eloquence to defending a strikingly material conception of the final resurrected state.[19] Tertullian makes the bold assertion that the flesh is the very hinge on which the soul's salvation turns (*caro salutis est cardo*). Spiritual blessings such as forgiveness, illumination, and deification are imparted via physical means: baptism, signing with the cross, the laying on of hands, feeding on Christ's body and blood.[20] Thus the outward and bodily come first; the inward and spiritual come second.[21] There is also something fitting about bodily resurrection: Would God let that flesh pass into oblivion that he has wrought with his own hands, animated with his own breath, sanctified with his sacraments, and crowned as "queen of his creation," "priestess of his religion," and "sister of his Christ"?[22] Decomposition and decay, dissolution and dispersion finally present no insurmountable obstacle, for restoring the flesh is easier than making it from scratch, and the Savior and Creator are one and the same.[23]

To deny the resurrection of the body is to divide the psychophysical unity of human nature. Soul and body are mutually co-inherent, so that even the most sublime intellectual operations take place "in the flesh, with the flesh, and through the flesh."[24] Tertullian accepts the Stoic doctrine that the soul is itself corporeal; from it all physical and perceptual activity is derived.[25] Thus future beatitude depends on the Spirit's transfiguration of the whole person, not a part. The fact that such bodily organs as teeth, stomach, and sexual organs have no foreseeable function in the resurrected state does not mean they will not exist; the equality with the angels mentioned by Jesus means simply that the blessed will be free from all physical necessity.[26]

---

18. See Kelly, *Early Christian Doctrines*, 163–66.

19. Most of the rest of this section is drawn from Cooper, *Life in the Flesh*, 65–68 (© Adam G. Cooper 2008). Reproduced with permission of the Licensor through PLSclear.

20. Tertullian, *Res.* 8 (PL 2:806).

21. Tertullian, *Res.* 8 (*ANF* 3:551).

22. Tertullian, *Res.* 9 (*ANF* 3:551–52).

23. Tertullian, *Res.* 11 (*ANF* 3:552–53).

24. Tertullian, *Res.* 15 (*ANF* 3:555).

25. Tertullian, *Res.* 17 (*ANF* 3:557).

26. Tertullian, *Res.* 60–62 (*ANF* 3:591–93).

Among martyrological accounts, the kind of theology of death, the body, and resurrection that we find here in Tertullian fueled a reinterpretation of death that enabled Christians to face threat and persecution with stoic contempt, and to exhibit an equal disdain for both physical pleasure and pain. A famous early example is found in the letter of Ignatius of Antioch to the Christians in Rome, in which the captive bishop welcomes his impending tortures with an almost pathological, masochistic glee:

> May I have the full pleasure of the wild beasts prepared for me; I pray they will be found ready for me. Indeed, I will coax them to devour me quickly—not as happens with some, whom they are afraid to touch. And even if they do not wish to do so willingly, I will force them to it. Grant this to me; I know what benefits me. Now I am beginning to be a disciple. May nothing visible or invisible show any envy toward me, that I may attain to Jesus Christ. Fire and cross and packs of wild beasts, cuttings and being torn apart, the scattering of bones, the mangling of limbs, the grinding of the whole body, the evil torments of the devil—let them come upon me, only that I may attain to Jesus Christ.[27]

Another account concerns the martyrdoms of Perpetua and Felicity who were executed in Carthage in AD 203. Quite probably they were members of the New Prophecy movement, to which Tertullian also attached himself. Their last days were recorded first by Perpetua herself while in prison, then by an eyewitness for posterity's sake, "to the glory of the Lord, as that you who know them by report may have communion with the blessed martyrs, and through them with the Lord Jesus Christ."[28] Of Felicity, who was heavily pregnant at the time, it was reported: "She was in great grief lest on account of her pregnancy she should be delayed [in being killed], because pregnant women are not allowed to be publicly punished."[29] But soon her worries were over. Going into labor four weeks early, Felicity bore a daughter. Now she was free to face the painful death she was longing for. She "rejoiced that she had safely brought forth, so that she might fight with the wild beasts; from the blood and from the midwife to the gladiator, to wash after childbirth with a second baptism."[30] The fame of these North African martyrs spread widely and helped solidify Christian resistance to coercive repression.

---

27. Ign. *Rom.* 5.2–3 (LCL 24:277).
28. *Passion of the Holy Martyrs Perpetua and Felicity*, pref. (*ANF* 3:699).
29. *Passion of the Holy Martyrs Perpetua and Felicity* 5.2 (*ANF* 3:703).
30. *Passion of the Holy Martyrs Perpetua and Felicity* 6.1 (*ANF* 3:704).

Origen, whose father had been killed by state-sponsored persecution and who eventually himself suffered despicable tortures before death, likewise had much to contribute to Christianity's debate with pagan intellectuals over Christ's physical existence and the spiritual redemption of the body. Origen never went as far as Tertullian's overt materialism, preferring the phrase "resurrection of the body" to "resurrection of the flesh." Indeed, the Alexandrian seems to have viewed human embodiment as the punitive consequence of a fall of pure intellects from a state of immaterial perfection through a process of satiety and "cooling" (*psychesthai*) by which they became terrestrially instantiated "souls" (*psychai*).[31] Later tradition judged Origen's ambivalence on such matters sternly, yet Origen bequeathed a number of key concepts about the flesh and its place in the divine economy which were taken up by mainstream orthodox tradition in both east and west. For a start, he loosely held with Irenaeus a tripartite view of the human being as body, soul, and spirit. By "spirit" they meant not God's Spirit but a faculty akin to moral conscience, which later writers came increasingly to associate with *nous* as a person's receptive spiritual center, his or her ineradicable capacity for self-transcendence.[32] As an essential part of the total human composite, spirit stands at the top of a hierarchy at the bottom of which is body, with soul mediating between the two. For Origen this tripartite structure had its parallel in Scripture in which the wise interpreter distinguishes between the plain narrative or letter (body), its moral or dogmatic content (soul), and mystical instruction (spirit).[33] This structure in turn characterizes the shape of the Christian life, in which the believer progresses from ascetic struggle to natural philosophy, finally arriving by ascent at contemplation or the vision of divine things.[34]

Far from sanctioning the denigration of the flesh, this threefold structure equipped Origen with the conceptual rationale with which to oppose Celsus's scornful contention, taken from the materialist philosopher Heraclitus, that bodies, especially dead ones, are "worse than dung."[35] To the contrary, Origen notes that it is precisely in virtue of its relation to a personal spiritual subject that even a cadaver is properly treated with due honor. Similarly, just as one is not free to disregard disciplined engagement with the "body" or text of Scripture, neither

---

31. Riemer Roukema, "Souls," in McGuckin, *A–Z of Origen*, 201.
32. See Lubac, *Theology in History*, 136–49.
33. Origen, *Princ.* 4.2.4 (Behr, 252–53).
34. Origen, *Princ.* 4.2.4 (Behr, 252–53); *Comm. Cant.*, prol. (Lawson, 44).
35. Origen, *Cels.* 5.24 (Chadwick, 282).

can one trivialize the contingent conditions of physical life implicit in the lifelong pursuit of moral virtue. Origen's penchant for allegorization never led him to abandon devotion to the written text, as his remarkable accomplishments in the science of text criticism demonstrate. Henri de Lubac has shown in his masterful study on patristic and medieval exegesis how, for Origen, the *historia* or bare narrative report presents the nonnegotiable basis (*fundamentum*) for penetrating Scripture's spiritual content. Encounter with divine realities in this life will always be bound to the bodily signs in which they are concealed and disclosed.[36]

In the sixth century a controversy arose in this connection in which Origen's name became embroiled. Certain enthusiastic monastic supporters of his legacy, finding additional inspiration in the writings of Evagrius and Didymus, found themselves expelled from their Palestinian monastery for entertaining speculations that were felt to undermine Christian belief in the physicality of the resurrected body and the damnation of evil spirits. It is quite possible that these "Origenists," as they were labeled, were simply inclined to more philosophical reasoning about their Christian faith, thinking through aspects of Christian teaching by means of Neoplatonic conceptual categories. But their opponents virulently attacked their ideas as impious and heretical:

> They say . . . that the risen body—first Christ's, then ours—is in the end totally annihilated . . . that in the restoration (*apokatastasis*) all intelligent beings, even the demons, will be able to create worlds; they say that our bodies will be raised in an ethereal and spherical form, and indeed that the Lord's body has already been raised thus; they say that we will be equal to Christ in the restoration.[37]

So sharply contested and politicized did the controversy become that even the emperor was drawn into the debate. Through an imperial decree in AD 543, and explicitly citing Origen as the problematic source, Justinian condemned teachings that propose a pretemporal creation and fall of souls, their spherical shape in the resurrection, the temporal limiting of damnation, and the eventual restoration of demons. This condemnation was reiterated ten years later with the so-called Fifteen Anathemas, composed by bishops just prior to their participation in the Fifth Ecumenical Council in the imperial capital, Constantinople.[38]

36. Lubac, *Four Senses of Scripture*, 41–82. See also the passages collated by Balthasar in Origen, *Spirit and Fire*, 86–112.

37. *Vita Cyriaci* 12; quoted in Daley, *Hope of Early Church*, 189–90.

38. Di Berardino and Studer, *Patristic Period*, 181.

Without ending speculations about human identity beyond death, however, these anti-Origenist anathemas were inadequate to address the outstanding intellectual problems posed by Christian eschatology. John Philoponus, the famous Aristotelian commentator and one of the keenest minds of the period, continued to think through the question whether our physical bodies as we know them are capable of the kind of existence implied by incorruptible life. He criticized earlier views, expressed for example by Gregory of Nyssa and Cyril of Alexandria, for failing to account for the inherent corruptibility of our current physical bodies, proposing instead the need in the eschaton for the essential and qualitative transformation of all physical natures, including the human form.[39]

We shall return to the question of *apokatastasis* in due course. In the meantime, we may round off this section by mentioning yet another of Origen's important, if controversial, contributions to reflection on the flesh. It concerned the relationship between the body and personal identity. Debating with both the spiritualizing intellectualism of pagan objectors and the naïve literalism of unthinking Christians, he contended that in view of the body's destruction following death and the radical physical transformation awaiting the baptized, personal and corporeal continuity will be preserved in the eschaton *not* by God omnipotently reconstituting the original material particles of each person's body, but by means of a certain corporeal *eidos* or *logos*.[40] This *eidos* or *logos* is a distinctive form or inner principle which, functioning like the *logoi spermatikoi* in Stoic cosmology, permanently constitutes a person's bodily existence as his or her own. With this reasoning goes the observation that, like a river, the underlying matter from which all bodies are constituted is naturally subject to continual flux, and is therefore incapable of providing bodily beings with ontological stability. Such stability must derive then not from the material body as such but from that body's native *eidos*, the determinative code which gives every species as well as every individual body its unique particularity and specific characteristics. When a person dies, this code is not destroyed, but ensures that the more refined luminous body with which the soul will be appropriately clothed in the resurrection, while as qualitatively different from the original body as a tree from its original seed, essentially constitutes the same person.[41]

---

39. Daley, *Hope of Early Church*, 195–96.

40. Origen, *Princ.* 2.10.3 (Behr, 133).

41. Origen, *Princ.* 2.10.3 (Behr, 133); *Cels.* 5.22–5.23 (Chadwick, 281–82). See also Chadwick, "Origen, Celsus, and Resurrection," 98–99.

Hereby the problem of continuing identity beyond death seems to have been resolved. Yet, as Bynum notes, the greater part of late antique theology was "unwilling to jettison material continuity in return for philosophical consistency.... They were willing to sacrifice philosophical coherence for the oxymoron of incorruptible matter."[42] And this was so, we might add, due to their sense of the vital material importance of Christ's own resurrection.

SALVATION AS ESCHATOLOGICAL VICTORY

The vision of salvation through Christ as a victory over hostile cosmic powers seems a far cry from the simple cures and healings Jesus performed as an itinerant preacher. The differences between the two analogies of salvation suggest rapid developments in the circumstances that shaped early Christian thinking about salvation and heavenly hope, among which many scholars would include sporadic persecution, social insecurity, economic strain, all heightened by the failed hope of Jesus' imminent eschatological return to judge the world and wrap up history as we know it. In such a context it is no wonder that people's sense of crisis came to be expressed in and further stimulated by vivid apocalyptic imagery: fire, flood, disaster, and cosmic violence that will destroy the known world.

But as Daley has argued, while it is true that after the death of Christ's first witnesses the Christian communities realized that "a re-orientation of the timeline of [their] eschatological hope" was needed, this did not involve the loss of urgency and expectation of Christ's imminent return, which have always marked authentic Christian hope in the nearness of God's saving victory.[43] The very prominence and persistence of apocalyptic versions of salvation in the early Christian centuries seem to support this claim. The Apocalypse of Peter, which ranked in status and popularity second only to the canonical Apocalypse of John, provides the earliest extant description of heaven and hell in a Christian document.[44] Listed in the Muratorian Canon, it reflects an influential tradition preceding the time of the Bar Kochba revolt. Both Clement of Alexandria and Methodius of Olympus cited it as divinely inspired

---

42. Bynum, *Resurrection of the Body*, 68, 112.

43. Daley, *Hope of Early Church*, 3.

44. Elliott, *Apocryphal New Testament*, 595. The text in question, reconstructed from Greek fragments and a longer Ethiopic version, is distinct from the Nag Hammadi tract of the same name. See Foster, "Christology and Soteriology," 226.

support for their belief that miscarried babies, even those conceived in adultery, are "delivered to care-taking angels."[45] According to Sozomen, it was still being read in the churches of Palestine every Good Friday right through to the late fourth century.[46]

The bulk of the text is occupied with a lurid description of the pain and torment awaiting sinners and apostates on the day of judgment. The horrifying scene is dominated by darkness and fire: overwhelming, cataclysmic, everlasting, cosmic fire. Everything burns—land, sea, air, sky. In the midst of this terror, Christ appears in glorious light, preceded by his cross. The dead are fully reconstituted in body and soul and gathered to await individual judgment. The punishments match the crimes: fornicating women are strung up by their hair, fornicating men by their genitals. Murderers' bodies are devoured by fire and worms. Women who aborted their unborn suffer drowning in foul poison, their breasts exuding milk that congeals into ulcer-causing parasites; while their children, delivered into the hands of the care-giving angels and set apart "in a place of delight," look on sighing and crying to God.[47] Slanderers and deceivers are tortured with fire, their lips excised, their eyes and tongues burned with red-hot pokers, their innards sluiced with burning liquid. And on and on the narrative goes, fleshing out the most violent agonies devised by Ezrael, the angel of wrath.

Predictably, the text moves on to a description, much briefer and more abstract, of heaven. It lingers only in its depiction of Moses and Elijah, beautiful in countenance, handsome in adornment, and in its vision of "a great garden, open, full of fair trees and blessed fruits, and of the odour of perfumes."[48] Yet even this, in the Ethiopic version at least, is not enough to quell Peter's dread of hell's horrors. He weeps for many hours, and is at last consoled by what appears to be a deliberate concession to a universalist doctrine of salvation: "My Father will give to them all the life, the glory, and the kingdom that passes not away.... It is also because of those who have believed in me that, at their word, I shall have pity on men."[49] Here there appears in nuce a doctrine proposed more explicitly in the Sibylline Oracles: sinners, even the unrighteous dead, may finally be saved through the intercession of the righteous. This

---

45. Clement of Alexandria, *Prophetical Extracts* 41.1 (PG 9:718); Methodius, *Symposium* 2.6 (Musurillo, 55).

46. Sozomen, *History of the Church* 7.19 (Aeterna, 283).

47. Apocalypse of Peter Ethiopic 8, in Elliott, *Apocryphal New Testament*, 605.

48. Apocalypse of Peter Ethiopic 16, in Elliott, *Apocryphal New Testament*, 610.

49. Apocalypse of Peter Ethiopic 17, in Elliott, *Apocryphal New Testament*, 612.

odd turn, along with Jesus' command to Peter that the vision of hell not be published abroad, suggests a motivational, rhetorical intention for the entire work. Its goal is to inspire fear of sin and judgment, to provide compelling rationale to keep company with the righteous and the angels, not to present a dogmatic statement about the final fate of unbelievers.[50]

Apocalyptically styled proposals of Christ's victorious reign were not limited to the teachings and texts of more marginal Christian communities. Prior to the fourth century, many leading Christian writers, drawing from the book of Revelation, the canonical Gospels, and various Old Testament prophecies, propounded a firm belief in an impending earthly reign of Christ. This tradition of millenarian Christianity apparently goes back to very early times, and seems most concentrated in central Asia Minor.[51] Eusebius reports the teaching of the early second-century figure Papias that "after the resurrection of the dead there will be a period of a thousand years, when Christ's kingdom will be set up on this earth in material form."[52] Such a doctrine, continues Eusebius, is surely based on a misinterpretation of apostolic writings. But Papias's views were apparently compelling, and it was "partly due to him that the great majority of churchmen after him took the same view."[53]

Another early writer who espoused a similar view was Cerinthus who, according to Irenaeus, was an infamous contemporary of the apostle John.[54] Quoting a text written around the year 200 by a Roman presbyter named Gaius, Eusebius names Cerinthus as source of the teaching that Christ would return to host a one-thousand-year-long wedding feast in Jerusalem:

> Then there is Cerinthus, who by revelations purporting to have been written by a great apostle presents us with tales of wonder falsely alleged to have been shown to him by angels. He declares that after the Resurrection the Kingdom of Christ will be on earth, and that carnal humanity will dwell in Jerusalem, once more enslaved to lusts and pleasures. And in his enmity towards the Scriptures of God, and his anxiety to lead men astray, he

---

50. See Foster, "Christology and Soteriology," 227–28.

51. See Daley, *Hope of Early Church*, 17–19.

52. Eusebius, *Hist. eccl.* 3.39 (Louth, 103).

53. We note Eusebius's disdain for Papias and his teachings: "I suppose he got these notions by misinterpreting the apostolic accounts and failing to grasp what they had said in mystic and symbolic language. For he seems to have been a man of very small intelligence, to judge from his books" (*Hist. eccl.* 3.39 [Louth, 103]).

54. Irenaeus, *Haer.* 3.3.4 (Unger, 34).

foretells a period of a thousand years given up to wedding festivities.[55]

Some fifty years later, another anti-chiliast, Dionysius of Alexandria, similarly attributed to Cerinthus the doctrine

> that Christ's Kingdom would be on earth: and the things he lusted after himself, being the slave of his body and sensual through and through, filled the heaven of his dreams—unlimited indulgence in gluttony and lechery at banquets, drinking-bouts, and wedding-feasts, or (to call these by what he thought more respectable names) festivals, sacrifices, and the immolation of victims.[56]

Yet among those who expressed a perspective similar to Papias and Cerinthus were the great apologists Irenaeus and Tertullian. Irenaeus expounded his millennial teaching over against various positions, the most influential of which was held by the followers of Valentinus. The Valentinians taught that at death, the spiritual, imbued with the divine seed of Achamoth, would ascend immediately to the Ogdoad, while the "psychics" (in the sense of earthly, natural) would dwell in the Hebdomad. In this scheme, there was no room for a salvation that included the body. But there were also Catholics skeptical of chiliasm, and Irenaeus directs his argument to them as orthodox Christians who, nonetheless, misreading the Scriptures, leave out a crucial step in the *ordo promotionis iustorum* and the *ordo resurrectionis*.[57] Like the gnostics, these Christians allegorized descriptions of an earthly reign of Christ in history, centered at a rebuilt Jerusalem. Irenaeus argued that such interpretations are proposed at the expense of actual reality. The physical and historical realism of a thousand-year terrestrial reign corresponds, in Irenaeus's mind, to the physical and historical realism of the human constitution and the credibility of the scriptural promises.

> For since there are real men, so must there also be a real establishment . . . that they vanish not away among non-existent things, but progress among those which have an actual existence. For neither is the substance nor the essence of the creation annihilated.[58]

---

55. Eusebius, *Hist. eccl.* 3.28.2 (Louth, 91).
56. Eusebius, *Hist. eccl.* 3.28.2 (Louth, 91–92); see also 7.25.2 (Louth, 240).
57. Irenaeus, *Haer.* 5.31.1–5.36.3 (PG 7:1208–24).
58. Irenaeus, *Haer.* 5.36.1 (*ANF* 1:566).

It is the present *mode* of this world that is passing away, argues Irenaeus, not the world itself.

Moreover, just as history under God has served a pedagogical and preparatory purpose, so the earthly reign of the righteous will serve a preparatory purpose, "the necessary purpose of training and gradually accustoming the righteous to apprehend God and his glory."[59] The orthodox non-chiliasts locate that preparatory stage in the vague intermediate state of an afterlife. The Valentinians view it as redundant and bypass it altogether. Irenaeus, by contrast, holds not only that such a preparation is needed for our progressive graduation to deification, but that it must engage and involve human beings and creation as they really are: fully physical, fully social, fully historical, fully alive. In this we detect a connection with Origen's conviction that we must understand that the world's consummation "shall happen not suddenly, but gradually and by degrees, during the passing of infinite and immeasurable ages, with the improvement and correction being accomplished slowly and by degrees."[60] Only this way of viewing history renders it intelligible, discerning within it a trajectory and goal congruent with the wise and saving guidance of its Creator.

In Tertullian's eschatological doctrine, a renewed earth with a renewed earthly city of God again feature as key final elements.[61] This world is old and worn out, "hoary with age" and the antichrist, close at hand, is "gaping for the blood . . . of Christians."[62] The oracles of the New Prophecy, which influenced Tertullian from AD 207 onwards, confirmed his take on biblical prophecies concerning a literal thousand year reign of the saints and the establishment of a divinely built city of Jerusalem let down from heaven to earth.[63] Tertullian cites contemporary Christian prophets who had foretold "that there would be for a sign a picture of this very city exhibited to view previous to its manifestation," and that exactly this prediction had been fulfilled and the apparition of the city observed forty mornings in a row in Judea.[64] He continues, "We say that this city has been provided by God for receiving the saints on their resurrection, and refreshing them with the abundance of all really

---

59. Hill, *Regnum Caelorum*, 19.

60. Origen, *Princ.* 3.6.6 (Behr, 227).

61. Osborn, *Tertullian*, 215.

62. Tertullian, *Spect.* 30 (*ANF* 3:91); *Fug.* 12 (*ANF* 4:124).

63. On precursors to the exuberant apocalypticism of the new prophecy, see Trevett, "Apocalypse, Ignatius, Montanism."

64. Tertullian, *Marc.* 3.25 (*ANF* 3:342).

spiritual blessings."⁶⁵ Like Irenaeus, Tertullian was propelled in this conviction by faith in the justice of God, hope in the nearness of Christ's second coming, and an anti-gnostic respect for matter: just as the pains of hell will be intensely physical, so must be the rewards and delights of paradise. Against Marcion, Tertullian argued that God is both lord and judge. He will punish unrepented sins. Threat of punishment motivates sinners to act well and keep the commands. The Marcionites' innate fear of sinning exposes a theological contradiction in their teaching, for such fear implies divine retributive justice.⁶⁶

The fear of eternal punishment, ever present in the teachings and writings of the so-called patristic period, was nonetheless never separated from a sense of the efficacy of the community in communicating salvation to the lost and helpless individual. The church's faith in Christ the Savior carries vicarious, salvific power. The unhappy solidarity of humanity in its alienation from God was seen to have its corollary in a happy solidarity of the baptized in salvation, manifest not only in the effective power of the church's intercession for sinners, but in the actual ritual practice of sponsorship of (either infant or unconscious) baptismal candidates. Among Augustine's numerous arguments against the Pelagians for their faulty theology of human freedom was his appeal to the long-standing practice of baptizing babies. Lacking volition and understanding, they nevertheless bear the wound of ancestral guilt and so rightly are baptized for the remission of sin. Yet it is not they who in the performance of the rite renounce the devil, nor profess faith in God, but their sponsor speaking on their behalf.⁶⁷ Salvation here is thereby viewed as a profoundly vicarious and communal process: it is through sacramental incorporation into the church and the integral dependence upon "universa societate sanctorum atque fidelium" that the individual finds his or her salvation.⁶⁸

Another source, this time a stylized story of Syrian provenance from sometime around the late fifth century, again attests to this nexus of universal hope for salvation and the intercessory efficacy of the Christian community for the lost, all couched in the language and imagery of radical apocalypticism. For over a millennium, this story passed as having come from Dionysius the Areopagite, the first-century convert of Paul the

---

65. Tertullian, *Marc.* 3.25 (*ANF* 3:343).
66. Tertullian, *Marc.* 1.27, 5.9–5.10 (*ANF* 3:292–93, 447–52).
67. Augustine, *Pecc. merit.* 1.34.63 (PL 44:146).
68. Augustine, *Letter* 98.5 (PL 33:362).

apostle.[69] It recounts the ecstatic vision had by a certain pious priest from Crete named Carpos. The vision concerned two retrograde parishioners of his who had fallen from the straight paths of the Lord. Carpos knew he was meant to intercede for them, to pray earnestly for their salvation. He knew that only mercy could win them to repentance. Instead, one night, overcome with bitterness, he prayed for their damnation. Troubled and angry, unable to sleep, he stood up in his bedroom before God, protesting that such impious people should be allowed to get away with their hell-bent waywardness.

Suddenly the room in which Carpos was standing was split in two. Above him the sky unfolded, a shining flame descended, and Jesus appeared with a host of angels in the heavenly court. Below him the floor opened and a dark chasm yawned, and he saw the two guilty parishioners slipping downwards at its edge. From the bottom of the pit serpents lashed, coiling themselves around the sinners' legs to drag them down. With the snakes appeared people, who also clawed and clasped at their feet. The two unfortunates "were trembling and pitiful; bit by bit they were starting to fall in . . . unwillingly and yet willingly as they were gradually ravaged by evil and at the same time persuaded by its charms."[70]

Carpos, furious with the spirit of raw vengeance, delighted in this spectacle of justice. Gripped with righteous rage, he raised his hand to beat the two men down, impatient to help them into hell. But then, glancing up, he saw Jesus rise from his throne. Moved by compassion, the Lord came down from heaven, reached out and, with angelic assistance, took the two men by their hands and drew them up, holding them close to himself, one on each side. Then Jesus spoke to Carpos:

> So your hand is raised up and I now am the one you must hit. Here I am, ready once again to suffer for the salvation of man and I would very gladly endure it if in this way I could keep men from sin. Look to yourself. Maybe you should be living with the serpents in the pit rather than with God and with the good angels who are friends of man.[71]

---

69. Dionysius the Areopagite (aka Pseudo-Dionysius), *Ep.* 8 (PG 3:1097–C3.1100D; also in Pseudo-Dionysius, *Complete Works*, 278–80). For the similarities between the vision of Carpos and the three eschatological myths of Plato in the *Gorgias*, *Republic*, and *Phaedrus*, as mediated by Proclus, see Hathaway, *Hierarchy in Pseudo-Dionysius*, 93–99.

70. *Ep.* 8, in Pseudo-Dionysius, *Complete Works*, 279.

71. *Ep.* 8, in Pseudo-Dionysius, *Complete Works*, 280.

Without denying the salutary value of fearing hell, the story reiterates Christ's saving solidarity with the wretched and warns against preemptive judgment.

UNIVERSAL *APOKATASTASIS*?

We may round up our analysis of the three main analogies of salvation in early Christianity by returning to the controverted topic of *apokatastasis*. One of the speculative questions it had raised, at least as it had been formulated within the later Origenian tradition, was whether it left open the possibility for a recurring fall, or even a recurring cycle of falls, of creatures from God. It was understood as a question related to creaturely freedom. According to Origen, it had been due to a lack of attention, a freely elected neglect of the good, that intelligent spirits first fell and precipitated the economy of terrestrial and historical existence. Having been saved and restored to that pristine unity with God, what is to prevent such a fall from recurring, without prejudice to created freedom?

Of course, dogmatic theology tended to exclude such open-endedness and instability from God's creative and saving purposes. Gregory of Nyssa's doctrine of *epektasis*, the eternal "stretching" of the human spiritual appetite in an insatiable desire commensurate to the infinite attractiveness of the divine beauty, aroused suspicion among medieval theologians for apparently holding final quietude of the creature's hunger for God forever beyond its reach. As for Origen, however, he had expressly characterized final salvation in terms of stability in the good. Perfection involves not only assent to the truth, but abiding in the truth, which Origen visualizes in terms of a perpetual feasting on infinite mysteries.[72] The perfect soul, having been rid of "all perception of wickedness," possesses the good, the God who is all.[73] The bodies of the saints, having been changed and spiritualized and glorified, "will abide forever and unchangeably by the will of the Creator."[74] The new heavens and earth will be "a dwelling and a resting-place for the pious."[75] Nothing can be added to those whose condition is complete.

But the emphasis on this future stability only sharpened the conundrum. How was the primeval stability upset and the original unity of souls in God dispersed? It was apparently not just Origen who

---

72. Origen, *Princ.* 2.11.7 (Behr, 144–45).
73. Origen, *Princ.* 3.6.3 (Behr, 225).
74. Origen, *Princ.* 3.6.6 (Behr, 228).
75. Origen, *Princ.* 3.6.8 (Behr, 229).

conceptualized the fall of souls in this way. In one passage, the universally revered theologian Gregory Nazianzen states that we are "a portion of God and have our source in heaven above."[76] Did this not perhaps imply the possibility of an eschatological future for the universe constituted by a simple return to this original protological immobility, and thus one theoretically open to a recurring fall? In any case, Gregory was invoked as an authority for a fully developed, three-stage cosmology: in the beginning, the entire universe existed in a state of rest (*stasis*) as a pristine intelligible unity or *henad* in God. From here it underwent motion (*kinesis*) by reason of loss of attention. Finally, it underwent generation (*genesis*) into actual existence in the multiplicity of beings that constitute finite creation.[77]

It was left to the erudite monastic theologian Maximus the Confessor to correct the adoption of such formulae in support of the faulty Origenist eschatology by reconstructing its cosmology with a schema more attentive to the biblical trajectory of all created history towards its sabbatical rest.[78] Against the problematic three-stage order Maximus proposes an alternative metaphysics which begins with the actual genesis of different beings from nothing by divine creation, proceeds to their natural motion and activity, and culminates in their final repose in God. Some of the passages in which he confronts this problem come over as very technical and laden with difficult philosophical concepts. But Maximus's worry with the problematic doctrine is not merely philosophical, but soteriological, anthropological, and pastoral. He argues that the doctrine of the *henad*, which holds that "stasis" or rest designates an actual original state from which rational beings fell through motion, fundamentally destabilizes the hope of eternal salvation in Christ inasmuch as it conceives this original state of union with God as metaphysically unstable. If it is true that rational beings once had a stable dwelling and foundation in contemplating the absolute beauty of God, yet subsequently grew satiated with God's beauty and fell away from him, then given the same circumstances, Maximus contends that "it must be assumed that under similar circumstances rational beings will necessarily undergo such changes indefinitely."[79] The implications are morally and existentially disastrous:

76. Gregory of Nazianzus, *Or. Bas.* 14.7 (Vinson, 43).

77. See Maximus the Confessor's summary of the problematic henadological doctrine in *Ambiguum* 7 (PG 91:1089C; also in *On the Cosmic Mystery*, 65).

78. See Maximus, *Ambiguum* 7 (PG 91:1068D–1101D); *Ambiguum* 15 (PG 91.1216A–1221B).

79. *Ambiguum* 7, in Maximus the Confessor, *On the Cosmic Mystery*, 46.

> If God can be abandoned once for the sake of experiencing something different, there is nothing to prevent this happening again and again. If reasonable beings are thus to be carried about and have no place to rest and cannot hope to have any abiding steadfastness in the good, what could be greater reason to despair?[80]

In Maximus's solution to the problem, the stable state of rest or union with God is placed not first in the metaphysical triad, but last, in keeping with the biblical doctrine of eternal Sabbath rest and the final recapitulation of all things in Christ the Son of the Father. In such a state, where our restless desire has finally found its ultimate goal in God, where God has become for us our "all in all," there can be no falling away, no interruption of joy, no loss of deification. This intimate participation in the divine nature has always been the goal of creation, "the blessed end for which all things were brought into existence."[81] It is for this union of all things to God in Christ, "that all the ages and the beings existing within those ages received their beginning and end in Christ."[82]

What, finally, becomes of those who resist assimilation to God, that is, who resist salvation? Maximus, like Origen, believed that eventually God will be manifest in creation as "all in all," the infinite cause complete and transparent in all its finite effects, "wholly in all beings in general and indivisibly in each particular."[83] Yet far from endorsing any kind of soteriological universalism, Maximus remained perplexed about the eventual mode of being for those who refuse the author and source of being. His thoughts come to a head in his comments on 1 Pet 4:17–18: "What will be the end for those who disobey the gospel of God? And 'if the righteous man is scarcely saved,' where will the impious man and the sinner appear?"[84] Maximus rephrases the question:

> In other words, what sort of end or judgement awaits those who have not only kept alive and active—both in soul and in body, both in will and in nature—the birth from Adam based on pleasure, but who embrace neither our God and Father, who appeals to them through His incarnate Son, nor the Mediator and Son Himself, who acts as ambassador for the Father, and who was Himself willingly sent, by the Father's counsel, to reconcile us

80. *Ambiguum 7*, in Maximus the Confessor, *On the Cosmic Mystery*, 46–47.
81. Maximus, *Ad Thal.* 60.3 (Constas, 428).
82. Maximus, *Ad Thal.* 60.4 (Constas, 429).
83. Maximus, *Amb.* 22 (PG 91:1257AB).
84. Maximus, *Ad Thal.* 61.1 (Constas, 434).

to the Father, to die for our sake, so that in Himself he might glorify us, illuminate us with His beauty and His own divinity?[85]

From here his answer focuses on the word "where," a term that indicates place. In Maximus's metaphysics, time and place are prerequisites of finite existence. All created things only have their being by being when and where.[86] By contrast, God is beyond every place. He is not somewhere but is beyond all where. For the saved, however, God has made himself their place. By grace he has become their abode and foundation, as the psalmist said: "Be thou to me a rock of refuge, a strong fortress, to save me" (Ps 71:3 RSV). The saved, therefore, will enjoy in the age to come a paradoxical mode of existence. Their where will be secure in the God who is beyond all where, and their life with him an existence without limits, transcending age, time, and place. But if they do not reach this goal without difficulty, that is, without guarding the grace of baptism through the sufferings of discipleship, what then of the impious? "Where" will that person appear, asks Maximus, who has rendered himself "unable to receive the presence of God, actualized in the state of well-being" and who has subsequently suffered "separation from divine life"?[87] The concepts where and how, like being itself, are unthinkable apart from the ontological and absolute ground of all place and quality.

Finally, unable positively to specify the kind of existence that characterizes such persons, and affirming the precariousness of his own status as a "sinner,"[88] Maximus concludes by repeating the original question, in this way leaving it to his readers, and himself, to discover the answer in a salutary life of repentance.[89]

BIBLIOGRAPHY

Arbesmann, Rudolph. "The Concept of *Christus Medicus* in St Augustine." *Traditio* 10 (1954) 1–28.
Brown, Peter. *The Cult of the Saints: Its Rise and Function in Latin Christianity*. Chicago: University of Chicago Press, 1981.
Bynum, Caroline Walker. *The Resurrection of the Body in Western Christianity, 200–1336*. New York: Columbia University Press, 1995.

---

85. Maximus, *Ad Thal.* 61.12 (Constas, 443).
86. Mueller-Jourdan, *Typologie spatio-temporelle*, 52.
87. Maximus, *Ad Thal.* 61.14 (Constas, 445).
88. Maximus postulates that perhaps "sinner" means someone "who has kept faith but, like me, transgresses the gospel commandments" (*Ad Thal.* 61.13 [Constas, 444]).
89. Maximus, *Ad Thal.* 61.350–61.352 (Constas, 445).

Chadwick, Henry. "Origen, Celsus, and the Resurrection of the Body." *HTR* 41 (1948) 83–102.
Clement of Alexandria. *Exhortation to the Greeks*. Translated by G. W. Butterworth. LCL 92. Cambridge, MA: Harvard University Press, 1919.
Cooper, Adam G. *Life in the Flesh: An Anti-Gnostic Spiritual Philosophy*. Oxford: Oxford University Press, 2008.
Crouzel, H., and V. Grossi. "Resurrection of the Dead." In *Encyclopedia of the Early Church*, edited by Angelo Di Berardino, translated by Adrian Walford, 2:732–33. New York: Oxford University Press, 1992.
Daley, Brian E. *The Hope of the Early Church: A Handbook of Patristic Eschatology*. Cambridge: Cambridge University Press, 1991.
Di Berardino, Angelo, and Basil Studer, eds. *The Patristic Period*. Translated by Matthew J. O'Connell. Vol. 1 of *History of Theology*. Collegeville, MN: Liturgical, 1996.
Dinkler, Erich. *Christus und Asklepios*. Heidelberg: Winter, 1980.
Dumeige, G. "Le (Christ) médecin." In *Dictionnaire de spiritualité: Ascétique et mystique, doctrine et histoire*, edited by Marcel Villier, vol. 10, cols. 891–901. Paris: Beauchesne, 1980.
Elliott, J. K., ed. *The Apocryphal New Testament: A Collection of Apocryphal Christian Literature in an English Translation Based on M. R. James*. Oxford: Clarendon, 1993.
Eusebius. *The History of the Church: From Christ to Constantine* [*Hist. eccl.*]. Edited by Andrew Louth. Translated by G. A. Williamson. Penguin Classics. London: Penguin, 1989.
Foster, Paul. "Christology and Soteriology in Apocryphal Acts and Apocalypses." In *The Oxford Handbook of Early Christian Apocrypha*, edited by Andrew Gregory and Christopher Tuckett, 213–32. Oxford Handbooks. Oxford: Oxford University Press, 2015.
Gregory of Nazianzus. *Select Orations* [*Or. Bas.*]. Translated by Martha Vinson. FOTC 107. Washington, DC: Catholic University of America Press, 2003.
Hamann, A. "Purgatory." In *Encyclopedia of the Early Church*, edited by Angelo Di Berardino, translated by Adrian Walford, 2:725. New York: Oxford University Press, 1992.
Harnack, Adolf. *The Mission and Expansion of Christianity in the First Three Centuries*. Edited and translated by James Moffatt. 2 vols. London: Williams and Norgate, 1904–8. https://www.ccel.org/ccel/h/harnack/mission/cache/mission.pdf.
Hathaway, Ronald F. *Hierarchy and the Definition of Order in the Letters of Pseudo-Dionysius: A Study in the Form and Meaning of the Pseudo-Dionysian Writings*. The Hague: Martinus Nijhoff, 1969.
Heyne, Thomas. "Were Second-Century Christians 'Preoccupied' with Physical Healing and the Asclepian Cult?" *StPatr* 44 (2010) 63–69.
Hill, Charles E. *Regnum Caelorum: Patterns of Millennial Thought in Early Christianity*. 2nd ed. Grand Rapids: Eerdmans, 2001.
Ignatius of Antioch. *Epistle to the Romans* [*Rom.*]. In *I Clement, II Clement, Ignatius, Polycarp, Didache*, edited and translated by Bart D. Ehrman, 268–83. Vol. 1 of *The Apostolic Fathers*. LCL 24. Cambridge, MA: Harvard University Press, 2003.
Irenaeus. *Against the Heresies (Book 3)* [*Haer.*]. Edited and translated by D. J. Unger. ACW 64. New York: Newman, 2012.
Kelly, J. N. D. *Early Christian Doctrines*. 3rd ed. London: Longman, 1972.
Larchet, Jean-Claude. "Le Christ médecin." In *Thérapeutique des maladies spirituelles*, 319–44. Paris: Cerf, 1991.

Lubac, Henri de. *The Four Senses of Scripture.* Vol. 2 of *Medieval Exegesis.* Translated by E. M. Macierowski. RRRCT. Grand Rapids: Eerdmans, 2000.

———. *Theology in History.* Translated by Anne Englund Nash. San Francisco: Ignatius, 1996.

Maximus the Confessor. *On Difficulties in Sacred Scripture: The Responses to Thalassios* [*Ad Thal.*]. Translated by Maximos Constas. FOTC 136. Washington, DC: Catholic University of America Press, 2018.

———. *On the Cosmic Mystery of Jesus Christ: Selected Writings from St. Maximus the Confessor.* Translated by Paul M. Blowers and Robert Louis Wilken. Crestwood, NY: St. Vladimir's Seminary Press, 2003.

McGuckin, John Anthony, ed. *The SCM Press A–Z of Origen.* SCM Press A–Zs. Louisville, KY: Westminster John Knox, 2006.

Methodius. *The Symposium: A Treatise on Chastity.* Edited and translated by Herbert Musurillo. London: Longmans, Green and Co., 1958.

Mueller-Jourdan, Pascal. "The Foundation of Origenist Metaphysics." In *The Oxford Handbook of Maximus the Confessor*, edited by Pauline Allen and Bronwen Neil, 149–63. Oxford Handbooks. Oxford: Oxford University Press, 2015.

———. *Typologie spatio-temporelle de l'ecclesia byzantine: La mystagogie de Maxime le Confesseur dans la culture philosophique de l'antiquité tardive.* VCSup 74. Boston: Brill, 2005.

Origen. *Contra Celsum* [*Cels.*]. Edited and translated by Henry Chadwick. Cambridge: Cambridge University Press, 1980.

———. *Contre Celse* [*Cels.*]. Edited and translated by Marcel Borret. 5 vols. SC 132, 136, 147, 150, 227. Paris: Cerf, 1967–76.

———. *On First Principles* [*Princ.*]. Edited and translated by John Behr. 2 vols. Oxford Early Christian Texts. Oxford: Oxford University Press, 2019.

———. *The Song of Songs, Commentary and Homilies* [*Comm. Cant.*]. Edited and translated by R. P. Lawson. ACW 26. Mahwah, NJ: Newman, 1956.

———. *Spirit and Fire: A Thematic Anthology of the Writings of Origen.* Edited by Hans Urs von Balthasar. Translated by Robert J. Daly. Washington, DC: Catholic University of America Press, 1984.

Osborn, Eric. *Tertullian: The First Theologian of the West.* Cambridge: Cambridge University Press, 1997.

Peters, F. E. *Greek Philosophical Terms: A Historical Lexicon.* New York: New York University Press, 1967.

Porterfield, Amanda. *Healing in the History of Christianity.* New York: Oxford University Press, 2005.

Price, Richard. *The Acts of the Council of Constantinople of 553: With Related Texts on the Three Chapters Controversy.* Translated Texts for Historians 51. Liverpool: Liverpool University Press, 2009.

Pseudo-Dionysius. *The Complete Works.* Translation by Colm Luibheid. Classics of Western Spirituality. Mahwah, NJ: Paulist, 1987.

Sozomen. *A History of the Church in Nine Books.* Las Vegas: Aeterna, 2014.

Trevett, Christine. "Apocalypse, Ignatius, Montanism: Seeking the Seeds." *VC* 43 (1989) 313–38.

Vagaggini, Cipriano. *The Flesh, Instrument of Salvation: A Theology of the Human Body.* Translated by C. U. Quinn. New York: Society of St. Paul, 1969.

5

The End-Times Throughout History
The Problem of the Year 1000

MARIO BAGHOS

The end of the present world order has been envisaged in many different ways by various cultures throughout history. The Christian expectation that the Lord Jesus will one day return to judge the living and the dead, renewing the world in light of God's kingdom, has been anticipated by the church since its very beginnings. Indeed, the *Catechism of the Catholic Church* has systematized the belief in the last things by addressing them under the following categories: death, judgment, heaven, and hell.[1] This paper chronologically addresses the Christian expectation of the end-times in relation to relevant sources, including the New Testament, late antique and medieval chronographers, and patristic writings. It will define apocalypticism, eschatology, and millenarianism (or millennialism), all of which are related terms, in order to account for the various ways in which the "end-times" have been construed in the aforementioned sources. The focal point comprises the expectation of Western medieval chronographers that the world would come to an end around the year 1000, as well as the related phenomenon of the end-times being ushered in by a final ruler or king. These related expectations—with the former equating to millenarianism proper—constitute a deviation from the ecclesial and patristic expectation that

---

1. *CCC* 1021–22, 1038–41, 1023–29, 1033–37.

God's kingdom can be experienced in the here and now within the Mass or liturgy.

What makes this millenarian deviation even more problematic is its preponderance in post-Enlightenment historiography, beginning in the nineteenth century but especially manifested among modern scholars of apocalypticism such as the late Norman Cohn, whose *Pursuit of the Millennium* remains, over seventy years after its publication, the benchmark scholarly work in this field.[2] The inheritors of Cohn's approach include Richard Landes,[3] Catherine Wessinger,[4] John Gray,[5] Stephen H. Webb,[6] Paul Boyer,[7] Eugen Weber,[8] Richard Kyle,[9] Damian Thompson,[10] to name a few. All these figures consider Christian eschatology to be equivalent to apocalypticism and millenarianism; thereby preferring what I believe is a reduction of eschatology—or at very least a subset of it—to eschatology proper. This is problematic because eschatology is inherently related to soteriology, to our salvation. This chapter will argue that the misleading conflation of eschatology, apocalypticism, and millenarianism is a result of scholars bypassing traditional reflection and teaching on the "last things" as well as neglecting the eschatological reality of the Mass, which we participate in by God's grace. This was more or less bound to happen on account of the secular nature of the contemporary academy, especially the discipline of historiography. But it is compounded by the reading of early Christian eschatological sources and themes through the lens of Western medieval chronographers who expected the world to end around the year 1000, an approach standardized by Cohn's *Pursuit*. It is the ecclesial/participatory perspective that, this chapter will argue, should be retrieved in scholarly discussions on the end-times.

---

2. Baghos, "Nuancing the 'Millennium.'"
3. Landes, "Millenarianism/Millennialism, Eschatology, Apocalypticism," 2:1094, 1110.
4. Wessinger, *Oxford Handbook of Millennialism*, 4.
5. Gray, *Black Mass*, 4–5, 19.
6. Webb, "Eschatology and Politics," 503.
7. Boyer, "Growth of Fundamentalist Apocalyptic," 519.
8. Weber, *Apocalypses*, 4, 148, 151, 153, 229, 233.
9. Kyle, *Last Times Are Here Again*, 24.
10. Thompson, *End of Time*, xii, 60–61, 69, 130–32.

DEFINITIONS AND METHODOLOGY

Etymologically, apocalypticism derives from the Greek word ἀποκάλυψις (*apokalypsis*), meaning "revelation," and indeed many apocalyptic texts are concerned with the revelation of either heaven or hell disclosed by God to a prophet, seer, or saint. This form of apocalypticism is manifested in the last book of the New Testament from which the apocalyptic genre derives its name. The book of Revelation is just one of many apocalyptic texts that were popular among both Jews and Christians in the first few centuries AD.

Revelation takes up themes that were already present in the Old Testament. For example, the prophets Isaiah and Micah were given "revelations" concerning the coming of the Messiah: the former pronouncing to King Ahaz—within the context of continued "revelations" to him by the God of Israel—that "the virgin is with child and shall bear a son, and shall call him Immanuel" (Isa 7:14), and the latter that this child would be born in Bethlehem.[11] Both of these prophecies can be considered "apocalyptic" without being relegated to the end of the world.[12] In a similar vein, the book of Daniel (9:24–25) was interpreted by the early church as pointing to the birth of the Messiah, whereas the same prophetic book (7:13–14) records the prophet's vision of the "Son of Man" and the "Ancient of Days" who gives the former power and dominion over all the nations of the earth; and this was taken as referring to the end-times.

This brings apocalypticism into an explicit relationship with eschatology, a term that derives from the Greek τα ἔσχατα (*ta eschata*),[13] which means the "last things." While associated with death, judgment, heaven, and hell, the "last things" concern the end of the world, which is marked by the second coming of Christ, who describes himself—in light of Old Testament and intertestamental prophecies—as the "Son of Man," before whom "all nations will be gathered" before he returns "in his glory" (Matt 25:31–32). The second coming is described in a more nuanced way

---

11. "But you O Bethlehem of Ephrathah, who are one of the little clans of Judah, from you shall come forth for me one who is to rule Israel, whose origin is from old, from ancient days" (Mic 5:2). All Scripture quotations in this chapter are taken from the NRSV.

12. In this chapter, though, I will for the sake of convention use the term "apocalypticism" in relation to the catastrophic end of the present world order. One will be able to determine whether or not I am primarily referring to its "revelatory" dimension from the context.

13. *PGL* 551.

by St. Paul as "the day of the Lord" (1 Thess 5:2)¹⁴ when "the Lord himself, with a cry of command, with the archangel's call and with the sound of God's trumpet, will descend from heaven, and the dead in Christ shall rise first" (1 Thess 4:16–17).¹⁵ Its universal or cosmic scope is highlighted in Acts 3:21 when St. Peter declares that Jesus "must remain in heaven until the time of universal restoration (ἀποκαταστάσεως πάντων) that God announced long ago through his holy prophets."¹⁶

There are various features that are associated with the second coming of Christ: the resurrection of the dead and judgment of humanity, the defeat of the devil/sin/death, described in various ways in the book of Revelation—such as their casting into hell—and the final "transformation of the cosmos"¹⁷ into a "new heaven and a new earth" (Rev 21:1). These features of the eschaton, however, can also be considered as having been immanently revealed (that is, "apocalyptically") by Christ, primarily to the church which is his body. This can be most explicitly discerned not only in St. John's vision of these end-times as recorded in Revelation, but Christ's teaching about the end-times (Matt 24:1–51), and also in relation to his resurrection from the dead, which is considered the basis for the expectation that he will return to resurrect and judge both the living and the dead. But Christ's life-restoring, or resurrectional, activity was not limited to either his own resurrection or the end-times, for in the Gospels he is depicted as raising from the dead an unnamed young girl (Matt 9:18–26; Mark 5:35–43; Luke 8:40–56), the widow's son at Nain (Luke 11:7–17), and Lazarus (John 11:38–44); not to mention that Matthew's Gospel links Christ's death on Golgotha with the opening of nearby tombs, so that "many bodies of the saints who had fallen asleep were raised" (27:52).

---

14. This concept is used in the Old Testament almost exclusively in relation to judgment: Isa 2:12; 13:6, 9; Ezek 13:5, 30:3; Joel 1:15; 2:1, 11, 31; 3:14; Amos 5:18, 20; Obad 15; Zeph 1:7, 14; Zech 14:1; Mal 4:1.

15. Paul refers once again to the mode of the general resurrection in 1 Cor 15:51–52: "Listen, I will tell you a mystery! We will not all die, but we will all be changed, in a moment, in the twinkling of an eye, at the last trumpet. For the trumpet will sound, and the dead will be raised imperishable, and we will be changed." In relation to this, Gordon D. Fee debunks the idea, current in modern biblical scholarship, that St. Paul expected the second coming to occur imminently (*Letters to the Thessalonians*, 175–76).

16. Frederick Fyvie Bruce compares the word "restoration" or *apokatastasis* used here with "Paul's picture of a renovated creation coinciding with the investiture of the sons and daughters of God" in Rom 8:18–23 (*Book of the Acts*, 85).

17. St. Basil of Caesarea refers to the "transformation of the cosmos" (μεταποιηθῆναι τὸν κόσμον) throughout his homilies on the six days of creation (*Hexaemeron* [PG 29:12C; author's translation]).

These resurrectional occurrences at the hands of the one who is life giver (John 10:1)[18] and who holds "the keys of Death and Hades" (Rev 1:18) are therefore to be seen as anticipating both his own resurrection and the general resurrection at the end-times marked by Christ's second coming, when, according to Revelation, God's kingdom, the new Jerusalem (Rev 21–22)—with Christ-God enthroned at its center—will be permanently established. But Christ is also depicted as preaching during his earthly ministry "the kingdom of God" which "has come near" (Mark 1:14) in a way that is associated with his physical presence. This means that the kingdom inaugurated by Christ and the resurrected life that it promises were believed by the earliest Christians as having *already* begun in Christ's ministry—namely in the church he established—but were as *not yet* fulfilled. This is known in scholarship as the "already–not yet" tension.[19] In other words, any references in the New Testament to Christ as the principal agent in inaugurating the kingdom of God/heaven (Mark 1:15; Matt 3:2), the new Jerusalem, eternal life (John 6:58), salvation (Luke 19:9), paradise (Luke 23:43), etc., point to the fact that God's kingdom was believed to have already been established by Christ (and the descent of the Spirit at Pentecost) but not yet consummated on a cosmic scale. The particular mode in which the "already–not yet" tension between God's kingdom—having already come in the church, but not yet having been consummated—unfolds in the ecclesial space is with a transformation of lifestyle, beginning with and marked by repentance[20] and initiated by the sacrament of baptism (Matt 28:19; Acts 2:41; 19:5) and frequent participation in the Eucharist (John 6:53; Luke 22:19–20; Acts 2:46; 1 Cor 11:23–27), so that the resurrectional life of Christ, expected by Christians to occur generally at the eschaton,[21] might be bestowed upon them in the here and now, making them "partakers of the divine nature" (2 Pet 1:4).

---

18. "I came that they may have life, and have it abundantly."

19. Dockery, *Biblical Interpretation*, 185.

20. I prefer to use this phrase insofar as it is etymologically more consistent with Christ's exhortation μετανοεῖτε, which appears in most translations of Mark 1:15; Matt 3:2; 4:17 as "repent," which includes this idea but is more nuanced in indicating that the act of sincere remorse must compel one to "transform" (indicated by the prefix μετά) one's mind (νοῦς).

21. With some rising to blessedness and others to the purification of fire. See, for instance, the parable of the last judgment (Matt 25:31–46) and St. Gregory of Nyssa's reflections on this topic in Baghos, "Reconsidering *Apokatastasis*," 405–15.

This "already–not yet" eschatological tension, with Christ at its center,[22] is often ignored in much modern scholarship and among many Christians where eschatology is construed exclusively in relation to the "last things" and as "apocalyptic," but not in the sense that denotes revelations from a heavenly realm or as relating to God's kingdom already manifested by Jesus. In such a rendering, the nuances of eschatology—specifically its Christocentricity and thus its "already–not yet" tension—are not taken into consideration. Instead, this "apocalypticism" is associated with the devastating end of the world, "mere anarchy" to allude to W. B. Yeats's famous poem "The Second Coming."[23] While prevalent in scholarship and popular literature on this subject, this rendering nevertheless consists of a reductionism that does not account for the participatory dimension of the eschatological experience as reflected in the New Testament sources and as believed by the earliest Christians, by traditional Christians throughout history, and by many Christians today. That is, it fails to account for the fact that the foretaste of the kingdom to come within the ecclesial context—specifically the Mass or liturgy—is eschatological, and that it has as both its source and goal participation in the grace of the God-man Jesus Christ, in the life of the Trinitarian God. There is ample literature on this topic, but to quote one representative passage from St. Maximus the Confessor, a seventh-century patristic author who was rediscovered by *ressourcement* scholars in Roman Catholic milieus in the twentieth century:

> Every Christian should be exhorted . . . to frequent God's holy church and never to abandon the holy synaxis [eucharistic gathering] . . . because of the grace of the Holy Spirit which is always invisibly present, but in a special way at the time of the holy synaxis. This grace transforms and changes each person who is found there and in fact remolds him in proportion to what is more divine in him and leads him to what is revealed through the mysteries which are celebrated . . . according to the order and progression from preliminaries to the end of everything.[24]

Maximus here considers the eucharistic liturgy in the light of the Eastern Church's views on deification, which is the transformation of the believer by the grace of God into a god by grace. His comments that the liturgy,

---

22. What can alternately be described as an eschatology that is "realized" within the church but is, admittedly, framed by a future eschatology that is yet to come.

23. "Mere anarchy is loosed upon the world, / The blood-dimmed tide is loosed" (Yeats, *Collected Poems*, 158–59).

24. Maximus the Confessor, "Church's Mystagogy" §24, 206–7.

specifically the Eucharist, offers an insight into "the end of everything" can be read through the lens of what takes place in the Eucharist: a communion with Christ, which, at his second coming at the eschaton, will be permanent and will endure forever.

In any case, it is certainly true that, throughout history, some Christian leaders and groups have chosen to ignore Jesus's exhortation that "about that day or hour no one knows" (Matt 24:36). Instead, they have fueled what we can call "apocalyptic anxiety"—sometimes with a view to exploiting the masses—so that the many centuries since the birth of Christianity have witnessed their share of "doomsday prophets" heralding the catastrophic end of the world and leading their followers to self-destruction. The eschaton, when viewed through the lens of a radical literalism in relation to the day or the hour of Christ's second coming, has thus often had negative connotations and results. The apocalypse thus understood is often related to the "thousand-year" period of the rule of Christ with his saints mentioned in Rev 20:3–4 and 6.[25] This "thousand-year" period was often interpreted allegorically by the church in light of the numerological significance of the number ten (and multiplications thereof) as denoting totality.[26] Thus, according to St. Augustine, the thousand-year period in Revelation, being a multiplication of ten, represents—along with the numbers one hundred and one thousand[27]—totality or perfection.[28] When related to the reign of Christ and his saints, the "thousand years" therefore do not necessarily mean a reign that would literally last for this specific length of time, but the perfect reign of Christ with his saints, which Augustine also described as occurring in the here and now within the church as it travels throughout history, yet not consummated until the eschaton proper.

PINPOINTING THE YEAR 1000

In spite of the above definition of eschatology, since the church's beginnings many Christians have interpreted the end-times as happening

---

25. After this rule, Satan is described as being loosed from his prison before his final defeat and the permanent transfiguration of the present world order.

26. Hiscock, *Symbol at Your Door*, 19.

27. Since for St. Augustine, in the New Testament, "a hundred is sometimes used as the equivalent of totality," he then argues "how much more is a thousand an equivalent of totality," but does not explore the implications further (*City of God* 20.7.287, 20.7.289).

28. This view is reiterated in modern times by James L. Resseguie, who affirms that "a thousand years represents a total and complete period" (*Revelation of John*, 244).

in their immediate contexts. Saint Paul hopefully expected the eschaton to occur imminently, and later, in the second century, the Montanists believed that the new Jerusalem was about to descend over the city of Pepuza in Asia Minor. In late antique Western Europe the concern for chronography, for calculating the precise date of the end of the world— perhaps hastened by the fall of the city of Rome at three consecutive junctures in the fifth century AD[29]—motivated scholars to begin their dating systems with a literalistic reading of the creation narrative in the book of Genesis, or anno mundi (the year of the world). While the scholarship (e.g., Landes) has shown that the Byzantines exhibited very little interest in calculating the precise date of the end of the world until the rise of Islam began to threaten the boundaries of the empire, major Western chronographers including Lactantius (d. 320), Hilarianus (late fourth century), Beatus of Liébana (d. ca. 800), John of Modena (mid-700s), and Hlotharius of Saint-Armand (ca. 800) subscribed to what Landes has called the "sabbatical millennium," that the world would end around the turn of the year 6000,[30] which would inaugurate the seventh millennium of either the reign of antichrist (postmillennialism) or the rule of Christ with his saints outlined in the book of Revelation (20:4–5, 12–13)—i.e., premillennialism. At this juncture we should explain that millenarianism has been subject to various interpretations, including premillennialism, postmillennialism, and amillennialism, that have been succinctly described by G. K. Beale as follows:

> Some believe that the millennium will occur after the second coming of Christ [premillennialism]. . . . Postmillennialism has held that the millennium occurs towards the end of the Church age and that Christ's climactic coming will occur at the close of the millennium. . . . Others believe that the millennium started at Christ's resurrection and will be concluded at his final coming [amillennialism].[31]

I will not delve into these now. Suffice it to state that the sabbatical millennium was calculated as taking place at three distinct dates—AD 500, 800, and at the approach of AD 1000.[32] Lactantius and Hilarianus believed that it would occur in AD 500, whereas Beatus, John of Modena,

---

29. Rome was sacked in AD 410 by the Visigoths, in 455 by the Vandals, and in 476 by Odoacer.
30. Landes, "Fear of Apocalyptic Year," 110.
31. Beale, *Book of Revelation*, 973.
32. Landes, "Fear of Apocalyptic Year," 111.

and Hlotharius pinpointed the year 800.[33] You will have noticed that I am using the anno Domini dating system, but in fact both of these dates were reckoned according to anno mundi computations as AM 6000.[34] Anno mundi was of course replaced by Dionysius Exiguus's dating system that he developed in the sixth century, and that begins with Christ's incarnation, what we call anno Domini;[35] but this did not become increasingly popular in Western Europe until the eighth century. Thus, the belief in the end of the world taking place around the year 1000 can be identified in the writings of those who, like Thietland of Einsiedeln (mid-tenth century), Adso of Montier-en-Der (d. 992), and the Cluniac monk Rodulfus Glaber, used the anno Domini system and interpreted the thousand-year duration in Rev 20:3–4 literally.

We have seen that this seems not to have been the case in the Byzantine East, where the passage of the years 6000 (i.e., AD 500) and AM 6500 (AD 1000) were not noted by historians.[36] We cannot like Landes, however, let Byzantine Christendom off the hook, because apocalyptic anxiety did in fact take place in Byzantium, but it was just not associated with millenarianism but with the rise of Islam in the seventh century. Indeed, based on earlier sources like the Tiburtine Sibyl, the Apocalypse of Pseudo-Methodius—which was written in the seventh century—describes the advent of the emperor of the last days, who would defend Christians against their marauding enemies and deliver the Roman Empire over to Christ upon the latter's return.[37] This motif of the last emperor would become prominent after the fall of Constantinople—the capital of Byzantium—to the Ottomans on May 29, 1453, and persists to this day in many Orthodox Christian milieus that have inherited the Byzantine legacy.[38] The West also had its version of this last emperor motif: the fact that the Carolingian ruler Charlemagne's coronation deliberately took place around the above-mentioned second juncture of the year 6000, on December 25, 801, is telling of the fact that the eschatological emperor motif was current in Western Europe also.[39] That it spread further west is attested to by the association of this motif, since the tenth century, with King Arthur and his return from near death

33. Landes, "Fear of Apocalyptic Year," 113.
34. Landes, "Fear of Apocalyptic Year," 113–14.
35. Mosshammer, *Easter Computus*, 3, 7–8.
36. Landes, "Fear of Apocalyptic Year," 122.
37. The most recent translation of this text is by Garstad.
38. Kessareas, "Signs of the Times."
39. Latowsky, *Emperor of the World*, 14–15.

to restore Britain,[40] and that it persisted is confirmed by the belief that Frederick Barbarossa, who died while leading the third crusade, would also come back to life and slay God's enemies just before the eschaton.[41]

The reason why this paper focuses on Western, as opposed to Eastern, apocalyptic literature is because the former exerted an influence on contemporary historians of apocalypticism like Norman Cohn insofar as they read early Christian eschatological literature through this lens. The Byzantine material, while addressed in more recent decades by Paul J. Alexander,[42] Donald M. Nichol,[43] and Benjamin Garstad,[44] has had more of an influence on the self-conscious representation of the respective nationalisms of Eastern Orthodox countries as they entered modernity, including Greece, Russia, etc., and the historiographical representations of their pasts and destinies by proponents of these nationalisms.[45]

THE CATASTROPHIC END OF THE WORLD

In any case, the late *Annales* historian of mentalities Georges Duby affirmed that in Western Europe this apocalyptic mentality reached its crescendo in the eleventh century: "The world was growing older; the end of time could not be far away. Eleventh-century humanity lived in expectation of it. His sense of human history had to prepare him for that transition." For Duby, this sense of an aging world that was about to come to an end was related to the natural environment: "The people struggled almost barehanded, slaves to intractable nature and to a soil that is unproductive because it is poorly worked."[46] Duby in fact based his observations on the firsthand accounts of the chroniclers of the epoch such as Rodulfus Glaber, who described the abundant evils that "afflicted all parts of the world about the year 1000 after the birth of Our Lord" as a

---

40. Writing in the twelfth century, Geoffrey of Monmouth affirms that in AD 542 Arthur is mortally wounded in his battle against Mordred and is taken to the isle of Avalon for his wounds to heal (*History of the Kings* 7.261). Upon this was predicated the legend that he would return one day to restore Britain before the second coming (Padel, "Nature of Arthur," 10).

41. Latowsky, *Emperor of the World*, 142–43.

42. Alexander, *Byzantine Apocalyptic Tradition*.

43. Nichol, *Immortal Emperor*.

44. Pseudo-Methodius, *Apocalypse* (trans. Garstad).

45. Kessareas, "Signs of the Times," 81.

46. Duby, *Age of the Cathedrals*, 80.

prelude to the end of the world.⁴⁷ According to Glaber, it was around this time that Mount Vesuvius erupted, "spewing forth, by more mouths than usual, sulphurous fire and a great many rocks" so that as a result "Italy and Gaul were devastated by violent conflagrations, and Rome itself largely razed by fire."⁴⁸ Also, "a terrible plague attacked mankind; it was like a hidden fire which consumed and severed from the body any limb which it afflicted";⁴⁹ and a "dire famine forced people to eat not just the flesh of unclean animals and reptiles, but also that of men, women, and children."⁵⁰ These descriptions of volcanic eruptions, fires, plagues, and the ensuing famine and cannibalism constitute the background to Duby's assertion that Western Europeans believed they were held prisoner by the natural world, which, according to Archbishop Wulfstan of York and Worcester, was, in this period, actively turning against people because of their many sins.⁵¹

From Duby we can infer that the inimical natural environment produced in the minds of some Europeans a preoccupation with the belief that the world would immediately end. Certain passages in the Scriptures, if taken out of context, could even be used to justify such a scenario. Does Christ not warn of "earthquakes, famines, and pestilences in various places" (Luke 21:11; see also Matt 24:7; Mark 13:8) in his discourse on the second coming? Duby related the turbulence in the material world to an increasing fear in the supernatural world. He went on to elucidate that the Christians of this period "felt utterly crushed by mystery, overwhelmed by the unknown world their eyes could not see, the tireless, admirable, disturbing world whose reign went beyond mere appearances."⁵² Duby did not elaborate on the unseen world, but one can infer that this negative dimension to spirituality can be discerned in the obsession with the antichrist and demonology—reflected in the writings of Thietland and Adso already mentioned—that took place in this period. These trends were in fact thoroughly assessed by Norman Cohn in his

---

47. Glaber, *Five Books of Histories* 2.12, 75.

48. Glaber, *Five Books of Histories* 2.13, 75.

49. Glaber, *Five Books of Histories* 2.14, 77.

50. Glaber, *Five Books of Histories* 2.17, 83.

51. Wulfstan of York wrote that "many parts of creation also oppress us and fight against us, as it is written: 'The circumference of the earth will fight for God against the foolish.' That is, in English, the whole world will fight greatly, because of sins, against the proud who refuse to obey God. The sky fights against us when it sends us fierce storms and severely damages cattle and fields" (*Homily* 3.30–3.40, in Godden, "Millennium, Time, and History," 169).

52. Duby, *Age of the Cathedrals*, 9.

The Pursuit of the Millennium and *Europe's Inner Demons*, and I defer to these monumental works for more details.

The preoccupation with negative spiritual elements or figures such as antichrist was also noticed by Abbo of Fleury, who, while not himself subscribing to the belief that the world would end around the year 1000, nevertheless testified to the apocalyptic tension. He wrote:

> Concerning the end of the world, as a youth I heard a sermon preached to the people in the Paris church to the effect that as soon as the number of one thousand years was completed, Antichrist would arrive, and not long after, the Last Judgment would follow. . . . For a rumor had filled almost the entire world that when the Annunciation fell on Good Friday, without any question it would be the end of the world.[53]

If inimical situations produce apocalyptic expectation, it is easy to see why the belief that the world would end around the year 1000 became so popular. So far, I have mentioned only Italy and Gaul (France), but this expectation of the end-times was not restricted to the European continent. To give just a few examples, in 1014, the above-mentioned Wulfstan of York and Worcester wrote as follows in his "Sermon of the Wolf to the English": "Beloved, know what the truth is: this world is in haste and it is nearing the end, and therefore things are in the world ever the worse as time passes, and so it must necessarily get worse before Antichrist's time."[54] Along with Wulfstan's writings, those of "Aelfric, bishop of Eynsham (c. 990), the anonymous Blickling homilies (before 971), and the Vercelli homilies (compiled around 1000)" all pointed to the end of the world occurring imminently, around the year 1000.[55]

In addition to the chronological fixation with the year 1000, many millenarian movements arose between the eighth and fourteenth centuries that were led by certain charismatic, self-proclaimed messiahs who affirmed that they were in fact God's vessels chosen to bring about the apocalyptic "last things." From wandering preachers such as Adalbert of Soisson,[56] Eon the Breton,[57] and Tanchelm of Antwerp[58]—who took

---

53. Abbo of Fleury, *Apologeticus ad Hugonem et Rodbertum reges Francorum*, PL 139:471–72 (translated from the Latin with assistance from Chris Baghos).

54. Wulfstan of York, *Homilies* 20.1–20.6, in Godden, "Millennium, Time, and History," 172.

55. Szittya, "Domesday Bokes," 379.

56. Cohn, *Pursuit of the Millennium*, 42–44.

57. Cohn, *Pursuit of the Millennium*, 44–46.

58. Cohn, *Pursuit of the Millennium*, 46–50.

up Christ's messianic prerogatives and extorted their followers for money and material goods—to the ragged Tafurs, led by their eponymous king who pillaged towns and villages during the First Crusade (a form of the last ruler motif),[59] and later with some trends in the Fraticelli or Brotherhood of the Free Spirit[60]—these movements all had one thing in common: a preoccupation with the immanent and catastrophic end of the present world order. Even the Crusades can be interpreted apocalyptically insofar as they were fought in this period to reclaim the terrestrial city of Jerusalem, since the celestial one—the new Jerusalem promised in Rev 21—had not in fact come around the year 1000. This is in spite of the fact that, from the perspective of the "already–not yet" tension, the new Jerusalem has always inhered proleptically within the church. In any case, it is not coincidental that the "peace of God" movement that swept the European continent in 1033 and was marked by truces between warring nations took place a thousand years after the death and resurrection of Christ.[61] (The reasoning for this was that, if Christ was to return imminently, then peace should be made between nations before the last judgment.)

CONCLUDING REMARKS

In light of what I have argued above about the eschaton's "already–not yet" dimension, all of the aforementioned examples of apocalyptic anxiety can be said to come out of a radical misunderstanding of how the end-times should be approached from a Christian perspective. For it is in the church that Christ is present in the Eucharist and as the source and goal of the church's experience in the Spirit. The sort of radical apocalyptic trends based on a misreading of the "millennium" mentioned in Revelation, and precipitated by inimical social, political, and religious factors, persisted in the Reformation. This time, however, the Reformers interpreted the Roman Catholic Church and the pope in terms appropriated from the demonological terminology of medieval apocalyptic literature: devils, antichrist, the end-times—all were expected as an imminent possibility once again.[62]

59. Cohn, *Pursuit of the Millennium*, 65–67.
60. Cohn, *Pursuit of the Millennium*, 182.
61. Le Goff, *Birth of Europe*, 46–47.
62. There are antecedents to this depiction of the Roman Catholic Church and its pontiff in the writings of thirteenth-century spiritualists. See Cohn, *Europe's Inner Demons*, 62. An indicative text from the Reformation period is Martin Luther's *Treatise on*

I have taken us up to the 1500s, but in reality the belief in the imminent end of the world—the doomsday apocalypse—has kept cropping up in Western and Eastern Europe, and throughout the world, until the present day. In the East it was always bound up with the destiny, or the reclaiming, of either Jerusalem or Constantinople from various Muslim caliphates or sultanates. Every time it has appeared, it has traumatized people unnecessarily, or worse. And contemporary scholars in the discipline of historiography, instead of nuancing the topic of eschatology and distinguishing it from radical millenarian apocalypticism, group all of these together in their approach to the early Christian period in order to make not just Christ and the earliest disciples (Paul, etc.)—but Christians of every age—conformable to the portrait of either being crippled by their fear of the world ending, or of wanting it to end.

But by and large, the experience of Christians, especially Catholics but also Orthodox, has held that something of God's eschatological kingdom can already be partaken of within the ecclesial context. It is jarring that scholars have missed this; for it can be assumed that while a handful of Western chronographers whose writings have come down to us believed that the world would soon end, nevertheless Christians throughout Western Europe were still regularly attending Mass to participate in God's kingdom within the church, albeit as a foretaste. (This is to mention nothing of medieval mystics who experienced God directly via visions, etc.) It is a truism that Christians believe that the second coming will happen and that the world will one day end, but from all of the above it is clear that an unhealthy fixation with it—facilitated these days by fundamentalist conspiracy theories, far-right populist leaders, and radical leftist approaches to ecocide—can lead to the destruction of psychological well-being, even to one's life and the lives of others. The answer, I believe, to all of our anxieties and fears lies in the same apocalyptic tradition of Christianity, but read properly, in its holistic, "already–not yet" form, which anchors the eschatological experience precisely within the church's eucharistic and liturgical space.

BIBLIOGRAPHY

Alexander, Paul J. *The Byzantine Apocalyptic Tradition*. Edited by Dorothy de Ferranti Abrahamse. Berkeley: University of California Press, 1985.
Augustine of Hippo. *The City of God Against the Pagans: Books XVIII.36—XX*. Translated by William Chase Greene. Cambridge, MA: Harvard University Press, 2001.

---

the Power and Primacy of the Pope, which includes a chapter that described the Catholic Church and its structures as the antichrist ("Marks of the Antichrist").

Baghos, Mario. "Nuancing the 'Millennium' in the Writings of Norman Cohn." *Literature and Aesthetics* 33 (2023) 37–54.

———. "Reconsidering *Apokatastasis* in St Gregory of Nyssa's *On the Soul and Resurrection* and the *Catechetical Oration*." In *Cappadocian Legacy: A Critical Appraisal*, edited by Doru Costache and Philip Kariatlis, 387–415. Sydney: St Andrew's Orthodox Press, 2013.

Beale, G. K., ed. *The Book of Revelation: A Commentary on the Greek Text*. Grand Rapids: Eerdmans, 1999.

Boyer, Paul. "The Growth of Fundamentalist Apocalyptic in the United States." In *The Continuum History of Apocalypticism*, edited by Bernard J. McGinn et al., 516–44. New York: Continuum, 2003.

Bruce, F. F. *The Book of the Acts*. Rev. ed. NICNT. Grand Rapids: Eerdmans, 1988.

Cohn, Norman. *Europe's Inner Demons: The Demonization of Christians in Medieval Christendom*. Rev. ed. London: Pimlico, 2005.

———. *The Pursuit of the Millennium: Revolutionary Millenarians and Mystical Anarchists of the Middle Ages*. New York: Oxford University Press, 1970.

Dockery, David S. *Biblical Interpretation Then and Now*. Grand Rapids: Baker, 1992.

Duby, Georges. *The Age of the Cathedrals: Art and Society, 980–1420*. Translated by Eleanor Levieux and Barbara Thompson. Chicago: University of Chicago Press, 1983.

Fee, Gordon D. *The First and Second Letters to the Thessalonians*. Rev. ed. NICNT. Grand Rapids: Eerdmans, 2009.

Geoffrey of Monmouth. *The History of the Kings of Britain*. Translated by Lewis Thorpe. Penguin Classics. London: Penguin, 1966.

Glaber, Rodulfus. *The Five Books of the Histories*. Edited and translated by John France. Rodulfus Glaber Opera. Oxford: Oxford University Press, 2002.

Godden, Malcolm. "The Millennium, Time, and History for the Anglo Saxons." In *The Apocalyptic Year 1000: Religious Expectation and Social Change, 950–1050*, edited by Richard Landes et al., 155–80. New York: Oxford University Press, 2003.

Gray, John. *Black Mass: Apocalyptic Religion and the Death of Utopia*. London: Penguin, 2008.

Hiscock, Nigel. *The Symbol at Your Door: Number and Geometry in Religious Architecture of the Greek and Latin Middle Ages*. Aldershot, UK: Ashgate, 2007.

Kessareas, Efstatheos. "'Signs of the Times': Prophecy Belief in Contemporary Greek Orthodox Contexts." *Social Compass* 70 (2023) 73–90.

Kyle, Richard. *The Last Times Are Here Again: A History of the End Times*. Grand Rapids: Baker, 1998.

Landes, Richard. "The Fear of an Apocalyptic Year 1000: Augustinian Historiography, Medieval and Modern." *Speculum* 75 (2000) 97–145.

———. "Millenarianism/Millennialism, Eschatology, Apocalypticism, Utopianism." In *Handbook of Medieval Culture*, edited by Albert Classen, 2:1093–112. Berlin: de Gruyter, 2015.

Latowsky, Anne A. *Emperor of the World: Charlemagne and the Construction of Imperial Authority, 800–1229*. Ithaca, NY: Cornell University Press, 2013.

Le Goff, Jacques. *The Birth of Europe: 400–1500*. Translated by Janet Lloyd. Oxford: Blackwell, 2005.

Luther, Martin. "The Marks of the Antichrist." In *The Book of Concord: The Confessions of the Evangelical Lutheran Church*, translated by Theodore G. Tappert et al., 299–306. Philadelphia: Fortress, 1959.

Maximus the Confessor. "The Church's Mystagogy." In *Selected Writings*, edited by George C. Berthold. Classics of Western Spirituality. Mahwah, NJ: Paulist, 1985.

Mosshammer, Alden A. *The Easter Computus and the Origins of the Christian Era*. Oxford Early Christian Studies. Oxford: Oxford University Press, 2008.

Nichol, Donald M. *The Immortal Emperor: The Life and Legend of Constantine Palaiologos, Last Emperor of the Romans*. Cambridge: Cambridge University Press, 2002.

Padel, O. J. "The Nature of Arthur." *Cambrian Medieval Celtic Studies* 27 (1994) 1–31.

Pseudo-Methodius. *Apocalypse—An Alexandrian World Chronicle*. Edited and translated by Benjamin Garstad. Dumbarton Oaks Medieval Library. Cambridge, MA: Harvard University Press, 2012.

Resseguie, James L. *The Revelation of John: A Narrative Commentary*. Grand Rapids: Baker Academic, 2009.

Szittya, Penn. "Domesday Bokes: The Apocalypse in Medieval English Literary Culture." In *The Apocalypse in the Middle Ages*, edited by Richard K. Emmerson and Bernard McGinn, 374–97. Ithaca, NY: Cornell University Press, 1992.

Thompson, Damian. *The End of Time: Faith and Fear in the Shadow of the Millennium*. London: Sinclair-Stevenson, 1996.

Webb, Stephen H. "Eschatology and Politics." In *The Oxford Handbook of Eschatology*, edited by Jerry L. Walls, 500–17. Oxford Handbooks. New York: Oxford University Press, 2008.

Weber, Eugen. *Apocalypses: Prophecies, Cults and Millennial Beliefs Throughout the Ages*. London: Random House, 1999.

Wessinger, Catherine, ed. *The Oxford Handbook of Millennialism*. Oxford Handbooks. New York: Oxford University Press, 2011.

Yeats, William B. *The Collected Poems of W. B. Yeats*. Hertfordshire, UK: Wordsworth, 1994.

6

"Purgatory"

An Approach Through Syriac Typology

Joseph Azize

Can Christians satisfactorily discuss the afterlife and purgatory, given the obscurity of Scripture, the lack of any consistent tradition, and the vagaries of analytic theology? Here I rehabilitate the ancient method of "typology," involving reasoning from analogies. I explore the ancient Semitic wisdom, which sees the world as comprising antetypes produced on the pattern of divine types (i.e., archetypes).[1] I consider the approach of Ephrem († ca. 373) to paradise, Gehenna, and Sheol, a scheme parallel but not reducible to Latin concepts. Finally, I suggest that typological patterning allows us, within limits, to speculate both downwards and upwards: if what we experience here reflects an archetype, however imperfectly, then we can use that experience for "theosophical" contemplation of divine realities. Since, in this life, mortification and suffering are typical accompaniments of purification, then, true to type, they are to be expected in the next life, for the same purpose. Typological reasoning does not argue against, but discerns with, wisdom. For the believer, its insights are a sound support in life.

---

1. There is no one consistent terminology for typology: a matter that reflects the history of the approach and the hitherto-unremarked linguistic differences between its vocabulary in Greek, Syriac, and Latin. Taking my cue from certain New Testament and patristic documents, I use "archetype" and "type" for whatever is original; and "antetype" for the copy made from the type/archetype. My reasons for adopting the spelling "antetype" rather than "antitype" are set out in Azize, "Beauty," 164.

ISSUES IN ESCHATOLOGY

Eschatology raises complex questions: the fate of the deceased, judgment, heaven, hell, purgatory, the parousia, the millennium, and resurrection. Solutions offered by analytic schools of theology, and even its foundation assumptions, are increasingly seen as theoretical, ideologically grounded, and unpersuasive: in 1959, Kaufmann averred of modern theologians that

> out of the New Testament they pick appropriate verses and connect them to fashion an intellectual and moral self-portrait which they solemnly call "the message of the New Testament" or "the Christian view." . . . Theologians do not just do this incidentally: this is theology. Theology is like doing a jigsaw puzzle in which the verses of scripture are the pieces . . . [which] makes the game . . . pointless [since] you do not have to use all the pieces, and the pieces that do not fit may be reshaped after pronouncing the words "this means." That is called exegesis.[2]

I doubt that time has altered matters, except that interest in academic theology is ever more restricted to its practitioners. Further, with the riddle of purgatory, we are unable to appeal to reliable direct perception, as a botanist can produce a specimen of a leaf. Yet, eschatology remains a lively topic in the modern world, Christian or otherwise, although questions of the afterlife and spiritualism do not presently enjoy the currency they did in the Victorian and Edwardian periods.

The Bible is replete with allusions and hints relating to doctrines that are implied, but the content of which is neither expressly declared nor explained. In particular, the treatment of life after death in Scripture, taken as a whole, is neither transparent nor systematic. Consider 2 Macc 12:42–46.[3] This does not inform us of the state of the deceased sinners, where they may be, how long their condition endures, when and how they are loosed from their sins, and whether they rise in physical bodies. But it emerges from 2 Maccabees that to pray for the deceased is a "holy

---

2. Kaufmann, *Critique of Religion*, 157.

3. "And so betaking themselves to prayers, they besought him [i.e. the Lord], that the sin which had been committed might be forgotten. But the most valiant Judas exhorted the people to keep themselves from sin, forasmuch as they saw before their eyes what had happened, because of the sins of those that were slain. And making a gathering, he sent twelve thousand drachms of silver to Jerusalem for sacrifice to be offered for the sins of the dead, thinking well and religiously concerning the resurrection, (For if he had not hoped that they that were slain should rise again, it would have seemed superfluous and vain to pray for the dead,) And because he considered that they who had fallen asleep with godliness, had great grace laid up for them. It is therefore a holy and wholesome thought to pray for the dead, that they may be loosed from sins" (DR).

and wholesome" thing, i.e., an effective operation both for the living who pray and the dead for whom they pray. Apart from questions of the parousia of Christ, the interim place and condition of the deceased, and the relation between body and soul at the resurrection, the main outlines of the fully developed Catholic doctrine of purgatory are to be found here. Even among those fathers who accepted 2 Maccabees, there was disagreement as to whether the deceased slept awaiting judgment, remained in the "bosom of Abraham" or some other obscure state, or were immediately consigned to their eternal fate; whether the physical body had to be raised to be reunited with the soul, and if so what form that body took.[4] Passages such as John 11:11 and Mark 5:39 are explicable on the basis that the dead sleep in a slumber from which only the voice of God can awaken them.[5] As we shall see, this is the chief Syriac way of envisaging the fate of the deceased from the time of death to judgment, certainly into the time of Ephrem.[6] Some New Testament passages which speak of union with Christ after death do not make reference to Hades or the bosom of Abraham.[7] Depending on how one reads Scripture, this can be taken as an internal contradiction, as complementarity, or as an anomaly which cannot now be resolved.

Then, there are New Testament passages of which the original meaning seems to have been a matter of conjecture throughout church history, e.g., 1 Pet 3:19 and 1 Cor 15:29. Some areas we consider worthy of inquiry were neglected in the ancient church: the afterlife was hardly mentioned in the first centuries, unlike the doctrine of the Trinity, where the early tradition soon interpreted and expounded the sparse scriptural references.[8] As Daley remarked concerning the Odes of Solomon, the chief concern was salvation won by Christ, and "the Christian experience of ecstatic worship as a foretaste of the eschaton" casting into the background the world, judgment, and resurrection.[9] It has been observed that the New Testament focuses upon the resurrection and the last judgment (i.e., the *positive* aspect of the faith), rather than to what one might call the negative dimensions of hell and the afterlife geography.[10] This situation still, by and large, prevails in the East. The Orthodox are

---

4. See Bercot, *Dictionary*, 191–97; 559–64; Daley, *Hope of Early Church*, throughout.
5. McIntyre, *John*, 124.
6. This is the burden of Guinan, "Where Are the Dead?"
7. Some passages are gathered and compared in Bremmer, *Afterlife*, 57.
8. See Bercot, *Dictionary*, 652–57.
9. Daley, *Hope of Early Church*, 16.
10. Bremmer, *Afterlife*, 57; Bernstein, *Formation of Hell*, 207–26.

certain that Christians are obliged to pray for the deceased, and that these prayers are of benefit for the souls,[11] but have offered diverse theories as to the condition of souls awaiting final judgment, how they might be assisted by prayers offered on their behalf, whether they suffer, and if so, whether the suffering is expiatory or satisfactory, i.e., do their trials sanctify and cleanse them in some way, or are they purely penalties to be paid as a sort of debt for sin?[12] Some Orthodox "preserve instead a reverent and agnostic reticence."[13]

This last way was, broadly, also the Syriac one, until comparatively modern times. In the ancient Syriac world, there was no expectation that Christians should be unanimous about the complex questions listed in the first paragraph of this article. The East was content to proceed with the traditional open outlook, while the Latin West, in the twelfth century, systematized the teaching of the church.[14]

There are equivalent concepts to purgatory in other religions, e.g., in Hinduism and Buddhism (where one is purified through karmic suffering),[15] and in Islam (although the temporary punishment is there said to be administered in hell).[16] It is apparent that, pretty well universally, it is considered that most of us are neither so bad that we deserve eternal damnation, nor so virtuous as to have merited to enter heaven immediately. Even a number of Protestant theologians agree that if nothing impure can enter heaven (Rev 21:27), it is distressing to observe how few offer any appearance of unmixed holiness. Despite the emphatic rejection of purgatory by Luther and Calvin, some Protestants have covertly reintroduced the idea of a postmortem purification or made it a moment-of-death event.[17]

Also, Christians have long contemplated many hard cases where classes of humanity, through no fault of their own, are denied heaven. Thus, unbaptized children were thought to pass to a peaceful state of

11. Ware, *Orthodox Church*, 259.

12. Ware, *Orthodox Church*, 259.

13. Ware, *Orthodox Church*, 259–60.

14. Walls, *Purgatory*, 27. Le Goff, *Birth of Purgatory*, initiated modern studies of purgatory in the Latin Church. For developments, see Walls, *Purgatory*, 33–34; Bremmer, *Afterlife*, 67.

15. Stoeber, "Hindu-Christian Dialogue," 40–41, 43; Williams, *Mahāyāna Buddhism*, 95.

16. Lange, *Paradise and Hell*, 155–57.

17. This is the puzzle that Walls, *Purgatory*, explores. Calvin's opinion of purgatory was not entirely favorable: "Purgatory is a deadly device of Satan . . . it undermines and overthrows our faith" (*Institutes* 3.5.6, 438–39).

limbo, and virtuous pagans were allowed a natural felicity, while neither were often thought to be admitted to heaven (texts such as Mark 16:16 seem to make baptism a nonnegotiable prerequisite for salvation). Their claims to felicity, if not bliss, were such that Dante had a limbo for virtuous pagans in the foyer of hell, while to Ripheus of Troy and the emperor Trajan, he accorded positions in heaven itself (*Par.* 20). Many apparently good people never heard the Gospel either because of when or where they lived. Artificial and fanciful exceptions point to the strength of the feeling that more people deserved salvation than seemed to be destined for it, if the church's doctrine was absolutely correct. Incidentally, there is a certain endorsement of this in the Gospel of Luke. When Jesus says that: "It is easier for a camel to go through the eye of a needle than for a rich person to enter the kingdom of God," the hearers asked: "Then who can be saved?" Jesus's response was "What is impossible with man is possible with God" (Luke 18:25–27).[18]

Belief in an afterlife is resilient, even among atheists,[19] hence the need for Christians to speak about the afterlife in ways which atheists and other non-Christians will understand. It is possible, I would suggest, to approach questions of the hereafter through a way of thought called "typology."[20] One of the very chief exponents of this method was Ephrem the Syrian.

EPHREM

Ephrem († ca. 373) served in the churches of Nisibis and Edessa, probably as a deacon, and committed to a celibate life.[21] Together with hymns, he produced verse homilies and prose commentaries.[22] Brock's classic study *The Luminous Eye* has made Ephrem's achievement accessible. Since much of Ephrem's work is not well indexed, I footnote reliable secondary authors, but also provide references to the original hymns, where needed, for to establish Ephrem's thought requires substantial cross-reference.

Ephrem's understanding of the afterlife is the traditional Semitic one: there is heaven, paradise, hell, and Sheol. He once suggests that there is a place that is analogous to "purgatory," and makes several references to purification of the deceased. Ephrem accepted that there had to be

18. All biblical quotations are my own, unless otherwise stated.
19. Lawton, "Everyone Believes in Afterlife."
20. For my own approach to this, with etymological notes, see Azize, "Beauty."
21. Ephrem, *Hymns on Faith*, 4–12.
22. Ephrem, *Hymns on Faith*, 13.

some sort of commerce between the material and spiritual worlds, but also that to fully comprehend spiritual realities was beyond the human mind, unless instructed by revelation. What mattered to Ephrem was the possibility of salvation, and while intellectual understanding could help, its role was limited: the mysteries of God were not to be argued over.[23] For Ephrem, the physical world comprises heaven (more accurately translated as "the skies"), the earth, and the abyss of waters. This scheme dates back to ancient Mesopotamian times[24] and sheds light on Christian Scriptures: there are three heavens (2 Cor 12:2), composed of diverse stones (Exod 24:9–10; Ezek 1:26–28; 10:1).[25]

These three worlds: sky, earth, and abyss, coexisted with and provide the framework for an imaginative scheme of three invisible regions "outside of the ordinary spatial and temporal order. These are Paradise, Sheol, and Gehenna."[26] There were two underworld realms: Gehenna or hell, and Sheol. This second, as in the Hebrew conception, is "the underworldly abode of the dead, the collective destination of all human beings who return to the dust from which they were formed as the consequence of Adam's sin, wherein they await the eschatological resurrection."[27] All souls went there, whether righteous or not (Enoch and Elijah were spared it, but even Moses descended).[28] Sheol is beneath the earth but above the abyss of water, however, still, *it cannot be perceived* and seems to not quite be in this world: the nature of a supernatural reality is indicated by analogy with the physical world.[29] Sometimes Ephrem described Sheol as a series of graves, sometimes as one cavern; as the realm of God, Death, or Satan; sometimes as giving birth to Christ in his resurrection, and on yet other occasions as "the stomach of Death

---

23. Brock, *Luminous Eye*, 46–51. Brock cites the prose *Commentary on the Diatessaron*, which has broadly been accepted as by Ephrem since a Syriac version was discovered in 1957 (McCarthy, *Diatessaron*, 25). See also Ephrem, *Hymns on Faith*, 2.24, 67.11–67.13.

24. Horowitz, *Mesopotamian Cosmic Geography*, xii.

25. Horowitz, *Mesopotamian Cosmic Geography*, 9.

26. Buchan, *Christ's Descent to Dead*, 35.

27. Buchan, *Christ's Descent to Dead*, 35.

28. Buchan, *Christ's Descent to Dead*, 54, 58. See Nisibene hymns 6, 35, 36, 39, 53, in Ephrem, *Hymns and Homilies*, 91, 127, 132, 140, 153. These show that even Simeon and John the Baptist are in Sheol, not *paradise*.

29. Buchan, *Christ's Descent to Dead*, 54; see *Nisibene Hymn* 36.7.

the devourer."³⁰ Sometimes Death is praised for his impartiality, and at others, he is reviled for it.³¹

In Ephrem, paradise is not the same as heaven, which is, as in the Mesopotamian conception, the three-storied dwelling of God and his immortal court.³² Further, Gehenna, "the place of fiery torment for the wicked" is not the abode of any human souls until the day of judgment, and paradise and heaven are different, the first of these being the Edenic home created for humanity, still somehow available, if inaccessible and not to be perceived with our physical senses.³³ Paradise is neither earthly nor unearthly. It is a "liminal space . . . intended to serve as the venue for Divine and human communion."³⁴ Yet, through the sacramental life of the church it is possible to "mystically participate" in paradise.³⁵ In the "Letter to Publius," Ephrem emphasized how even to speak of eschatology, judgment, paradise and Gehenna was necessarily to speak metaphorically and speculatively: thus, when Matthew (25:33) speaks of right and left at the judgment, these are only names: there is not really either a right or a left.³⁶

More modern, arguably, than any Latin churchman before the twentieth century, Ephrem said that, even in speaking of Gehenna,

> maybe it is that the Gehenna of the wicked consists in what they see, and it is their very separation that burns them, and their mind acts as the flame. The hidden judge who is seated in the discerning mind has spoken, and has become for them there the righteous judge who beats them without mercy and with the torments of contrition. Perhaps it is this which separates them out, sending each one to the appropriate place.³⁷

Hence, Buchan states that: "In Ephrem's view, no single, univocal, or totalizing account can ever convey the full complexity of the invisible reality of Paradise, or, by extension, of Sheol or Gehenna."³⁸ I would

---

30. Buchan, *Christ's Descent to Dead*, 54–57; see *Nisibene Hymns* 38, 53.
31. Buchan, *Christ's Descent to Dead*, 57–58; see *Nisibene Hymns* 38, 52, 53.
32. *Genesis* 1.4, in Ephrem, *Selected Prose Works*, 77.
33. Buchan, *Christ's Descent to Dead*, 35, 37–39, 46–47; see *Nisibene Hymn* 38.
34. Buchan, *Christ's Descent to Dead*, 47.
35. Buchan, *Christ's Descent to Dead*, 282–83; "Hymn on the Unleavened Bread" 17.8–12 (cited in Brock, *Luminous Eye*, 101); Beggiani, "Typological Approach," 548.
36. Buchan, *Christ's Descent to Dead*, 42–44; citing "Letter to Publius" 9.3.
37. Buchan, *Christ's Descent to Dead*, 44; citing "Letter to Publius" 22.
38. Buchan, *Christ's Descent to Dead*, 42.

note here that the same is also true of Jacob of Sarug, whose view of the afterlife exhibits, if anything, more diversity than that of Ephrem.[39]

We now return to Sheol and concepts of purgatory. There is no torment of the dead in Sheol, which is the big difference between it and hell (Gehenna). It is characterized "by rest and peace and freedom from misery, filled with silent, happy, and tranquil dead."[40] There is neither torment in Sheol nor opportunity for repentance; it is where the deceased may "rest in peace."[41] Yet, in the *Hymns on the Nativity* 13.2, he has the Hebrew daughters sing: "Today let Eve rejoice in Sheol, for behold the Son of her daughter as the Medicine of Life came down to save the mother of His mother."[42] Sheol is not the same here as in the Old Testament (Ps 6:5). Ephrem does not, so far as I am aware, allude to this difference, but it could be explained by the new birth and freshness which comes upon all creation at the incarnation (this is the sustained theme of the lengthy first of the *Hymns on the Nativity*).[43]

In the tenth of the *Hymns on Paradise*, Ephrem implies that since so many people of diverse conditions pass to the next life, one might hope that some of these will be purified in the next life, and find forgiveness, even if they were not baptized Christians. The soul which is not intrinsically worthy might nonetheless be saved. In hymn 10.13–10.15, we read:

> The river of humanity consists of people of all ages, with old, young, children and babes, infants in their mothers' arms, and others still unborn in the womb. . . . Blessed the sinner who has obtained mercy there, and is deemed worthy to be given access to the environs of Paradise; even though he remains outside, he may pasture there through grace. As I reflected I was fearful again because I had presumed to suppose that there might be between the Garden and the fire a place where those who have found mercy can receive chastisement and forgiveness. . . . His divine cloud hovers over all that is His; it drips dew even on

---

39. Guinan, "Where Are the Dead?," 545–50. Jacob of Sarug usually speaks of human death as a "dissolution": e.g., in *Creation of Adam*, using the verb *š.rō*; but also features the motif of the trial of the otherworldly passage over a sea of fire (Guinan, "Where Are the Dead?," 342–45). Guinan states, on the basis of a personal communication from Aelred Cody, that the theme is to be found in earlier "West Syrian liturgical texts" ("Where Are the Dead?," 549). I have found such a reference only in the Maronite anaphora *Šarar*, but this is known only in a form that postdates Jacob of Sarug.

40. Buchan, *Christ's Descent to Dead*, 58–60; see *Nisibene Hymns* 36, 38, 52, 64, 66.

41. Buchan, *Christ's Descent to Dead*, 60, 295; *Nisibene Hymn* 48.12.

42. Ephrem, *Hymns*, 137.

43. Ephrem, *Hymns*, 63–74.

that fire of punishment so that, of His mercy, it enables even the embittered to taste of the drops of its refreshment.[44]

Clearly, Ephrem does not have an authoritative tradition behind him, so he has to work from first principles, chief of which are the justice and the mercy of God. He is also, apparently, agitated by the unfairness of those who perish in the womb or as infants being denied paradise. So Ephrem says that sinners can be admitted into "the environs" of paradise and find mercy, and he wonders if mercy cannot be granted in Sheol and in a place which approximates to purgatory. But in the *Commentary on the Diatessaron* 10.4 and 10.6, he takes this to the furthest degree when he says that even the sin against the Holy Spirit might be forgiven in the other world.[45]

The postmortem purification contemplated by Ephrem is also related to the mystery of Love, for Love is a unifying power, and nothing can be brought into a unity with something different unless there is an affinity: union is not agglomeration. Thus, in *Hymns of Faith* 32, Love is described as "the keeper of the heavenly treasure," and so it would stand to reason that salvation cannot be achieved until one is perfected in Love. Obviously, this rarely happens in our world, so the human experience continues to the day of judgment itself.[46]

To summarize my contentions so far, Ephrem has an ancient scheme of the universe, which he adapts in the light of the Christian revelation. It consists of the three heavens (the abode of God and his angels); the earth, the abyss of waters; and in a parallel but eternal universe, paradise, Gehenna (hell), and Sheol. He has the concept of purgatory, and he speculates that there may be a place between Gehenna and paradise where there is cleansing and forgiveness, but also that one can be purified and saved from the suffering in Gehenna. This is his view of the physical universe, and it was never reducible to Latin categories. But a parallel can be drawn, and in the end, the two schema are identical: those who died too good for hell, but not yet deserving of heaven, may be purified and cleansed.

---

44. Ephrem, *Hymns on Paradise*, 152–53.
45. McCarthy, *Diatessaron*, 167–68.
46. "Letter to Publius 25," in Ephrem, *Selected Prose Works*, 355–56.

TYPOLOGY

While typology includes a method of reading the Bible, it is not restricted to that, although in the Latin understanding of typology it is simply interpreting the Old Testament in terms of the New.[47] To be sure, in Rom 5:14 Adam is said to be a type (*tupos*) of the one coming (i.e., Christ), and in 1 Cor 10:9–11 Paul says that the disasters which struck the Israelites in Sinai happened "as types" (*tupikōs*) as a warning to us. The typological connections between the two Testaments are real. But the method, as developed in the Semitic world, always was broader than that. I shall suggest that we should think of "typology" as a "theosophy" rather than as a "theology." In the first instance, the *Shorter Oxford Dictionary* defines *theosophy* as: "Any system of speculation which bases the knowledge of nature upon that of the divine nature: often with reference to Boehme." It then refers to Blavatsky's Theosophical Society. On the other hand, *theology* is also defined as: "The study which treats of God, His nature and attributes, and His relations with man and the universe." The dictionary also notes that "natural theology" is "theology based upon reasoning from natural facts apart from revelation." Typology often moves from "natural facts" to divine ones and is a theosophy which not only bases the knowledge of nature upon that of the divine nature but also, as I shall demonstrate, bases the knowledge of the divine nature upon that of nature.

As evidenced in contemporary fashions, theology is today often openly articulated in terms of political and social ideologies (e.g., feminism and post-colonialism). From the perspective of typology, this is to invert the proper order: ideologies should be read in the light of theosophy or theology, not the other way around. Typology is the discerning of patterns: there is no right or wrong. At the end of the day, one perceives a pattern, or one does not. The Syriac writers never attempted to expound the basis of their method, it has to be inferred from that work itself,[48] although Ephrem saw that his attitude was not that of the controversialist thinkers of his time, when the Arian dispute was fracturing the church.[49] If modern philosophy and theology are analytic, typology is synthetic.

If theology combines "scattered scriptural references according to meaning and function," this operation is still not synthetic, because

---

47. Even the erudite Daniélou, *From Shadows to Reality*, has this limitation.
48. Murray, "Theory of Symbolism," 3.
49. Murray, *Symbols of Church*, 89.

Scripture is being dismembered to be remade into a new creature.[50] I opened this chapter with Kaufmann's critique of this practice. It is not beside the point that he also stated that:

> Confronted with Scriptures of which some are richly ambiguous while others make unequivocal but often unacceptable demands, the theologian accepts all of them and gives a univocal interpretation of all at once. If it is really univocal it represents a vast impoverishment . . . in no case can a theology really do justice to the Scriptures because it refuses to take into account their heterogeneity and their deep differences.[51]

I suggest that ancient typology is immune from this attack. The Syriac practitioners of typology never made any attempt to systematize the teaching, because they assumed it to be a unified and coherent whole. Their actual doctrines were those they had received through the apostolic tradition and were now developing and passing on. It is tempting to simply assert that the chief element in this tradition was Scripture, but the sacramental system, especially baptism and the Eucharist, were no less significant.[52] I cannot delve into it here, but the Syriac and Orthodox traditions rely upon the sacraments for the understanding of the Holy Spirit as much as they do upon Scripture, and they see the church's sacraments in Scripture.[53] Typologically, this is entirely proper, for the pattern of creation reflected in Scripture and the sacraments is beyond time. Hence, Buchan says that Ephrem saw "the world as a coherent collection of interrelated signs and types whereby visible realities reveal the invisible reality of Divine truth."[54]

By means of eternal signs and types, the *ineffable* truth is directly expressed in words, although those words cannot capture the truth. It is, perhaps, like shining variously colored lights from the other side of a misty valley: what one sees from the other side is the direct result of the lighting, and objectively reflects something of the origin, but it is altered because of the foggy medium through which it must pass. One can fairly accurately describe what is seen, but we cannot know the *nature* of the

---

50. Bernstein, *Formation of Hell*, 318.

51. Kaufmann, *Critique of Religion*, 162.

52. For a similar perspective from the Byzantine world, see Constas, "Middle State of Souls," 120.

53. Beggiani, "Typological Approach," especially 547–48, 551–54, and on sacraments of vocation, 555–57.

54. Buchan, *Christ's Descent to Dead*, 26. So too Beggiani, "Typological Approach," 543–44.

lights in themselves due to our circumstances. The distinction between cataphatic and apophatic ways thus breaks down. Murray says that Ephrem's theology of names operated "between apophatic and cataphatic poles."[55]

It is rather foreign to typology to say that an insight of the applicability of an archetype is wrong. It is as pointless to fault the typological drawing of connections as it would be to criticize "Hail to thee, blithe Spirit! Bird thou never wert" for self-contradiction. Typology does not "combine scattered scriptural references," "according to meaning and function" but *draws* upon Scripture as an organic reality. Thus, in speaking of the creation, Jacob of Sarug writes that Sunday, the first day, was "full of mysteries [rō.ze] and laden with types [ṭ.3een ṭuf.se]" (lit., bearing types).[56] He then relates it to night and day, and to Jacob and Esau, "who, like day and night, did not resemble one another. Esau, the first-born, was of a dark color, like the night."[57] To the analytic mind this is fanciful. Yet, it is impossible to assert that Jacob is *wrong*. All that can be said is that he has discerned a pattern which we might think strained. However, Jacob develops this, affirming that in both cases the better followed the lesser, that the light of day became the foundation of existence. In this way, types fructify not only in the intellect but also the imagination of the hearer. If the mind can countenance the connection, the connection holds.[58]

So, as in the example of Jacob and Esau, day and night, the typological perspective enables us to move from earthly antetypes to heavenly types or archetypes. Typology is thus complementary to analytic theology, each having certain advantages and limitations, because "the typology found in nature and in Scripture is not just an interpretive tool, but is of the very essence of things."[59] A further example is Ephrem's celebrated observation of how, when a bird takes flight, it makes a cross out of its

55. Murray, "Theory of Symbolism," 12.

56. Jacob of Sarug, *First Day* 8.489. The verb ṭa'en has a primary meaning of "bear" as in bearing fruit and in pregnancy. The active participle, used here, is also employed for items imbued with symbolic meaning (Payne Smith, "ṭen," *Syriac Dictionary*, 179, col. 2).

57. Jacob of Sarug, *First Day* 8.500–8.501.

58. In today's Maronite Divine Liturgy, at the fraction, the English translation has that the host is a "forgiving ember," which "glows with heavenly mysteries." The Syriac reads: gam.ru.tō m.⊠as.yō.nee.tō w.mal.yat rō.ze men raw.mō ("the pardoning coal full of mysteries/signs, meaning types from on high"). It has the nuance that the eucharistic host is a sign on multiple levels.

59. Beggiani, "Typological Approach," 544, noting in Syriac typology "the Incarnation is the summit of Creation, and was prepared for throughout history."

body by lifting its wings: "When it has matured and has flown in the air, it stretches out its wings in the symbol of the cross."[60] In *Hymns on Faith* 24, Ephrem avers that all which stands upright does so through the cross:

> The cross is the seal and mould of created things.
> By its length and breadth—by its shape—everything is sealed.
> The cross that bears every bird on two wings
> Through its strength all stands.[61]

For Ephrem, "The Bible contains *raze*, revelatory symbols of Christ because the whole world does."[62] *Raze* is one of many terms that can be used for types. With this perspective, it is not Ephrem's interpretation, which is arbitrary, but our interpretation of God's creation which is overly narrow, forcibly refusing the Creator in his works, and his patterns in its forms and manifestations.

Finally, typological interpretation is not exclusive: simply because I have spoken of a bird as a type does not mean that I cannot speak of it in other ways. The crucifixion is a type, but it is also history, and it can also be discussed in terms of analytic theology. In *Hymns of Faith* 26.3 Ephrem admits he cannot understand the six wings of the Seraphim, why they need wings to fly, and whether it is true or is a parable. Wickes comments that even if the wings are figurative, "it is difficult to explain what the figures represent."[63] But the typologist neither amends nor abandons the text: the engagement with the mystery simply continues.

A MODERN TYPOLOGICAL APPROACH TO PURGATORY

A. C. Charity states that typology is related to analogical thought:

> Either the broad study, or any particular presentation, of the quasi-symbolic relations which one event may appear to bear to another—especially, but not exclusively, when these relations are the analogical ones existing between events which are taken to be one another's "prefiguration" and "fulfilment." The second definition is a comparatively dogmatic and idealistic one, intended to apply only to Christian typology . . . according to this

---

60. Ephrem, *Hymns on Faith* 18.2, 148.

61. Ephrem, *Hymns on Faith* 24.8, 166.

62. Murray, "Theory of Symbolism," 5. He alludes to the timeless Semitic heritage of typology, seeing roots in ancient Mesopotamia and parallels in the gnostic Gospel of Philip (11–12).

63. Ephrem, *Hymns on Faith*, 173.

definition, Christian typology is "the science of history's relations to its fulfilment in Christ."[64]

When ancient texts include anomalies, clear contradictions, or absurdities (which we would think cry out for clarification or resolution) this is but a reflection of the ancient assumption that there are some things of which we cannot know the full truth: they must be spoken of enigmatically or not at all. Thus, Ephrem's contradictory descriptions of Sheol may move the mind to dwell on each picture as an aspect of the whole, accepting that there is a Sheol, a place of sleep where there may perhaps also be some more active joy; and that it can be depicted as a cavern, or a cemetery (or possibly both). Inconsistent descriptions convey that no description can be complete. Perhaps where the intellect is inadequate the feeling aspect of faith, hope and love will loom larger.

Now, "mystery" as translation of the Syriac *razō* does not simply mean an unknown. The eucharistic *razō* does not mean that nothing is known about the Eucharist. On the contrary, a great deal is known about it, and an endless amount can be understood, it is just that our comprehension will never be complete. But while one will always see new perspectives on the Eucharist, there will always be dimensions of it extending beyond our understanding, no matter how bright one moment of enlightenment may be. The earthly is a "mystery" or *razō* of the heavenly, and one aspect of that can be expressed when we say that it is an antetype of the divine archetype, manifesting for us the pattern of heaven. I suspect that the Hellenic and rabbinic rules of interpretation, *a minori ad maius* (and all its related formulations) and *qal wahomer*,[65] respectively, are similar, but not quite the same as typology.[66] Typological reasoning is a different category: it is an analogical movement between two tiers of the universe, knowing that there is a divinely established pattern, while the others are a basic rule of common sense. We can arrive at the same insight by another path: the Word of God created the world, not just an ordinary but a divine Word, full of the infinity of meaning and revelation, so that the meaning we discern in the world (if our understanding is not distorted by sin) is objectively a manifestation of the Word of God, on an earthly plane.[67]

---

64. Charity, *Events and Their Afterlife*, 1, noting "the fundamental analogical process in poetry," which "hints at an order that dwells deep within things" (4).

65. Lit., "light and heavy": if something applies in this instance, how much more will it apply in this other and weightier circumstance.

66. These have often been studied, e.g., the republished lecture in Hayes, *Early Rabbinic Culture*, 393–418.

67. I am expanding the available material, e.g., Beggiani, "Typological Approach."

This brings us now to the need for a contemporary approach to typology. Two or more phenomena, classes, or sets of circumstances "are generally said to be analogous if they share a common pattern of relationships among their constituent elements, even though the elements themselves differ." This probably uniquely human ability of "representational reasoning" (i.e., to perceive truth through analogy) is a higher function of the mind, which seems to be related to the rostral prefrontal cortex.[68] It had been noted that while this area seemed to correlate with intelligence in humans, yet some people who suffered damage there nonetheless performed extremely well in IQ tests. It now appears that those tests were not looking for what is called "fluid intelligence." Since "analogical reasoning is a key component of many 'fluid intelligence'–type tests, but not of IQ tests that measure intelligence as an average across disparate tasks," the IQ test results were unexpectedly high.[69] I am paraphrasing, but not, I think unfairly, to say that standard IQ tests look for a certain narrow type of intellectual activity, while the more fluid intelligence that moves between diverse objects and fields, often operating by analogy, is not so well observed by them. The relevance of this to a contrast of analytic theology and the theosophy of typology should be patent: theology tests for a relatively narrow range of understanding, a range that the typologist can see and engage in, but to which he is not limited.

There have been many attempts to understand how it is that, by using analogy, humans can perceive truths which lie beyond the knowledge which the senses can provide.[70] People can see analogical connections where there are deliberately induced superficial similarities, and the making of analogies can be learned, and seems to be easier where there is a "functionally relevant relation," especially if expressed in a causal system which includes a relational scheme.[71]

This is precisely, almost ideally, the situation in the Christian, especially the Eastern Christian scenario: God the Omnipotent Creator guarantees the clear causal system; and the relations within creation and between God and his creation are likewise assured, and are happily and memorably hierarchical and imbued with moral value.[72] In fact, not

68. Holyoak and Lee, "Causal Relations by Analogy," 459.

69. Burgess, "Riddle," 1627–28.

70. Kassler, *Newton's Sensorium*, 127, on Isaac Newton's *sensorium* theory.

71. Holyoak and Lee, "Causal Relations by Analogy," 460–61.

72. Space does not allow me to deal with the fascinating area of comparing and contrasting "the univocal, equivocal, and analogical senses of being" (Desmond, "Analogy,"

much is accounted to be mere accident in the East: the typological idea of the pattern of heaven upon earth has a wide embrace, because it is recognized that when divine images are realized upon the earth and in humanity, they may be distorted (hence the many references in Christian liturgy to the warping of the image of God in humanity). A development of this is found in the prayer: "Thy will be done as in heaven so on earth." The order in Matt 6:10, and in many translations, is the reverse of the English: it begins with heaven, it acknowledges that the earth should be ordered according to this pattern, but it is not.[73]

Therefore, typological thought can be applied to the concept of purgatory not only by proceeding from the archetype (which has been partially revealed) to the antetype, but in the opposite and complementary direction. We know enough about the archetype to know that it has to do with suffering and purification to somehow prepare us for the kingdom of heaven (or, in Ephrem's terms, paradise). If we commence, in this case, with the antetype (our experience of suffering as purification) we can extrapolate to the archetype (suffering as purification in the state of purgatory). This is really all that needs to be said: there is suffering here that can change people for the better, so there must be a divine form of suffering and cleansing there. Polkinghorne has hints of this when he looks at the way the potential of all creation has unfolded as a *process* then:

> One may expect that similar characteristics will persist in appropriate ways as expressions of God's will for creation's destiny beyond its death. In other words, eschatological discontinuity will not be so abrupt as to be an apocalyptic abolition of the old. . . . There must be sufficient continuity for the new to be seen to arise . . . out of the old. . . . Yet there must also be enough discontinuity so that the new is not just a repetition of the old.[74]

The application of this to the idea of purgatory is that we can reason to suffering and purification in the next world (continuity), the end of which is perfection in Christ so as to be fitted for the beatific vision (discontinuity). "Discontinuity" is not so accurate a term as the more perfect ordering of all experiences and processes to the divine purpose of universal salvation. Independently of my own research, Constas had

---

72). Desmond states: "Analogy is a way of figuring, in light of being itself as open to figuration" (75).

73. I hope to cover this in future research.

74. Polkinghorne, *God of Hope*, 15; but the same sort of reasoning is found throughout the volume.

in 1991 made a similar analogical move, but reasoning from the life of Christ (a classic source of archetypes in typology) and his death as "a universal prototype (cf., Col. 1:18)."[75]

We often employ this type of reasoning when we attribute human qualities and attributes to God. Sometimes this is entirely wrongheaded, e.g., when some people fondly imagine that God has faults and limitations. But on other occasions it may be possible, e.g., when we speak of the love, mercy, or faithfulness of God. It is necessary, indeed, to sometimes attribute human qualities to God but in a divine not a human manner. Jesus does this in Luke 11:11–13, to take but one of many examples, and says: If *you* would do that, how much more will God do it. The fact that this sort of reasoning has antecedents in Jewish ideas of *qal wahomer* would go to show that it is a Semitic way of thinking.

Eastern Christian religious culture lost a great deal when, under the influence of the christological controversies, it adopted the culture of Hellenic philosophy. Murray observed that when Ephrem was most philosophical, he was "probably being forced, however unwillingly, to take up some of the Arians' weapons, though he is always able to maintain his chosen position based on the primacy of symbols and the analogical validity of human language."[76] Constas notes a similar development in Byzantium: there the church had long tolerated a "muddle" of opinions on the "middle state" of souls, but were moved to articulate their beliefs and come to a "doctrinal identity" when they "encountered the Latin doctrine of purgatory" at the Councils of Lyons (1274) and Ferrera-Florence (1438–39).[77]

However, the analytic approach seeks certainty: and this is, arguably, an unnecessary and even futile imperative. In a talk delivered in 1974, John G. Bennett (1897–1974), the Catholic mystic and former pupil of G. I. Gurdjieff, stated that it was very difficult for us to understand what was wrong with "doubt" and why doubt was what he called an "evil suffering":

> Doubt is the condition where one is asking for evidence and proof and refuses to accept anything unless it is shown. Where does this come from? It comes from one's own egoism and the wish to have something without having earned it. We need to grasp that this doubt is a sin.

---

75. Constas, "Middle State of Souls," 83.
76. Murray, "Theory of Symbolism," 14.
77. Constas, "Middle State of Souls," 94, 124.

In this world the next step in front of us is always clear and we can always tell at the very moment what we have to do. When it comes to tomorrow there may be questions and uncertainties, but if we say: "How can I go on unless I am given some assurance about tomorrow?" we are making an illegitimate demand. Many people suffer from this kind of inner questioning and agonizing. On the surface it can appear to be justified but it is both a self-indulgence and a manifestation of egoism. When we see doubt is a wrong kind of suffering then our attitude changes. We see that it is not necessary to have certainty. There is a difference between asking questions and demanding answers. We can live perfectly well knowing what is to be done at this moment without any certainty as to the outcome or as to what will happen tomorrow.[78]

In the case of the teaching on purgatory, the main practical values are the consolation that while some traits and traces in us might not be eradicated in this life, yet if we have honorably struggled with them, God in his mercy may forgive us and save us, admitting us to his paradise. Much else could be considered, not least in the writings of Clement of Alexandria. Yet, before being distracted, it is valuable to hold clearly before our mental eyes the ancient Semitic way of reasoning we today call "typology," a method which used image and a sense or feeling of fitness, in a balanced way, with intellectual endeavor, but in doing so, it transforms the endeavor into an equally artistic one.

BIBLIOGRAPHY

Azize, Joseph. "Beauty in the Syrian Eastern Christian Tradition." In *Beauty and Christian Tradition*, edited by Matthew Del Novo et al., 161–79. Strathfield, Aus.: St Pauls, 2020.
Beggiani, Seely Joseph. "The Typological Approach of Syriac Sacramental Theology." *TS* 64 (2003) 543–57.
Bennett, John G. *Talks of Beelzebub's Tales*. Repr., York Beach, ME: Samuel Weiser, 1988.
Bercot, David W. *A Dictionary of Early Christian Beliefs*. Peabody, MA: Hendrickson, 1998.
Bernstein, Alan E. *The Formation of Hell: Death and Retribution in the Ancient and Early Christian Worlds*. Ithaca, NY: Cornell University Press, 1993.
Bou Mansour. *La pensée symbolique de Saint Ephrem le Syrien*. Kaslik, Leb.: Bibliothèque de l'Université Saint-Esprit, 1988.
Bremmer, Jan N. *The Rise and Fall of the Afterlife*. London: Routledge, 2002.

---

78. Bennett, *Talks of Beelzebub's Tales*, 130.

Brock, Sebastian. *The Luminous Eye: The Spiritual World Vision of Saint Ephrem the Syrian*. Kalamazoo, MI: Cistercian, 1985.

Buchan, Thomas. *"Blessed Is He Who Has Brought Adam from Sheol": Christ's Descent to the Dead in the Theology of Saint Ephrem the Syrian*. Gorgias Studies in Early Christianity and Patristics 13. Piscataway, NJ: Gorgias, 2004.

Burgess, Paul W. "Riddle Is to Conundrum as the Frontal Pole Is to . . . ?" *Brain* 139 (2016) 1627–30.

Calvin, John. *Institutes of the Christian Religion*. Translated by Henry Beveridge. Peabody, MA: Hendrickson, 2008.

Charity, A. C. *Events and Their Afterlife: The Dialectics of Christian Typology in the Bible and Dante*. London: Cambridge University Press, 1966.

Chrysostom, John. *Homilies on First and Second Corinthians*. Edited by Philip Schaff. Vol. 12 of *NPNF*[1]. Peabody, MA: Hendrickson, 2012.

Constas, Nicholas. "'To Sleep, Perchance to Dream': The Middle State of Souls in Patristic and Byzantine Literature." *Dumbarton Oaks Papers* 55 (2001) 91–124.

Daley, Brian E. *The Hope of the Early Church: A Handbook of Patristic Eschatology*. Cambridge: Cambridge University Press, 1991.

Daniélou, Jean. *From Shadows to Reality: Studies in the Biblical Typology of the Fathers*. Translated by Wulstan Hibberd. London: Burns and Oates, 1960.

Desmond, William. "Analogy and the Fate of Reason." In *The Oxford Handbook of Catholic Theology*, edited by Lewis Ayres and Medi Ann Volpe, 72–94. Oxford Handbooks. New York: Oxford University Press, 2019.

Ephrem the Syrian. *Hymns*. Translated by Kathleen McVey. Classics of Western Spirituality. Mahwah, NJ: Paulist, 1989.

———. *Hymns and Homilies of St. Ephrem the Syrian*. Translated by John Gwynne. N.p.: Veritatis Splendor, 2012.

———. *The Hymns on Faith*. Translated by Jeffrey T. Wickes. FOTC 130. Washington, DC: Catholic University of America Press, 2015.

———. *Hymns on Paradise*. Translated by Sebastian Brock. Crestwood, NY: St. Vladimir's Seminary Press, 1990.

———. *Selected Prose Works*. Edited by Kathleen McVey. Translated by Edward G. Mathews and Joseph P. Amar. FOTC 91. Washington, DC: Catholic University of America Press, 1994.

Guinan, Michel D. "Where Are the Dead? Purgatory and Immediate Retribution in James of Sarug." In *Symposium Syriacum 1972*, edited by I. Ortiz de Urbina, 541–50. OrChrAn. Rome: Pontificium Institutum Orientalium Studiorum, 1974.

Hayes, Christine, ed. *Classic Essays in Early Rabbinic Culture and History*. Classic Essays in Jewish History. London: Routledge, 2018.

Holyoak, Keith J., and Hee Seung Lee. "Inferring Causal Relations by Analogy." In *The Oxford Handbook of Causal Reasoning*, edited by Michael R. Waldmann, 459–74. Oxford Library of Psychology. Oxford: Oxford University Press, 2017.

Horowitz, Wayne. *Mesopotamian Cosmic Geography*. Winona Lake, IN: Eisenbrauns, 1998.

Jacob of Sarug. *Jacob of Sarug's Homilies on the Six Days of Creation: The First Day*. Edited and translated by Edward G. Mathews Jr. Piscataway, NJ: Gorgias, 2009.

———. *Jacob of Sarug's Homily on the Creation of Adam and the Resurrection of the Dead*. Edited and translated by Edward G. Mathews Jr. Piscataway, NJ: Gorgias, 2014.

Kassler, Jamie C. *Newton's Sensorium: Anatomy of a Concept*. Dordrecht: Springer Nature, 2018.

Kaufmann, Walter. *Critique of Religion and Philosophy*. London: Faber & Faber, 1959.

Lange, Christian Robert. *Paradise and Hell in Islamic Traditions*. Themes in Islamic History. Cambridge: Cambridge University Press, 2015.

Lawton, Graham. "Why Almost Everyone Believes in an Afterlife—Even Atheists." *New Scientist*, Nov. 20, 2019. https://www.newscientist.com/article/mg24432570-500-why-almost-everyone-believes-in-an-afterlife-even-atheists/.

Le Goff, Jacques. *The Birth of Purgatory*. Translated by Arthur Goldhammer. Chicago: University of Chicago Press, 1984.

McCarthy, Carmel. *Saint Ephrem's Commentary on Tatian's Diatessaron*. Oxford: Oxford University Press, 1993.

McIntyre, John. *The Holy Gospel According to Saint John*. London: Catholic Truth Society, 1899.

Murray, Robert. *Symbols of Church and Kingdom: A Study in Early Syriac Tradition*. Rev. ed. Piscataway, NJ: Gorgias, 2004.

———. "The Theory of Symbolism in St. Ephrem's Theology (1)." *ParOr* 6 (1975–76) 1–20.

Payne Smith, Robert. *A Compendious Syriac Dictionary*. Edited by Jessie Payne Smith. Repr., Winona Lake, IN: Eisenbrauns, 1998.

Polkinghorne, John. *The God of Hope and the End of the World*. New Haven, CT: Yale University Press, 2002.

Stoeber, Michael. "Hindu-Christian Dialogue on the Afterlife: Swami Vivekananda, Modern Advaita Vedānta, and Roman Catholic Eschatology." *International Journal of Hindu Studies* 27 (2023) 33–65.

Walls, Jerry L. *Purgatory: The Logic of Total Transformation*. Oxford: Oxford University Press, 2012.

Ware, Timothy. *The Orthodox Church: An Introduction to Eastern Christianity*. Rev. ed. Harmondsworth, UK: Penguin, 1980.

Williams, Paul. *Mahāyāna Buddhism: The Doctrinal Foundations*. 2nd ed. Library of Religious Beliefs and Practices. London: Routledge, 2009.

7

Human Persons Defined by Their End
Eschatology and Anthropology Within the Thought of Romano Guardini

Paschal M. Corby OFM Conv.

INTRODUCTION

Nature is teleologically defined. The nature of a thing receives its form from what it is in its state of flourishing. The same holds for human nature. Along with more base creatures, human beings are defined according to their physiological inclinations to life, self-preservation, and reproduction. But according to their spiritual nature, reflective of their creation in the *imago Dei* (Gen 1:27), the human person is projected beyond time and space. Human nature is, therefore, only fully realized in its end. Recognizing this teleological projection, Joseph Ratzinger succinctly states: "We do not understand man when we ask only where he comes from. We understand him only when we also ask where he can go. Only from his height is his essence really illuminated."[1]

The purpose of this chapter is to investigate this connection between human nature and teleology, or more specifically, between anthropology and eschatology. This will be achieved by drawing on the wisdom of one of Ratzinger's greatest influences, the Italian-German theologian Romano Guardini. Questions of anthropology exist at the heart of Guardini's theology. Guardini scholar Robert A. Krieg defines him as "a

---

1. Ratzinger, *Images of Hope*, 58–59.

theologian of personal existence."[2] Ratzinger himself, in his papal address to a conference on "The Spiritual and Intellectual Legacy of Romano Guardini," draws out the theological milieu of Guardini's anthropology. "Guardini did not want to know one thing or many things, he aspired to the truth of God and to the truth about man."[3] More specifically, Guardini's anthropology is situated within an eschatological framework. It seeks to understand the human person in reference to the eternal Word, and in the Word's movement from (*exitus*) and return to (*reditus*) the bosom of the Father. This is the "arch" along which every human person is called to travel, suggests Guardini, towards the full realization of himself before God.[4]

TRINITARIAN THEOLOGY OF THE WORD

Guardini's anthropology is deeply rooted in a Trinitarian theology of the Word that he adopts from Saints Augustine and Bonaventure.[5] Within this theology, the Word, the Second Person of the Holy Trinity and Son of the Father, is the form of all reality both internally (within the Trinity) and externally (in creation). In the words of Guardini: "Because the Father's Word, the *Logos*, is the expression of all that must be expressed, of the very essence of God, it is also the expression of the essence of all finite things. For whatever can be, is, in that it reflects God. Thus the prototype of all things is to be found in the *Logos*."[6] This "exemplarism," borrowed from the theology of Saint Bonaventure, maintains that the movement of the Word from the Father (as his self-expression) becomes the form of all things external of God, in human beings and creation.[7]

Bonaventure identifies a threefold expression of the Word (*Verbum triplex*): "Of the Uncreated Word by whom all things are brought forth; of the Incarnate Word by whom all things are restored; and of the Inspired Word by whom all things are revealed."[8] The Uncreated Word defines

2. Krieg, "Theology of Human Person," 473.

3. Benedict XVI, "Address," para. 3.

4. Guardini, *Last Things*, 18.

5. See Frývaldský, "Dio dialogico."

6. Guardini, *Conversion of Augustine*, 11.

7. Frývaldský writes: "The Second Divine Person that stands in the middle (medium) between the Father and the Spirit has the active role of being the Mediator in the creation of the universe. Since the Word represents the medium and model of creation, the truth of things can be known only in the light of the same Word (*Verbum lux mentis*)" ("Dio dialogico," 82–83).

8. Bonaventure, *Collations on Six Days* 3.2.

the internal speech of the Father in his "eternal generation of the only begotten Son as *Verbum aeternum* or *natum*."[9] The Incarnate Word is that exterior manifestation within "the temporal creation of the cosmos, the *Verbum temporale* or *creatum*."[10] The Inspired Word (*Verbum inspiratum*) is the inhabited Word, through the action of the Holy Spirit, in the heart of the believer through which one participates in the redemptive work of Christ.[11] All things come into existence through the Word (John 1:3). Accordingly, for Bonaventure, Word (*Verbum*) "is the most excellent and appropriate name for the Son of God because it expresses his relationship with the Father from whom he is generated, the cosmos which was created through him, the flesh that clothed him in the incarnation and the truths he revealed in the power of the Holy Spirit."[12]

UNCREATED WORD

The Father eternally begets (sends forth) the Son, his Word and self-expression. The being of the Son is, therefore, defined by this *exitus*, this going forth from the Father. But since this distinction is contained within a more profound unity, the Son's going forth is matched by his return (*reditus*), which propels the Word back to its source in the bosom of the Father. Having his being in the Father, the Son finds his "home" in this return. Within the mystery of the Trinity, this action takes place "in the boundless intimacy of love which is the Spirit."[13] The Holy Spirit—the love that unites them—is the path along which the Son goes forth and returns to the Father.

Guardini images this movement as speech. The Son "is the Father's eternal, spoken Word."[14] This Word, as we read in John's Prologue, is eternally "with" the Father. As Guardini interprets, "an eternal speech" happens within God:[15] "He is the speaking God and the spoken Word: Father and Son";[16] "the speaker (Father), the one spoken (Son), and the loving comprehension of the eternal speech (Spirit)."[17] This speech is

9. Johnson, "Bonaventure's Theology of Word," 356.
10. Johnson, "Bonaventure's Theology of Word," 356.
11. Frývaldský, "Dio dialogico," 83.
12. Johnson, "Bonaventure's Theology of Word," 356.
13. Guardini, *Conversion of Augustine*, 4.
14. Guardini, *Conversion of Augustine*, 4.
15. Guardini, *Word of God*, 4.
16. Guardini, *Conversion of Augustine*, 11.
17. Guardini, *World and Person*, 349.

unlike human speech, for human utterances depart from the speaker, seeking "one who shall receive it, and if it does not find him it vanishes in space."[18] God's Word is different. It is not an utterance spoken into nothingness. It does not vanish into space. God's *logos* remains, and does so "independent of whether a creature exists which could hear Him."[19] This is because the Word is within God himself. He is his own answer (*Antwort*), for "in God there is a true 'I' and 'Thou.'"[20] The Word remains "with" the Father in the Holy Spirit. And this abiding is the assurance that God's Word "does not become a second God,"[21] but exists as "union and abiding, intimacy and faithfulness, fulfillment and eternity."[22]

INCARNATE WORD

The intra-Trinitarian procession and return of the Word from the Father, in the Holy Spirit, becomes the form of God's action in history: in the act of creation (of the person and the world), and in the act of the incarnation of the Word.

The incarnation is the most dramatic expression of the Father's speaking forth his Word. While the Word eternally abides in the Father (as noted already), the incarnation might be imaged as a moving away from the Father—the creation of a distance between Father and Son—that approximates the distance between God and creation. This *exitus*—this establishment of a distance—is revealed in the kenotic hymn of Phil 2. The Son "empties himself" of his glory to assume the slave form of the "likeness of men" (Phil 2:6–7). This moving away from the Father reaches its climax on Calvary, with Christ's cry of abandonment (Matt 27:46). "In the final fulfillment of the redeeming oblation," writes Guardini, "in the blackest darkness of the doom of death, even the nearness of the Father withdrew, and he was left quite alone."[23]

From this point of distance, the Son is drawn back into the Father's embrace. The Father raises him from the dead and seats him by his side (Eph 1:20). After his resurrection, Christ entrusts the Magdalene with a message for his disciples: "Go to my brethren and say to them, I am ascending to my Father and your Father, to my God and your God" (John

18. Guardini, *Word of God*, 6.
19. Guardini, *World and Person*, 349.
20. Guardini, *Word of God*, 7, 8.
21. Guardini, *Word of God*, 8.
22. Guardini, *Word of God*, 6.
23. Guardini, *Meditations on the Christ*, 79.

20:17). It was a message already proclaimed before his death: "It was from the Father that I came, when I entered the world, and now I am leaving the world, and going on my way to the Father" (John 16:28).

However, a note of caution must be added here. For Guardini, distance does not equate with separation. While the distance between the Father and the Son in his incarnation and passion is *felt*, it is not an ontological reality. The communion of love that they share is eternal and is only intensified through these saving events. This coincides with what Carlo Caffarra writes: "In death, the greatest distancing from the Father, the Son finds himself closest to the Father through *perfect* obedience to him; here the Son, as man, fully reveals himself in his Sonship."[24] His moving away from the Father, therefore, is only apparent. The Son and the Father are one (John 10:30). Whoever sees the Son sees the Father (John 14:9). While he is sent forth by the Father, Christ speaks and acts and exists only from the plenitude of that source. As Guardini writes: "What Jesus declares, he owns. He possesses the God of whom he speaks. There is no duality here, only unity."[25] And again: "The presence of the Father is so close to our Lord, and his oneness with him such an interior thing, that the living Jesus Christ is simply the Father become visible."[26]

Guardini adds that if Christ suffers any alienation or estrangement, it is primarily realized in his human relationships. From the moment of his incarnation, he exists as a being in *passage*.[27] He does not belong to the world. He comes from the Father. And precisely because of that unique relationship that he shares with the Father in the Holy Spirit, he is ultimately alone on this earth. In his *Mediations on Christ* Guardini writes: "His sense of aloneness among the rest of men sprang from this being one with the Father, for he was different from them. And at the same time, he was able to endure this isolation because of this very oneness."[28]

He came to his own, and they received him not (John 1:11). His disciples misunderstand him (Luke 9:45). One betrays him, another denies him, all but one abandons him as he is lifted up on the cross.

---

24. Caffarra, *Living in Christ*, 41; emphasis in original. Or, as Michael Hanby writes, in his submission to death "the Son assumes a position of infinite distance from the Father precisely *because* he is the perfect image of the Father's love," asserting "both the unity, identity and equality between the Father and Son *and* a difference between the Father and the Son which is infinitely *greater* than that between God and creation" (*Augustine and Modernity*, 54; emphasis in original).

25. Guardini, *Meditations on the Christ*, 59.

26. Guardini, *Meditations on the Christ*, 86.

27. Guardini, *Meditations on the Christ*, 18.

28. Guardini, *Meditations on the Christ*, 101.

Even his most perfect disciple, his blessed Mother, senses an increasing distance opening up between her and her divine Son. Of this Guardini writes that "it is as if a gulf opens up between him and her"[29] as she contemplates "the infinite distance out of which he comes."[30] Though he was hers in the most intimate fashion—took his human nature from her, drew life from her—yet he necessarily "grew away from her, went on past her."[31] Or, as Hugo Rahner contends, from the moment of Mary's yes to divine motherhood there existed a resignation to his death, a death that she realized daily in the "parting from him during his life on earth" and "her complete loss of him in the fullness of his manhood."[32]

But Christ's isolation and distancing from those around him had its source in his obedience to the will of the One who sent him. He was not distracted by those who think, not as God, but as the world (Matt 16:23). He was not tied to any worldly consideration but totally transfixed by the Father's will. Thus, he comes to the cross unattached, alone "on the sharpest pinnacle of Creation, in the presence of God."[33] The cross is, therefore, both the extremity of the Son's *exitus* and the moment of his return. It is the point of intersection between going "from" and returning "to" the Father. Similarly, the cross signifies the extremity of humanity's alienation from God, but it is also the beginning of its redemption, its return. The darkest moment in human history, in which man kills God, becomes the source of light and life. When raised high on the cross, the distance between Christ and the world is overcome, drawing all to himself (John 12:32). His cross shatters the monotony of our finite lives. In the words of Ratzinger it becomes "the fishhook of God, with which he reels up the entire world to his height."[34]

According to Bonaventure, sin had destroyed humanity's compass in navigating its return to God, possessing no power within itself to restore it. "Only Jesus Christ, the Word made flesh, can rescue us from this path of alienation and lead us back to God."[35] He draws us to himself, and into his life and place before the Father.[36] In his incarnation he has assumed our humanity, and through his death and resurrection he has

---

29. Guardini, *Meditations on the Christ*, 8.
30. Guardini, *Meditations on the Christ*, 9.
31. Guardini, *Meditations on the Christ*, 11.
32. Rahner, *Our Lady and Church*, 106.
33. Guardini, *Meditations on the Christ*, 13.
34. Ratzinger, *Images of Hope*, 76.
35. Delio, *Simply Bonaventure*, 79.
36. Guardini, *Last Things*, 113.

opened a way for us; that we might go forth "with Christ to the hands of God."[37] Thus, the action of the Word in history restores the person to his or her path. Even more, as Guardini writes, in and through Christ "the world is oriented toward God in the way in which he willed it in creating it."[38] God's action in history lays bare the fallen nature of the world, with its tendency toward self-enclosure and sin. He judges the world and rejects it as unholy. But he does so in love. For the Son—his Word—"places himself on the side of the world, takes its guilt upon himself, and becomes for it the living 'way' to God."[39]

GOD'S WORD AND HUMANITY

As suggested above, the incarnation of the Word, as the exemplary form of the eternal procession of the Word within God, is also the form of his creation of the world and humanity. Concerning the being of the human, Krieg highlights three main ideas which underpin Guardini's theological anthropology. In the first place, personhood exists primarily in God. Human beings participate in the divine personhood. Accordingly, they are persons in an analogical sense. In the second place, this participation comes about only through God's free choice to "communicate" himself to human beings. God's will creates and sustains the person in his or her being. As Krieg interprets: "The 'I-Thou' relationship that exists between God and the divine word has opened itself to include creation, especially human beings. In other words, creation possesses within itself, in a derivative manner, the character of the 'you' or 'thou' to whom God speaks as an 'I.'" Finally, the human person definitively enters into this "I-Thou" relationship only through grace, through Christ in the Holy Spirit. "As Divine Word, Christ is the mediator between God and creation, and each human being is called upon to undergo a conversion to Christ."[40]

With Guardini we recall that God creates *by speaking*. "Not by letting the world spring forth from himself, or by eternalizing himself in it, or by imagining it; but by his word, his command."[41] God's creative word—his "let it be" spoken in the book of Genesis—is recapitulated in the prologue of John's Gospel. As Guardini suggests: "St. John tells us the deeper secret of that which Genesis shows us at work, for behind the

---

37. Ratzinger, *Images of Hope*, 76.
38. Guardini, *World and Person*, 317.
39. Guardini, *World and Person*, 320.
40. Krieg, "Theology of Human Person," 464.
41. Guardini, *Word of God*, 9.

word that turns outward in divine creation, there is the interior word of the divine life. The former is a free radiation of the latter, free because creation is not of necessity but comes from God as deliberately willed action."[42] The primary procession of the Word from the Father is the guarantee of the free act of creation. Creation exists as a similitude of God's eternal sending forth of the Son. It is only in this sense that we can say that God creates freely; that he has no need of creation. For without the priority of the spoken Word, God would remain unknown to himself and would need creation to express himself or mirror his thought.[43]

Within creation, this Word form of being is most clearly expressed in the creation of the human person. Created in the image of God (Gen 1:27), he or she is marked by Trinitarian relations of communion/love. Contemporary interpretations of Trinitarian anthropology insist that "the image of God means, first of all, that human beings cannot be closed in on themselves." Systems of isolation can betray the essence of humanity, for "to be the image of God implies relationality."[44] Furthermore, in modeling the relations of the Blessed Trinity—of the Father's being "for" the Son, the Son being "from" the Father, and the Holy Spirit being "with" them both—the mode of being in relationship is more precisely defined. Accordingly, Ratzinger will say: "Man, for his part, is God's image precisely insofar as the 'from,' 'with,' and 'for' constitute the fundamental anthropological pattern. Whenever there is an attempt to free ourselves from this pattern, we are not on our way to divinity, but to dehumanization, to the destruction of being itself through the destruction of the truth."[45]

However, according to a distinctly Augustinian-Bonaventurian anthropology, "the human person is in the image of God not in a general sense of being like God but in a specific sense of being like the Son . . . Just as the Word is the expressed 'image' of the Father, the human person is created to be an expressed 'image' of the Word."[46] The human person, therefore, possesses a Word form. It is within the space between Father and Son—between Speaker and spoken Word—that the human person

---

42. Guardini, *Word of God*, 9.

43. Frývaldský writes that from an Augustinian-Bonaventurian perspective, the Second Person of the Holy Trinity is conceived "as the Word in which is eternally expressed and manifested the Truth of the Father. Without this Word, God would be 'mute,' that is 'unknown' to himself, and would need the world in order to know himself" ("Dio dialogico," 87).

44. Ratzinger, *In the Beginning*, 47.

45. Ratzinger, "Truth and Freedom," 28.

46. Delio, *Simply Bonaventure*, 72.

exists. He is defined by this relationship. Guardini himself speaks of the human being as one who is intended both to hear God's word and respond to it, not only for himself, but on behalf of the whole of creation as the world is drawn into the "I-Thou" relation. "All things are words of God spoken to that creature which by its nature is destined to stand in the 'Thou'-relation to God. Man is the one who is meant to be the hearer of the world-word. He is also meant to be the one who answers. Through him all things should return to God in the form of an answer."[47] His existence as a person in his being an I is immediately dependent on God's existence as his Thou.[48]

In realizing oneself as an image of the Word, the human person is marked by a twofold nature of dependence and transcendence. Just as the Son exists from the Father, so the person finds his or her being from the Creator. It is the realization of a fundamental dependence that is expressed in terms of relation. As Ratzinger writes: "He must recognize that he is not self-sufficient and autonomous. He must give up the lie of unrelatedness and of arbitrariness. He must say Yes to his neediness, Yes to the other, Yes to creation, Yes to the limits and precepts of his own essence."[49] The acceptance of his dependence is a manifestation of humility. Such humility does not diminish human dignity. Guardini insists that the "kind of humility which, in order to honor God, debases man" is not Christian.[50] Rather, through the humble acknowledgment of his created nature, the person is free to live in the image of God.

However, in imaging the Word/Son, human persons are instinctually conscious that they are created for something more. The person senses "that this present existence is not the real and true one, that it must become new and different and so attain to its proper reality."[51] His spirit aspires to transcendence, seeking something surer; something more permanent. "What he desires is the real transformation, the genesis of something entirely new from which man would at last receive his proper self."[52]

Throughout history, human beings have expressed this desire for transcendence (or immortality) in various ways. Frequently it has taken the form of a vicarious sharing in the life of another; what Joseph

---

47. Guardini, *World and Person*, 355.
48. Guardini, *World and Person*, 353.
49. Ratzinger, *Church, Ecumenism, and Politics*, 255.
50. Guardini, *Learning the Virtues*, 65.
51. Guardini, *Word of God*, 43.
52. Guardini, *Word of God*, 44.

Ratzinger has referred to as "man's conviction that he has no permanence on his own and hence can live on only if he lives in another."[53] This consciousness has been variously expressed through hopes of surviving through one's offspring, memory, fame, or even the Marxist concept of the perfect society. But Guardini warns that such hopes cannot stand up to the depths of the human desire for permanence. "Man is not saved from death when a child is born to him," he writes, "for this child in turn must die. He is not saved from perishing if he leaves a great work, for in its time this also shall perish. He does not overcome the powers of annihilation if he is remembered by men for his noble deed, for in time these men will also forget."[54] Placing one's hope in temporal realities is unsustainable. Their objects lack permanence for they themselves will pass away.

Thus, Guardini cautions that "if transitoriness is to be overcome this can only be done by means of something which does not pass away."[55] Or, as Ratzinger interprets, the hope of living on in another can only be assured if God remembers us. Because "only *he* remains; only *his* thought is reality."[56] This external reference point for humanity's identity and nature saves them from the suffocating claustrophobia of self-reference, so paralyzing in our contemporary world. It frees him to move towards his end. On this Guardini is insistent. One can realize oneself only in light of eternity. "The shape of man's life," writes Guardini, "is not a growth and unfolding from within, culminating in a return upon itself."[57] And more explicitly: "For his nature does not realize itself in the development of a predisposition closed in upon itself, but in that it is drawn above and beyond itself into a communion of life with God."[58] Therefore, the shape of a person's life seeks its form and symbol not in "the self-enclosed circle, but an arch that reaches out toward something that in turn comes to meet it."[59] It is the arch that the Word (in whose image we were created) eternally travels, in his movement from and to the Father. He "carries

---

53. Ratzinger, "What Comes After Death?," 258; emphasis in original.

54. Guardini, *Word of God*, 47.

55. "And that not merely in the sense in which poets use the words, but in actual truth. St Paul says that this 'something' exists—it is Christ. When you turned to him and united yourselves to Him, a new life awakened in you through the Holy Spirit, a life over which death has no power" (Guardini, *Word of God*, 47).

56. Ratzinger, "What Comes After Death?," 258.

57. Guardini, *Last Things*, 18.

58. Guardini, *Pascal*, 65.

59. Guardini, *Last Things*, 18.

man's nature to God and back again from God to man."[60] This is the arch along which humanity returns to God.

In defining the person according to his or her end, we can understand Guardini's assertion that "man can only be man if he dares to be more than 'man.'"[61] To understand his meaning, we must return to his anthropological principle that the human person is created in the image of the Word; in light of the Word made flesh. It is, therefore, only in the God-man, Jesus Christ, that the "more than man" is revealed. It is only in him that "the mystery of man" is illuminated; that the truth of human nature is made manifest.[62] In his twofold nature as God and man, Christ is the form—the archetype—of humanity in its creation and its end. According to Guardini: "Only he who is more than man, who truly and by nature '*passe infiniment l'homme*,' is at once perfectly and archetypally man. His personality, his life, his way of thinking, his destiny are the canon of the humanity intended by God."[63]

It follows that if Christ is the rule or *canon* of human nature, the person can only be himself or herself in relation to him. One realizes oneself only by being conformed to Christ and, with him, returning to the Father. This contextualizes our place in the world. "Man does not belong exclusively to the world," writes Guardini; "rather he stands on its borders, at once in the world yet outside it, integrated into it yet simultaneously dealing with it because he is related directly to God."[64] Drawing again on the thought of Pascal, Guardini reflects that "man, as he is today, is something which cannot be understood by itself. He cannot be reduced to the limit of the natural world or the human order. He is by nature *ad Deum creatus*, ordained to be laid hold of by the encounter with God and drawn into a living participation in the divine nature."[65]

The human person's end as participation or communion in God also relativizes the mode of his or her being in the world, necessitating the transformation of his or her nature in the life to come. Concerning the state of that nature Guardini writes:

> The new life that will now be ours after death is not the prolongation of earthly life into the world to come. It is not just the fulfillment of the original urge to live; that would make of death

60. Guardini, *Last Things*, 27.
61. Guardini, *Pascal*, 66.
62. Second Vatican Council, *Gaudium et Spes* §22.
63. Guardini, *Pascal*, 72.
64. Guardini, *Power and Responsibility*, 93.
65. Guardini, *Pascal*, 64–65.

merely a transition from one form of life into another, through some power of transformation inherent in our nature—comparable to the butterfly emerging from a chrysalis. What Christ accomplished and proclaimed was not a matter of natural necessity, but of grace. The new life is the gift of God's free creative power. It is at the same time man's fulfillment; for man's mystery is this: that his life, in the last analysis, is not under an inexorable law, but results from his encounter with God and with his loving freedom.[66]

The end of the person in God does not arise by means of laws of nature (of physics or genetics). It is the fruit of an encounter with the living God in Jesus Christ through which his life is given "a new horizon and a decisive direction."[67]

From this, Guardini can confidently claim that "man is comprehensible only in God, because only in him is his essence fulfilled."[68] Without God the human being remains a mystery, for it is God's creative act that makes and sustains the person in his or her being. "Because he turns to me with the evocative power of his love I become myself and exist as myself. My special character is rooted in Him, not in myself. When God beholds me it is not as when a man looks upon another man, a finished being regarding another finished being, but the glance of God creates me."[69] Accordingly, human nature is only completed in the beatific vision; of God's eternal glance enjoyed by those who return to God. The human capacity to image the Word is not exhausted with the act of creation (or emergence) from God, but, conformed to the Word's trajectory, finds its fulfillment in return. Indeed, Guardini specifically identifies the return as ultimately significant for the identity of humanity, asserting that the complete person "is determined not at the beginning, but at the end."[70] It is not that the beginning is irrelevant. It is rather that it remains shrouded in mystery. In his or her beginning—or *exitus* from

---

66. Guardini, *Last Things*, 28.

67. Benedict XVI, *Deus Caritas Est* §1. Benedict writes: "Being Christian is not the result of an ethical choice or a lofty idea, but the encounter with an event, a person, which gives life a new horizon and a decisive direction." His dependence on Guardini is evident. He had previously written: "As we are taught by Guardini, the essence of Christianity is not an idea, not a system of thought, not a plan of action. The essence of Christianity is a person: Jesus Christ himself" ("Guardini on Christ," 55).

68. Guardini, *Conversion of Augustine*, 5.

69. Guardini, *World and Person*, 207–8.

70. Guardini, *Last Things*, 18.

God—the human person is a being in potential. He or she is incomplete and alone is incapable of attaining that completeness.

THE PERSON'S PRECARIOUS SITUATION IN THE WORLD

From the perspective of his "not yet" realized nature, the human person's situation is precarious. He is oriented towards blessedness but is not sure of attaining it. He is destined to return but struggles along the way. Interpreting Pascal, Guardini writes: "Man is suspended between angel and beast, '*et le malheur veut, que qui veut faire l'ange, fait la bête.*'"[71] More precisely:

> Man had but two possibilities: to exist above or below himself. If sin means that he tumbled down from the communion of grace with God, then it also means that he fell below what is truly human. "Nature" in man is not that which it is thought to be in modern times; it is not a self-sufficient notion, intelligible of itself. It needs an ultimate determination, which ensues in the attitude to God. As soon as it is simply considered as a primary, self-determined category, intelligible by itself, it becomes ambiguous, misleading, even demonic. Human nature can only be elevated above itself or precipitated below itself. What is now in man is nature thrown into confusion: a subnature, that "similarity to the beasts" and the same time that "greatness" reminiscent of man's original vocation.[72]

As Guardini suggests, there is no such thing as a "natural" human in his postlapsarian existence. Sin has subverted his nature. Within this distortion there exists a constant tension "between what man is and what he would like to be; between that which has been realized and that which remains to be accomplished."[73]

Bearing this tension, suggests Guardini, is the virtue of patience. Patience is the antithesis of the hubristic desire to control. While modernity perceives patience as "something dull and insignificant, a miserable means by which a narrow life seeks to justify its own poverty," Guardini maintains that patience exists as a uniquely human virtue.[74] Animals, in their instinctive relation to nature's laws, are incapable of patience or

71. Translation: "And misfortune wills that whoever wants to play the angel, plays the beast" (Guardini, *Pascal*, 46).
72. Guardini, *Pascal*, 65–66.
73. Guardini, *Learning the Virtues*, 39.
74. Guardini, *Learning the Virtues*, 35.

impatience. Only those creatures who can rise above what already exists and desire what is not yet realized are so capable. In this one recognizes the link between patience and hope. Patience exists between what we are and what we would like to be; between the "here-and-now" and the "not yet." It is not simply a matter of waiting but demands accepting what is given and living with limitations. As Guardini notes, those who are unwilling to make this concession live in a state of constant conflict with their own existence.[75] He gives the example of Goethe's Faust, who rejects reality and spurns his destiny. After renouncing hope and faith, Faust curses patience as something feeble and cowardly. While, in the modern imagination, Faust exists as a type of "liberated man" who takes his future into his own hands,[76] Guardini suggests that he is a slave to fantasy and immaturity. Real maturity involves acceptance of the reality of what is, and it is only with this humble acceptance that we have "the power to change and to reshape it."[77]

MORAL SIGNIFICANCE

Guardini's teleological anthropology has, I suggest, real moral significance. In the first place it coincides with the end of the moral life as beatitude or communion with God. At the end of the person's arch is God, and he travels along this arch in freedom. Freedom is essential to the realization of man's end. Unlike the Marxist temptation to control and impose upon humanity on their way towards an immanent utopia, the path towards the person's end in God is paved by freedom. "One cannot free man ... by lining with concrete the channels along which it [the human spirit] must move," writes Ratzinger.[78] Humanity is liberated only through their free submission to God's Word, in dialogue with his truth and love.

In waiting on humanity's submission, Guardini admits that God's sovereignty in the world might appear to be weak. "He can only command, require, admonish, lovingly urge, that man, whose salvation depends upon it, recognize the truth and obey it; beyond that he 'must' leave room for freedom."[79] Accordingly, while God's will is supreme, yet within the sphere of history, "He cannot enforce the doing of his will,

75. Guardini, *Learning the Virtues*, 39.
76. See Bloch, *Principle of Hope*, 3:1013–22; Hedges, *Framing Faust*, 192–93, 198. See also Ratzinger's critique in *Yes of Jesus Christ*, 42–43.
77. Guardini, *Learning the Virtues*, 40.
78. Ratzinger, *Turning Point for Europe?*, 91.
79. Guardini, *Last Things*, 34.

since it can only be accomplished freely."[80] However, this weakness is only apparent, for God's call to humanity to return has its own dynamic force.

> God calls man but also draws him so that he can approach him (cf., John 6:44). Man goes across from himself to God and this resignation enables him for the first time to enter into full possession of himself. Grace is this manner of existence founded on this relationship. It signifies a share in God but it is God who has made that share possible. It denotes a continuing reception of divine love through which the real self develops.[81]

Still, God must wait on the person's response. The patience that we spoke of earlier is also—indeed primarily—a virtue of God. God does not simply create. He also "upholds and sustains" and "does not become weary of it."[82] God's patience is expressed in his faithfulness to his creating word. (Guardini contrasts this divine patience to the divine impatience of the Hindu god Shiva, who creates but grows tired of his creation, beginning over and over again.) However, in the reality of the end to which humanity inevitably moves, freedom (and patience) is finite. At the end of the person's arch—his or her path of return to God—the "closed sphere of history will be opened" and the freedom to say "Yes and No will be gone."[83] What this means in eschatological terms is that, beyond time and space, we encounter the absolute Otherness of God. "God confronts man in His Holy Essence. . . . The look he casts on man becomes the Judgment, a Judgment that determines man's true being and the shape of his eternal destiny."[84] Within that divine gaze we perceive our true selves, and—according to whether or not our lives have conformed to that true self—we receive our judgment and the "shape of our eternal destiny."

Beyond these considerations for personal judgment, humanity's eschatological orientation has further moral significance. In recognizing ourselves in our end, we are moved to gaze upon the whole of humanity through eschatological eyes. We are drawn to acknowledge the inherent goodness of the human person as destined for communion with God. Following Ratzinger's determination that the measure of the human person is not limited to our origins but is only realized in the heights of our end, he adds: "And only when this height is perceived does there awaken an absolute reverence for man that considers him still holy even

80. Guardini, *Last Things*, 33–34.
81. Guardini, *Freedom, Grace, and Destiny*, 128.
82. Guardini, *Learning the Virtues*, 36.
83. Guardini, *Last Things*, 34.
84. Guardini, *Last Things*, 34.

in his humiliation. Only from there can we really learn to love the human condition in ourselves and in the other."[85]

From the perspective of our end in God, we perceive the inherent goodness of what it means to be a human being. Guardini likens this perception to purity of vision: the experience of being seen in one's truth, and the capacity to gaze upon God in his truth. In this world, sin distorts our vision. It creates an illusion. But in the end, our vision will be restored, and "it shall be revealed that the world exists only in consequence of its being known by God—the world and we ourselves also. I shall realize that I exist only because God knows me. My being known by God is my reality, and I become real in the measure that my life and action are in harmony with the knowledge of God."[86] And, according to Guardini, "this will be eternity, the essential and unending. All else shall pass away. . . . One day there shall be nothing but pure brightness, quiet genuineness, the perfectly fulfilled presence of this 'face to face.'"[87]

From this clear vision of ourselves, we are graced to look upon our neighbor through new eyes. We learn to reverence the other as one who, like us, is made for God. From this, Ratzinger offers a reformulation of Kant's categorical imperative: "We must always see in other human beings persons with whom we shall one day share God's joy."[88]

CONCLUSION

The uniqueness of the human experience lies precisely in our creation in the *imago Dei*. Accordingly, our being is not merely "natural" (in the sense of the rest of the natural world), but "supernatural" in its orientation towards God. Accordingly, Guardini insists that the human person in this world "is not a complete being."[89] He or she is a being in becoming, emerging from God and moving along the arch of return. From this perspective, the human person is "only defined in his being by his religious decision, by his relationship to the Holy God."[90]

In keeping with this teleological orientation, human persons will not be satisfied with anything less than communion with God. This aspiration and capacity for transcendence puts a lie to contemporary

---

85. Ratzinger, *Images of Hope*, 58–59.
86. Guardini, *Word of God*, 98.
87. Guardini, *Word of God*, 98.
88. Ratzinger, *In the Beginning*, 49.
89. Guardini, *Pascal*, 84.
90. Guardini, *Pascal*, 84.

materialist and reductionist claims that limit human beings to the product of an evolutionary process. The person cannot be reduced to his or her DNA. He is also spirit, reaching towards infinity and the totality of being. It is in this context that we recall the words of Ratzinger quoted at the beginning of this essay, that the uniqueness of the person is only realized in light of their end. Human greatness is not limited to the present but is defined by the future.

The purpose of the chapter was to investigate the connection between anthropology and eschatology within Guardini's thought. It is founded on a Word-centered theology that sees the whole of reality, and human nature in particular, as conforming to the Son's movement from (*exitus*) and return to (*reditus*) the Father. This is the "arch" along which every person is called to travel, towards the full realization of himself or herself before God. Within this dynamic, it is asserted that the movement toward, or return to, God is ultimately determinant of human nature. For human beings exist really and truly only as God sees them. And the depth of this reality is perceived only before the immensity of the divine. Hence, it is only before God that the human person is complete.

BIBLIOGRAPHY

Benedict XVI. "Address of His Holiness Benedict XVI: The Guardini Foundation's Congress on 'The Spiritual and Intellectual Legacy of Romano Guardini.'" Vatican, Oct. 29, 2010. https://www.vatican.va/content/benedict-xvi/en/speeches/2010/october/documents/hf_ben-xvi_spe_20101029_fondazione-guardini.html.

———. "*Deus Caritas Est*: On Christian Love." Vatican, Dec. 25, 2005. https://www.vatican.va/content/benedict-xvi/en/encyclicals/documents/hf_ben-xvi_enc_20051225_deus-caritas-est.html.

———. "Guardini on Christ in Our Century." Translated by John M. Haas. In *The Essential Pope Benedict XVI: His Central Writings and Speeches*, edited by John F. Thornton and Susan B. Varenne, 53–55. New York: HarperCollins, 2007.

———. *See also* Ratzinger, Joseph.

Bloch, Ernst. *The Principle of Hope*. Translated by Neville Plaice et al. 3 vols. Cambridge, MA: MIT, 1986.

Bonaventure. *Collations on the Six Days* [*Collationes in Hexaemeron*]. Translated by José de Vinck. Works of Bonaventure 5. Paterson, NJ: St. Anthony's Guild, 1970.

Caffarra, Carlo. *Living in Christ: Fundamental Principles of Catholic Moral Theology*. Translated by Christopher Ruff. San Francisco: Ignatius, 1987.

Delio, Ilia. *Simply Bonaventure: An Introduction to His Life, Thought, and Writings*. New York: New City, 2001.

Frývaldský, Pavel. "Il Dio dialogico e la persona umana: La dimensione trinitaria dell'antropologia di Romano Guardini." *Theol* 11 (2021) 77–95.

Guardini, Romano. *The Conversion of Augustine*. Translated by Elinor Briefs. Providence, RI: Cluny, 2020.

———. *Freedom, Grace, and Destiny: Three Chapters in the Interpretation of Existence.* Translated by John Murray. New York: Pantheon, 1961.

———. *The Last Things: Concerning Death, Purification After Death, Resurrection, Judgment, and Eternity.* Translated by Charlotte E. Forsyth and Grace B. Branham. London: Burn and Oates, 1954.

———. *Learning the Virtues That Lead You to God.* Translated by Stella Lange. Manchester, NH: Sophia Institute, 1998.

———. *Meditations on the Christ: Model of All Holiness.* Translated by Peter White. Manchester, NH: Sophia Institute, 1998.

———. *Pascal: A Study in Christian Consciousness.* Translated by Brian Thompson. Providence, RI: Cluny, 2022.

———. *Power and Responsibility: A Course of Action for the New Age.* Translated by Elinor Briefs. Chicago: Regnery, 1961.

———. *The Word of God: On Faith, Hope, and Charity.* Translated by Stella Lange. Providence, RI: Cluny, 2022.

———. *The World and the Person: And Other Writings.* Translated by Stella Lange. Washington, DC: Regnery Gateway, 2023.

Hanby, Michael. *Augustine and Modernity.* Routledge Radical Orthodoxy. London: Routledge, 2003.

Hedges, Inez. *Framing Faust: Twentieth-Century Cultural Struggles.* Carbondale: Southern Illinois University Press, 2005.

Johnson, Timothy J. "Anthropology, Cosmology, and Bonaventure's Theology of the Word." In Deus Summe Cognoscibilis: *The Current Theological Relevance of Saint Bonaventure*, edited by Amaury Begasse de Dhaem et al., 353–66. BETL. Leuven: Peeters, 2018.

Krieg, Robert A. "Romano Guardini's Theology of the Human Person." *TS* 59 (1998) 457–74.

Rahner, Hugo. *Our Lady and the Church.* Translated by Sebastian Bullough. Providence, RI: Cluny, 2019.

Ratzinger, Joseph. *Church, Ecumenism, and Politics: New Endeavors in Ecclesiology.* Translated by Michael J. Miller et al. San Francisco: Ignatius, 2008.

———. *Images of Hope: Meditations on Major Feasts.* Translated by J. Rock and G. Harrison. San Francisco: Ignatius, 2006.

———. *In the Beginning: A Catholic Understanding of the Story of Creation and the Fall.* Translated by Boniface Ramsey. Grand Rapids: Eerdmans, 1995.

———. "Truth and Freedom." Translated by Adrian Walker. *Comm* 23 (1996) 16–35.

———. *A Turning Point for Europe? The Church in the Modern World: Assessment and Forecast.* Translated by Brian McNeil. 2nd ed. San Francisco: Ignatius, 2010.

———. "What Comes After Death?" Translated by Michael J. Miller. In *Dogma and Preaching: Applying Christian Doctrine to Daily Life*, edited by Michael J. Miller, 255–59. San Francisco: Ignatius, 2011.

———. *The Yes of Jesus Christ: Spiritual Exercises in Faith, Hope and Love.* Translated by Robert Nowell. New York: Crossroad, 1991.

———. *See also* Benedict XVI.

Second Vatican Council. "*Gaudium et Spes*: On the Church in the Modern World." Vatican, Dec. 7, 1965. https://www.vatican.va/archive/hist_councils/ii_vatican_council/documents/vat-ii_const_19651207_gaudium-et-spes_en.html.

8

Imago Dei as an Eschatological Promise
Genesis 1:26–27 in Light of Ratzinger's Augustinianism

Tegha A. Nji

INTRODUCTION: "LET US MAKE MAN IN OUR IMAGE AND LIKENESS"

> The luminous word of God with which Genesis begins the account of the creation of man combats all threats to man caused by calculations about power and usefulness: Let us create man in our image and likeness—*faciamus hominem ad imaginem et similitudinem nostram*, in the words of the Vulgate (Gn 1:26). But what does this word mean? What is the divine likeness present in man?[1]

The above-quoted words stand at the heart of Joseph Ratzinger's message in his little-known 1996 address, "The Likeness of God in the Human Being." In this address, Ratzinger recalled the horrors of World War II and the terrifying killings of the mentally ill in the Third Reich as a threat to humanity itself. He writes, "When the mystery of God, his inviolable dignity, which is present in each and every man, is not respected, then not only are individuals threatened, but humanity itself is endangered."[2]

---

1. Ratzinger, "Likeness of God," 16–17.
2. Ratzinger, "Likeness of God," 16.

This "mystery of God" in man refers to the "image and likeness of God" (henceforth abbreviated as *imago Dei*). According to Ratzinger, the *imago Dei*, precisely because it sets the human person in relationship to God, constitutes the unassailable foundation of human dignity regardless of mental, physical, social, economic, political, or whatever status. The ultimate implication of this exalted human dignity is the vocation of man to love God for eternity. Therefore, the *imago Dei* is a pledge God makes to the human person, that we will live with him forever. It is an eschatological promise. Founded on the above-mentioned address, but extending to his prior and subsequent theological works, this present study is concerned with the theological presuppositions and ramifications of this promise.

Accordingly, this chapter seeks to answer two questions: First, how is the *imago Dei* an eschatological promise and what are the theological implications of such an assertion? Second, what are the theological sources of Ratzinger's characterization of the *imago Dei*? The answer to the first question lies in Ratzinger's deeply relational characterization of the *imago Dei*, such that the human person's coming into existence is at the same time a response to a vocation to be "God's partner in dialogue."[3] If for Ratzinger the first proposition of the Christian faith and the fundamental orientation of Christian conversion is that "God is,"[4] then, the second most important one is that this God has revealed the fullness of his love for us and to us in his Son Jesus Christ, who is the very "measure" of what it means to be human and *the* perfect "image of God" according to whom we are both created and re-created (Rom 11:36; Col 1:16; 2 Cor 3:18; 4:4).[5] With respect to the second question, this chapter will demonstrate how Ratzinger's relational characterization of the *imago Dei* is deeply Augustinian, with important nuanced redactions influenced by his reading of St. Bonaventure, of course, to the extent that Bonaventure himself is an Augustinian.[6] All these accounts are deeply biblical.

Methodologically, we proceed in two parts, treating the above-mentioned aims in reverse: part 1 attends to the Augustinian roots of

3. Ratzinger, *Introduction to Christianity*, 355.

4. Ratzinger, "God Exists."

5. Ratzinger, "Homily." The theme, "Christ as the measure of what it means to be human," runs throughout Ratzinger's writings.

6. Fernand Van Steenberghen notes, "It is as a theologian, and only as such, by the spirit of his theology and by its principal doctrines, that St. Bonaventure belongs to the Augustinian school, or to an Augustinian trend in theology" (*Aristotle in the West*; as quoted in Foshee, "St. Bonaventure," 163n1).

Ratzinger's relational understanding of the *imago Dei*; and part 2 considers how this understanding shapes Ratzinger's eschatological vision.

THE AUGUSTINIAN ROOTS OF RATZINGER'S RELATIONAL UNDERSTANDING OF THE *IMAGO DEI*

Two preliminary remarks are important here: First, the fact that Augustine's own views were deeply influenced by his context; and second, that even within Augustine's own corpus are found significant developments, and even retractions. In this study, however, the focus is not on these developments and/or retractions but on the mature position of Augustine.[7]

Imago Dei in Pre-Augustinian Traditions

Here, we present a summary of the Jewish, mythical, philosophical, and early Christian perspectives on the *imago Dei*, precisely as the context within which Augustine articulates his own views.

First, Gen 1:26–27—let us make man according to our own image and likeness—is the foundational text for Augustine. This text is referred to as a monolith, for it does not appear again in the Jewish Scripture, except through implicit references. For example, Ps 8 resembles the text of Gen 1:26–27 in form and language. Genesis 9:6 prohibits the shedding of human blood because of mankind's creation in God's image. Sirach 17:2 furthers the interpretation of Gen 9:6, rooting the greatness of man in his being created in God's image and likeness. Wisdom 2:23 adds the crucial aspect of immortality, a sharing in God's own life, as a function of the *imago Dei*. The text reads, "God created man for incorruption, and made him in the image of his own eternity" (RSV). Many Midrashic traditions, such as the Gemara, interpret the Gen 1:26–27 text in terms of human dignity.[8] For example, the Gemara states, "Great is human dignity, as it overrides a prohibition in the Torah" (Ber. 19b:9–13).[9] More recently,

---

7. I am presupposing here both Gerald Boersma's elaborate treatment, *Augustine's Early Theology*; and Matthew Puffer's more succinct account, "Human Dignity." Read together, both authors offer profound insights to the developments of the understanding of *imago Dei* in the thought of Augustine.

8. Gemara is an essential component of the Talmud, a collection of rabbinical commentaries on the Mishnah, which is itself a written collection (in sixty-three books) of Jewish oral tradition.

9. Jewish liturgy and blessings (such as the *Siddur*) praise God for creating man in

Rabbi David Wolpe, while referring to the question of human dignity, described Gen 1:26–27 as "Judaism's greatest gift to the world."[10]

Second, even predating the Jewish tradition, there is some evidence for the limited usage of *imago Dei* language in referring to kings in their roles in some Mesopotamian and ancient Near Eastern cults. This notwithstanding, the Genesis text remains radically unique in its description of every human person as an *imago Dei*, thereby providing the latter as the foundation of human dignity.[11]

Third, with respect to ancient philosophical traditions, that which came very close to the *imago Dei* language was the pre-Socratics' "divine spark of reason," or as Stanley Grenz calls it, "the divine origin of human intelligibility." For Grenz, this translates in Aristotle to the definition of man as a "rational animal."[12] However, it was the (Neo-)Platonic tradition, itself not unfamiliar with the "divine spark" tradition, that had the greater philosophical influence on Augustine.[13] In Plato, for instance, the light and sun are similes for enlightenment (*Resp.* 6.516b). This is particularly true in his famous Allegory of the Cave (*Resp.* 7). Generally, Plato sees philosophical insights as thought that cannot be expressed verbally but which must be pursued by a constant communion with the thought, as it comes to birth in the soul, suddenly, like a light that is kindled (*Ep.* 7.341c–d). Such "thoughts" are the true realm of being of which earthly realities are "images." This matures into his theory of Forms, which had a significant influence on Augustine, mediated especially through the Neoplatonist Plotinus.[14] Summarily, Augustine was influenced by the following aspects of this tradition: (1) Plotinus's cosmology, which, like Plato's, argues that the world emanates from the One, present in all things but not one single thing. (2) Through a relational dialectic, the material order is an image in that it at once "reflects" the One and "fails" to capture the One. (3) The nature of the material order as image includes not only a movement from the One (*exitus*) but also a dynamic desire to return to the One (*reditus*).[15] For Plotinus, and later for Augustine, the failure to reflect the One happens when the image does not recognize that it

---

his image: "Blessed are You, LORD our God, King of the universe who made me in His image" (Feld and Uhrbach, *Siddur Lev Shalem*, 103). See t. Ber. 6:18; b. Menaḥ. 43b.

10. Wolpe, "Strangers in the Land," para. 7.
11. Middleton, *Liberating Image*, 26–27.
12. Grenz, *Social God*, 143–44, 50.
13. Rowland, *Divine Spark of Syracuse*, esp. chs. 1 and 2.
14. See Plato, *Tim.* 29a–b; cited in Boersma, "Plotinian Image," 145n28.
15. Boersma, "Plotinian Image," 146.

is "existing in a participatory relationship with immaterial and eternal being."[16] The fuller Plotinian process comprises four stages, viz., genesis, conversion, contemplation, and radiance.[17]

Fourth, even before Augustine, some of the early Christian apologists and writers like Irenaeus, Tertullian, and Origen had already adopted and adapted philosophical categories in their interpretation of Gen 1:26–27. Augustine would generally follow their lead, nuances notwithstanding. For instance, Tertullian insisted on the otherness of Christ as *the* image of God, and of man's mere analogical participation in *this* image. This sounds like Plotinus's "mirroring and failing to mirror the One." From the Greek words *kat' eikona tou theou* (Latin: *ad imaginem Dei*; English: *according* to the image of God), Tertullian argued that human persons were created "toward" the image of God, though in some instances he uses the expression "Man *is* the image of God."[18] Unlike Irenaeus's physicalist language—God with his two hands (Son and Spirit) made man in the resemblance (image) of his Son—Tertullian's language is more spiritual. However, both essentially agree that the whole person, not just a part of him, is made in the image of God, hence overcoming any anthropological dualism.[19] Unlike Clement of Alexandria, who in some instances does not make a distinction between image and likeness, both Irenaeus and Tertullian distinguish between the two.[20] They both understood image in substantialist terms. For Irenaeus it is primarily rooted in reason,[21] while for Tertullian, it is a "spiritual stamp" endowing man with certain divine elements: an immortal soul, free will, and rational capacity.[22] Likeness, on the other hand, is understood by both of them as referring to the Holy Spirit of God, breathed into man and thereby conferring upon him

---

16. Boersma, "Plotinian Image," 146.

17. Plotinus, *Ennead* 5.1.3. See also *Ennead* 5.3.8; Aubin, "L'image dans l'oeuvre de Plotin." All cited in Boersma, "Plotinian Image," 150–52.

18. Tertullian, *Spect.* 2; Boersma, "Hilary of Poitiers," 25.

19. Irenaeus writes, "For by the hands of the Father, that is, by the Son and the Holy Spirit, man, and not [merely] a part of man, was made in the likeness of God" (*Haer.* 5.6.1 [*ANF* 1:531]). With regard to Tertullian, Boersma notes that for the latter, the intellectual and volitional faculties of the human soul are expressions of the image of God ("Hilary of Poitiers," 26–27). Tertullian writes, "Man himself . . . is not only a work of God—he is His image, and yet both in soul and body he has severed himself from his Maker" (*Spect.* 2 [*ANF* 3:80]).

20. At other times, however, Clement of Alexandria distinguishes the two: image and likeness. See Hutabarat et al., "Understanding of the Image," 6; Litwa, "You Are Gods."

21. Simango, "*Imago Dei*," 174.

22. Boersma, "Hilary of Poitiers," 26; Tertullian, *Marc.* 2.5.

a spiritual dynamic that puts him in relationship with God. According to this tradition, the fall resulted in a considerable "loss," or better still diminution, but not eradication of the likeness of God in man.[23] The latter was fully restored only by Christ's redemptive passion.

Another emerging characterization of likeness in these early Christian writers was its dynamic rather than static nature: it transforms the whole man for eternity.[24] Origen speaks several times about making progress daily in being transformed more fully into the likeness of Christ, according to whose image we have been made.[25] As Andrew Louth explains, the Greek word used for likeness in Gen 1:26 is *homoiōsin* (accusative singular feminine of *homoiōsis*) and it suggests a process rather than a state. A state (static) would have been *homoiōma* or *homoiotēs*.[26] Louth sees here an influence of Platonism, since the latter often conceived of philosophy's goal as the "likening" of its practitioner to God, "assimilation to God" (*homoiōsis theō*).[27] For the Christian, this "assimilation" takes place through the very creative *Logos* or Reason. This explains the above-noted association of *imago Dei* with rationality. For to be rational (*logikos*) means to participate in the *Logos*, that is, "in the One who was incarnate as Christ (cf., Jn 1:14)."[28] The perfection of the Christian counterpart of the Platonic "assimilation to God" is *theōsis* or deification, which, in fact, brings us back to our thesis: that the *imago Dei* is an eschatological promise. The full argument for this thesis necessitates a consideration of the Augustinian position, a nuanced appropriation of the foregoing.

Augustine's Characterization of the *Imago Dei*

The mature position of Augustine on the *imago Dei*, the position Ratzinger retrieves, can be summarized in the following sixfold movements:

1. Augustine offers a more nuanced understanding of the separation between image and likeness. He reads Gen 1:26–27 like a Hebraism:

---

23. Origen likewise affirms as follows: "For the image of God always remains, even if you yourself draw 'the image of the earthly' over it in yourself" ("Homilies on Genesis," hom. 8.4).

24. Irenaeus, *Haer.* 5.6.1; Tertullian, *Bapt.* 5; Boersma, "Hilary of Poitiers," 26.

25. Origen, "Homilies on Genesis," hom. 1.13.

26. Andrew Louth, in Louth and Conti, *Genesis 1–11*, i.

27. *Theatetus* 176b is the text often cited by the fathers in this regard (Andrew Louth, in Louth and Conti, *Genesis 1–11*, l).

28. Andrew Louth, in Louth and Conti, *Genesis 1–11*, xlix–l.

image clarifying and reinforcing likeness, and vice versa.[29] Even in his earlier work, *De Genesi ad litteram imperfectus liber* (ca. AD 393-400), sections of which he later retracted, Augustine writes, "Perhaps 'likeness' was added after 'image' as a clarification. It shows that the image was not merely like God (i.e., participating in the concept of likeness) but that the image was itself the absolute Likeness that makes all other things alike" (*Gen. imp.* 16.58 [Image]). By the time he writes *De Trinitate* (AD 400-426), he uses image and likeness almost interchangeably.

2. Augustine characterizes the *imago Dei* as both an intrinsic human capacity and as an act to love God. Because it is intrinsic, it cannot be destroyed, not even by sin. It can only be forgotten or dulled as a result of sin.[30] As a capacity, it is shared by all human persons, but as an act it requires faith, the actual desire for God, a response to God's grace and love.[31] This compares to what he says regarding the desire for happiness in all peoples, even in the pagan philosophers, whereas it is through faith alone that this desire can be actualized.[32]

3. Augustine retains the localization of the *imago Dei* in the rational soul or mind (*Trin.* 14).[33] Here, he follows the early Christian writers like Irenaeus and Tertullian but develops a much more elaborate psychological account of how the rational soul is an *imago Dei*, while avoiding dualism. Right from *De genesi contra Manichaeos* and *De diversis quaestionibus* (q.12), he speaks of the body's participation in the image of God, when it is well ordered toward the rational soul, thereby participating remotely in the life of the soul.[34] He specifically treats the question of the body's participation in immortality and

---

29. Neither the Vulgate (*ad imaginem et similitudinem*) nor the Septuagint (κατ' εἰκόνα ἡμετέραν καὶ καθ' ὁμοίωσιν) preserves the Hebrew text's double usage of the preposition "according to" before both "image" and "likeness" (C. John Collins, *Genesis 1-4*, 62).

30. This is a retraction of his earlier position that "the image of God can be lost," as articulated in *Contra Adimantum* (AD 396) and in *De Genesi ad litteram imperfectus liber* (between 393 and 400). See TeSelle, *Augustine the Theologian*, 258-59; Puffer, "Human Dignity," 73.

31. Augustine, *Trin.* 14.4.6; 14.8.11; 14.12.15.

32. See Augustine, *Trin.* 10.10.14; 10.1.3; 13.3.6; 15.12.21; *Civ.* 19.

33. In fact, he espouses this view even in the earlier text, *De Genesi ad litteram imperfectus liber*. Therein, he writes, "Rational souls are called 'wise' because of God's wisdom. This label 'wise' is not applicable any further: we do not apply it to any beast, and far less to trees; nor to fire, air, water, or earth" (*Gen. imp.* 16.59 [Image]).

34. Boersma, "Epilogue," 259.

the likeness of the Son of God in *Trin.* 14. There he writes, "For this [the body], too, is called an image of the Son of God, in which we shall have, as He has, an immortal body, being conformed in this respect not to the image of the Father or of the Holy Spirit, but only of the Son, because of Him alone is it read and received by a sound faith, that 'the Word was made flesh.' [Jn 1:14]."[35]

4. Following from the above, the *imago Dei* relates to eternal life and to immortality of both the body and the soul. In *De Trinitate*, from book 8 onwards (see 13.8.11; 14.4.6), every now and then, Augustine touches on the idea that true blessedness cannot be attained save by man becoming immortal. This immortality is the promise of the afterlife, whereby man comes to fuller participation in God's life.[36] It is not simply immortality of the soul alone, for that would mean a part of man would then be absent, thereby compromising the conditions of "completeness and permanence" needed for perfect blessedness. Rather, it is "blessedness in all the good things of human nature, that is, of both soul and body," and this requires faith.[37] He expresses the same view in *Civ.* 12.[38] Augustine, therefore, ties together *imago Dei*, immortality, and eternal life.

5. Trinitarian theology, Christology, and pneumatology all coincide in Augustine's anthropology or psychology in *De Trinitate*. The central argument of Augustine's anthropology is that man is created in the image and likeness of the Triune God. In retractions that he later added to *De Genesi ad litteram*, he argues as follows: "When it is said that God made man in his own image, it is meant in the image of the Trinity itself."[39] This image of God is discernible in the human rational, intellectual, spiritual soul or mind.[40] From its mirroring of the Trinity, there follows the mind's capacity to contemplate divine

---

35. Augustine, *Trin.* 14.18.24. See bks. 13–15.

36. For instance, *Trin.* 14.4.6 speaks of the immortality of the rational soul in terms of the soul bearing the image of the Creator (the Trinity), which is immortally implanted (Cavadini, "Trinity and Apologetics," 72–73).

37. Augustine, *Trin.* 13.20.25.

38. For example, ch. 22 is devoted to the topic "That the Bodies of the Saints Shall After the Resurrection Be Spiritual, and Yet Flesh Shall Not Be Changed into Spirit." Book 13.17–13.24 discusses different aspects of the immortality of the body and soul.

39. "Ita dictum est: *Fecit Deus hominem ad imaginem Dei*, tamquam diceretur ad imaginem suam, quod est ipsa Trinitas" (Augustine, *Gen. imp.* 16.61 [CSEL 550]). See *Retract.* 1.18.

40. Augustine, *Trin.* 15.3.5. See *Tract. Ev. Jo.* 3.4; *Trin.* 9–10; *Gen. imp.* 16.55; *Faust.* 24.2; *Gen. litt.* 6.27; *Conf.* 13.22; *Civ.* 11.2; *Spir. et litt.* 28.48.

truths by remembering God (*memoria*), knowing or understanding him (*intelligentia*), and loving God, which is ultimately to participate in God's divine life (*participatio*).[41] Fallen man, however, left to himself, is incapable of such remembrance, understanding, and loving of God. Yet in and through Christ, who bestows the grace of conversion, renewal, and adoption, and by the power of the Holy Spirit, man can so ascend beyond self to God. This is a transformation into Christ, who is the perfect image of God, the firstborn of all creation, and in this consists the goal of the human person as an *imago Dei*.[42]

6. Augustine characterizes the *imago Dei* in terms of dynamic relationality. Far from some solipsistic understanding of the human mind in terms of a self-referential remembering, knowing, and loving, Augustine proposes a dynamic relational perspective. For instance, in *Civ.* 11, he presents contemplation of the image of God in ourselves as the necessary means by which we arise beyond self to God. It is in God that "our being [*esse*] will have no death, our knowledge [*nosse*] will have no error, and our love [*amare*] will know no check. In our present state, we believe that we possess these three not on the testimony of others, but because we ourselves are aware of their presence, and because we discern them with our own most truthful inner vision [*interiore . . . aspectu*]."[43] Thus, even when Augustine speaks of *imago Dei* as intrinsic to human nature, "human nature" as used here must "transcend the human person; it finds intelligibility in its exemplar, the Holy Trinity."[44] It is a participation in God.[45] In their reading of *De Trinitate*, Boersma and Williams agree that for Augustine, "The mind as independent individuality cannot image God. . . . The image of God, in short, is realized when we come to be *in conscious relation to the divine act* that establishes the possibility of relation; when we see ourselves acting

41. *Trin.* 12.7.12.

42. This is the central thesis of *De Trinitate* seen from an anthropological perspective. See esp. bks. 9–15. The earlier bk. 4 is particularly devoted to showing how Christ, the Son, redeems and perfects us in body and soul. Compare to *Trin.* 13.20.25.

43. *Civ.* 11.28. English translation, with slight modifications, is taken from Cavadini, "Trinity and Apologetics," 75.

44. Boersma, "Epilogue," 256.

45. *Participatio* is a central theme in Augustine's thought, and several studies have been dedicated to a treatment of this. See Annice, "Theory of Participation"; Bonner, "Augustine's Conception of Deification"; Teske, "Image and Likeness"; Boersma, "Plotinian Image."

out the self-imparting of God by consciously yielding ourselves to be known and loved by God."[46] From the very beginning, therefore, *imago Dei*, according to Augustine—and Ratzinger elaborates this point—implies a supernatural orientation, such that the human person cannot be conceived independently of God. It is by his analogical participation in God that man's *being* in the image of God is sustained.[47]

RATZINGER'S RETRIEVAL OF AUGUSTINE: FROM A RELATIONAL UNDERSTANDING OF *IMAGO DEI* TO ESCHATOLOGY

From the above, we have seen how early Christian writers stressed the distinction between image and likeness without a corresponding robust explanation of how to simultaneously hold this distinction and the unity of the two so as to avoid separating them. We have likewise seen how Augustine, for his part, even while oscillating between separation and unity, ends up with a more nuanced position that favors unity over separation. This notwithstanding, it is not until the scholastic era that we find a systematic explanation for simultaneously affirming the distinction and unity of image and likeness. The genius of Ratzinger's Augustinianism is, in part, how he adopts this explanation through his reading of the scholastic *Doctor Seraphicus*, St. Bonaventure, to develop the nuances of Augustine's mature position vis-à-vis eschatology.

In his above-referenced 1996 address, we find one of the most succinct presentations of Ratzinger's perspective in this regard. Though he does not mention Augustine by name, he adopts an Augustinian stance and pushes the latter's thoughts into their fullest implications. He writes,

> The orientation towards eternal life is what makes man the created counterpart of God. . . . An orientation towards eternity, therefore, is an orientation towards the eternal communion of love with God, *and the image of God thus bears the marks of its nature beyond earthly life*. It *cannot* be determined in a *static* fashion and bound to some particular quality, but is a *prosthesis* of time beyond earthly life. It can be understood only with reference to its tension regarding the future, in its *dynamic* impulse towards eternity. Those who deny the existence of eternity and

---

46. Boersma, "Epilogue," 256; Williams, "Sapientia and Trinity," 320.

47. Boersma, "Epilogue," 256. At the background here are the following words of St. Paul, "In God we live and move and have our being" (Acts 17:28).

who see man as a merely terrestrial creature do not have any possibility—from the very outset—of penetrating the essence of the likeness of God.[48]

What immediately jumps out of this quotation are some crucial characterizations of *imago Dei*: it is dynamic as opposed to static, it puts man in relationship with God from the beginning, and it bears within it an upsurge toward eternity. In what follows, we will examine more closely how these categories are taken up and/or accounted for in the works of Ratzinger in a way that argues for our thesis, that the *imago Dei*, as revealed in the Genesis text, and as appropriated by Augustine, is an eschatological promise. We shall structure our argument here around the following four aspects: the *imago Dei* as a divine imprint, the intertwining of creation and election, the process of hominization, and temporality and the eschatological promise.

Image and Likeness: A Dynamic Divine Imprint

For Ratzinger, the image and likeness of God in man is like an imprint that results from the breath of God. God breathing into man is what makes him a living being and not simply a "lifeless" creature from the dust of the earth (Gen 2:7; John 20:22). This breath sets him in a "direct relationship with God," the God who has called him by name: "I have called you by name, you are mine" (Isa 43:1).[49] Accordingly, Ratzinger observes, in the human person, heaven and earth touch one another; in him God enters his own creation.[50] Man thus cannot understand himself in static isolation or self-absorption, but always in a tending toward God, or in Ratzinger's own words, "in [a] dynamic impulse towards eternity."[51] Ratzinger points to the incarnate *Logos* as the effulgence of this relatedness of man to God. The very creative *Logos* becomes man, the perfect man through whom God enters his creation in a more definitive fashion, binding himself forever with his creation, not just as a relatable

---

48. Ratzinger, "Likeness of God," 17; emphasis added.
49. Benedict XVI, *Divine Project*, 69.
50. Ratzinger, *In the Beginning*, 44–45. See John 1:1–4: "In the beginning was the Word, and the Word was with God, and the Word was God. He was with God in the beginning. Through him all things were made; without him nothing was made that has been made. In him was life, and that life was the light of all mankind" (NIV).
51. Ratzinger, "Likeness of God," 17.

Other but also as an invocable Other. He comes from God and thus establishes the "true form" of man's being as destined for God.[52]

Read in the context of Ratzinger's overall theological vision, "true form of man's being" as used here is synonymous to the likeness of God. Again, recalling the point made earlier, likeness is used in this case as a distinctive quality from image. Ratzinger's point, then, is that it is the incarnate Christ who perfects in us the likeness of God received at creation, which was dulled by sin. While this is essentially an Augustinian position, Ratzinger, following Bonaventure, offers a more nuanced and developed account of the relationship between image and likeness, in a way that upholds both their distinction and their unity, without separating likeness into a second substance beside image. We can summarize his argument as follows: At creation, man is gifted with the image and likeness of God, the divine imprint. Likeness expresses a similitude, a "vital directedness towards God."[53] It is like the "form" of the image of God gifted at creation, precisely in the sense that it makes the human being related to God from the very beginning of his existence. Thus, likeness is not a separate substance different from image but a quality of image, its actuality or form.[54] Both Ratzinger and Bonaventure compare likeness thus understood to grace—as that which comes from Godself, or in fact, as the gift of Godself—which transforms sinful humanity and more readily conforms us to God.[55] Recalling Augustine's distinction between (and not separation of) "capacity" and "act" with respect to the image of God in man, the point we seek to make here is that for Ratzinger, following Augustine and Bonaventure, image could be likened to a "capacity," and likeness to the "form" that actualizes the capacity, such that image is always already an actual capacity. It is this capacity that places the human person in direct relationship to God from the very first instance of his creation.[56] Therefore, man is always

52. Benedict XVI, *From Baptism*, 334.

53. DeClue, "Theology of Divine Revelation," 117; citing Ratzinger, *Offenbarungsverständnis*, 334.

54. Ratzinger, *Offenbarungsverständnis*, 334: "Die Ähnlichkeit ist also nicht etwa eine neue Substanz, sondern ein Akt, der sich an der Substanz des Bildes ereignet: Deshalb ist der Ausdruck 'Ähnlichkeit' in Grunde bezeichnender als die Gegenüberstellung von 'Schöpfungsbild' und 'Bild der Neuschöpfung'" ("The likeness is therefore not really a new substance, but an act, which itself inheres in the substance of the image: That is why the expression 'likeness' is fundamentally more meaningful than the juxtaposition of 'image of creation' and 'image of the new creation'").

55. Ratzinger, *Offenbarungsverständnis*, 334; citing Bonaventure, 1 Sent. d17 p1 q4c; 2 Sent. d27 a1 q2c.

56. Ratzinger notes, "With Augustine [*Trin.* 14.8.11] the image of God is interpreted

the image and likeness of God at one and the same time. What sin does then is that it dulls the likeness received at creation, such that man fails to live out fully his relatedness to God, but it cannot destroy his being in the image of God (which of course always includes the likeness of God). In the end, then, even the likeness of God in man can only be weakened by sin but never completely destroyed either, lest man ceases to be God's image since the image cannot be without the likeness and vice versa.[57] This further explains why Ratzinger often uses *imago Dei* (image of God) to mean image and likeness of God. Or as we see in the mature Augustine, likeness is used as a kind of linguistic clarification of image, an emphasis. Therefore, Christ's grace, by re-creating man, perfects this likeness, that is, increases the vitality of man's relationship with God, which is in turn a perfection of the very same image of God received at creation. Put another way, in the new creation, grace perfects the very same image of God in man by *in-forming* it with a renewed divine likeness. It is this likeness, precisely as a relational quality, that can increase or decrease in man. It is this likeness which essentially defines *imago Dei* as a relational quality, such that whenever we speak of the image of God in man (with or without adding likeness), we are speaking of the relational quality of being ordered toward God. In Ratzinger's words, "likeness ultimately consists in unification [*Vereinigung*] with God."[58] Here, the substantialist, relational, and functional views of the *imago Dei* coincide.[59] This brings us to consider the connection between creation and election.

---

as capacity for God, qualification to know and love God. That is what for Augustine gives the idea of man as the image of God its dynamic aspect; man is the image of God to the extent in which he directs himself to God" ("Commentary on *Gaudium*," 5:121). Ratzinger adopts this position of Augustine, following Bonaventure, while contrasting it with Aquinas's stance. Augustine's position emphasizes more strongly the actuality of the *imago*, that is, the direct relatedness of man to God by virtue of the image of God in man, whereas the Thomistic position, as Ratzinger argues, articulates this relatedness less directly, through "three stages of representation within the one *imago*: the *intellectualitas* as such, the *intellectualitas in actu*, the *intellectualitas actu Deum cognoscens*" (*Offenbarungsverständnis*, 331). See DeClue, "Theology of Divine Revelation," 116.

57. In the 1996 address, Ratzinger criticizes Luther and the Reformation theologians for holding that sin destroys the image of God in man ("Likeness of God," 18).

58. Ratzinger, *Offenbarungsverständnis*, 334: "Die Ähnlichkeit bestehe letzterdings in der Vereinigung mit Gott."

59. The substantive (or substantialist) view highlights the *imago Dei* as man's essential nature. The relational view conceives of the *imago Dei* in terms of man's relationship with God. The functional view emphasizes the fact that it accords man a certain role, such as stewardship over creation.

Creation as Election

If the *imago Dei*, given to man at creation, so sets him in a direct relationship with God, then it means he is elected into God's friendship (and the life of blessedness) from the very moment of his creation by God. Salvation or eternal beatitude is not an afterthought on God's part. On this point, Ratzinger commented, "We cannot separate man's becoming man and his knowledge of God precisely because he is 'the image' of God."[60] For Augustine, Bonaventure, and Ratzinger, every other creature is more fittingly said to bear only vestiges or shadows of God insofar as he is their Creator—by sheer causality—while man alone is properly image of God since he alone has God as "object of knowledge (*obiectum*)."[61] At the same time, it is this knowing and loving of God that is at the heart of man's vocation and destiny, of his election from the very moment of creation. Like Bonaventure, Ratzinger affirms that "the doctrine of man's divine imagery is identical with the doctrine of the natural desire of man for God," which means that being thus created, man is already offered an invitation to desire his Creator as his final destiny.[62] There are strong resonances here of the Pauline doctrine of election: "For [God] chose us in [Christ] before the creation of the world ... he predestined us for adoption to sonship through Jesus Christ, in accordance with his pleasure and will" (Eph 1:4–5). Our very existence is a factor of *ex-sistere* (to stand forth, out of): We come into being (stand forth) out of (*ex*) nothingness in response to the invitation of love, "Let us make man," and we find our fullest meaning by *ex-sistere* (going out from self) toward the One who calls. In short, we find ourselves only in our dialogical relatedness.

Relationality and the Eschatological Finality of Hominization (*Menschwerdung*)

"The essence of an image," Ratzinger writes, "consists in the fact that it represents something.... Its nature as an image is that it goes beyond itself and that it manifests something that it is not."[63] Therefore, human beings, precisely as images of God, cannot be closed in upon themselves.

---

60. Ratzinger, "God Exists," s.vv. "Is God Also Mother?"

61. DeClue, "Theology of Divine Revelation," 110; Ratzinger, *Offenbarungsverständnis*, 318.

62. Ratzinger, *Offenbarungsverständnis*, 321; DeClue, "Theology of Divine Revelation," 111.

63. Ratzinger, *In the Beginning*, 47.

Imago Dei is the capacity for relationship; it is the human capacity for God. This capacity is concretely lived, above all in thinking and praying. Through thinking, human beings are revealed to themselves as beings of word, and through praying, as beings of love. They are beings "moving toward Another, oriented to giving themselves to the Other and only truly receiving themselves back in real self-giving."[64] This logic is rooted in the very life of the Trinity, who, according to Augustine, is indeed the God in whose image we are created. In addition to this, Ratzinger affirms that God himself is "self-obligation in triune love and thus pure freedom," therefore, to be in an image of this God, man cannot be enclosed in his finitude but must recognize that he is not self-sufficient or autonomous.[65] In the words of *Introduction to Christianity*, man is from the beginning "God's partner in dialogue." Seen from above, he is a being addressed by God, and seen from below, he is the being that can think of God, the being open to transcendence. Like Augustine, Ratzinger adds, "The point here is not whether [man] really does think of God, really does open himself to him, but that he is in principle the being who is in himself capable of doing so, even if in fact, for whatever reasons, he is perhaps never able to utilize this capacity."[66] As God's partner in dialogue, his ultimate vocation is to participate in the eternal perichoretic dialogue, the communion of love of the Triune God. His being an *imago Dei*, therefore, in Ratzinger's words, "can be understood only with reference to its tension regarding the future, in its dynamic impulse towards eternity."[67]

Ratzinger agrees with Augustine, Ambrose, Tertullian, and Irenaeus, that it is in and through Christ that man's impulse towards eternity finds its fulfillment. He who became man is he in whom and through whom man is taken up into the divine love of God, precisely since he is the perfect image of God according to whom we are being transformed from glory unto glory (2 Cor 3:18; see also 4:4). The human being, therefore, is a "preliminary project in anticipation of Christ."[68] Put another way, Christ is the fundamental idea of the Creator, and human beings are predestined "to be molded into the image of his Son, who is thus to become the firstborn among many brothers."[69] Therefore, there arises an existential tension within the human person, who, though finite, is at the same time

64. Ratzinger, *In the Beginning*, 48.
65. Ratzinger, "Freedom and Liberation," 69.
66. Ratzinger, *Introduction to Christianity*, 354.
67. Ratzinger, "Likeness of God," 17.
68. Ratzinger, "Likeness of God," 17.
69. Ratzinger, "Likeness of God," 17; drawing on Rom 8:29; 1 Cor 15:49; 2 Cor 4:6.

called to partake of infinity. His being is caught between "clay and spirit, earth and heaven, terrestrial origins and divine future."[70] Human beings are beings *en route*, in transition. They are not yet themselves; they must ultimately become themselves.[71] This *becoming* is what Paul means by "being transformed into [Christ's] image with ever-increasing glory" (2 Cor 3:18). Thus, becoming Christlike is the eschatological promise made to man, a promise fulfilled in Christ's own resurrection and ascension. "Christ [is] the 'last man' (ἔσχατος ᾽Αδάμ: 1 Cor 15:45)—the final man, who takes man into his future, which consists of his being, not just man, but one with God."[72] Two christological affirmations coincide here, namely, Christ as image of God and Christ as Last Adam/Man.

This coincidence has important implications for Ratzinger. For instance, it is as the Last Adam that Christ is both the perfection of what it means to be human and the perfection of the *imago Dei in hominem*. He is the exemplary man in whom and through whom the process of hominization comes to fruition. In Augustinian style, Ratzinger delineates a threefold movement in the process of hominization: (1) The Rubicon of becoming man was first crossed in the movement from nonexistence into being, God fashioning man from the earth. (2) There was the crossing from merely being an animal to *logos*, that is, from simply being "there" to becoming mind through the breath of divine life. (3) The ultimate process of finality is in the creative *Logos*, God himself merging with man, that man might realize the fullness of his being. At this point, man reached the highest potential of his development, a culmination of the "process that began when a creature of dust and earth looked out beyond itself and its environment and was able to address God as 'You.'"[73] In short, in Christ, the incarnate *Logos*, man is most fully himself, and hominization reaches its goal. Having overstepped the bounds of humanity, Christ has brought humanity more intimately to herself by bringing her to the Father. Humanity finds itself by going beyond itself in Christ and with Christ, toward the altogether truly Other, the God of whom it is an image.[74] As Ratzinger reiterates, "Man finds his center of gravity, not inside, but outside himself . . . in the mystery of God."[75] Human existence finds its "in-itself-ness outside itself and can

70. Ratzinger, "Likeness of God," 17.
71. Ratzinger, *In the Beginning*, 48–49.
72. Ratzinger, *Introduction to Christianity*, 234.
73. Ratzinger, *Introduction to Christianity*, 235.
74. Ratzinger, *Introduction to Christianity*, 234–36.
75. Ratzinger, *Principles of Catholic Theology*, 171.

find its true center only in *ex-sistere*, in going-out-from-itself."[76] Indeed, "Christ is the *beginning of the future*, the already *inaugurated finality* of the being man."[77] At this point, one thing remains to be considered: how this eschatological promise of the *imago Dei* relates to our concrete reality of time and history here and now.

History, Temporality, and the Eschatological Promise

Ratzinger describes the *imago Dei* in terms of a tension, a pulling of time into eternity, or a *"prosthesis* of time beyond earthly life."[78] Coupled with the above-mentioned expressions—"beginning of the future" and "inaugurated finality"—which suggest the idea of an "already but not yet," it is apparent that the *imago Dei* points to paradoxical coexistences that cannot be ignored: temporality and eternity, history and finality, or present and future. This sounds very much like the aporia of time in Augustine's *Confessions*. The implied question could be phrased thus: How does the eschatological promise, precisely as pertaining to man's coming into being as an *imago Dei*, account for the concrete lived history of the human subject as a being of time? Does the fulfillment of this promise imply a jettisoning or annihilating of time and history, a certain disembodiment?

Ratzinger, like Augustine, disavows a disembodied eschatology. His response to the above questions is formulated in the context of his criticism of two extreme views. On the one hand is the view that "salvation history is an anti-thesis to metaphysics" (held by Karl Barth, Emil Brunner, Oscar Cullmann), and on the other hand is the view that "eschatology is an anti-thesis to salvation history" (held by Rudolf Bultmann, Philipp Vielhauer, and Hans Conzelmann).[79]

The first extreme overemphasizes the historical in-breaking of God's word or revelation in history over and against metaphysics, to the extent that all "human actions" are rejected as mere "religion."[80] This raises serious challenges for the Christian faith itself. For instance, it threatens

---

76. Ratzinger, *Principles of Catholic Theology*, 190.

77. Ratzinger, *Introduction to Christian*, 262; emphasis added.

78. Ratzinger, "Likeness of God," 17; emphasis added.

79. Ratzinger offers a detail treatment of this in *Principles of Catholic Theology*, 171–90.

80. Ratzinger, *Principles of Catholic Theology*, 175, 176. Ratzinger has in mind especially Karl Barth's rejection of natural religion. See Barth, "Religion as Unbelief," in *Church Dogmatics*, 1.2:299.

the very unity and harmony between the ontology (identity) of Jesus, the "is" of the Chalcedonian definition—"Jesus *is* God"—and the historical inbreaking of this "is" in the revelatory historical event of the incarnation.[81] The second extreme, by its radical eschatological reinterpretation of the message of Jesus (salvation history), threatens the very integrity of the concrete historical meaningfulness of the incarnation. Begun by J. Weiss and A. Schweitzer, it was Bultmann, Ratzinger observes, who would bring to full term the implications of the Barthian claim that a Christianity not wholly, entirely, and absolutely eschatological has wholly, entirely, and absolutely nothing to do with Christ.[82] For Bultmann, word takes preeminence over event, in fact, salvation history is rejected. The real salvation history is simply the word, the kerygma (proclamation), and this is itself reduced to the eschatological. Consequently, salvation is de-temporalized, and eschatology is "purified" of all temporal determinatives.[83]

Ratzinger rejects both extremes and proposes a twofold non-annihilating dialectic of word-and-event against the second extreme, and of metaphysics-and-event against the first extreme. Both dialectics are rooted in the "*prae* of God's action," that is, the apriority and exceedingly greater nature of God's action vis-à-vis human understanding. With respect to the word-and-event dialectic, what this means is that the revelatory event of God is deeper than the "proclamation" of this event (word), which is in fact an interpretation of the latter in human language.[84] Therefore, word or proclamation or kerygma is only a "moment" in the whole revelatory event, and so, it can neither exhaust it nor invalidate it, but must simultaneously acknowledge its historical as well as eschatological breadth and depth. With respect to the metaphysics-and-event dialectic, Ratzinger's point is that there exists a reciprocal validation of the one by the other: the event of revelation makes sense only if the ontological identity of God who reveals is upheld, while the being of this God is made known only in the event of revelation.

In all, the genius of Ratzinger's proposal here lies in his re-centering of the Christian kerygma on the resurrection of Jesus as the definitive starting point. In this schema, the theology of the resurrection is what grounds the theological metaphysics of the Sonship of God: Jesus *is* God,

---

81. Ratzinger, *Principles of Catholic Theology*, 182.

82. Ratzinger, *Principles of Catholic Theology*, 176; referring to Karl Barth's *Römerbrief.*

83. Ratzinger, *Principles of Catholic Theology*, 176–77.

84. Ratzinger, *Principles of Catholic Theology*, 186.

indeed. Also, the resurrection is that definitive eschatological event which happens beyond history and time, but which at the same time touches upon history and time, since the once dead person, Jesus Christ, is no longer dead. He himself, in his very same person, is eternally alive in his individuality and uniqueness.[85] Therefore, the resurrection of Jesus, while illuminating the metaphysics of his divine Sonship, pulls time or history beyond itself into its finality, without at the same time annihilating the latter. Accordingly, in and by the resurrection, the eschaton has broken into history and time, thereby breaking history, and likewise humanity, out of themselves, toward God. Consequently, the fulfillment of the eschatological promise made to man—in virtue of his being an *imago Dei*—does not annihilate his lived historical consciousness. Hence, we can affirm, it is *this* man, in all his historicity and temporality, who has been redeemed by the Last Man. At the same time, this in-breaking of the eschaton is a promise still being fulfilled in the historical man.

CONCLUSION

We have demonstrated that, for Ratzinger, the *imago Dei* orients the human person, from creation, toward an eschatological fulfillment. Also, we have seen how he develops this in dialogue with Augustine, and likewise Bonaventure. Additionally, we have shown how Christ is the centerpiece in the whole process, both as the creative *Logos* and as the perfect image of God into whom we are being transformed. By his dying and rising, Christ has become the Last Man who brings humanity into its future. We could therefore say that for Ratzinger, the resurrection is the christological resolution of the Augustinian aporia of time. Ratzinger sums up this aporia as follows: "Augustine traverses the varied landscapes of his own being and comes across *memoria*, 'memory.' In memory, he finds past, present and future gathered into one in a peculiar way [*distentio*, that is, tension] which, on the one hand, offers some idea of what God's eternity might be like, and, on the other, indicates the special manner in which man both is bound to time and transcends time."[86] It is only man, precisely as an *imago Dei*, who experiences this *distentio*. The *Confessions* is a depiction of this *distentio* in Augustine's own life: from his obsession with God's creatures (his past sinfulness), his search for saving knowledge (*attentio*, present), and his realization that true happiness lay only in the future (*expectatio*). This future is in Christ, who is the

85. Ratzinger, *Principles of Catholic Theology*, 187. See 184–87.
86. Ratzinger, *Eschatology*, 182; referring to Augustine, *Conf.* 10.

eschatological fulfillment of God's purpose for creation, the perfect image of God into whom we are being transformed or configured. Despite his appeal to the paschal mystery and Christ as Mediator,[87] Augustine does not develop an argument as to how this aporia is overcome. Supplying this lack in Augustine constitutes a unique contribution of Ratzinger to Augustinian scholarship.

Following Bonaventure's theology of history, Ratzinger sees Christ as the center and hinge of being, time, and history. Imagine a perfectly hinged pendulum that swings to left and to right until it comes to a harmonious stop, with both the leftward and rightward movements resting in perfect equilibrium. This is an analogy of how all time and history, hinged on Christ, swings from past (left) to future (right). He is the integrating space in which the past and future of man touch each other. With respect to the past, it is in Christ that all was created; it is in him that the burden of original sin was overcome through the historical events of his incarnation and the paschal mystery. With respect to the future, he is the Last Man, the revelation and beginning of the definitive mode of human existence, the finality of human history, and the perfection of man as the image of God. It is in him that man approaches his perfect harmonious equilibrium, when the now past and future will be united in an eternal present. Therefore, incorporated into Christ, our now or today is the historical experience of becoming, in which the past is always slipping into the present and the present anticipating the future. In concrete Augustinian and Ratzingerian terms, this means the forgiving of our past, the perfecting of our everyday through grace, and the bringing of the whole of man into the fullness of Christ in the eschaton. Thanks to the resurrection, the dawn of the new creation, that is, the reconfiguration of the first creation, the eschaton already touches upon history and stretches it forward. Past, present, and future coincide as "God conquers man's past—conquers sin—by calling him into a future in Christ."[88] Put differently, the resurrection, man's re-creation, is ultimately a fulfillment of the eschatological promise of man's first creation in *imago Dei*. Specifically, here, we come upon a demonstration of the thesis we set out with. Like Bonaventure, Ratzinger adopts a progressive circular shape of time and human history, as opposed to Aristotle's simply linear conception of time, as an infinite line without ordering. In terms familiar to Plotinus and Augustine, he redefines the teleology of time in terms of a progressive circular movement of *egressus* (from God to humanity) and

---

87. Augustine, *Conf.* 10.33. See bks. 10–13.
88. Ratzinger, *Principles of Catholic Theology*, 188. See 187–90.

regressus (from humanity back to God), in and through the person of Christ.[89] Christ is that all-encompassing integrating space, in whom the "we" of human beings, God's images, and in fact, all of creation, bearing vestiges of God, gather on the way to the Father even as all were granted existence in and through him.[90]

BIBLIOGRAPHY

Annice, M. "Historical Sketch of the Theory of Participation." *New Scholasticism* 26 (1952) 49–79.

Augustine. *The City of God* [*Civ.*]. Translated by Marcus Dods. New York: Random House, 2010.

———. *The Confessions of Saint Augustine* [*Conf.*]. Translated by Albert C. Outler. Repr., Louisville, KY: GLH, 2019.

———. "De Genesi ad litteram imperfectus liber" [The literal interpretation of Genesis: Unfinished book; *Gen. imp.*]. Augustinus, n.d. https://www.augustinus.it/latino/genesi_incompiuto/genesi_incompiuto.htm.

———. *De Genesi ad litteram libri duodecim: eiusdem libri capitula. De Genesi ad litteram imperfectus liber [Gen. imp.]. Locutionum in Heptateuchum libri septem.* Edited by Joseph Zycha. CSEL 28/1. Vienna: Verlag der Österreichischen Akademie der Wissenschaften, 2013.

———. The Literal Interpretation of Genesis: Unfinished Book [*De Genesi ad litteram imperfectus liber*; *Gen. imp.*]. Roger Pearse, Aug. 2020. Translated by Isabella Image. Revised by Roger Pearse. https://www.roger-pearse.com/weblog/wp-content/uploads/2020/08/Augustine-De_Genesi_Imperfectum_Image-v4.pdf.

Barth, Karl. *Church Dogmatics*. Edited by G. W. Bromiley and T. F. Torrance. 14 vols. Edinburgh: T&T Clark, 1956–77.

Benedict XVI. *The Divine Project: Reflections on Creation and Church*. Edited by Michael Langer and Karl-Heinz Kronawetter. Translated by Chase Faucheux. San Francisco: Ignatius, 2022.

———. *From Baptism in the Jordan to the Transfiguration*. Translated by Adrian J. Walker. Vol. 1 of *Jesus of Nazareth*. San Francisco: Ignatius, 2007.

Benedict XVI. *See also* Ratzinger, Joseph.

Boersma, Gerald P. "The Analogical and Embodied Imago Dei." In *Augustine's Early Theology of Image: A Study in the Development of Pro-Nicene Theology*, 189–223. Oxford Studies in Historical Theology. Oxford: Oxford University Press, 2016.

———. "Epilogue: The *Imago Dei* in *De Trinitate*." In *Augustine's Early Theology of Image: A Study in the Development of Pro-Nicene Theology*, 254–66. Oxford Studies in Historical Theology. Oxford: Oxford University Press, 2016.

———. "Hilary of Poitiers." In *Augustine's Early Theology of Image: A Study in the Development of Pro-Nicene Theology*, 19–50. Oxford Studies in Historical Theology. Oxford: Oxford University Press, 2016.

---

89. Joseph Ratzinger, *The Theology of History in St. Bonaventure*; cited in Christopher Collins, "Joseph Ratzinger's Theology," 50–54.

90. Ratzinger, "Notion of Person," 116–17.

———. "The Plotinian Image." In *Augustine's Early Theology of Image: A Study in the Development of Pro-Nicene Theology*, 135–64. Oxford Studies in Historical Theology. Oxford: Oxford University Press, 2016.

Bonner, Gerald. "Augustine's Conception of Deification." *JTS* 37 (1986) 369–86.

Cavadini, John C. "Trinity and Apologetics in the Theology of St. Augustine." *Modern Theology* 29 (2013) 48–82.

Collins, Christopher. "Joseph Ratzinger's Theology of the Word: The Dialogical Structure of His Thought." PhD diss., Boston College, 2012. http://hdl.handle.net/2345/2564.

Collins, C. John. *Genesis 1–4: A Linguistic, Literary, and Theological Commentary*. Phillipsburg, NJ: P&R, 2006.

DeClue, Richard G. "Ratzinger's Theology of Divine Revelation." PhD diss., Catholic University of America, 2021.

Feld, Edward, and Jan Uhrbach, eds. *Siddur Lev Shalem for Shabbat and Festivals*. New York: Rabbinical Assembly, 2013.

Foshee, Charles N. "St. Bonaventure and the Augustinian Concept of Mens." *Franciscan Studies* 27 (1967) 163–75.

Grenz, Stanley J. *The Social God and the Relational Self: A Trinitarian Theology of the Imago Dei*. Louisville, KY: Westminster John Knox, 2001.

Hutabarat, Franklin, et al. "The Understanding of the Image of God in the Early and Medieval Church History." *European Journal of Theology and Philosophy* 1 (2021) 5–11.

Litwa, M. David. "You Are Gods: Deification in the Naassene Writer and Clement of Alexandria." *HTR* 110 (2017) 125–48.

Louth, Andrew, and Marco Conti, eds. *Genesis 1–11*. ACCS. Downers Grove, IL: InterVarsity, 2001.

Middleton, J. Richard. *The Liberating Image: The* Imago Dei *in Genesis 1*. Grand Rapids: Brazos, 2005.

Origen. "Homilies on Genesis." Translated by Ronald E. Heine. In *Homilies on Genesis and Exodus*, edited by Hermigild Dressler et al., 47–224. FOTC 71. Washington, DC: Catholic University of America Press, 2002.

Plato. "Epistles" [*Ep.*]. Translated by R. G. Bury. In *Timaeus, Critias, Cleitophon, Menexenus, Epistle*s, 383–628. LCL 234. Repr., Cambridge, MA: Harvard University Press, 2007.

———. *The Republic: Books 6–10* [*Resp.*]. Translated by Paul Shorey. LCL 276. Cambridge, MA: Harvard University Press, 1982.

Plotinus. *The Six Enneads*. Classics, n.d. Translated by Stephen MacKenna and B. S. Page. http://classics.mit.edu//Plotinus/enneads.html.

Puffer, Matthew. "Human Dignity After Augustine's *Imago Dei*: On the Sources and Uses of Two Ethical Terms." *Journal of the Society of Christian Ethics* 37 (2017) 65–82.

Ratzinger, Joseph. "Commentary on Introductory Article and Chapter 1 of *Gaudium et Spes*." Translated by W. J. O'Hara. In *Commentary on the Documents of Vatican II*, edited by Herbert Vorgrimler, 5:115–64. New York: Herder and Herder, 1969.

———. "Concerning the Notion of Person in Theology." *Comm* 17 (1990) 439–54.

———. *Eschatology: Death and Eternal Life*. Translated by Michael Waldstein. Revised by Aidan Nichols. 2nd ed. Dogmatic Theology 9. Washington, DC: Catholic University of America Press, 2007.

———. "Freedom and Liberation: The Anthropological Vision of the Instruction *Libertatis Conscientia*." Translated by Stephen Wentworth Arndt. In *Anthropology and Culture*, edited by Nicholas J. Healy and David L. Schindler, 52–69. Vol. 2 of *Joseph Ratzinger in* Communio. RRRCT. Grand Rapids: Eerdmans, 2010.

———. "God Exists: But What Does This Mean for My Life?" Benedictus XVI, 1973. https://www.benedictusxvi.com/the-question-of-god?q=%2Fthe-question-of-god&cHash=c171eae000654c54bf9a0e3eb9bedd4d.

———. "Homily of His Eminence Card. Joseph Ratzinger: Mass 'Pro Eligendo Romano Pontifice.'" Vatican, Apr. 18, 2005. https://www.vatican.va/gpII/documents/homily-pro-eligendo-pontifice_20050418_en.html.

———. *In the Beginning: A Catholic Understanding of the Story of Creation and the Fall*. Grand Rapids: Eerdmans, 1995.

———. *Introduction to Christianity*. Translated by J. R. Foster. Rev. ed. Communio. San Francisco: Ignatius, 2004.

———. "The Likeness of God in the Human Being." *Dolentium Hominum* 34 (1997) 16–19.

———. *Offenbarungsverständnis und Geschichtstheologie Bonaventuras: Habilitationsschrift und Bonaventura-Studien*. Gesammelte Schriften 2. Freiburg im Breisgau: Herder, 2009.

———. *Principles of Catholic Theology: Building Stones for a Fundamental Theology*. Translated by Mary Frances McCarthy. San Francisco: Ignatius, 2007.

———. See also Benedict XVI.

Rowland, Ingrid D. *The Divine Spark of Syracuse*. Mandel Lectures in the Humanities. Waltham, MA: Brandeis University Press, 2019.

Sefaria: A Living Library of Torah Texts Online. https://www.sefaria.org/.

Simango, Daniel. "The *Imago Dei* (Gen 1:26–27): A History of Interpretation from Philo to the Present." *Studia Historiae Ecclesiasticae* 42 (2016) 172–90.

TeSelle, Eugene. *Augustine the Theologian*. New York: Herder and Herder, 1970.

Teske, Roland J. "The Image and Likeness of God in St. Augustine's De Genesi Ad Litteram Liber Imperfectus." *Augustinianum* 30 (1990) 441–51.

Williams, Rowan. "Sapientia and Trinity: Reflections on the *De Trinitate*." In *Collectanea Augustiniana: Mélanges T. J. van Bavel*, edited by Bernard Bruning et al., 317–32. BETL 92. Leuven: Leuven University Press, 1990.

Wolpe, David. "Strangers in the Land of the Free." *Atlantic*, Jan. 31, 2017. https://www.theatlantic.com/politics/archive/2017/01/iranian-jews-immigration/515241/.

9

Punishment in the Eschaton
C. S. Lewis's Imagination at the Service of Aquinas's Theory

CHRISTIAN STEPHENS

This chapter proposes that C. S. Lewis's fictional narrative *The Great Divorce* communicates in an imaginative way the Thomistic account of punishment, and that such a project is fitting in a culture which may have particular difficulty in appreciating an eschatological divine punishment. In the first place, there will be a brief introduction as to why reference to divine punishment may be particularly difficult in contemporary culture. Second, Aquinas's account of punishment will be presented. This will begin by presenting it in the context of his understanding of evil and the goodness of justice, and the agents and proportionality of punishment. The emphasis will be that while punishment is necessarily something contrary to the will of the one punished, it is also something which flows naturally or automatically from sinful behavior. The second part of the paper will include examples of character's attitudes and experiences in Lewis's narrative which demonstrate or exemplify the point Aquinas is making. It is proposed that this combination of systematic thinking and imaginative storytelling can be an effective combination in communicating the plausibility and necessity of divine punishment in the eschaton.

"THE MEDICINE OUR CONDITION ESPECIALLY NEEDS"

In an essay titled "The World's Last Night," C. S. Lewis states that since the teaching of Christ's second coming "conflicts with our favourite modern mythology [some form of universal progressivism or evolutionism] . . . it is, for that very reason, to be the more valued and made more frequently the subject of meditation. It is the medicine our condition especially needs."[1] If Lewis is correct that we need to meditate more on the truths of divine revelation which are most contrary to our intellectual and cultural milieu, then the teaching about divine punishment is pertinent in contemporary study of the eschaton. The reason is that we live in a milieu that has been described by Phillip Rieff as "the therapeutic culture," and what Charles Taylor has called "expressive individualism" or "a culture of authenticity."[2] In contrast to other societies which see the purpose of culture as purifying and elevating the individual into a higher order than he or she is automatically capable of appreciating and contributing to, we live in an anti-culture where it is now the role of society to bend in support of the individual's spontaneous desires and identity. On account of this, "progress" tends to be measured by the removal of any laws or customs which are obstacles to the *libido dominandi* of the individual, and ethics is often reduced to simply managing one's own and others' feelings, ensuring that on the whole, everyone experiences more positive than negative emotions.

Since punishment, even on the most superficial understanding, is known to be something contrary to the desires of the one punished, it is thus immediately considered suspect, if not condemnable, by the therapeutic culture and expressive individualism. Not only because it makes another person feel unpleasant, but also because it would seem to imply an objective moral order violated by the one punished. The punisher must be suspected of cruelty and intolerance, particularly in the form of imposing his or her own subjective values on others. Even if there was in fact some moral wrongdoing, the punisher probably fails to appreciate the numerous psychosomatic and social causes of human behavior which render the person not only inculpable for the act, but perhaps even a very victim of it themselves. Those punished are assumed to be unnecessarily traumatized by the punishment; all that was likely needed was some form of educational and/or medicinal intervention.

---

1. "World's Last Night," in Lewis, *Essay Collection*, 49.

2. Taylor, *Secular Age*, 473–504; Rieff, *Triumph of the Therapeutic*, 232–61. See also Trueman, *Rise of Modern Self*, 35–79.

If we then consider that much of our intuitive and acquired theological reasoning entails moving analogically from creatures to the divine, given this widespread phobia or indignation regarding punishment, how is the typical person of our time supposed to come to terms with an eschatological divine punishment? Does God not understand or love us enough to either celebrate, or at least tolerate, who we are? Even if someone does offend him, is not he confident and magnanimous enough to leave them alone; is he so insecure as to need to taunt them?

THE TWO PILLARS OF PUNISHMENT: EVIL AND JUSTICE

In order to address these concerns, it is important to begin with a theory of punishment that is coherent and defensible in the natural order itself, in order to then apply it to the eschaton. This chapter will propose the Thomist account of punishment as one such instance. It stands on two pillars, which are its accounts of evil and justice. In the first place, according to Aquinas, there are two kinds of evil: the evil of *poenae* (translated as either punishment, penalty, or pain) and the evil of *culpae* (translated as fault, guilt, or sin).[3] The evil of *poenae* refers to any privation present in a person's form and integrity (its "first act/perfection"), whereas the evil of *culpae* is a privation present in the voluntary operation of the will (the person's "second act/perfection"). As a general rule, the line distinguishing the two types of evil is whether it is something *undergone* by the acting person contrary to their will, or whether it is something *voluntary and pursued*.[4] The evil of *culpae* is worse than the evil of *poenae*.[5] The first reason is that while the evil of pain or punishment is contrary to the creature's own private good, the evil of fault is contrary to both the divine good and the common good of the natural order. The second reason is that the good of human existence (first perfection) is ordered toward the good of the human act (second perfection), and the evil of fault entails the corruption of that human act itself. Therefore the evil of sin is always and absolutely evil, whereas the evil of punishment is only relatively evil to the one undergoing it, but it could be absolutely good all things considered.

---

3. Aquinas, *ST* I, q.48, a.5–6; q.64, a.3, r.3; *ST* I–II, q.21, a.1, r.3; a.2; q.42, a.3; q.83, a.1; *SCG* 2:83; *John*, 9.1; 11.1.

4. "As a general rule" because of the complicated situation of some sins being permitted as punishment for other sins. This is investigated below.

5. Aquinas, *ST* I, q.48, a.6; *ST* I–II, q.39, a.4; q.79, a.1, r.4; *ST* II–II, q.76, a.4.

The second pillar of the Thomist account of punishment is justice. As it exists in the acting person, justice is "a habit whereby a man renders to each one his due by a constant and perpetual will."[6] Since "justice alone, of all the virtues, implies the notion of duty," any enacting of what is fitting or due to another belongs to this virtue or one of its parts.[7] It is the greatest of the moral virtues since it perfects our rational appetite, and its object is that state of affairs which entails right relationship, order and harmony with other persons, one's community, and ultimately God.[8] Thus the goodness of the virtue of justice is grounded in the metaphysical goodness of order and right relation: "To render anyone his due has the aspect of good, since by rendering a person his due, one becomes suitably proportioned to him, through being ordered to him in a becoming manner."[9]

Aquinas ties together the relationship between sin, punishment and justice in a most succinct way when he says, "When anyone by reason of his unjust will ascribes to himself something beyond his due [the evil of *culpae*], it is only just that he be deprived of something else which is his due [the evil of *poenae*]."[10] Since by the evil of sin a person has indulged his will by taking a good that was not his, in order to correct that, he must now, contrary to his will, undergo the loss of a good that would otherwise be rightly his.[11] Thus punishment comes under the *ratio* of the virtue of justice since, as we saw, the object of the latter includes any notion of debt, duty, and right relation. Punishment is thus primarily retributive in its very object and end, and it is rehabilitative ("medicinal") and deterring as a matter of hoped for consequence or intention.[12] This does not mean that *anything* done in retaliation to evil is just: to punish well requires the virtue of *vindicatio* (vengeance) which, like the acts of all the moral virtues, requires prudence to reason and command well regarding the

---

6. Aquinas, *ST* II–II, q.58, a.1.

7. Aquinas, *ST* I–II, q.99, a.5, r.1; *ST* II–II, q.58, a.1; q.122, a.1.

8. Aquinas, *ST* I–II, q.46, a.7, r.2; q.66, a.4; q.100, a.2, r.2; q.113, a.1; *ST* II–II, q.57, a.1; q.58, a.2, a.4, a.12; q.104, a.6; q.122, a.1; q.123, a.12; q.181, a.1; *Job*, 1.4; Aristotle's "Nicomachean Ethics," 5.1–5.2.17; 8.1.

9. Aquinas, *ST* II–II, q.19, a.11; q.58, a.11; q.81, a.2; q.109, a.2; q.114, a.1; *SCG* 3.128.

10. Aquinas, *ST* III, q.49, a.6; *ST* I–II, q.87, a.6; *ST* II–II, q.108, a.4.

11. For this reason, the evil of punishment, the loss of a good contrary to the will of the person, is the opposite of happiness, which consists in the will resting in the attainment of the ultimate good (Aquinas, *ST* II–II, q.18, a.3; *SCG* 3.141).

12. Aquinas, *ST* II–II, q.68, a.1; q.99, a.4.

who, what, when, where, and why of punishment, including the potential side effects a course of action may entail.[13]

While punishment as primarily retributive might sound harsh, it is in fact what preserves the right relationship and dignity between all the actors and agents involved. First, it keeps the focus on what a person *deserves*, regardless of how rehabilitative or deterring of evil more imposition of suffering would be. As C. S. Lewis indicates, if the medicinal and deterring effects of punishment are primary, there is no reason why the person need be guilty of anything at all, or the severity of their act considered at all, before they are subjected to the "punishment."[14] Second, if the medicinal end were primary, it would make for the awkwardness of a potential criminal being warned, "Be careful, otherwise we'll make you a better person!" Surely, we should *always* be trying to help people be better, but we come across a limitation in the form of them having a right to certain goods or opportunities they may misuse. When people do the wrong thing, we do not take the consequence to be that now we will force them to be a better person (as if such a thing were possible).[15] Rather, they will now need to forego some good against their will, which it previously would have been unjust to deprive them of. Punishment and therapy are two different activities, even though they may both be serving a common end of harmony and right order.

Finally, it is worth noting that for Aquinas, punishment per se is only deserved by sin, whether it be original or actual.[16] Once the will is reoriented to the divine good, one may still experience evil-as-suffered, yet it now becomes not punishment strictly speaking (since it is accepted by the will voluntarily), but instead becomes the material of purification, satisfaction, and penance. The evil of pain and suffering can thus be satisfactory or meritorious if instrumentalized by a will infused with charity (as exemplified in the life of Christ and the saints). Saint Thomas mentions other goods which may be accomplished in and through evil

---

13. Aquinas, *ST* II–II, q.108; q.47, a.7.

14. Lewis, "Humanitarian Theory of Punishment," in *Undeceptions*, 239; "Letter 67," in *Essay Collection*, 423–24.

15. To *force* someone to perform a *morally good act* is a contradiction and thus is metaphysically impossible. "Force" suggests that it is contrary to the person's will, and yet a morally good act presupposes it is voluntary, and thus there is goodness *in the will*. At best, one can simply force another person to *imitate* the *external* component of a morally good act; but no one would think this is a morally praiseworthy act. Germain Grisez presents the implications of this for educators and formers, and how it is that through failing to understand this point they easily bring about the very opposite of what they thought they were accomplishing (*Beyond the New Morality*, 182–93).

16. Aquinas, *ST* I–II, q.76, a.2; q.85, a.5; q.87, a.7; *SCG* 3.141.

as suffered: these include preservation from future sins, growth in virtue, and as an example for others.[17] For these reasons, one must avoid hasty particular judgments about how or why someone is suffering.

THE AGENTS OF PUNISHMENT

With this background of Aquinas's theory of punishment now presented, in the next part of the chapter some more specific details will be explored. In particular, who or what are the agents of punishment, how is it to be determined what the punishment should be, and for how long? However, this time the theoretical explanation will be accompanied by examples from C. S. Lewis's *Great Divorce*. This is a fictional narrative written from the perspective of its protagonist who wakes up in the afterlife. Over the course of the story, he makes his way from the Valley of the Shadow of Death to, and then through, the Valley of the Shadow of Life, relying on his trustworthy guide to understand what is happening and why.[18] While pursuing (and undergoing) his own journey, he encounters about twenty-five other people whose own peculiar words and actions manifest their own character and, ultimately, destiny. In some cases, these persons do not even choose to begin their journey out of the Valley of the Shadow of Death, while others begin it without completing it. In either case, it results in the person's frustration and unfulfilled desire and is thus an instance of eschatological punishment.

Who or what renders punishment? Aquinas claims that the answer lies in the fact that all things exist and act from within an order which has other parts and a principle:

> All things contained in an order, are, in a manner, one, in relation to the principle of that order. Consequently, whatever rises up against an order, is put down by that order or by the principle thereof. And because sin is an inordinate act, it is evident that whoever sins, commits an offence against an order: wherefore he is put down, in consequence, by that same order, which repression [*depressio*] is punishment [*poena*]. Accordingly, man can be punished with a threefold punishment corresponding to the three orders to which the human will is subject . . . one,

---

17. Aquinas, *ST* I–II, q.87, a.2, r.1; q.98, a.2, r.3; *ST* II–II, q.39, a.4, r.3; q.68, a.1; q.83, a.8, r.1; a.16; q.108, a.4, r.2; *SCG* 3.141; *Matthew* 13.1; *John* 9.1.

18. Lewis, *Great Divorce*, 68.

inflicted by himself, viz. remorse of conscience; another, inflicted by man; and a third, inflicted by God.[19]

We see here that punishment is the *depressio* (lit., the submission, lowering or sinking) of *disorder* by the principle of that very order and its other parts. This creates an interesting tension by which punishment simultaneously results from the disordered will and yet is imposed on it. On the one hand, there is nothing accidental or arbitrary about who or what is doing the punishing: it is coming from the very others (metaphorically in the case of one's own conscience) that cause and constitute one's own community of being. In this way, the punishment is deeply *intrinsic* to a sinful character and actions when considered in its real context. Yet on the other hand, since all punishment is loss of goods contrary to the will of the person, its principle (or source) must be *extrinsic* to the principle of disorder, the will.[20] Thus all punishment is experienced as *imposed* on the person, despite the fact that its occurrence is the automatic or natural consequence of his or her own action. Take a simple example of a child, Sam, thinking it's "not fair" that they feel sick after trying to live on cake alone. He experiences a stomachache and fatigue that is not what he wants and which is "imposed" on him from "without," and yet at the same time, if he comes to a knowledge and appreciation of the kind of being he is (an animal who needs nutrition) and what cake is (sugar, flour, and fat), he will realize that there is nothing arbitrary about his ill health. It did not require someone else to intervene, and thus there is no one else to blame, and there is nothing "unfair" about it.

We have seen that Aquinas believes that punishment is administered by "the three orders" which regulate the human will. We will now give a brief explanation of each and explore how each of these can be found in Lewis's eschatological narrative.

Oneself

The first agent of punishment is the person's own reasoning and, as we have seen, this is called "the remorse of conscience." The unrepentant sinner experiences an internal punishment at the hands of "the order of his own reason" which naturally regulates his will.[21] In St. Thomas's postlapsarian

19. Aquinas, *ST* I–II, q.87, a.1.
20. Aquinas, *ST* I–II, q.42, a.3, r.1.
21. Aquinas, *ST* I–II, q.87, a.1.

anthropology, the natural inclination to virtue is diminished; however, it can never be totally destroyed since it is grounded in the very principle and ends of human nature itself.[22] The intellect and will still have the universal true and universal good for their objects respectively, and thus some basic inclination to them, however weakened. Saint Thomas says, "Even in the lost the natural inclination to virtue remains, else they would have no remorse of conscience."[23] The *remaining natural orientation* to the good is the principle of the unrepentant sinner's pain or remorse in suffering some degree of incompleteness, inconsistency, confusion, dejection, or absence of fulfillment.

Aquinas points out that

> the wicked reckon their sensitive and corporeal nature, or the outward man, to hold the first place. Wherefore, since they know not themselves aright, they do not love themselves aright, but love what they think themselves to be . . . the wicked have no wish to be preserved in the integrity of the inward man, nor do they desire spiritual goods for him, nor do they work for that end, nor do they take pleasure in their own company by entering into their own hearts, because whatever they find there, present, past and future, is evil and horrible; nor do they agree with themselves, on account of the gnawings of conscience.[24]

Life becomes burdensome and absurd to the person. He is doing what he wants, attempting to satisfy his disordered appetites (which he identifies himself with) and yet he is not happy, since he undermines the true goodness and intelligibility of his nature and ultimate end as a human person. Thus part of the punishment of sin is that the person lives "at odds with himself," because he desires pleasures associated with his fallen appetites, and yet he also continues to have inclinations that are in accordance with his nature and reason.[25] Put more pithily, it can be said that "man becomes a burden even to himself in being opposed to God through sin . . . [and] One sees in this that sin has its own punishment immediately."[26]

---

22. Aquinas, *ST* I, q.48, a.4; q.98, a.2; *ST* I–II, q.63, a.1; q.78, a.2; q.85, a.1–2, 4; q.93, a.6, r.2; q.106, a.3, r.3; *ST* II–II, q.10, a.4; *SCG* 3.12.

23. Aquinas, *ST* I–II, q.85, a.2, r.3.

24. Aquinas, *ST* II–II, q.25, a.7; *ST* I–II, q.29, a.4; q.32, a.7, r.3; q.33, a.2; *John* 8.4.

25. Aquinas, *Aristotle's "Nicomachean Ethics,"* 9.4.

26. Aquinas, *Job* 7.4; *ST* I–II, q.33, a.3; q.69, a.2, r.2; q.78, a.2; *SCG* 4.93; *Aristotle's "Nicomachean Ethics,"* 4.4.

Ultimately, it is the absence of charity (which integrates the person, purifying and drawing their affections from the arbitrary and many to the intelligible and one) that is the reason why the disintegrated person's affections are pulled in competing and incompatible directions.[27] For this reason, those without charity cannot have true peace or joy.[28] One essential aspect of peace is that a person be in harmony with himself: but his interior life is harmonized only by seeking the One who fulfills all desires, and this is God alone.[29] "There cannot be full joy in a created good because it does not give complete rest to man's desires and yearnings."[30] The more one possesses the Sovereign Good, the more one loves it and despises all else. In contrast, temporal goods appear to be satisfying before they are possessed, but after they are possessed, they are known better and the will thus moves on to something else, at times even despising the very same goods once longed for.[31]

Without exception, all of the unrepentant sinners presented by Lewis in the afterlife are aware of their own misery and lack of fulfillment (even though they cannot know the true degree of this). This explains the apparently contradictory combination of their attitudes and responses. On the one hand they are frequently whimpering, full of self-pity, and believing themselves to be victims. On the other hand, they frequently display malice, stubbornness, or aggressiveness. This brief exchange between a good spirit and the ghost of a vain lady who does not wish to be seen by others in her current appearance captures numerous points from Aquinas's theory:

> "But we were all a bit ghostly when we first arrived, you know. That'll wear off. Just come out and try."
> "But they'll see me."
> "What does it matter if they do?"
> "I'd rather die."
> "But you've died already. There's no good trying to go back to that."
> The Ghost made a sound something between a sob and a snarl. "I wish I'd never been born," it said. "What *are* we born for?"[32]

Clinging to her disordered desires to appear in a certain way, she experiences life as burdensome, and then finally unintelligible. Later on,

27. Aquinas, *ST* I–II, q.73, a.1, r.3.
28. Aquinas, *ST* II–II, q.29, a.3, r.1.
29. Aquinas, *Second Thessalonians* 3.2.
30. Aquinas, *John* 16.6.
31. Aquinas, *ST* I–II, q.2, a.1, r.3; *John* 4.2; 4.4.
32. Lewis, *Great Divorce*, 61; emphasis in original.

George MacDonald, the protagonist's guide, points out that in contrast to heaven, "Hell is a state of mind. . . . And every state of mind, left to itself, every shutting up of the creature within the dungeon of its own mind—is, in the end, Hell."[33] Thus we see that in a real sense, the most proximate agent of punishment is the person's own reason and interior life.

Other Creatures

The second source of punishment that Aquinas mentioned are those persons who have authority for the common good of the community of which the sinner is a member.[34] This would be the various levels of human government at the various levels of community. In *The Great Divorce*, Lewis does not make any mention of a human government or any kind of law enforcement. This is most likely to emphasize that the evil of pain and punishment is not by being "caught" by others, but the very nature of the attitude and actions. The characters are constantly blaming others around them for their suffering, and thus the presence of law enforcement may only help increase the pretense, and perhaps even lure in the reader (particularly those subscribed to the expressive individualism mentioned above) to believing the error.

We could, however, expand this category to consider punishment at the hands of others in a more general sense. If the virtues of charity, wisdom, and religion are the great moral unifiers of human society, then mortal sin, foolishness, and idolatry are their antitheses respectively.[35] And thus they are a (if not *the*) source of interpersonal and social conflict. Having turned from God, who is the Common Good of all to be enjoyed, and thus a principle of social harmony, the unrepentant sinner forfeits the possibility of social harmony and concord.[36] For Aquinas, following Aristotle, social concord is political friendship. It is a practical affair, and so it does not consist in holding the same opinion on speculative questions (a difference on which is compatible with friendship), but "it is concerned with things to be done," and not just any, but those considered *most important* and of a nature that it (actually or potentially) affects *all* involved. Concord is thus present when, on these matters, "they agree on what is useful, so that they vote for the same measures and work

---

33. Lewis, *Great Divorce*, 70. Later on, MacDonald points out that "to be afraid of oneself is the last horror" (81).

34. Aquinas, *ST* I–II, q.87, a.1.

35. Aquinas, *ST* I–II, q.73, a.1.

36. Aquinas, *ST* II–II, q.12, a.1, r.2; *Second Thessalonians*, 3.2.

together on projects they consider for their interests."[37] According to Aquinas, the evil cannot have this political friendship with each other (or with the virtuous) because (1) they are prone to unreasonably changing their minds and choices, (2) they unjustly want more than their share of advantages and less than their share of the burdens, and for this reason, (3) they positively inquire into the business of others for the purpose of interfering with their plans.[38] In summary, where "the common good of justice is not preserved, the common possession of concord among (a people) is destroyed."[39]

The unrepentant sinner inevitably neglects, downplays, or even sabotages other real beings, goods, and truths. Insofar as other persons recognize, preserve, promote, and pursue those other beings, goods, or truths (even in a sinful way), each party is going to experience a kind of mutual *depressio* (resistance or punishment) at the hands of the other. Each will be able to grab a hold of, and commit to, the particular truths or goods neglected by the other.[40] It is only by conversion back to the One who is Subsistent Truth and Goodness Itself that errors and disordered desires can be seen for what they are and abandoned, and all true and good aspirations be finally reconciled. In the absence of this, the conflict and divisiveness among the population itself is a kind of punishment inflicted by others.

Lewis's story is utterly saturated with interpersonal conflict and its consequent suffering. In the opening three pages alone, we see what recurs throughout the story: fights, arguments, lying, cheating, cursing, threats, conflict over perceived superiority or inferiority, and finally, the fear that there is not enough of something (despite this *always* being false). In fact, the quarrelling is so consistent that some of those living in the Valley of the Shadow of Death (with no intention of progressing out

---

37. Aquinas, Aristotle's "Nicomachean Ethics," 9.6.
38. Aquinas, Aristotle's "Nicomachean Ethics," 9.6; Second Timothy 2.4.
39. Aquinas, Aristotle's "Nicomachean Ethics," 9.6.
40. This goes a long way in explaining the conflict in contemporary partisan political discourse. Each side absolutely commits to voicing and representing a particular truth or goodness, contrary to the opposing party, who is neglecting or opposing that particular truth or goodness. On every issue, whether it be abortion, immigration, or taxation, each side has its favorite talking points and "dog whistles," rarely bothering to clear the space and time to incorporate the truth and goodness of other party's position into their own. Once one or both of the parties have absolutized (or idolized) something that is only contingent or conditioned, coherence and reconciliation become impossible.

of it) are constantly moving further away from each other, believing that if only they would be left alone they would have some peace.[41]

We could expand this category further to include punishment at the hands of nonhuman persons. According to St. Thomas's reading of the Scriptures, one of the penal effects of sin is an enslavement or subjection to the devil.[42] Christ calls Satan "the ruler of this world" (e.g., John 12:31) not because he is its creator or due to any natural right, but because the worldly have turned from the divine lordship to serve him.[43] Similarly, Christ implies that Satan is the "father" of sinners (John 8:44). Aquinas takes this to be true in the sense that human sinners "imitat[e] him who was the first to sin."[44] The devil's sin consisted in a prideful turning from the truth about his own nature and its ordering to God by desiring to find happiness by his own power, a murderous envy of the supernatural good offered to human persons, and a desire to order other beings to his own private end.[45] The person brings this demonic enslavement onto himself by consenting to the demonic suggestion and doing what the demons themselves did to incur their own fall.[46] This subjection is a fitting punishment: "For the order of Divine justice exacts that whosoever consents to another's evil suggestion, shall be subjected to him in his punishment."[47]

The more freely and easily one's activity is directed by the demons, the more it pervades the person's life, and the deeper the slavery.[48] According to Aquinas, the devil "reigns perfectly" over someone when he has brought them to "the last step of sin," which is glorifying in their sin. Such persons have so embodied the demonic disposition that they are *in*

---

41. Lewis, *Great Divorce*, 10–11. Jean Paul Sartre's eschatological play *No Exit* was performed and published within a couple of years of *Great Divorce*. It famously concludes with the character's insight: "So this is hell. I'd never have believed it. You remember all we were told about the torture-chambers, the fire and brimstone, the 'burning marl.' Old wives' tales! There's no need for red-hot pokers. HELL IS—OTHER PEOPLE!" (Sartre, *No Exit*, 50). It could also be a case study for how one's very own reasoning is an agent of punishment.

42. Aquinas, *Matthew* 6.3; 8.2; *Colossians* 2.3; *Ephesians* 1.5; 4.3; *First Timothy* 4.1; *SCG* 3.112; *John* 14.8; *Job* 20.2; 40.2.

43. Aquinas, *ST* I, q.65, a.1; *Matthew* 12.2; *John* 1.3; 7.5; 16.1; *Ephesians* 2.1; 6.3; *Second Timothy* 2.4.

44. Aquinas, *ST* I, q.114, a.3, r.2; *ST* III, q.8, a.7, r.2; *John*, 6.8; 8.6; 16.1; *Galatians* 3.3; *First Timothy* 5.2.

45. Aquinas, *ST* I, q.63, a.2–3; *SCG* 3.109–10; *Matthew* 4.1; *John* 8.6; *Job* 40.2.

46. Aquinas, *ST* I–II, q.80, a.4, r.2.

47. Aquinas, *ST* I, q.63, a.8; *ST* III, q.48, a.4, r.2; *Matthew* 18.1; 18.3; *Colossians* 2.3.

48. Aquinas, *John* 8.4.

principle hostile to God and his rule.[49] In St. Thomas's reading, these are those whom St. Paul calls "the children of wrath" (Eph 2:3). No longer sinning through ignorance or weakness, but now without any "faith in eternal realities nor hope in salvation," the demon can "lead them . . . wherever he wishes . . . doing whatever he pleases in them."[50] He suggests that "the child of wrath" has some awareness of the truth of their demonic enslavement, but tolerates it for the sake of trying to attain the goal of his disordered appetite.[51] The sinner accepts the demonic tyranny as part of the project of a life lived apart from God.

In *The Great Divorce*, there is a notable absence of demons as playing any central role in the story. Once again it could be surmised that this is to avoid any chance of the reader finding a purely external or arbitrary cause for the suffering of the unrepentant sinner. However, one could also add that this book was published four years after Lewis's masterpiece *The Screwtape Letters*, which was entirely dedicated to the demonic suggestion-slavery dynamic described above. Therefore, there was no need to rehearse this in the eschatological dimension.

In Lewis's portrayal, we see this completion of the human imitation of the demonic sin in the lost. Its egocentric and tyrannical dimension is present in their attempts to "extend Hell, to bring it bodily, if they could, into Heaven. There were tub-thumping Ghosts who in thin, bat-like voices urged the blessed spirits to shake off their fetters, to escape from their imprisonment in happiness, to tear down the mountains with their hands, to seize heaven 'for their own.'"[52] They believed it "better to reign in Hell than serve in Heaven."[53] The demonic envy is imitated in that they believe "they should be allowed to blackmail the universe: that till they consent to be happy (on their own terms) no one else shall taste joy: that theirs should be the final power; that Hell should be able to veto Heaven."[54] Finally, there are the deformed monsters who spend months and years trekking in the Valley of the Shadow of Life, enduring the pain, all so that they can curse and insult God as closely as they can.[55]

---

49. Aquinas, *Matthew* 4.1.
50. Aquinas, *Ephesians* 2.1.
51. Aquinas, *Matthew* 6.5.
52. Lewis, *Great Divorce*, 80.
53. Lewis, *Great Divorce*, 71.
54. Lewis, *Great Divorce*, 135.
55. Lewis, *Great Divorce*, 81–82.

God

Finally, God as the first principle, governor, and ultimate end of nature is the ultimate principle of punishment. In Aquinas's understanding, since the *evil of fault* (sin) is by definition the will being opposed to the divine love and wisdom, God can only permit this kind of evil, and not positively will it. However, God does will *the evil of punishment* (which is evil only in a relative sense, that is, to the person undergoing it) not for its own sake as if pain were an end in itself, but rather because he loves justice, and he loves the order of creation, which is its intrinsic good, and whose accomplishment manifests his glory, which is the ultimate end of all creation.[56] In the final analysis, while the evil of fault is the sinner's refusal to be voluntarily subject to the eternal law, the evil of punishment is their subjection to that same law in spite of their will.[57]

This need not mean that God *miraculously* punishes evil. As we have seen, the created order, whose principle and end he is, includes the conscience and other creatures, and so their own repression of evil is also God's. This is what Lewis leans into in *The Great Divorce*. God does not enter onto the scene as simply one character among others, and he does not act in any immediate or miraculous way. In not making a personal appearance, as in the absence of any human government and demons, Lewis again emphasizes the immediate relationship between the person's character and their suffering, giving no room for the sinner's proneness to a victim mindset at the hands of an arbitrary higher power. The second reason is that it also gives an opportunity to other creatures to share in God's own justice and mercy, both for their own good and that of the person they're engaging with. Lewis highlights the place of other persons as truly participating in and mediating God's love for others, thus highlighting again the place of right relation with other members of their community. For example, the employee, professor, and artist are all ministered to by their own former colleagues.[58] In each case, honesty, repentance, and reconciliation are the conditions for being able to progress in their journey.

---

56. Aquinas, *ST* I, q.19, a.9; q.48, a.6; q.49, a.2; *ST* I–II, q.39, a.2, r.3; q.79, a.4, r.1; q.87, a.3, r.3; *ST* II–II, q.19, a.1; *ST* III, q.1, a.1, r.3; *SCG* 1.96; 2.41; 3.144; *John* 9.1; 11.1; 17.3.

57. Aquinas, *ST* I–II, q.93, a.3, r.1; a.6, r.2.

58. Lewis, *Great Divorce*, 30, 37, 85–87.

THE PROPORTIONALITY OF PUNISHMENT

Since punishment comes under the lens of justice, it is essential that the severity of the punishment is proportionate to the severity of the sin, otherwise this would only introduce a *second* disorder in need of rectification.[59] Punishment is not about two wrongs making a right; it is about righting a wrong. Just as a doctor never cuts off a superior limb to save an inferior one, so too God never punishes the person with the loss of a spiritual good for the sake of preserving or obtaining bodily or external goods, but he does impose the loss of a lower good for the sake of a higher good.[60] Far from God's punishment for sin being harsh, St. Thomas insists that such punishment is in principle always less than what is deserved: the paying of a temporal punishment for disparaging a spiritual good is always insufficient since "a spiritual thing cannot be appraised at an earthly price."[61]

We will now consider three ways that Aquinas's theory preserves the proportion between sin and punishment, and how *The Great Divorce* provides examples of each.

We Lose the Good We Sin Against

The first way that we see the proportionality between a sin and its punishment preserved in Aquinas's theory is that we lose the good we sin against. This constitutes the "pain of loss [*poena damni*]."[62] Depending on the good one sins against, punishment can be eternal (if it is the loss of the Eternal Good), or temporal, with the latter ranging from the loss of virtue itself, to the disordering of natural powers, to bodily injury, and to loss of external goods.[63] Persons who sin against God's grace and inspiration thus lose these very gifts. When God is said to "blind their eyes and harden their hearts" (John 12:40), "give them up to a base mind and improper conduct" (Rom 1:28), or even "forsake" them (Ps 22:1), St. Thomas insists that this is meant to refer to God justly withholding his grace from the sinner, or at least not hindering him from acting on his disordered desires.[64] This withholding is a just punishment since, not

---

59. Aquinas, *ST* I–II, q.78, a.4; q.87, a.4; *ST* II–II, q.99, a.4.
60. Aquinas, *ST* I–II, q.114, a.10, r.3; *ST* II–II, q.43, a.7; q.108, a.4; *John* 9.1.
61. Aquinas, *ST* II–II, q.100, a.1.
62. Aquinas, *ST* I–II, q.87, a.4; *SCG* 3.144; 3.162; 4.90; *Matthew* 3.1.
63. Aquinas, *SCG* 3.141.
64. Aquinas, *ST* I, q.113, a.6; *ST* I–II, q.79, a.1, r.1; a.3; q.87, a.2; q.98, a.4, r.2; *ST*

only are people not *owed* God's gratuitous gifts but, in the final analysis, these are exactly what they have sinned against.

Ignorance of divine things as a punishment for sin is a constant theme in Aquinas's biblical commentaries, for the obvious reason that it is a constant theme in the Scriptures themselves:

- When one resists the truth out of wickedness, the wickedness itself blinds him.[65]
- Because they did not cling to the truth, *they were given over to errors.*[66]
- Those unwilling to believe the truth *will believe a lie.*[67]
- *They did not understand* because they did not believe.[68]

In each of these instances, there is a reference to voluntary ignorance and deception (the evil of fault), followed by an ignorance or deception which is against the will of the person (the evil of punishment). No one directly wills to be blind, in error, or believing lies as ends in themselves, but one justly incurs such a result by turning from the light insofar as it has been made known. The disordered will impedes the proper activity of the intellect, either by directing it to think about something else, or refusing to consider the divine matters at hand. Thus, the penal ignorance follows as a matter of cause and effect, with God's permission.[69] Just as in the previous section we saw Thomas identify the disordered will as both sin and punishment in itself, so here he says, "Their sin *and* punishment is their deception."[70]

Closely related to the penal ignorance of divine things is foolishness. It is opposed to wisdom, and it "denotes dullness of sense in judging, and chiefly as regards the highest cause, which is the last end and the sovereign good."[71] While Aquinas recognizes that sometimes this dullness can have nonvoluntary or involuntary causes, he says that in the case of "the worldly," this foolishness is caused by him "plunging his sense

---

II–II, q.10, a.1, a.6; q.159, a.1, r.3; q.164, a.1; *Matthew*, 5.12; 8.1; *John* 7.7; 10.5; *Romans* 1.7; *Job* 12.2.

65. Aquinas, *Second Timothy* 2.4; emphasis added.
66. Aquinas, *Matthew* 24.1; emphasis added.
67. Aquinas, *John* 5.7; emphasis added.
68. Aquinas, *John* 6.8; emphasis added.
69. Aquinas, *ST* I–II, q.79, a.3; *ST* II–II, q.10, a.1, a.6; *Matthew* 11.1; *John* 10.5; 15.5.
70. Aquinas, *Second Thessalonians* 2.3; emphasis added.
71. Aquinas, *ST* I–II, q.46, a.2; *ST* II–II, q.8, a.6, r.1.

into earthly things, whereby his sense is rendered incapable of perceiving Divine things."[72] This dullness includes "failing to perceive such evident signs of God," and so lacking the "common and confused knowledge of God which is found in practically all men."[73]

Since the context of Lewis's story is the eschaton, the good which the characters are sinning against is the eternal good, which is nothing other than God himself and our supernatural participation in his life. To reject God, and yet have happiness and eternal life, is asking for something that is metaphysically impossible since God *is* Subsistent Happiness and Eternal Life.[74] Therefore to sin against God is necessarily to lose this life. As per Aquinas's account of sin, it is not that these people encounter God as one more object among many; rather it is the case that they cleave to a particular creature as if it were their ultimate end and salvation, making an idol out of this creature. We see here an example of the penal ignorance of divine things and foolishness. The characters rarely if ever consider God at all. In fact, when the saintly spirits do implicitly or explicitly refer to God, the fallen always see it as a distraction from the real matter at hand, or an attempt to be manipulated.[75] Despite the extraordinary nature of their state and environment, it does not lead them to growth in faith, hope, and love: instead they foolishly think and act within the same naturalistic and immanent framework they have been operating in all along. One character believes that both the Valleys of the Shadow of Death and Life are created and orchestrated by a worldwide secret society, and "they" will not suck him in.[76] Another character insists that this experience of the afterlife is all a hallucination.[77] In the story, Lewis is at pains to show how it is the case that it is really *only* sins against God that finally determined the loss of the eternal good. The good spirits who make their way down to try to convince people to keep moving along the journey are often at pains to relativize the people's sins against others while back on earth, and to affirm that, as long as they are willing, those sins can be forgiven and all harm undone.[78] However it is the ghost's foolish judgment of everything else in light of those one or

---

72. Aquinas, *John* 14.4 (compare to 14.6); *ST* I, q.93, a.8, r.3; *ST* I–II, q.46, a.2; *ST* II–II, q.15, a.1, a.3.

73. Aquinas, *SCG* 3.38.

74. Lewis himself presents this point in his theoretical work. See *Mere Christianity*, 176; and *Problem of Pain*, 42.

75. Lewis, *Great Divorce*, 24, 42.

76. Lewis, *Great Divorce*, 52–53.

77. Lewis, *Great Divorce*, 81.

78. Lewis, *Great Divorce*, 26–30, 38–39, 73.

two creatures who continue to occasion sinning against the divine good, or more specifically, the divine mercy. They need to, so to speak, double down on their sin in order not to move forward towards heaven.

Since the unrepentant sin against their own nature, they also begin to lose this as much as is metaphysically possible. Aquinas notes that while the individual *act* of sin may be temporary by nature, it leaves an imprint on the person, and in particular it entails a loss of comeliness and beauty in the person's character. He calls this effect of sin a stain (*macula*).[79] In turning from the divine, and then cleaving to a creature instead, the person experiences a *dehumanization* or *depersonalization*, insofar as he or she sabotages or deforms the condition of his or her nature. There is a degrading narrowness since the spiritual faculties of intellect and will are deformed by being forced to submit to something other than he who is Subsistent Truth and Goodness.[80]

In Lewis's story, the characters do not remain ontologically unaffected, as if they simply continued to live a life consistent with their state on earth. Instead, since they are sinning against their own very nature and being, which comes from God and is ordered to him, the characters become less real insofar as they participate less in the divine likeness: the characters are ghosts, "man-shaped stains on the brightness of that air," unable to act on or change things in the Valley of the Shadow of Life.[81] At the same time as being less real, they are also not as dynamic and malleable in the features: "They were all fixed faces, full not of possibilities but impossibilities . . . all, in one way or another, distorted and faded."[82] They actually become shadows of their former selves, not merely in its reality, but also in its richness and multidimensionality.[83] To persist in a

---

79. Aquinas, *ST* I-II, q.86, a.1; q.89, a.1; q.109, a.7.

80. Aquinas, *ST* II-II, q.7, a.2; q.19, a.11.

81. Lewis, *Great Divorce*, 20–21, 25. Yet at the same time, the protagonist wonders whether it is in fact this world that is more real and substantial than what he and others were used to; that the change is in fact in the world, and not them.

82. Lewis, *Great Divorce*, 17.

83. At the end of the story, when Lewis tackles the difficult question of how one could ever be happy knowing a loved one is lost, one of his answers is that the kind of person one is remembering, with those more or less lovable features, no longer exists. There is only a remnant of the person, so small that all of the people and objects in the Valley of the Shadow of Death could be swallowed by a butterfly without affecting it (Lewis, *Great Divorce*, 137–38). Yet at the same time, persons need not simply accept this on testimony. The guide MacDonald states that "every one of us has interrupted that journey and retraced immeasurable distances to come down today on the mere chance of saving some ghosts," and yet those being purified realize eventually a limit to which one can hinder or slow their own journey for the sake of these others: "The sane would do no good if they made themselves mad to help mad men" (74–75).

state of unrepented sin in the afterlife is to persist seeking out something other than God as one's ultimate end and healing. This is an illusion, morally and ontologically, for *there is no other ultimate end of the person outside of God*. In the end, the alternative to God as one's ultimate end is not a creature—it is nothing. "The whole difficulty of understanding hell is that the thing to be understood is so nearly nothing."[84]

The Good We Love in a Disordered Way Afflicts Us

Second, the proportion between sin and its punishment is preserved by the fact that the good we love in a disordered way becomes a source of our affliction, and this constitutes "the pain of the senses" (*poena sensus*).[85] Our own sins form the matter we are punished with.[86] It is fitting that the created goods which we idolize "rebel" against our idolatry by simply being what they are (with their own finite being and essence), and as a result they are "disobedient" to our disordered will, "refusing" (so to speak) to be an accomplice to our attempts to impose our disordered will on the world.[87]

In Lewis's narrative, we see that each of the characters is positively tormented or disappointed by the good they prefer to the divine good. The Entrepreneur unnecessarily goes through tremendous toil, agony, and fear to try to carry back one real fruit to the Valley of the Shadow of Death, and all to no avail since it will not fit down there.[88] The Vain Lady who is so concerned about her appearance that she does not walk with everyone else is unnecessarily afflicted by her appearance.[89] The Oppressive Wife who insists that her holy husband absolutely needs her and is incapable of doing anything on his own is haunted by the fact that she can no longer control him and take pride in being his apparent savior.[90] The Husband who wants to be missed, needed, or pitied by his holy wife cannot bear the idea that she does not absolutely need him or does not suffer to see him suffering.[91] The Employer who insists that he

---

84. Lewis, *Great Divorce*, 77.
85. Aquinas, *ST* I–II, q.87, a.4; *SCG* 4.90.
86. Aquinas, *ST* I–II, q.85, a.5, r.3; *ST* II–II, q.99, a.4; *John* 2.2.
87. Aquinas, *ST* I, q.96, a.1; *ST* I–II, q.17, a.9, r.3; *ST* II–II, q.99, a.4; q.153, a.2, r.2; *SCG* 3.145; *SCG* 4.90.
88. Lewis, *Great Divorce*, 20–21, 47–49.
89. Lewis, *Great Divorce*, 60–62.
90. Lewis, *Great Divorce*, 94–95.
91. Lewis, *Great Divorce*, 121–33.

just wants his "rights" is tormented by this desire in a twofold manner: first, it leads him to interpret all talk about his need for charity, mercy, and gift as an insult to his dignity; and second, what he *is* getting is what he deserves (his rights).[92] Ironically, if he could only forget about his rights for a moment, he could begin to attain the happiness he is longing for. Those who traveled for years and counted on being thrilled to meet famous historical figures are disappointed by them.[93] Finally, Napoleon's obsession with military victory leads him to endlessly pace up and down blaming people for the loss.[94]

It was mentioned above that Aquinas believes there is a particular stain that is an effect of sin. We can add here that he believes these stains are diversified and customized by the particular sin (or creature) that causes it.[95] The disordered love in the will for this object is nothing other than the person's proportion, aptitude, or co-naturality for union with this particular thing.[96] Just as there is the love of a good which perfects and elevates the person by adapting him to the beloved, there is a "love of a good which is unsuitable to the lover, [and which] wounds and worsens him."[97] In each of the unrepentant we see them in the grip of a particular ideology, a particular pattern of thinking driven by a disordered desire, and it renders them unable to appreciate, seek after, and take rest in other goods. Despite all the ghosts being "unsubstantial," in Lewis's story "they differed from one another as smokes differ."[98]

Lewis does not present as examples of the damned anyone whose character or actions would make them candidates for such a punishment according to the secular or worldly vision. The only murderer mentioned is one who has repented and is saved.[99] Why does Lewis focus on people who apparently want to contribute to the economy, the academy, their marriage, or their children? In nearly all cases, the problem with these characters is that they have confused the means for the end; means which are otherwise perfectly fine in themselves, but have become dislocated

---

92. Lewis, *Great Divorce*, 26–30.
93. Lewis, *Great Divorce*, 11–12, 53.
94. Lewis, *Great Divorce*, 12.
95. Aquinas, *ST* I–II, q.86, a.1, r.3.
96. Aquinas, *ST* I–II, q.25, a.2; q.26, a.2; q.27, a.1, a.3, a.4; q.28, a.5; q.29, a.1, a.2; q.30, a.2; q.32, a.4, r.3.
97. Aquinas, *ST* I–II, q.28, a.5.
98. Lewis, *Great Divorce*, 106.
99. Lewis, *Great Divorce*, 26–31.

from their proper place in human life.[100] At the same time, they consider God (if at all) only as a means to serve their private end.[101] The protagonist's guide says: "There is but one good; that is God. Everything else is good when it looks to Him and bad when it turns from Him. And the higher and mightier it is in the natural order, the more demoniac it will be if it rebels."[102] In other words, the greater the natural good, the more it has a natural ontological likeness to the divine. However, this does not mean that pursuing or attaining such a good necessarily means moving towards the Divine himself. In fact, they could provide the motivation for greater sins. Sins which involve the disordered pursuit of more base goods, particularly if caused by weakness in the moment, tend to leave those who commit them with a sense of shame and depravity, and a corresponding sense of needing the mercy of God.[103] It is when we make idols out of the highest natural goods, that we encounter the sins that are the most difficult to recognize and repent of. Did not Christ himself say that it was the tax collectors and prostitutes who were entering the kingdom at hearing his preaching, and not those who trusted in their own righteousness (Matt 21:31)? Christ himself explicitly singles out the possibility of religious rituals, family relations, the pursuit of world peace, annihilating poverty, and even our own health, as obstacles to the kingdom.[104] Jesus knows that these highest of natural goods, those which appear to be what make up a "decent" life by the world's standards, are those that, if idolized, pose the greatest snare. Yet, from the perspective of the eschaton, while these might be greater temporal goods than mere pleasure, they are still temporal goods, and insofar as they are contrasted to the kingdom, or not ordered towards it, they become snares. These too will pass away and can be found purified and restored only by God's gift in the new heavens and the new earth.

Punishment Lasts as Long as the Sin

Finally, in Aquinas's account, the proportion between sin and its punishment is preserved in the sense that punishment, which is an effect of sin, remains only as long as the sin or disturbance of the order

---

100. Lewis, *Great Divorce*, 73.

101. Lewis, *Great Divorce*, 99.

102. Lewis, *Great Divorce*, 106. This is a frequent theme throughout Lewis's *Four Loves*.

103. Lewis, *Great Divorce*, 72.

104. For example, health (see Matt 5:29–30; 10:28), family (Matt 8:21–22; Luke 14:26), world peace (Matt 10:34), and annihilating poverty (John 12:8).

does.[105] This principle can be seen as ultimately flowing from the first two: one *keeps* losing the good they are sinning against, and one *keeps* being tormented by the good one clings to in a disordered way. In *The Great Divorce*, the characters are continually punished because they are continually sinning. It is not that they once committed a certain sin of which they've repented, and yet they continue to be punished for it. Rather, they continually deploy their free will in affirming the sin, despite pleas to the contrary. "There is always something they insist on keeping even at the price of misery. There is always something they prefer to joy—that is, to reality."[106]

In spite of being sorry for (or lamenting) the shame, confusion, and other evils of punishment which they are experiencing (which itself bears witness to the goodness of their nature), in unrepentant sinners this does not translate into repentance for the evil of fault specifically.[107] Even though they may see the causal connection between their choices and the state or circumstances under which they suffer, they do not repent of the act's sinfulness, but simply regret the disadvantage it has brought them.[108] In the Valley of the Shadow of Death, the lost rationalize their situation: "One will say he has always served his country right or wrong; and another that he has sacrificed everything to his Art; and some that they've never been taken in, and some that, thank God, they've always looked after Number One, and nearly all, that, at least they've been true to themselves."[109] This refusal to repent, even in spite of the extent of one's suffering, only manifests the evil of the will.

CONCLUSION

In this chapter we have seen that one major obstacle to the acceptance and understanding of the Catholic teaching on the eschaton is the element of punishment it contains. This is at least partly due to factors such as the therapeutic mindset which permeates contemporary secular liberal culture. Yet the doctrine and nature of punishment flows from an appreciation of the nature of evil and justice, both of which presuppose that there is a real order of reality that is not the arbitrary will of any creature. In this way we see that when a person acts in a disordered

---

105. Aquinas, *ST* I–II, q.87, a.3.
106. Lewis, *Great Divorce*, 71.
107. Aquinas, *ST* I, q.64, a.3, r.3; *ST* I–II, q.73, a.5, r.3.
108. Aquinas, *ST* I–II, q.78, a.2, r.3.
109. Lewis, *Great Divorce*, 70.

way, they justly incur a punishment from their own nature, others, and God, and this specifically consists in losing the good one sins against, being afflicted by the good one loves in a disordered way, and finally, the persistence of this punishment as long as the disorder lasts. We have seen that C. S. Lewis's novella *The Great Divorce* is able to capture in a narrative form the classical theological reasoning on this matter. Rather than the reality of eschatological punishment leading a person to question God's goodness, it ought first and foremost to raise awareness of how deeply horrific sin is. The example of concrete characters with their own attitudes, words, and actions helps to bring this home to the reader.

If the twentieth century was marked by the so-called demythologizing project, then the twenty-first century would do well to be marked by what might be called a remythologizing, that is, a popular and academic rediscovery and re-presentation of works like *The Great Divorce* as effectively communicating profound eschatological truths.

BIBLIOGRAPHY

Aquinas, Thomas. *Commentary on Aristotle's "Nicomachean Ethics."* Translated by C. I. Litzinger. South Bend, IN: Dumb Ox, 1993.

———. *Commentary on the Book of Job.* Translated by Brian Thomas Becket Mullady. Lander, WY: Aquinas Institute for the Study of Sacred Doctrine, 2016.

———. *Commentary on the Gospel of John.* Translated by Fabian R. Larcher. Lander, WY: Aquinas Institute for the Study of Sacred Doctrine, 2013.

———. *Commentary on the Gospel of Matthew.* Translated by Jeremy Holmes. Lander, WY: Aquinas Institute for the Study of Sacred Doctrine, 2013.

———. *Commentary on the Letters of Saint Paul to the Galatians and Ephesians.* Translated by Fabian R. Larcher. Lander, WY: Aquinas Institute for the Study of Sacred Doctrine, 2024.

———. *Commentary on the Letters of Saint Paul to the Philippians, Colossians, Thessalonians, Timothy, Titus, and Philemon.* Translated by Fabian R. Larcher. Lander, WY: Aquinas Institute for the Study of Sacred Doctrine, 2012.

———. *Commentary on the Letter of Saint Paul to the Romans.* Translated by Fabian R. Larcher. Lander, WY: Aquinas Institute for the Study of Sacred Doctrine, 2024.

———. *Summa Contra Gentiles.* Translated by Anton C. Pegis et al. Notre Dame, IN: University of Notre Dame Press, 1975.

———. *Summa Theologica.* Translated by Fathers of the English Dominican Province. New York: Benziger Brothers, 1948.

Grisez, Germain. *Beyond the New Morality: The Responsibilities of Freedom.* 3rd ed. Notre Dame, IN: University of Notre Dame Press, 1988.

Lewis, C. S. *Essay Collection: Faith, Christianity and the Church.* London: HarperCollins, 2000.

———. *The Four Loves.* New York: Harcourt, 1988.

———. *The Great Divorce.* London: HarperCollins, 1946.

———. *Mere Christianity*. London: HarperCollins, 2001.
———. *The Problem of Pain*. New York: Macmillan, 1947.
———. *Undeceptions: Essays on Theology and Ethics*. London: Bles, 1971.
Rieff, Philip. *The Triumph of the Therapeutic: Uses of Faith After Freud*. New York: Harper & Row, 1966.
Sartre, Jean Paul. *"No Exit" and Three Other Plays*. Translated by L. Abel. New York: Vintage, 1976.
Taylor, Charles. *Sources of the Self: The Making of the Modern Identity*. Cambridge, MA: Harvard University Press, 1989.
Trueman, Carl R. *The Rise and Triumph of the Modern Self: Cultural Amnesia, Expressive Individualism, and the Road to Sexual Revolution*. Wheaton, IL: Crossway, 2020.

10

Cosmos and *Contrapasso*
Subject, Sin, and Suffering in Dante's *Inferno*

DANIJEL UREMOVIĆ

INTRODUCTION

Though all "books have their fate," they do so "according to the mind of the reader."[1] The fate of Dante Alighieri's *Commedia*—too often to be read (or at least remembered) only as far as its first *cantica*, the *Inferno*—is hardly an exception.[2] Yet, as regrettable as such a fate may be, its necessary ties to the particular ideas, convictions, and presuppositions of a modern readership shed light upon what the "final things" actually mean to the world today.

The bizarre tortures of the *Inferno*, poetically fitted to the crimes of various historical and mythical figures, even to the modern secular mind, often appear as the most captivating and memorable features of the *Comedy*. That any of the three canticles should today draw new readers from outside the world that formed the poet and his work is something of a marvel—that the dark circles of hell should prove the most popular among the *cantiche*, even more so. Though a manifestly Christian worldview and the burden of its belief in the afterlife might give the *Commedia* every reason to be met today only with indifference, its regular appearance in new translations and editions witnesses instead to its enduring influence and appeal. While it may point to the brilliance of

---

1. Terentianus Maurus, "De litteris," line 1286: "Pro captu lectoris habent sua fata libelli."

2. Citations from *Commedia* here refer to the parallel edition prepared by Robin Kirkpatrick, whose translation, introductions, commentary, and notes provide an invaluable aid for understanding Dante's vision.

the poet or the courage of his readers, this warm welcome by even secular modernity more often points to the separation of Dante's verse from his vision: hell—in this view—as the relic of an age finally given over to more rational and discerning views of reality, can finally be approached not as an object of superstitious fear, but more freely and soberly according to the potent imagery that even now is able to paint a convincing picture of modern man, his world, and his struggles.[3]

The danger only increases when this popular approach seeps into the Catholic imagination. Here, even for the completionists who might retain their copies of the *Purgatorio* and *Paradiso*, the scenes of the *Inferno* can all too easily be viewed simply in terms of their externally dealt punishments, in a state that is more maturely viewed under the aspect of *chaos* or *absence* and with no real connection to the remaining states that follow death, nor to the God that sustains them. Catholic eschatology, if its approach mirrors anything of the popular approach to Dante, can remain equally fixated on the purely punitive or "chaotic" aspects of hell, even if for ostensibly different reasons.[4]

Our task here will be to show, against such interpretations, how hell, for Dante, is a manifestation not simply of God's justice and might, but equally of his goodness and love. Beyond the tortures that might frighten believers or excite sceptics, the brilliance of Dante's *Inferno*, we will suggest, comes from its essentially positive presentation of the sacred order that reaches even as far as the eternally condemned. A sketch of the metaphysics underpinning the *Inferno* and a tour through three of its circles will reveal how one can perhaps better understand hell as

---

3. E.g., Kopić, *Prekogroblje po Danteu*, 5; referencing Osip Emilyevich Mandelstam, *Razgovor o Dante*.

4. Kirkpatrick notes a similar problem in the reception of Dante's great work. He explains that "Italians even now tend to warn readers away from this *cantica* [the *Paradiso*] on the grounds that the passions and excitements of the *Inferno* have dwindled here to an endless sequence of doctrinal debates. No unprejudiced reader is likely to arrive at the same conclusion. . . . This translation attempts to reveal something of how exhilarating the *cantica* can be if one abandons the presumption that the only proper subject for literature is darkness and disaster. Dante . . . would not have written the *Inferno* and *Purgatorio* if he had not known from the first the extent to which intelligence is fulfilled in the perception and propagation of the good" (Kirkpatrick, introduction, lxxiii). See also Romano Guardini's assessment: "The romantic evaluation has also contributed to the false interpretation, which appreciates the *Inferno* above all, hesitantly allows the *Purgatorio* to pass, and feels that there is nothing to be done with the *Paradiso*" ("*Divina Commedia*," 494). Again, Mary Taylor, citing similar attitudes, notes how the *Paradiso*, as "the least read of the three canticles," may seem to many "as less concrete than the others . . . and less interesting—even boring" (even if, for her, it is "the most beautiful") ("Sparkling of Holy Ghost," 521).

the superabundant presence of a loving God (rather than his definitive absence and withdrawal from the creature), and eternal suffering as the logical outworking and expression of individual character (rather than a divine "settling of scores").

By shedding some light on this universal order (*cosmos*) and the correlation of punishment and crime (*contrapasso*), we hope to encourage the reader of the *Inferno* to persevere in his journey with Dante, that under the light of the *Paradiso*, he may better appreciate the *theo*-centric order of which hell is but a part. Only from these heavenly heights can hell ever be properly counted as part of a *comedy*—that is, as part of the epic triumph of good over evil.

THE ORDER OF HELL AND ITS ONTOLOGICAL GROUNDING

"Dante," writes Friedrich Nietzsche, "committed a crude blunder when, with a terror-inspiring ingenuity, he placed above the gateway of his hell the inscription, 'I too was created by eternal love.'"[5] For Christians and nonbelievers alike, these words articulate a legitimate concern raised by the simultaneous belief in a benevolent God and an eternal hell. Nevertheless, for Dante, the notion of love as something coextensive with creation[6] means that even hell falls within a divine arrangement characterized by truth, goodness, and beauty, and not an abstracted form of justice.

Even in its apparent lawlessness, Dante's stratified vision of hell and its extravagant tortures reveal an understanding of the order that underlies any creaturely opposition to it: "When No is said to God, the louder Yes resounds!"[7] Placing the ultimate priority on God as the ground of all being, Dante appreciates the analogy that obtains between the goodness, truth, and beauty of God, and that of his creation—hell included.[8] For this reason also, hell, "as old as the world," has inscribed on its gates the triple name of God: "Divine Power, Highest Wisdom," but also "First Love."[9] As a work of divine art, it remains a reality

---

5. Nietzsche, *Genealogy of Morals*, 28.

6. See Taylor, "Sparkling of Holy Ghost," 540–42.

7. Balthasar, *Studies in Theological Styles*, 83.

8. Taylor, "Sparkling of Holy Ghost," 536, 539–40; Balthasar, *Studies in Theological Styles*, 105; Mazzeo, "Analogy of Creation."

9. Balthasar, *Studies in Theological Styles*, 38; citing Hugo Friedrich. Even with justice set above all three, it is a *giustizia orribil arte*.

ontologically dependent on God, so that even the crudest images of the *Inferno* rely on sacred types to make their point.[10] Be it the hellish renditions of the *Vexilla Regis*,[11] or the parodic inversion of the Trinity at hell's icy core,[12] the *disorder* of the underworld is ultimately seen to be parasitic on the intrinsic *order* of reality. The same notion stands behind the poet's ongoing reference to love as a principle of motion;[13] his use of language and its abuse as markers for order and chaos, respectively;[14] and, of course, the inverted hierarchy of hell's circles. "The laws of the abyss," despite the dark shadow cast upon it, never fully "break down."[15] Bearing these marks of the divine, hell, for the poet, falls under the same theological order as the entirety of creation.

The reach of this metaphysical continuity is, however, complicated by several features of Dante's work. The force with which the Christian

---

10. *Inf.* 1.100, 1.103–1.105; 14.6; 21.16.

11. *Inf.* 34.1. See also the hymn "Vexilla Regis Prodeunt," in Catholic Church, *Breviarium Romanum* 2:850–51, 864. The pre-Urban text can be found in the supplement Nova et Vetera, *Hymni Antiqui*, 4.

12. *Inf.* 34.37.

13. A principle of motion that, importantly, begins in heaven (as the "love that moves the sun and other stars" [*Par.* 33.145]) and runs throughout creation (*Par.* 29.10–29.18; see Taylor, "Sparkling of Holy Ghost," 546n97, 547n101), even to the depths of hell, where chaotic movement of the shades is ultimately guided by a *perverted* love (see our examples below). Though a category foreign to modern cosmologies, "love," for Dante, stood as the marker of an "intentional"—that is, teleological—cosmic order. See Balthasar, *Studies in Theological Styles*, 42, 86, 90–91; Guardini, "*Divina Commedia*," 331–36, esp. 332.

14. While language and communication may fall apart in the *Inferno*, the basic structure and possibility of speech always remain. In this way, while language—as a window into reality—can be twisted, confused, or misguided, it is never abandoned entirely. Thus, even the disorder of hell's soliloquous ranting, as the perversion of language, is in truth the perversion of an enduring love, motion, and order. See Balthasar, *Studies in Theological Styles*, 85–86; Robin Kirkpatrick's notes in *Inf.* 367; Taylor, "Sparkling of Holy Ghost," 530–36; Lombardi, *Syntax of Desire*, 134–40.

15. *Purg.* 1.46. See Balthasar's comments on this "edifice of the 'eternal law'" (*Studies in Theological Styles*, 82). Concerning the image of light throughout the *Commedia*, see Guardini, *Studi danteschi*, 259–60. Robin Kirkpatrick, in his introduction to *Par.*, explains Dante's own distinction between the terms *luce* or *lume*, *raggio*, and *splendore*. Though in the *Inferno*, *luce* and *lume* appear most often in reference to a light beyond hell (in a former earthly existence or in the foregone glory of heaven), they do on occasion denote a light (however dim) within their realm (e.g., *Inf.* 3.73–3.75; 3.133–3.135; 4.103–4.105, and [the Italian text of] 29.37–29.39) (lxx–lxxi). Beyond these specific terms, however, Guardini notes the *light* of the burning walls around hell, the flaming rain falling on pimps, and the fiery pits of the simonists and liars, so that even in the darkness of hell, it is again the "misuse" or "perversion" of light, and not its total absence, that "darkens" hell.

difference is seen to touch upon Dante's hell can admittedly seem limited. The otherworldly backdrop of all the *cantiche*, the noted inscription at hell's entry, and even its very topography shaped by the crucifixion, still, for the likes of Balthasar, fail to provide a properly christological and Trinitarian form to the *Inferno*.[16] Moreover, its apparently reductive sense of love (i.e., as mere form, punitive justice) as well as the absence of any true "motion" (of which this love is the principle) ultimately suggest, for the Basel theologian, an analogical or even equivocal tie between hell and divine goodness.[17]

The poet's purposes, it must be admitted, do remain obscured at times by various features of the text that weave together the secular with the sacred, and markers of order with those of chaos. For this reason, however, the *Comedy*'s characterization as "the narrative of an intellectual and spiritual struggle"[18] perhaps best accounts for the interplay of motion and stagnation, the clarity of faith and an all-too-human pity for the condemned,[19] the triumph of truth and the continued striving of sinful self-delusion. The allowance for both shadows and highlights in the *Inferno* need not be taken as implicating the "equivocity" of Dante's hell. Rather, art's cataphatic fallback can quite naturally enable the free use of these varied tones to bring out here God's objective order, here the creature's resistance to it. Even if one determines that Dante's picture of hell lacks the full definition offered by Christian revelation alone, the underlying primacy of truth, order, goodness, and love nevertheless holds true, and is itself what allows for the occasional space that doubt or delusion are seemingly granted in order to lay bare the inner struggle of the poet or those he encounters along the way.

It is perhaps with the lifting of this veil in the *Purgatorio* that this first play of imagery becomes apparent. On Mount Purgatory, hell's "exile . . . is transformed into the condition of pilgrimage, of a quest for distant truth."[20] While a basic pattern of *contrapasso* might be identified as the

16. See Guardini's comments in "*Divina Commedia*," 493–97.

17. See, however, Kirkpatrick, introduction, xlix. References to Scripture outnumber those to classical literature.

18. Kirkpatrick, introduction, xv.

19. As, for example, in canto 5, discussed below. See Guardini's comments in this regard in *Studi danteschi*, 353. That Dante himself moves between these moments of pity and more sober judgment, while also presenting his own moral and intellectual limits, is not to be neglected. In these, the "pilgrimage" character of the poem is deepened and comes to bear directly upon the text's presentation of truth and falsehood in hell.

20. Kirkpatrick, introduction, xv.

common form of both hell and purgatory, the presence of hope marks a fundamental difference in the final meaning of justice in the first and second *cantiche*. It is on the basis of this hope that the ethical schema of the *Inferno* gives way to a markedly Christian ascent through the terraces of the capital sins.[21] As such, it is upon this hope that communion is able to be restored and perfected, so that hell's confused ranting now opens up to genuine and intelligible exchange, and the shared lot of sinners in fruitless suffering is traded for a common striving towards authentic freedom.

That which in the *Inferno* appeared as the total breakdown of order, communion, and meaning is thus quickly recovered by Dante in the *Purgatorio*. In both the *Inferno* and the *Purgatorio*, however, a singular law ultimately governs, so that the perfection or failure of language, motion, and all other markers of divine order is hinged upon the sinner's Yes or No. The triumph of this divine order, even against the sinner's protest, itself rules out any "equivocal" reading of Dante's hell. Guardini's explanation and interpretation of this order in the *Comedy* is worth recalling in its connection to the problem we noted at the outset: "Modernity says: the world is material. . . . And yet, it is not so, for in the world there is a divine planning. To see it as chaos is the result of the refusal to understand reality." His aetiology is as follows: "The Middle Ages still had alive in their memory the terrible experience of that centuries-old chaos, consequent of the collapse of the ancient world and the absurd destruction of the migration of peoples." In consequence, it "could not bear the sick luxury of chaotic pleasure," so that all within the *Commedia* is ultimately a "constructing from above":[22] a recognition of divine goodness that reaches even as far as hell. It is, however, at the intersection of character, act, and suffering in the portraits of the damned that Dante brings this grand metaphysical picture into sharper focus.

---

21. On this point, Kirkpatrick identifies an important difference between the ordering of hell and purgatory that is frequently overlooked. The capital sins, probably the most obvious candidate for a Christian ethical schema by which to organize the condemned, are instead a division reserved for the *Purgatorio*, with the *Inferno*, by contrast, being organized around the rational order of reality and sins against it. While order is thus present in both these *cantiche*, it is hope (through the liberating recognition of sin as such) that finally enables an ascent, even if the suffering of both appears to follow a materially identical pattern of the punishment fitting the crime (Kirkpatrick, introduction, lxxvii). See also *Purg*. xiv. Concerning the "pilgrim" character of the poem, see Guardini, "Divina Commedia," 302–8, esp. 306: "There is no continuity of passage from one sphere of value to the other, only a jump, a surrender, a risk."

22. Guardini, "Divina Commedia," 482.

CRIME AND PUNISHMENT

Though mentioned only once by Dante, *contrapasso* provides the basic pattern of punishment that runs throughout his *Inferno*.[23] While contrary to his intention, as we will suggest, it may appear to propose a strictly extrinsic or voluntaristic origin to hell's punishments.[24] In this view, the suffering of the condemned has its cause outside of the sinner and within the will of God. There remains, it would seem, no genuine causal connection between crime and punishment beyond the punitive: as a creative display of divine omnipotence, punishment is dealt to the sinner from without.

A closer reading of the text, however, reveals a stronger formal tie between the sin and suffering of the *Inferno*. Rather than a poetic "payback" from on high, Dante's *contrapasso* serves a view of eternal punishment as the logical outworking of sin, the natural expression of a person's character as (de)formed by their actions.

In its simplest formulation, *contrapasso* holds that the punishment accords with the crime. Neither the externalist nor the internalist picture is excluded from this definition, though such turns of phrase as the *vendetta di Dio* may well appear to favor the former.[25] These expressions, however, are perhaps best read again from within the poet's internal struggle, for which reason, it would seem, the *Inferno* can freely move about in the chiaroscuro of chaos and order, lucidity and delusion, indeed, between human understanding and divine truth. The precise case of Dante's meaning is, quite naturally, to be determined from his text; and the merit of his vision (whatever it is shown to be), against the enduring questions of Catholic eschatology.

The version of *contrapasso* that we will suggest most properly represents the poet's understanding of sin, however, might be better expressed in the view that *the sin is the punishment itself*. Balthasar, commenting on this theme, notes how *contrapasso*

---

23. *Inf.* 28.142.

24. As the reductive sense of a *poena talionis* might be seen to require. See Kopić, *Prekogroblje po Danteu*, 13. Etymologically, *contrapasso* (*contra* and *patior*) denotes a "suffering from the opposite," which Kopić states can appear as an analogous, contrary, or analogous *and* contrary punishment. Nevertheless, while its most basic meaning lies in this sense of proportionality, *contrapasso* need not exclude an internalist interpretation of sin and its "sentence." See Kirkpatrick, introduction, lxxx–lxxxii. See also Balthasar, *Studies in Theological Styles*, 91.

25. *Inf.* 14.16–14.18; 24.118–24.120. See also *Purg.* 33.34–33.36.

so lays hold of the sinner from within that the punishment becomes the complete expression of his guilt. In fact, content and form are so intertwined that the sinner himself presses toward the place of his punishment and eagerly embraces its particular form.[26]

For this reason, the discrepancy between the states of the damned, those undergoing purification, and those in heavenly glory is, for Guardini, a variance most properly in the appropriation of values: "In hell, we encounter values in so far as they are negated"; in purgatory, these values "appear at the same time *in modo conversionis* or *in statu nascendi*,"[27] being "approved in intention but as yet unrealized in action"; and in paradise, as "completely accepted and immersed in a loving communion with the holy God."[28]

Thus, what we see in the poet's encounters with the condemned runs far deeper than divine retribution. In the residents of hell, we instead discover the intersection of individual character (formed by free decision) and suffering. Here, to speak even of an *internal cause* of infernal punishment might prove still too sharp a distinction. Balthasar's unity of "content and form" appreciates the heart of the matter: it is not simply that the individual is responsible for the punishment that might follow death; rather, he opts for such disfiguration, harm, and unhappiness by the very acts that bring these about. There exists, as it were, a certain concomitance of act, character, and its experienced effect. Any of the *Inferno*'s scenes might serve to make the point. Here, however, a glance at the lustful, the blasphemers, and the thieves will suffice to illustrate Dante's understanding of *contrapasso* along these lines.

I. Lust

In canto 5 of the *Inferno*, Dante encounters the souls of those given over to lust. Now thrown about on the winds of a violent storm, their punishment recalls the storm of passion that governed their lives on earth.[29] An initial reading may well suggest an externalist view of sin and punishment, inasmuch as the force of the storm seems to be an exterior power acting upon the condemned. Nevertheless, Dante's description of

---

26. Balthasar, *Studies in Theological Styles*, 86; citing *Inf.* 5:7–5.8.
27. That is, as transformed or emergent values.
28. Guardini, "*Divina Commedia*," 214.
29. *Inf.* 5.31–5.48.

and conversation with these figures suggest a closer link between their crime and its punishment.

When first seeking the attention of "those two who go conjoined," referring to Francesca da Rimini and Paolo Malatesta, Dante is told to "invoke the love that draws them on."[30] Though they "look so light upon the wind" the principle of motion suggested by Virgil is in fact the interior drive of their passions.[31] Having called upon such a love, "the wind . . . swept them nearer," revealing the interior nature of the habit by which these souls move about.[32] Dante likewise makes a point of the freedom behind these movements: "Come, if none forbids," he cries, and "by their own steady will" do they come.[33]

While the poet is clear about the proximity of punishment to sin, there nevertheless remains a question as to how such a force—if it is truly *interior*—could continue to exercise such influence upon these souls. Herein lies a secondary feature of all hell's tortures. While the souls of the lustful clearly detest their current misfortunes, they nevertheless remain the product of their free election. The choice for sin, aside from its entailed choice for self-inflicted suffering, has the further implication of a choice *against* reality, such that in choosing to sin, they first renounce the truth. Forgoing the truth about God, the sinner then plays the victim, as though Francesca's was the "generous heart,"[34] and all could be resolved *if only* "the Sovereign of the universe were still our friend."[35] There is no truthful admission of culpability, only the confused attempts at self-justification. From here follows the surrender of the related human truth: "love," in its most hellish construal, masks the reality of Francesca and Paolo's actions, such that they freely continue down the path of self-delusion.[36] Convinced of their innocence, they are eternally set upon the course they chose while still living. Such is the isolating effect of sin that the only momentary relief these souls seem to find is in their brief exchange with the poet—a short-lived moment of the communion and transcendence that their eternally ratified decisions now otherwise exclude.[37]

30. *Inf.* 5.77–5.78.

31. Further suggested by their representation "as doves . . . called by their desires" (*Quali colombe dal disio chiamate*) (*Inf.* 5.82).

32. *Inf.* 5.79.

33. *Inf.* 5.81–5.84.

34. *Inf.* 5.100.

35. *Inf.* 5.91–5.92.

36. One of the most striking features of the canto is its shamelessly equivocal use of the word "love" (*amore*). On this theme, see Robin Kirkpatrick, in *Inf.* 333–35.

37. "Whatever you may please to hear or say, / we, as we hear, we, as we speak,

II. Blasphemy

Like the lustful, the blasphemer shades (i.e., souls) of canto 14 are presented by Dante as the products of their own choosing. Alongside the usurers (who charge for an empty product) and the sodomites (whose acts are equally empty on account of their fruitlessness), the blasphemers have their empty words matched to the backdrop of a barren desertscape.[38] There, fire unceasingly rains down upon them as they crawl or lay supine upon the sand.[39]

The clearest correlation of sin and punishment is given here by one such blasphemer. Introducing himself to his guests, Capaneus plainly states that what he, "once living, was," is "so [now] dead."[40] The irony, however, lies in the difference between his own perception of reality, and the actual truth of the matter. Far from dying a "hero,"[41] Capaneus remains the same isolate and lifeless blasphemer that he was on earth. His correlation of sin and suffering echoes the declaration of personal innocence that we encountered in the lustful, though to no avail. "This punishment, in consequence, is yours," retorts Virgil: "No agony, except your own great rage, would serve as proper answer to your ire."[42] Thus, it is not that God exacts recompense for one's crime in an eye-for-eye system of justice. It is rather that the immediate and interior consequences of blasphemy are their own punishment. The only difference is that now, in hell, these effects are fully exposed and secured for all eternity.

---

assent, / so long—as now they do—these winds stay silent" (*Inf.* 5.94–5.96). For Dante's understanding of community and individuality in hell, see Belliotti, *Dante's Deadly Sins*, 300–302. See also Guardini: "There is no communion here, but anger, bitterness, envy, hate. . . . It is the same fate that binds them into groups, so that this order is not rooted in feeling, even less in love. The men are chaotically disconnected one from another. What holds them in order is the coercion of the sentence, which has passed into their psychophysical existence and finds its expression in the conditions of the surrounding context. But it has not passed into their will, and so acts only as an external constraint causing them suffering. They are in themselves separated . . . against God's will for them, against their authenticity" ("*Divina Commedia*," 265–66). Compare this to the thieves, discussed below, in whom this rupture of true communion is especially evident.

38. The common theme uniting these diverse sinners is the sterility of their actions. In their financial, sexual, and verbal exchanges, these souls dealt ultimately in the empty and fruitless. As usury charges for what does not exist, and as no life comes from the act of sodomy, so too are the words of the blasphemer vain, barren, and false.

39. *Inf.* 14.13–14.30.
40. *Inf.* 14.51.
41. *Inf.* 14.46.
42. *Inf.* 14.64–14.66.

Again, blasphemy entails the further effects of self-isolation and the perversion of truth that we earlier suggested to be a proper characteristic of all hell's circles. In his mind, Capaneus remains the victor: "No sweet revenge he'd have on me!" he tells himself.[43] As his earthly blasphemy was confused and unintelligent, even now his words lack clarity and direction.[44] Though we noted the use and abuse of language to be a common theme in the *Commedia* (as among the various markers of a sacred order and one's departure from it), the case of blasphemy draws special attention to it. The divine gift of intellect is realized in a special way through the power of speech *soli homini datum*.[45] By virtue of its object, blasphemy proves the greatest misuse of this gift. And as far as sin directs its injury not merely to its object, but also to its very subject, this attack on the divine order necessarily affects the one who speaks. Locked into his own sin, his exchange with Dante is better characterized as a monologue, with any genuine communion between his interlocutor and God forgone.

III. Theft

As a final example, the punishment of thieves outlined in canto 25 points yet again to the convergence of subject, sin, and suffering. Here, the men who in a former life deprived others of their property now have their most basic possession—their own human form—continually taken away. Gruesome reptiles strike at the condemned, robbing them of their proper bodily form and claiming it for themselves, only to have this "exchange" repeated shortly after, to their loss.

The law of this circle—supply and demand—from the view of those lacking their human form, can appear finally to suggest a strictly external origin of divine retribution: having deprived others, these sinners are now themselves to be deprived. Likewise, the serpents that bind the hands of these thieves seem an equally reactive answer to the offense against property. If the act itself effects and sustains the punishment (according

---

43. *Inf.* 14.60.

44. Virgil's response to Capaneus is critical here. In answer to the confused ramblings of the blasphemer, Rome's poet presents a clear and truthful account of the king's perdition, finally offering something intelligible to the conversation. Dante's use of language as a marker for truth and order is particularly prominent here, given that the blasphemer is the preeminent offender through language against the truth, having that highest Truth as the object of his speech (*Inf.* 14.61–14.72).

45. Dante Alighieri, *De Vulgari Eloquentia* 1.2.1; cited in Imbach, *Potret pjesnika kao filozofa*, 31.

to the view of *contrapasso* given thus far), could this be anything other than a divine imposition upon the sinner? Yet this limited supply and insatiable demand is not merely the law of the marketplace—it is the law of appetite, and thus the immediate expression of one's person. Dante's play on number ("neither two nor one," etc.) highlights the boundary between property and possessor obscured by theft.[46] This focus not on material but spiritual values becomes apparent in light of the medieval understanding of property, recalled by Guardini: "In those distant times, the order of property seems to have originally been a sacred order,"[47] so that "theft, in its original sense, was the removal of things that were closely tied to the personal 'I': clothing, weapons, ornaments. . . . These forms of property constituted an extension of the person," being, as it were "saturated with . . . [the] spiritual energy" of the owner.[48] This order reveals "not a material mode of thought, but rather the opposite: a spiritualization . . . of those things that were, in the strict sense of the term, property."[49]

In the final balance then are counted not goods taken or owed, but that which was most fundamentally "lost," the gift of self. For man, "a microcosm, which contains in itself all nature"—"the mineral, vegetative, animal, and even angelic"—the act of theft represents a surrender of those highest powers, which in their right function would otherwise accord with the spiritual order of human property.[50] "What is a mode of thought and ethical behavior in the thief," in whom "mine and thine" thus "disappear," "has, in the serpent, attained its objective form."[51]

The rule of this interior law is likewise visible when considering the sinners in their transitional serpent form. Here, the condemned, in their continued act of thievery, perpetuate the cycle by which they, in turn, will suffer loss. While sin's effects are rightly shown to dehumanize and depersonalize, one cannot utterly forget the true subject beneath the reptilian form that is lined up to "inflict" the punishment: it is the fellow thief that binds and restricts the creeping hands of the co-condemned. As such, even communion can only attain as far as this parodic "exchange" and "participation" of thieves in their common *lot* (and *choice*). As with

---

46. *Inf.* 25.67.
47. Guardini, *Studi danteschi*, 405.
48. Guardini, *Studi danteschi*, 304.
49. Guardini, *Studi danteschi*, 304.
50. Guardini, *Studi danteschi*, 303. See also Guardini, "*Divina Commedia*," 219–20; Imbach, *Potret pjesnika kao filozofa*, 31.
51. Guardini, *Studi danteschi*, 409.

the other shades considered thus far, the sentence is dealt not from without, but freely from within.

THEOLOGICAL APPLICATIONS

While Dante remains, first and foremost, a poet, we have seen his presentation of hell to be far more than the product of poetic license or an untempered medieval imagination. His understanding of a cosmological order and the connection between sin and punishment are not without serious value for philosophical and theological reflection. Thus, while we cannot claim the poet to say more than he himself does, we may happily apply the key ideas and themes of his *Commedia* to some of the enduring questions of Catholic eschatology, moral theology, and anthropology.

Having examined this use of *cosmos* and *contrapasso*, our final section will propose three such applications of Dante's vision: first, for the metaphysical question of the relationship between a loving God and the creation of hell; second, for an internalist understanding of punishment as the natural consequence of sin; and third, for the formulation of a pastoral examination of sin grounded in sound anthropology.

I. The Metaphysical Question of Hell

Dante's dedication to a far-reaching, theocentric cosmology has drastic implications for our understanding of hell. His view of this realm as a work of love and beauty seems to require a qualification of the conventional designation of hell as "life without God" or his "absence." The problem is quickly apparent to the metaphysician: as long as God remains the ground of our being, a postmortem state characterized by his absence may well tend closer to an annihilationist view of hell than to anything markedly Catholic. As long as hell is real, it is so in a relationship of dependence upon God, by which it enjoys its claim to be a work, not only of justice, but also of beauty and love.

While hell has historically been discussed in terms of absence and chaos, we find an alternative model in Dante that instead takes up the categories of presence and order. Rather than regard hell's occupants as in a definitive separation from God, could it not be that they enjoy the superabundance of his glorious presence, such that even in the sinner's No to God, "the louder Yes" of the Creator's goodness yet "resounds"?[52] Of

---

52. Balthasar, *Studies in Theological Styles*, 83.

course, the aspect of absence—a legitimate formulation of the tradition—need not be forgone entirely. Here Dante and, say, the catechism, may simply mark the difference between the subjective experience of *separation* brought by hell's self-isolation and the objective reality of God's *presence* that endures over and above it.[53] Neither the "separation" noted by the catechism nor the stronger absence that one might equally ascribe to hell need be viewed as contradicting this notion, inasmuch as this choice for self-exclusion or the experience of absence remains on the part of the creature. Here one can draw the parallel with the (naturally, limited) human analogy, wherein strained personal relations can make confrontation notably more painful than avoidance. How much greater, then, would be the pain of the sinner before his Creator, from whom he cannot escape: *Si descendero in infernum, ades*.[54]

II. Crime as Punishment

The metaphysical connection between God and hell dovetails with the "internalist" view of sin and suffering found in the *Inferno*. If God remains the ground of all being (hell inclusive) then the common situation of saints and sinners in the presence of God leaves one hard-pressed to find any locus of guilt and suffering exterior to the person. Standing before their God and eternally convinced of their innocence, mortal sinners opt for a continual rejection of him in whom we, nevertheless, "live and move and have our being" (Acts 17:28).

Furthermore, recognizing the interior nature of punishment as the direct outworking of sin as contrary to human nature—thus, ultimately, as self-harm—one appreciates how it is by the personal decision of unrepentant sinners that individuals freely choose hell, in a way that, even in terms of punishment, cannot be so easily attributed to God as its proper cause. In a voluntarist understanding of God, there is perhaps little issue with the externalist picture. Yet, for the lengthier Catholic tradition, committed to a God of order, reason, and truth, the co-identification of sin and suffering found in *contrapasso* better presents both mankind as the cause of his own suffering and unhappiness, as well as the truth of the immutable God who wills that none "should perish" (2 Pet 3:9).[55]

---

53. See *CCC* 1035.

54. "Though I descend into hell, you are there" (Ps 138:7 Vulgate).

55. On some of the difficulties faced by the voluntarist-intellectualist divide, see Stump, "Dante's Hell"; Benedict XVI, "Faith, Reason and University."

III. Sin and Unhappiness: Anthropological Hamartiology

Finally, Dante's approximation of sin and punishment has further merit in its derivative anthropology and what it suggests about sin for those of us yet living. Thus, while first providing an account of sin's effects after death against a considered theodicy, it also works in the opposite direction to explain the deformation wrought by sin for the living.

Consider the case of lust, blasphemy, and theft explored above. The punishment that these souls undergo is not simply a description of their final state, but also of the person they were while living. Capaneus was not far off the mark: what the sinner will be in hell, he is already in his present state (only now without the hope of reform). Thus, those who blaspheme in this life isolate themselves, then and there, from the ground of their existence. Through the initial abuse of language aimed at God, the blasphemer in turn distorts all subsequent relations he enjoys with the created order, himself included. His words cause him to lay spiritually supine, powerless beneath the all-powerful God.

Likewise, lust has its parallel effects on the sinner while living. Though not by the winds of a physical storm, those so completely given over to their passions surrender something of their rationality and humanity while yet alive. No longer moving in accord with the dictates of divine law and reason, they move only along the path determined by the law of appetite. Consequently, their view of reality becomes so distorted as to cloud even their most basic assessments of truth and falsehood, right and wrong. One cannot but notice the similarities between Francesca's confused defense of love and our own contemporary abuse of the term: part of what is so pitiable about her speech is that it belongs to the same fallout with truth that underlies our modern crisis in human relationships.

As for the thieves, a similar disregard of a sacred order undermined not only the spiritual good of those to whom such possessions belonged, but even the spiritual good of him who claimed it. This descent into sin necessarily implies a descent into properly unhuman behavior, viewing the material order within the parameters of animal appetites. It is not without reason that the traditional qualification around theft ultimately depends on this personal, spiritual value of property: theft, properly speaking, denotes the unlawful gain of another's property, in defiance of their spiritual value. So much so, that "there is no theft . . . if refusal is contrary to reason and the universal destination of goods," as when "the only way to provide for immediate, essential needs . . . is to put at one's disposal and use the property of others."[56]

In these examples and beyond, Dante takes the classical account of virtue ethics and unveils its eternal significance. Our decisions in this life are thus never singular events, but over time serve to form (or deform) one's character.[57] The subsequent applications of this earthly *contrapasso* are numerous. What if, for instance, the designation of mortal sin as the loss of charity was seriously viewed as the foretaste of the decay to be realized eternally in hell, with such effects as those given by Dante hinting at a fragmentation of the person that begins even now?[58] What if even venial sin, rather than being the confessional's "free pass," was understood to contribute to the daily destruction of the person, even if without the immediate danger of damnation?[59] What if, in turn, one's "fundamental option" was instead seen as the ultimate reference point of *contrapasso*, gathering to itself all subsequent decisions for or against God as the formative influences of man's most basic disposition?[60]

The pastoral function of this anthropocentric hamartiology is also hopefully here apparent.[61] Far from confining one's examen to the fearful reflection on Boschian hellscapes, Dante's understanding of sin as its own punishment, and its entailed anthropology, should serve to highlight the positive truth about human action and the contribution it makes to one's flourishing and happiness. "I do not understand what I do" because sin blinds my sense of reality, as it did for Francesca, Paolo, Capaneus, and

56. CCC 2408.

57. On the "reflexive" effect of human action, see Wojtyła, "Person and Act," 199–204; and John Paul II, *Laborem Exercens* §§4–6.

58. CCC 1855–56, 1861.

59. CCC 1855, 1863. There is good reason, accordingly, for the practice of devotional confessions, which, though containing only venial offenses, nevertheless aid the work of human formation and the development of right habits and dispositions.

60. One interesting question raised by the *Inferno* concerns the placement of souls guilty of various offenses. Belliotti identifies the problem, resolving it with the suggestion that particular sins determine overall character. Thus, while a person may be given over to many vices, a particular fatal flaw accounts for subsequent ones, in a way concerned more with character and interior disposition than exacting justice for specific transgressions (*Dante's Deadly Sins*, 163). Consider, for example, Kirkpatrick's reference to Count Ugolino della Gherardesca, and his punishment, not as a cannibal, but as a traitor (Kirkpatrick, introduction, lxxvii).

61. In no negative or exclusive sense of the term. Naturally, for the Catholic, a theo-centricity is always implied. Here, an anthropocentric hamartiology or moral theology is simply one that begins with the agent rather than their material actions, in accordance with the scholastic maxim *agere sequitur esse*. See Aquinas, *Providence*, 69; *Scriptum Super Sententiis* 3.3.2.1.

the Florentine thieves. Likewise, "what I hate I do" (Rom 7:15), above all, because in sinning, I ultimately decide against my own happiness.

In this view, love, as a principle of movement, enjoys a greater metaphysical force than might often be realized within the realm of moral theology or pastoral practice. More than the throwaway description for what is lacking in man's poor choices, love—precisely as a principle of movement—reveals how a Christocentric reality now enables our hope for reform, prevents this possibility in hell, underscores the personal change in purgation, and most essentially characterizes the perfect motion of heavenly beatitude.

Though this cosmic explanation might seem to entail an exception with regard to hell, it is rather the definitive rejection of this possibility that marks the critical line of difference: what remains available to man in this life is not simply absent in hell, but holds true for every state that follows death, such that each choice for sin, venial or mortal, is not simply a difference of greater or lesser charity lost, but a choice against the very principle of our being (and against our being itself). As we have already seen, the movement in hell is only as stagnant as the love directing it.

In this way, too, the marvel of grace becomes even clearer: what injured humanity cannot achieve on its own is yet enabled by the principle of God's love. Even more astoundingly, the notion of mortal sin and conversion precisely as a spiritual death and new life, respectively, are all the more apparent when viewed as the *loss* and *restoration* of *charity*, that is, of our most fundamental principle of movement. In this also, the mercy of postmortem purification shows itself as that gratuitous measure for man's ultimate destination, in keeping with an understanding of sin's (de)formative power: in man's heart remains not only love, the principle of movement for one made in God's image and likeness, but also the hope to be sustained in this movement until it is perfected.

The shortcomings noted by Balthasar might well enjoy some merit, insofar as the metaphysical scaffolding of Dante's *Inferno* was not so visibly built upon the Christ event that gives it is surest support, its most radical meaning. Nevertheless, the clear vision of hell as a work of love and beauty need not be undermined by the sin that, as we saw, has its natural expression, in eternity, in the sufferings told by the poet. Rather, it is only within these confused figures and the twisted accounts of their own lives that the quality of divine love is ever obscured. Where even Dante's sympathies and compassion are sometimes misplaced, we hardly find cause to dismiss the ties otherwise made between the fruit of God's enduring love and majesty, and the sufferings that flow from the free decision for sin. Love might well appear then only under the face of punitive justice, yet the restriction of love to this form—as when Dante speaks of the *vendetta di Dio*—lay not on the choice of God, but of the sinner.

CONCLUSION

The discipline of eschatology, as clouded as it may already appear by speculation, perhaps has little to gain from the additional musings of a medieval poet. The thirteenth century remains at a near-equal historical distance from the authority of Scripture as it does from so many of the developments in eschatology following more recent theological reflection. More than that, as a work of poetry, it might be the graver error to treat the *Commedia* as even feigning such a serious attempt at theological clarification. Even on a shelf below one's Bible and *Summa*, it appears that the *Commedia* must defend its place in any properly Christian treatment of hell.

Beyond a Thomistic lexicon or almost syllogistic turns of verse, Dante does, however, in his picture of hell and its residents, reveal a clear vision for human life and especially for human freedom. Though artistic license might be thought to detract from the poet's occasional theological insight, we may instead find in Dante's understanding of human nature, the goodness of creation, and the end to which all are called a surer remedy for another (far graver) excess of imagination.

In our brief examination of the *Inferno*, we have encountered challenges to the popular conceptions both of Dante's *Commedia* and of hell as such. Having explored the metaphysics of the *Inferno* and the pattern of punishment given by the use of *contrapasso*, we saw the poet's understanding of both to rest upon a fundamental commitment to cosmic order, whereby hell is a work of beauty and love (as much as justice), and the punishment of sin, a natural consequence of the departure from this order (rather than any creative payback). Here we found a means of navigating the problems faced by certain historical formulations of the teaching on hell. Thus, against models of chaos and absence, we saw that Dante's hell could be better appreciated in terms of presence and order (with the suffering in question understood as the rejection, rather than elimination, of these). Likewise, the moral question of divine justice found a further resolution in Dante's *contrapasso*, whereby sin and punishment approach each other as a singular decision of the individual against God's order, as against their own happiness and beatitude. From here, a practical function of Dante's implied anthropology (with its understanding of the formative role of human habits) brought to light the disfiguring effects of sin even now in the earthly lives of men. Against popular conceptions of medieval piety, Dante offers a fundamentally positive vision of man and the world (including hell) as creations of beauty, goodness, and love. Could it then be under the aspect of comedy, the triumph of this beauty, goodness, and love over evil, that Catholic eschatology best fulfills its duty—to itself and the world—of accounting "for the hope within" (1 Pet 3:15)?

BIBLIOGRAPHY

Aquinas, Thomas. *Providence*. Translated by Vernon J. Bourke. Vol. 3 of *Summa Contra Gentiles*. Notre Dame, IN: University of Notre Dame Press, 1975.

———. *Scriptum Super Sententiis*. Edited by M. Fabianus Moos. 3 vols. Paris: Lethielleux, 1929.

Balthasar, Hans Urs von. *Studies in Theological Styles: Lay Styles*. Vol. 3 of *The Glory of the Lord: A Theological Aesthetics*. San Francisco: Ignatius, 1986.

Belliotti, Raymond Angelo. *Dante's Deadly Sins: Moral Philosophy in Hell*. Hoboken, NJ: Wiley-Blackwell, 2013.

Benedict XVI. "Faith, Reason and the University: Memories and Reflections." Vatican, Sept. 12, 2006. https://www.vatican.va/content/benedict-xvi/en/speeches/2006/september/documents/hf_ben-xvi_spe_20060912_university-regensburg.html.

Catholic Church. *Breviarium Romanum*. 2 vols. Bonn: Nova et Vetera, 2008.

Dante Alighieri. *The Divine Comedy*. Edited and translated by Robin Kirkpatrick. 3 vols [*Inf.; Purg.; Par.*]. Penguin Classics. London: Penguin, 2006-7.

Grčić, Marko, and Božidar Petrač, eds. *Svijet i Dante: Tekstovi pjesnika i mislilaca 20. stoljeća o Danteu u povodu njegove sedme stoljetnice smrti*. Zagreb: Alfa, 2021.

Guardini, Romano. *"La Divina Commedia" di Dante i principali cencetti filosofici e religiosi*. Translated by Oreste Tolone. Vol. 19.2 of *Opera omnia*. Brescia: Morcelliana, 2018.

———. *Studi danteschi*. Translated by Oreste Tolone. Vol. 19.1 of *Opera omnia*. Brescia: Morcelliana, 2012.

Imbach, Ruedi. *Potret pjesnika kao filozofa: O filozofiji Dantea Aligherija*. Translated by Maja Herman Duvel. Zagreb: Istina, 2022.

John Paul II. "*Laborem Exercens*: On Human Work." Vatican, Sept. 14, 1981. https://www.vatican.va/content/john-paul-ii/en/encyclicals/documents/hf_jp-ii_enc_14091981_laborem-exercens.html.

Kirkpatrick, Robin. Introduction to *Inferno*, by Dante Alighieri, edited and translated by Robin Kirkpatrick, xi–civ. Vol. 1 of *The Divine Comedy*. Penguin Classics. London: Penguin, 2006-7.

Kopić, Mario. *Prekogroblje po Danteu*. Zagreb: Matica Hrvatska, 2021.

Lombardi, Elena. *The Syntax of Desire: Language and Love in Augustine, the Modistae, Dante*. Toronto: University of Toronto Press, 2007.

Mazzeo, Joseph Anthony. "The Analogy of Creation in Dante." *Speculum* 32 (1957) 706–21.

Nietzsche, Friedrich. *The Genealogy of Morals*. Dover Thrift Editions: Philosophy. Mineola, NY: Dover, 2003.

Nova et Vetera. *Hymni Antiqui: Hymni Breviarii Romani ad Laudes et Horas Diei ex Antiphonale Romano Romæ MCMXII*. Bonn: Nova et Vetera, 2008.

Stump, Eleonore. "Dante's Hell, Aquinas's Moral Theory, and the Love of God." *Canadian Journal of Philosophy* 16 (1986) 181–98.

Taylor, Mary. "The Sparkling of the Holy Ghost." *Comm* 46 (2019) 520–65.

Terentianus Maurus. "De litteris, de syllabis, de metris." In *Grammatici Latini*, edited by Heinrich Keil, 6:325–413. Leipzig: Teubner, 1923.

Wojtyła, Karol. "Person and Act." In *"Person and Act" and Related Essays*, edited by Antonio López et al., translated by Grzegorz Ignatik, 95–414. Vol. 1 of *The English Critical Edition of the Works of Karol Wojtyła/John Paul II*. Washington, DC: Catholic University of America Press, 2021.

11

Reading Backwards
The Senses of Scripture and Eschatological Exegesis

SUSANNA EDMUNDS OP

INTRODUCTION

The book of Revelation unveils the ultimate realities underlying divine revelation and salvation history. When Scripture is read canonically, the book of Revelation functions as a teleological magnet, uniting the diverse literary genres by revealing their common goal. Yet the search for the literal sense of the book of Revelation has become mired in debates over historical contexts and literary influences. Furthermore, despite contemporary shifts towards theological exegesis, hermeneutics such as canonical or typological interpretation can be difficult to apply to apocalyptic literature.[1] In the words of St. Thomas Aquinas, the things of eternity "do not stand figuratively for other things; all other things stand figuratively for them."[2]

Yet recent work reconnecting the fields of Scripture and metaphysics may open avenues for reclaiming the teleological function of the book of Revelation. In his 1988 Erasmus lecture,[3] Cardinal Ratzinger (later, Pope

---

1. "Theological exegesis" is used by Ratzinger, among others, to describe an interpretation that is open to the insights of historical-critical approaches but recognizes them as tools rather than ends in themselves. For Ratzinger's usage, see Ratzinger, *Verbum Domini* §34. The phrase is popular among exegetes of the Reformed tradition but is also being employed by biblical Thomism. See Dauphinais and Levering, introduction, xiii; McGuckin, "Theological Exegesis," 197; Lombardo, "Inspiration, Authorial Intention," 826.

2. Aquinas, *Quodlibetal Questions* 7.6.2.ad5.

3. Various editions of this address have been published in English. This chapter

Benedict XVI)[4] called for renewal in biblical interpretation, not through a simplistic return to patristic or medieval reading methods, but rather by a fruitful "synthesis of historical and theological methods, of criticism and dogma."[5] To achieve this synthesis, he argued, we must examine our metaphysical framework to assess its compatibility with the worldview proposed by Scripture.

Ratzinger suggests that the principles of metaphysical participation and analogy, as employed by St. Thomas Aquinas,[6] can provide an "open philosophy" capable of grappling with "the possibility that God can work in history and enter into it without ceasing to be himself."[7] Participation and analogy are frameworks within Aquinas's metaphysics of creation that hold the infinite distance between the creature and the Creator in tension with their intimate union, made possible by the Creator's capacity for immanence and the creature's capacity for transcendence. Although Ratzinger is no Thomist, he finds this framework to be the best expression of the creature-Creator reality envisioned by the Bible itself, and he proposes that it may make it possible for contemporary thinkers "to recover the presuppositions necessary for an understanding of the Bible."[8]

In the subsequent three decades, proponents of biblical Thomism have begun to explore the implications and possibilities that analogy and participation hold for biblical interpretation.[9] This chapter seeks to build on this work by examining the implications of metaphysical analogy for the traditional fourfold senses of Scripture and the possibilities therein for bringing the book of Revelation into fruitful dialogue with the rest of the canon. We will begin with a brief overview of the rise and fall of the senses of Scripture, followed by an application of the metaphysics of analogy to the senses of Scripture. To conclude, we will sketch the

---

draws from the longer version, which is more explicitly metaphysical and Thomistic: Ratzinger, "Biblical Interpretation in Conflict."

4. Hereafter, Ratzinger, as most of his biblical work was published under this name.

5. Ratzinger, "Biblical Interpretation in Conflict," 7.

6. Ratzinger, "Biblical Interpretation in Conflict," 23. Although he does not himself seek to outline those principles, he includes extensive references to the work of Maximino Arias Reyero, which can thus be read as a guide to Ratzinger's thought on this question. See especially Arias Reyero, *Thomas als Exeget*, 106–7, 161, 193–96, 204.

7. Ratzinger, "Biblical Interpretation in Conflict," 22.

8. Ratzinger, "Biblical Interpretation in Conflict," 23.

9. A name coined by Matthew Levering, who was inspired by Servais Pinckaers (Levering et al., "Biblical Thomism," 10). Biblical Thomism covers a rich variety of scholarship, characterized by attention to Aquinas's scriptural commentaries and the use of Scripture in his systematic treatises. See Vijgen, "Biblical Thomism."

possibilities that this approach offers for biblical eschatology through a brief case study examining the gates and foundation stones of the heavenly Jerusalem as described in Rev 21.

PART 1: THE SENSES OF SCRIPTURE

Dei Verbum recommends three tools for fostering theological exegesis without disregarding the insights of historical and literary criticism: reading canonically, reading within the analogy of faith, and reading in dialogue with tradition.[10] These tools seek to lift each book of the Bible out of the limits of its immediate context and bring it into the broader context of the community of faith, the natural habitat of the inspired word of God. One traditional method of achieving this broadened horizon is the fourfold senses of Scripture. The catechism summarizes this approach by quoting a medieval couplet: "The Letter speaks of deeds; Allegory to faith; the Moral how to act; Anagogy to our destiny."[11] It recognizes that the various words and deeds of salvation history need to be considered as melodic strands in an orchestral score, which may sound pleasing in isolation but only reveal their full truth when brought into harmony with other strands. By identifying the multifaceted dimensions of a text's meaning, connections can be identified between the two testaments and between a variety of scriptural genres, thus transforming the literal sense of the passage from a solo into a symphony.

The fourfold division of the senses of Scripture and its corresponding nomenclature was formalized and popularized by St. Thomas Aquinas.[12] However, unlike some of his predecessors and peers, his interpretation and application of the spiritual sense was governed by a metaphysical framework of signification.[13] Following Augustine, Aquinas recognized that just as words signify things (*significatio vocum*), so too, things themselves function as signs (*significatio rerum*).[14] This is a consequence

---

10. Second Vatican Council, *Dei Verbum* §11.

11. Traditional, but attributed to Augustine of Dacia (*CCC* 118). In common practice, the allegorical sense sees the Old Testament anticipating the life of Christ and the church; the moral sense draws practical applications from the events of salvation history; and the anagogical sense looks for ways in which both the Old and New Testaments anticipate the eschaton and the four last things.

12. Aquinas, *ST* 1.110; Williamson, *Catholic Principles*, 172.

13. Holmes, "Participation and Meaning," 104–7. For the importance of metaphysics for Aquinas's approach, see Huizenga, "Literal and Spiritual Senses."

14. For the influence of Augustine on Aquinas's approach and the areas of continuity and discontinuity between Aquinas and the church fathers, see Dahan, "Thomas

of the metaphysics of creation, which recognizes that the Creator has written not only the book of Scripture, but also the book of nature.[15] Since Scripture is the inspired word of God, it carries both a literal sense, the realities signified by its words, and a spiritual sense, the signification of these realities. Such figurative reading is not an arbitrary imposition of the reader's imagination onto the text; rather it is the reader's recognition of the divine authorship of both the Bible and the very realities of salvation history. The spiritual senses are the meaning attached to reality not by the reader, but by the divine author who authored both the book of Scripture and the book of nature.[16]

This symphonic reading strategy was largely lost during the Reformation and Enlightenment, following the late medieval shift away from a metaphysics of participation.[17] However, contemporary movements in exegesis have sought ways to reclaim the theological fruitfulness of the spiritual sense without compromising the insights gained through historical-critical approaches.[18] In its 1993 document "The Interpretation of the Bible in the Church," the Pontifical Biblical Commission (PBC) defines the spiritual sense of Scripture as "the meaning expressed by the biblical texts when read under the influence of the Holy Spirit, in the context of the paschal mystery of Christ and of the new life that flows from it."[19] This christological and pneumatological hermeneutic enables three levels of readings to be brought into symphony: the world of the text, the paschal mystery, and the reader's own life and circumstances. The PBC acknowledges these to be not just interpretive levels, but indeed, three "levels of reality."[20] It thereby alludes to the relationship between

---

d'Aquin et l'allégorie." Yet Aquinas is able to go beyond Augustine, thanks to a more developed metaphysics of participation (Holmes, "Participation and Meaning," 106). This allows him to clarify Augustine's apparent rejection of the "intrinsic worthiness of the Old Testament realities" (Holmes, "Participation and Meaning," 112n44).

15. For an overview of the Christian understanding of the "book of nature," especially in the early and medieval period, see Tanzella-Nitti, "Two Books," 235–40. Unlike Augustine and Bonaventure, Aquinas does not deal explicitly with this concept but rather assumes it. His thought on the topic underlies his teaching on the relationship between truths known by reason and truths known by faith (*ST* 1.1.10) and on the divine names (*ST* 1.13).

16. Nichols, *Discovering Aquinas*, 32–33.

17. The decline in a participatory understanding of history can be associated with the rise in nominalism, with its implications for exemplar causality, and to voluntarism, with its implications for final causality (Levering, *Participatory Biblical Exegesis*, 19).

18. PBC, "Interpretation of the Bible" 1.A.introduction.

19. PBC, "Interpretation of the Bible" 2.B.2.

20. PBC, "Interpretation of the Bible" 2.B.2.

our interpretation of the Bible and our understanding of reality, that is, our metaphysical framework.

Despite its acknowledgment of the relationship between the senses of Scripture and the structure of reality, the PBC remains wary of "enclos[ing] the Christian message within the constraints of a particular philosophy"[21] and proposes instead a literary approach to the spiritual sense. It thus loses the anchor of objectivity traditionally found in the metaphysical framework of *significatio vocum* and *significatio rerum*. Requiring new interpretive criteria to safeguard the spiritual senses of Scripture from "interpretations of a wildly subjective nature,"[22] the PBC seeks objectivity in the original author's communicative intent.[23] Therefore, it advises that typological connections must be "based on the way in which Scripture describes the ancient reality and not simply on the reality itself."[24]

While this method may be more palatable for exegetes formed in the schools of historical and literary criticism, it curtails the scope of the spiritual sense, limiting the christological interpretation of the Old Testament to those passages which the New Testament itself interprets christologically.[25] To use an example that will be relevant to our case study, the account of Joshua's crossing of the Jordan River could be considered within this approach as a type of baptism, as it seems to be a literary reworking of the exodus crossing, which itself is explicitly named as a foreshadowing of baptism in the New Testament (1 Cor 10:1–2). However, features that are unique to Joshua's crossing, such as the memorial of twelve river stones which he sets up on the far shore, cannot be read christologically, as there is no scriptural or magisterial precedent for doing so.[26]

---

21. PBC, "Interpretation of the Bible" 1.A.4. The philosophy highlighted by the PBC as an example of this danger is Bultmann's existentialist interpretation (2.A.2).

22. PBC, "Interpretation of the Bible" 2.B.1.

23. In this sense, the PBC's approach resembles that of the Protestant Reformers, who largely retained typological interpretation so long as it was between "two items that stand in a historical relation of anticipation and fulfilment" (Vanhoozer, *Is There a Meaning*, 118).

24. PBC, "Interpretation of the Bible" 2.B.2.

25. The examples given by the PBC are Adam as a figure of Christ and the flood as a type of baptism (Rom 5:14 and 1 Pet 3:20–21, respectively) (PBC, "Interpretation of the Bible" 2.B.2).

26. In addition to christological connections that have been sanctioned by the canon itself, the PBC allows for interpretations that draw their authority from the magisterium or the patristic tradition, categorizing these readings under the "fuller sense" of the text (*sensus plenior*) (PBC, "Interpretation of the Bible" 2.B.3). Texts that lack

The limits of this purely literary approach seem to be acknowledged by Ratzinger in his 2008 post-synodal apostolic exhortation *Verbum Domini*. While he affirms the PBC's insight that the spiritual sense captures "the meaning expressed by the biblical texts when read, under the influence of the Holy Spirit, in the context of the paschal mystery of Christ and of the new life which flows from it," he also quotes the traditional fourfold nomenclature of the medieval couplet.[27] Most importantly, however, the exhortation proposes a theological framework for interpretation based on the metaphysics of creation, within which it may be possible and palatable for contemporary exegetes to recover multifaceted interpretation based not on textual rereadings but on the sacramental nature of reality and history.

Ratzinger calls this framework the "analogy of the Word of God," by which he means not only our analogous uses of the phrase "the Word of God," but the more fundamental recognition that the Word of God is an analogous reality.[28] God speaks his one Word in "many and various ways" (Heb 1:1),[29] especially through the "two incarnations" spoken of by the church fathers, Christ's incarnation "in human language and in human flesh,"[30] as well as through the two books of creation and Scripture.[31] In this analogical framework, the metaphysics of creation, the theology of inspiration, and the incarnation can each be seen as a participatory reality, a breaking forth into time and space of the one eternal Word of God. Therefore, it is not only possible, but essential, for these realities to be read in symphony.

While this framework does not negate the literary understanding of the spiritual sense advocated by the PBC, it provides a robustly metaphysical approach with a greater capacity to plumb the depths of the Word of God. This approach allows an openness to the full spectrum of divine revelation, expressed not only in Scripture but also in nature, through salvation history, and by the Incarnate Word himself. It recognizes

---

such authoritative rereadings cannot be read christologically, and indeed, according to some members of the PBC, gain nothing from being read in the light of the paschal mystery: for example, the Shema, the Decalogue, prophetic ethics, and Ps 23, according to Fitzmyer, *Interpretation of Scripture*, 95. Similarly, Zenger proposes that the books of Amos and Jonah "do not need the New Testament for their message to be complete" (Williamson, *Catholic Principles*, 134).

27. Ratzinger, *Verbum Domini* §37.
28. Ratzinger, *Verbum Domini* §7.
29. All Scripture quotations in this chapter are taken from the NRSVCE.
30. Harrington, *Record of Revelation*, 20.
31. *CCC* 2500.

that the realities of creation, history, and revelation are capable of symbolic signification, akin to the mechanism of poetic metaphor, and that this signification is not a human imposition but rather a consequence of a dual metaphysical participation, the participation of created existence in God's subsisting being and the participation of created essence in God's wisdom and providence. In short, Ratzinger's "analogy of the Word of God" gives contemporary expression to the Thomistic metaphysics of creation and signification. Therefore, since Ratzinger himself does not provide practical guidance for putting this framework into practice, it seems fitting to consider whether Aquinas's fourfold senses of Scripture can be reclaimed as a suitable interpretive approach for contemporary theological exegesis.

PART 2: AN ANALOGICAL APPROACH TO THE SENSES OF SCRIPTURE

In order to recover Aquinas's metaphysical approach to exegesis, it is necessary to recover his metaphysical mindset. As seen in Ratzinger's description of the "analogy of the Word of God," philosophical participation has a remarkable capacity for expressing the symphonic relationships between Creator and creature, eternity and history, Word and text. In Aquinas's metaphysics of creation, participation is traditionally coupled with analogy, a means of considering various instances of a participated perfection and identifying their similarities not in spite of their dissimilarity, but rather in light of it. Here, we will briefly outline the metaphysics of analogy in order to appreciate the fourfold senses of Scripture as an analogical framework which gives expression to the participatory realities described in Ratzinger's "analogy of the Word of God."

Linguistically, analogous concepts lack precision; therefore, in the words of philosopher W. Norris Clarke, "one gets to the meaning of such terms not by clear definitions . . . but rather by running up and down a spectrum of typical examples and grasping in a synthetic insight what is common to them all."[32] Metaphysical analogy works in a similar way. A multiplicity of analogues provides a real glimpse of the prime analogate in which they participate, without ever exhausting its transcendence. As the multiplicity of the senses of Scripture is a consequence of the participation of all divine revelation in the one eternal Word, the structures of metaphysical analogy can provide a fitting way of expressing

32. Clarke, *One and the Many*, 50.

the relationships between the various senses and the way in which they lead beyond created multiplicity to eternal Truth.

Two forms of analogy underlie Aquinas's metaphysics of creation: the analogy of intrinsic attribution and that of proper proportionality.[33] As will be seen, the twinning of these two forms of analogy has the potential to provide a framework whereby the spiritual senses can be explored in their fullness without being untethered from the foundation of the literal sense. The analogy of attribution can be demonstrated in the analogous uses of "health."[34] Health can belong properly only to a living organism. However, medicine (a cause of health) and urine (a sign of health) can also be called healthy. These are analogous use of the terms, as health belongs to them only by relation to a living organism, the prime analogate.[35] Health is thus attributed to different substances in analogous ways.

However, while "health" is a quality that can be attributed to organisms in a primary way and to medicine in a secondary way, no such quality, not even being, can be considered as a "neutral point of reference" attributed to both God and creatures.[36] When applying the analogy of attribution to the Creator, it must be understood by way of participation. Any quality attributed both to God and creatures refers to a perfection which belongs to God essentially and to creatures only by varying degrees of participation and likeness. Furthermore, there is no fixed distance between the degree to which the quality is found in God and the degree to which it is found in a Creature. The "goodness" of the saints or the "goodness" of a flowering apple tree, for example, belong to a totally different order compared to the "goodness" of God, because of a difference in mode. Goodness is found in created things as is proper to their mode of created being; goodness is found in the Creator according to his mode of uncreated being, *ipsum esse subsistens*.

This divine transcendence is expressed in the second form of analogy, that of proper proportionality. While the analogy of attribution

---

33. While there remains some debate over the degree to which Aquinas favored one of these forms of analogy over the other, this is beyond the scope of this chapter. It suffices here to emphasize the need for both forms as complementary frameworks expressing two facets of analogical participation.

34. Aristotle, *Metaphysics*, 2:1584–85; Aquinas, *ST* 1.13.5. While some argue that this is a nominalist or logical analogy, we follow Velde in reading it as "embedded in a metaphysical account of the causal relationship between creatures and God" (*Aquinas on God*, 109).

35. Hütter, "According to the Wisdom," 221.

36. Velde, *Aquinas on God*, 113.

does indicate a proportionality between the analogues, for example, the proportional relationship between the health of my dog and the healthiness of the medicine I give to it, the analogy of proper proportionality indicates a harmony in the "proportion of the proportion." Aquinas provides the example, understanding is to mind as sight is to eye.[37] Understanding is not proportional to sight; rather, it is the relationship between understanding and the mind that is proportional to the relationship between sight and eye.[38] Recognizing this "proportion of the proportion" is necessary for any analogy between the creature and God, as it expresses their utterly different modes of existence and their "lack of common measure," yet without creating a chasm of equivocity.[39] While the analogy of attribution expresses the reality of similitude between the Creator and creatures, the analogy of proper proportionality protects the dissimilitude.[40]

The two forms of analogy can both be employed when bringing various passages of Scripture into dialogue. The analogy of attribution recognizes that Christ, the Incarnate Word, is the prime analogate to whom all other expressions of the Word of God point and from whom they derive their revelatory power. Therefore, all parts of Scripture can be read christologically, and the Gospels stand above all other books of the Bible as their interpretive key. The analogy of attribution thus identifies the primacy of the allegorical sense of Scripture above the other senses. It is useful, then, when attempting a moral reading of an Old Testament text, or an anagogical reading of a New Testament epistle, to first identify the allegorical sense of the text, that is, the way that it anticipates or echoes the life of Christ.[41]

While analogy of attribution highlights the participation of all revelation in the Incarnate Word, the analogy of proper proportionality highlights the role of the receiving subject, which limits the perfection according to the mode of the analogue. For Scripture, this mode is the text's literal sense with all its historical and literary particularities. This

37. Long, "Thomas Aquinas," 177. Long points out that while mathematical examples (e.g., 3:6 :: 25:50) are initially helpful, they do not capture the proportionality between the ratios, since they can be resolved univocally (e.g., 1:2).

38. Although our mind is quick to grasp the likeness between understanding and sight, it can do so only with reference to the mind and the eye, even if this is not conscious. In contrast, there is a direct proportion between "dog" and "dog's breakfast" that needs no third or fourth term.

39. Nichols, *Discovering Aquinas*, 153.

40. Betz, "After Barth," 69.

41. Smith, *Sermons of Thomas Aquinas*, 168. This same practical point about the primacy of the christological analogate is expressed by the PBC in its guidelines for exegetical "actualization" (PBC, "Interpretation of the Bible" 4.A.2).

is not to be understood as a limitation on the application of the spiritual sense, but rather a key to unlock further dimensions of interpretation. It is precisely through the limitations of the receiver, in this case, the text's literal sense, that the perfection, that is, the life of Christ, finds multifaceted expression. Like stones in a brook, which cause the river to murmur as its water tumbles over them, the particularities of genre, authorial intent, and *Sitz im Leben* cause each passage of Scripture to reveal another dimension of the mystery of the Gospel.[42]

This function of the literal sense is a consequence of the incarnation. As expressed by Fr. Francis Martin, "The word enters into a culture and a linguistic grid: he becomes 'flesh' in language."[43] Just as we encounter the hylomorphic reality of the human person through the flesh of the human body, so too, we encounter new dimensions of the eternal Word through the "flesh" of the literal sense. And yet, just as we recognize that it is insufficient to stop at the level of flesh when we are seeking to encounter another person, so too, while the literal sense is indispensable for exegesis, it is also insufficient, for we seek not only to know but to encounter the realities envisioned by the text.[44] By unveiling the spiritual sense of a passage within twinned analogical frameworks employed by Aquinas, the exegete is able to explore new horizons while remaining anchored in the text's christological analogate (analogy of attribution) and literal sense (analogy of proper proportionality).

PART 3: CASE STUDY (REV 21)

The spiritual sense of Scripture seeks to decode the metaphors that providence has written into the fabric of creation and history.[45] Recovering the metaphysical understanding of the spiritual sense, therefore, allows the book of Revelation to reclaim its function as something like a "final cause" for the whole of the canon, unveiling the telos of all creation. This is especially true of the later chapters of the book, which directly

---

42. Robinson, *Inspiration and Revelation*, 280.

43. Martin, *Sacred Scripture*, 245. In the words of Erich Przywara, "The one eternal truth of God reveals itself noetically in creaturely truth in the same way that divine being reveals itself ontologically in creaturely being—that is, within the variety produced by this 'togetherness' and 'succession'" (*Analogia Entis*, 144).

44. Explaining the theological and philosophical warrants for such a bold quest is the accomplishment of Wright and Martin, *Living God in Scripture*.

45. In the words of Ratzinger's Thomistic source, "The literal sense calls for the spiritual sense in the same way that our experience of motion calls for an unmoved mover" (Arias Reyero, *Thomas als Exeget*, 204).

deal with the final judgment, heaven, and hell. We will consider here the heavenly Jerusalem, as described in Rev 21, as an eschatological case study. By exploring the spiritual senses of this text through the mechanisms of metaphysical analogy, we seek primarily to expand the exegetical horizons of apocalyptic literature. However, as Scripture is the soul of theology, it is no surprise that doing so can also provide insights into current questions in eschatology.[46]

The passage in question reads as follows:

> Then one of the seven angels who had the seven bowls full of the seven last plagues came and said to me, "Come, I will show you the bride, the wife of the Lamb." And in the spirit he carried me away to a great, high mountain and showed me the holy city Jerusalem coming down out of heaven from God. . . . It has a great, high wall with twelve gates . . . and on the gates are inscribed the names of the twelve tribes of the Israelites. . . . And the wall of the city has twelve foundations, and on them are the twelve names of the twelve apostles of the Lamb. . . . The foundations of the wall of the city are [twelve jewels]. . . . And the twelve gates are twelve pearls. (Rev 21:9–10, 12, 14, 19, 21)

This vision seems to present a harmonious and synergistic coupling of the twelve tribes of Israel, represented by the city gates, and the twelve apostles of the Lamb, represented by the city's foundation. In its literal sense, this symbolism provides a theological affirmation of the continuity between the old and new covenants, both of which are brought to fulfillment in the eschaton.[47] Yet when considered canonically, this coupling creates two areas of tension, both concerning the fittingness of having the names of the apostles inscribed on the foundation stones.

The first set of tensions arises when the text is brought into dialogue with its theological parallels in the New Testament, where stone imagery is predominantly applied to Christ. He is the stone rejected by the builders,[48] which has become the foundation for the church (1 Cor 3:11). The notable exception is Jesus's naming of Simon Peter as the rock on which the church will be built (Matt 16:8). Yet even here, Jesus makes no reference to the twelve apostles per se. Finally, while some passages do refer to the apostles or the community of believers as stones,[49] they do so

---

46. Second Vatican Council, *Dei Verbum* §24.
47. Universidad de Navarra, *Revelation*, 147.
48. Mark 12:10; Acts 4:11; Rom 9:32.
49. Eph 2:20; 1 Pet 2:4–8.

always in reference to Christ as the cornerstone, and thus as the prime analogate of the analogy.[50] The book of Revelation does not.

A second tension arises from considering the text in dialogue with its Old Testament anticipations. It would seem more logical to link the foundation with that which comes first, namely, the tribes of Israel, representing the whole history of salvation which provided the foundation for Christ's coming and the establishment of the church. Moreover, the foundation stones are described as precious jewels,[51] which, despite slight discrepancies in naming, can be connected to the twelve stones worn on the breastplate of the high priest whereby the people of Israel were carried into the holy place to be remembered before the Lord.[52] Replacing the names of the tribes with those of the apostles may be taken as implying a rejection of Israel's history or a hermeneutic of rupture.[53]

Coupling these tensions with the apparently minor role played by the apostles in the book of Revelation, J. Massyngberde Ford concludes that link between the foundation stones and the apostles is a later addition to the text, an observation that she supports with grammatical analysis.[54] Whether this conclusion is plausible is not proper matter for evaluation by the exegetical approach proposed in this chapter, which does not critique but rather utilizes well-established findings of historical-critical and literary methods. Instead, the key question is what to do with such findings, especially when they highlight apparent contradictions between various stages of redaction. Many modern exegetical methods would seek to dissolve the tension by dissecting editorial layers and hypothesizing the communicative intentions of the original community of authorship. In contrast, theological exegesis based on the metaphysics of creation seeks to discern the literal sense[55] by bringing the text, with all its ambiguities and contradictions, into dialogue with other parts of the canon to which it can be connected through the spiritual senses. Textual tensions are not

---

50. Ford, *Revelation*, 334.

51. A literary allusion to the prophecies of Isa 54:11 and Tob 13:16.

52. Exod 28:15-21, 29.

53. Naming the gates after the apostles would have been equally problematic, given the association between the gates and the twelve tribes in Ezekiel's vision. See Ezek 48:30-35.

54. Ford, *Revelation*, 333. The grammatical findings are largely seconded by Aune, *Revelation 17-22*, 1155-57.

55. Understood according to the definition of the PBC, by which the literal sense is "that which has been expressed directly by the inspired human authors" (PBC, "Interpretation of the Bible" 2.B.1).

problems to be solved; rather, they function as exegetical prompts which unveil deeper facets of the mystery.[56]

This proposal begs the question of whether the spiritual senses can indeed be applied to the book of Revelation. Aquinas is right to say that Revelation lacks an allegorical or moral sense, in that the things of eternity "do not stand figuratively for other things." But he goes on to say that this is because "all other things stand figuratively for them."[57] That is, in its literal sense, Revelation expresses the anagogical sense of all other passages.[58] This fits with Aquinas's insistence that the teaching of any spiritual senses must be elsewhere explicated in the literal sense.[59] Each of the spiritual senses, therefore, can be applied to the book of Revelation, not by reading forward from anticipation to fulfillment, but rather backwards, from fulfillment to anticipation, from telos back to pedagogical prefigurement.

According to the logic of the analogy of attribution, the prime analogate should first be identified, namely, the christological text that provides the most fundamental insight into the mystery. There are two places where Jesus is connected to foundation stones: Jesus declares to Simon, "You are Peter, and on this rock I will build my church" (Matt 16:18); and "No one can lay any foundation other than the one that has been laid; that foundation is Jesus Christ" (1 Cor 3:11).[60] Already we find a discrepancy: the one foundation is sometimes Peter, and sometimes Christ.

Analogical analysis turns this impasse into an exegetical springboard. The analogy of proper proportionality calls us to examine each text within its literary, historical, and canonical context, and to thus identify the proportionality between the pedagogy of the texts, without forgetting the disproportionality of the texts' claims. In the Gospel, Jesus declares Peter to be blessed not because of his profession of faith per se, but because of its source: "Blessed are you, Simon son of Jonah! For flesh

---

56. I am indebted to Dr. Robert Tilley of the Catholic Institute of Sydney for this insight.

57. Aquinas, *Quodlibetal Questions* 7.6.2.ad5.

58. Noting, of course, that the literal sense of the book of Revelation includes the decoding of its extensive figurative language in accordance with its apocalyptic genre.

59. Aquinas, *Quodlibetal Questions* 7.6.1.ad3; *ST* 1.1.10.ad1. This is consistent with Augustine, *Doctr. chr.* 2.6.8.

60. An alternative set of christological texts surround the analogues of structures and dwellings, especially the temple, e.g., 1 Pet 2:4–8; John 2:19. Although these are of immense importance for the exegesis of Rev 21 and the new Jerusalem, they are of secondary importance for Rev 21:14 and are thus set aside for now.

and blood has not revealed this to you, but my Father in heaven" (Matt 16:17). He is blessed because he hears the word of God and keeps it.[61] Peter thus becomes an embodied parable, the man who builds his house on the rock of Christ's words.[62] As a result, he himself is declared to be the rock, the foundation of the church. Because Peter built on Christ, Christ will build on Peter; and while Peter built his life on Christ by listening to his words, Christ will build his church on Peter by speaking his words through him.[63]

The pedagogy of the rock analogy is established in the second half of the verse, where Jesus promises that the gates of hell will not prevail against the church (Matt 16:18b). In warfare, a city's firm foundation stone is essential to its defense; but the promise of victory over an enemy's gates implies an offensive strike. Thus, it is not Peter, the foundation, who will be victorious, but that which is built on Peter, namely, the church built by Christ. Yet the pedagogy of the passage remains Petrine: if believers wish to build their lives on the rock of Christ's teaching and to be part of the victorious church built by Christ, they must build their lives on Peter, that is, on the apostolic teaching which is founded on and defended by Peter and his successors.[64]

A proportional pedagogy governs the second christological text, in which Christ is named as the foundation of the church. The literary context is Paul's rebuke of the Corinthians for the divisions that have arisen between those instructed by Paul and those claiming to follow the teachings of Apollos. Paul uses the analogy of a building to emphasize that all their teaching is based on one foundation, namely Christ, and that as this foundation has already been laid, it cannot be shaken, changed, or divided. At the time of writing, very little "foundation" had been laid for the institutional church: only the gospel events themselves and the proclamation of the gospel by the apostles in the years following Pentecost. These, then, must be the foundation to which Paul refers. Regardless of who their teacher was, the Corinthians have all received

---

61. See Luke 11:27.

62. See Matt 7:24–25.

63. This causal relationship is confirmed by the reverse scenario in the following verses, where Peter becomes a stumbling block by following human logic rather than the divine word. See Matt 16:22–23.

64. This interpretation is confirmed liturgically by the collect for the feast of the Chair of St. Peter (Feb. 22): "Grant, we pray, almighty God, that no tempests may disturb us, for you have set us fast on the rock of the Apostle Peter's confession of faith" (Catholic Truth Society, *Roman Missal*, 864).

the one gospel message, based on the one person of Christ and his one paschal mystery.

Thus, in naming Christ as the foundation of the church, Paul is perhaps making a doctrinal statement, but for the pedagogical purpose of exhortation. He is urging the Corinthians to be reunited by returning to the wellspring of their faith, the apostolic teaching on which both Paul and Apollos are building. The church does not, therefore, have two foundations, sometimes Peter and sometimes Christ. Nor is Jesus's naming of Peter as the rock a contradiction of his own role as the church's one foundation. Rather, it is his revelation of the means by which this one foundation is to be established in time and space. The Corinthian situation addressed by Paul illustrates the importance of understanding this connection between Christ and Peter, between the one paschal mystery and its unfolding in history through the one fount of apostolic teaching.

These christological roots of Rev 21 thus resolve the first tension noted above, namely how the twelve apostles can be the foundation stones of the heavenly Jerusalem when it should be Christ who is the church's one foundation. The apostles, and, by participation, their successors both in the college of bishops and in the ministry of the Word, are foundation stones in so far as they are privileged means by which the unifying foundation of faith in the Gospel is provided to each generation. Indeed, this highlights the significance of the text specifying that they are apostles *of the Lamb* (Rev 21:14).[65] The grammatical awkwardness of this phrase may indicate a redactor's insertion, but in divine providence, it functions as an exegetical prompt highlighting the source of the foundation's firmness. This is confirmed by consideration of the analogous moral sense. All believers are indeed "living stones [being] built into a spiritual house" (1 Pet 2:5) but only in so far as their lives are built on the firm foundation of Christ's teaching (Matt 7:24–25), which is promulgated through the ministry of the apostles.

To resolve the other tension noted above, that of the relationship between the apostles and the tribes, it is necessary to look to the allegorical sense of the foundation stones. Textual criticism can link Rev 21 with literary analogues such as the description of the first tabernacle, the construction of the Solomonic Temple, and the messianic prophecies of Isaiah and Ezekiel.[66] However, a metaphysical framework allows us to also consider conceptual analogues. One such example, alluded to above,

---

65. Harrington, *Understanding the Apocalypse*, 259.
66. Respectively: Exod 25–27; 1 Kgs 6; Isa 65:17–25; Ezek 40–48.

is found in the book of Joshua. Woven through the narrative of Joshua's crossing of the Jordan River are references to twelve river stones, which are set up by Joshua at Gilgal as a memorial of the twelve tribes and their triumphant crossing.[67] As will be seen, these stones are analogous in several ways to the foundation stones of the new Jerusalem; thus, consideration of their role in salvation history may shed light on the pedagogy of the stones and gates of Rev 21.

While significant historical-critical attention has been given to Joshua's Gilgal shrine, textual tensions within the river-crossing narrative highlight the need to also examine the stones themselves. These tensions derive from two textual ambiguities. The first concerns Joshua's command to "take twelve men from the tribes of Israel, from each tribe a man" (Josh 3:12), the explanation of which is withheld for five verses, during which the entire crossing is described. It thus seems to be either a deliberate plot diversion or a mistaken fragment. The second ambiguity surrounds the existence of a second set of twelve stones. When the narrative eventually returns to these twelve men called forth by Joshua, he commands them to "take twelve stones from here out of the midst of the Jordan, from the very place where the priests' feet stood, and carry them over with you, and lay them down in the place where you lodge tonight" (Josh 4:2). However, after this action and its explanation is given, the narrator adds, "And Joshua set up twelve stones in the midst of the Jordan, in the place where the feet of the priests bearing the ark of the covenant had stood; and they are there to this day" (Josh 4:9). Although the Septuagint specifies that these are twelve "other" stones, the Masoretic text lacks "other."[68]

Theological exegesis does not seek to resolve these ambiguities, but rather to turn the tension into transcendence. As above, the analogy of proper proportionality leads us to consider the stones in their original context and to examine their pedagogical function. Canonically, the book of Joshua lies between the Pentateuch and the historical books. Joshua is a "new Moses," indeed, an ideal Moses, "without flaw or hesitation . . . the ideal leader of Israel, one who keeps the teaching of Moses in its entirety . . . the prototype of the ideal king."[69] Joshua thus forms a bridge between the prophetic leadership of the Mosaic covenant and the royal governance of the Davidic covenant, and his establishment of the

---

67. Hahn, *Catholic Bible Dictionary*, s.v. "Gilgal."

68. Boling and Wright suggest that "other" was dropped from the Masoretic text by haplography (*Joshua*, 158).

69. Coogan, "Joshua," 111. See also Bergsma and Pitre, *Old Testament*, 291, 294.

twelve memorial stones serves as an anticipation of the kingly task of constructing the Jerusalem temple and of governing right worship.[70]

It is fitting, therefore, that Joshua's Gilgal shrine became the site of the first Passover in the land, as well as a place of governance for both Samuel and Saul.[71] Yet despite this, it eventually becomes associated with corrupt worship, beginning with Saul's disobedient sacrifice and culminating in the denouncements of the prophets Hosea and Amos.[72] Given that a redaction of the book of Joshua was likely associated with the monarchical reforms of Hezekiah,[73] a reform which featured the centralization of worship in Jerusalem and the denouncement of rival sanctuaries, it is possible that the passages glorifying the establishment of Gilgal posed a conundrum for a pro-monarchical redactor.[74] Boling suggests, therefore, that the fragmentary reference to the twelve men in Josh 3:12 and the uncontextualized description of Joshua placing stones on the riverbed are remnants of an earlier text in which both sets of stones featured more prominently.[75] While the redactor could not completely eliminate the Gilgal stones, he creates a textual ambiguity which diverts the reader's focus from the stones of Gilgal towards the embedded river stones. Given that these stones mark the place where stood the priests carrying the ark of the covenant, this redirection functions as a subtle nod to the Jerusalem temple.[76]

This historical context suggests that the textual tension between the two sets of river stones points to a broader tension in which the redactor found himself, between the ideal Israel promoted by the monarchial reforms coming out of Jerusalem, and the historical Israel, for whom Gilgal had been a place of both of victory and defeat, of law and rebellion, of worship and idolatry. The twelve memorial stones on the riverbank, the foundation of Gilgal, were meant to have a catechetical function, bearing witness to the glory of God and the unity of Israel (Josh 4:21–24). With the destruction of Gilgal, this pedagogy had to be carried by the twelve stones that remained lying on the riverbed, with an added dimension:

70. Bergsma and Pitre, *Old Testament*, 291.
71. Respectively: Josh 5:10; 1 Sam 7:16; 10:8; 1 Sam 11:15.
72. Respectively: 1 Sam 13:9–14; Hos 4:15; 9:15; 12:11; Amos 4:4; 5:5.
73. Although it was likely also revised during the exile (Coogan, "Joshua," 111).
74. Boling and Wright, *Joshua*, 179–80.
75. Boling and Wright, *Joshua*, 171, 180.
76. The stones and Gilgal are a necessary chapter in the history of Israel; additionally, the redactor might have needed to retain reference to the stones due to the persistence of a catechetical custom, described in the text, in which children are to ask their parents about the meaning of the stones (Boling and Wright, *Joshua*, 174).

their hiddenness is a silent reminder of the faithlessness that led to the ruin of the visible memorial, and of the already-but-not-yet tension of Israel's existence. Thus, in the pedagogy of the book of Joshua, the underwater stones serve as an anchor of hope, a reminder of the firmness of God's promise which endures, though the fidelity of his people waxes and wanes.[77] Yet without the visible Gilgal stones, enshrined in catechetical memory, these underwater stones would be forgotten. It seems that the immanent, tangible working out of God's promises in history, through fallible instrumental causes, can bear witness to these promises, regardless of the fidelity or failure of the instruments.

A proportional pedagogy can therefore be discerned between three sets of analogues: Simon Peter and Christ; the Gilgal stones and the riverbed stones; the twelve gates and the twelve foundations. The eternal Word of God and the unshakable truth of apostolic teaching form a firm foundation for the church, the bride of the Lamb. Yet this transcendent truth would not be known were it not for the immanent, tangible unfolding of Christ's mission, beginning with the history of Israel, culminating in Christ's earthly life, and continuing in the wayfaring church. The twelve gates named after the twelve tribes thus represent the breaking forth of the kingdom of God in time and space. Like all gates, these derive their stability not from themselves but from their foundations, that is, from the eternal truth of the Gospel. Thus, the promises offered by the temporal expressions of the kingdom are not ultimately fulfilled through temporal means but through the transcendence of divine grace.[78] And yet, while gates add vulnerability to a city's defenses, it is precisely this vulnerability that allows a gate to serve as an entry point into the city. Hence, the limitations and messiness of salvation history, typified by Gilgal and embodied in Simon Peter, are the very means of grace chosen by God to draw all people to himself.

PART 4: ESCHATOLOGICAL CONCLUSIONS

The dichotomy of the gates and the foundation stones is thus not primarily to be understood as a reference to the dichotomies of old and new

---

77. Approaching Joshua through this hermeneutic may enable a more nuanced reading of the book, which is easily dismissed as triumphalist, and uncover points of convergence between the books of Joshua and Judges.

78. As the catechism explains, "The kingdom will be fulfilled . . . not by a historic triumph of the Church through a progressive ascendancy, but only by God's victory over the final unleashing of evil, which will cause his Bride to come down from heaven" (*CCC* 677).

covenants and Old and New Testaments. Rather, all of salvation history is built on the firm foundation of the Gospel, epitomized by apostolic teaching and embodied by the twelve apostles. And all of salvation history is a visible, temporal gateway into the fulfillment of God's providence, which employs instrumental causes while simultaneously transcending them. This is not to downplay the radical newness of the Gospel, which fulfilled Israel's eschatological hopes with an unimaginable superabundance. Rather, it is to emphasize that God is able to do new things without causing rupture. Indeed, it seems to be a scriptural expression of the metaphysical framework called for by Ratzinger, an "open philosophy" capable of grappling with "the possibility that God can work in history and enter into it without ceasing to be himself," and, we might add, without compromising the nature of history as a created reality with its own proper integrity.[79]

This reading of Rev 21 through the lens of the fourfold senses of Scripture can shed light on contemporary issues in eschatology, especially concerning the relationship between history and the eschaton. But more fundamentally, the relationship between the literal and spiritual senses of Scripture can itself provide a model for an analogical approach to the seemingly dichotomous relationships which characterize eschatological tension. For example, rather than viewing the transition from the old creation to the new creation from a hermeneutic of rupture, as has been posited by some, it may be fruitful to consider creation as a sort of *significatio vocum* or literal sense which stands in an analogous relationship to the *significatio res* of the new creation.[80]

Similarly, perhaps the false extremes of inner-worldly utopianism and otherworldly escapism[81] can be approached in a parallel manner to the allegorical and anagogical senses, which can seem to be at odds and yet can be brought into dialogue via their shared christological prime analogate. In this life, all work towards building up the kingdom draws its value from its character as an extension of the mission of Christ, and thus as an anticipatory signification of the kingdom which he has already-but-not-yet established. In turn, the ultimate reality of the kingdom is nothing more or less than the fulfillment of this mission. As such, it relies

---

79. Ratzinger, "Biblical Interpretation in Conflict," 22.

80. International Theological Commission, "Current Questions in Eschatology" 4.3.

81. International Theological Commission, "Current Questions in Eschatology" 2.

entirely on the immanent expressions of the kingdom as the means by which all creation is drawn to its transcendent fulfillment.[82]

We thus enter the new Jerusalem through the pearly gates of the twelve tribes of Israel; that is, we work for the coming of the kingdom through our participation in the drama of salvation history. Though they are marked by the groanings of creation and the fallibility of the saints, we are confident that these gates are firmly established on the dazzling foundation stones of the twelve apostles and the hope-filled truth of the Gospel. The wedding feast of the Lamb has begun, and his bride is being prepared to welcome him (Rev 19:17).

BIBLIOGRAPHY

Aquinas, Thomas. *Quodlibetal Questions*. Translated by Turner Nevitt and Brian Davies. Oxford: Oxford University Press, 2019.

———. *Summa Theologica*. Translated by Fathers of the English Dominican Province. New York: Benziger Brothers, 1925.

Arias Reyero, Maximino. *Thomas von Aquin als Exeget*. Einsiedeln, Switz.: Johannes, 1971.

Aristotle. *Metaphysics*. In *The Complete Works of Aristotle*, edited by Jonathan Barnes, 2:1552–728. Princeton, NJ: Princeton University Press, 1984.

Aune, David E. *Revelation 17–22*. WBC. Nashville: Thomas Nelson, 1998.

Bergsma, John, and Brant Pitre, eds. *A Catholic Introduction to the Bible: The Old Testament*. San Francisco: Ignatius, 2018.

Betz, John R. "After Barth: A New Introduction to Erich Przywara's *Analogia Entis*." In *The Analogy of Being: Invention of the Antichrist or Wisdom of God?*, edited by Thomas Joseph White, 35–87. Grand Rapids: Eerdmans, 2011.

Boling, Robert G., and G. Ernest Wright. *Joshua*. AB 6. New York: Doubleday, 1982.

Catholic Truth Society. *The Roman Missal: English Translation According to the Third Typical Edition*. London: Catholic Truth Society, 2010.

Clarke, W. Norris. *The One and the Many: A Contemporary Thomistic Metaphysics*. Notre Dame, IN: University of Notre Dame Press, 2001.

Coogan, Michael David. "Joshua." In *The New Jerome Biblical Commentary*, edited by Raymond E. Brown et al., 110–31. London: Burns & Oates, 1990.

Dahan, Gilbert. "Thomas d'Aquin et l'allégorie." *St* 24 (2021) 103–15.

Dauphinais, Michael, and Matthew Levering. Introduction to *Reading John with St. Thomas Aquinas: Theological Exegesis and Speculative Theology*, edited by Michael Dauphinais and Matthew Levering, xiii–xxvi. Washington, DC: Catholic University of America Press, 2005.

Fitzmyer, Joseph A. *The Interpretation of Scripture: In Defense of the Historical-Critical Method*. Mahwah, NJ: Paulist, 2008.

Ford, J. Massyngberde. *Revelation*. AB 38. Garden City, NY: Doubleday, 1975.

---

82. This approach to eschatology could benefit from further consideration within the framework of Erich Przywara's *analogia entis*, which grapples with the dynamic rhythm of truth "in-and-beyond" history (Betz, "After Barth," 54–64).

Hahn, Scott, ed. *Catholic Bible Dictionary*. New York: Doubleday, 2009.
Harrington, Wilfred J. *Record of Revelation: The Bible*. Chicago: Priory, 1965.
———. *Revelation*. SP. Collegeville, MN: Liturgical, 1993.
———. *Understanding the Apocalypse*. Washington, DC: Corpus, 1969.
Holmes, Jeremy. "Participation and the Meaning of Scripture." In *Reading Sacred Scripture with Thomas Aquinas: Hermeneutical Tools, Theological Questions and New Perspectives*, edited by Piotr Roszak and Jörgen Vijen, 91–113. Textes et études du Moyen Age 80. Turnhout, Belg.: Brepols, 2015.
Huizenga, Leroy A. "The Literal and Spiritual Senses of Sacred Scripture." In *Healing Fractures in Contemporary Theology*, edited by Peter John McGregor and Tracey Rowland, 91–117. Eugene, OR: Cascade, 2022.
Hütter, Reinhard. "According to the Wisdom of God—From Effect to Cause, from Creation to God: A *Relecture* of the Analogy of Being According to Thomas Aquinas." In *The Analogy of Being: Invention of the Antichrist or Wisdom of God?*, edited by Thomas Joseph White, 209–45. Grand Rapids: Eerdmans, 2011.
International Theological Commission. "Some Current Questions in Eschatology." Vatican, 1992. https://www.vatican.va/roman_curia/congregations/cfaith/cti_documents/rc_cti_1990_problemi-attuali-escatologia_en.html.
Levering, Matthew. *Participatory Biblical Exegesis: A Theology of Biblical Interpretation*. Notre Dame, IN: University of Notre Dame Press, 2008.
Levering, Matthew, et al. "Biblical Thomism: Its Actuality and Approaches." *St* 24 (2021) 10–12.
Lombardo, Nicholas E. "A Voice Like the Sound of Many Waters: Inspiration, Authorial Intention, and Theological Exegesis." *NV* 19 (2021) 825–69.
Long, Steven A. "Thomas Aquinas, the Analogy of Being, and the Analogy of Transferred Proportion." In *The Discovery of Being and Thomas Aquinas: Philosophical and Theological Perspectives*, edited by Christopher M. Cullen and Franklin T. Harkins, 173–92. Washington, DC: Catholic University of America Press, 2019.
Martin, Francis. *Sacred Scripture: The Disclosure of the Word*. Naples, FL: Sapientia, 2006.
McGuckin, Terence. "Saint Thomas Aquinas and Theological Exegesis of Sacred Scripture." *NBf* 74 (1993) 197–211.
Nichols, Aidan. *Discovering Aquinas: An Introduction to His Life, Work, and Influence*. Grand Rapids: Eerdmans, 2003.
Pontifical Biblical Commission. "The Interpretation of the Bible in the Church." Catholic Resources, Apr. 23, 1993. https://catholic-resources.org/ChurchDocs/PBC_Interp.htm.
Przywara, Erich. *Analogia Entis: Metaphysics—Original Structure and Universal Rhythm*. Translated by John R. Betz and David Bentley Hart. Grand Rapids: Eerdmans, 2014.
Ratzinger, Joseph. "Biblical Interpretation in Conflict: On the Foundations and the Itinerary of Exegesis Today." Translated by Adrian Walker. In *Opening Up the Scriptures: Joseph Ratzinger and the Foundations of Biblical Interpretation*, edited by José Granados et al., 1–29. RRRCT. Grand Rapids: Eerdmans, 2008.
———. "*Verbum Domini*: On the Word of God in the Life and Mission of the Church." Vatican, Sept. 30, 2010. https://www.vatican.va/content/benedict-xvi/en/apost_exhortations/documents/hf_ben-xvi_exh_20100930_verbum-domini.html.

Robinson, H. Wheeler. *Inspiration and Revelation in the Old Testament*. Oxford: Oxford University Press, 1946.

Second Vatican Council. "*Dei Verbum*: On Divine Revelation." Vatican, Nov. 18, 1965. https://www.vatican.va/archive/hist_councils/ii_vatican_council/documents/vat-ii_const_19651118_dei-verbum_en.html.

Smith, Randall B. *Reading the Sermons of Thomas Aquinas: A Beginner's Guide*. Steubenville, OH: Emmaus Academic, 2016.

Tanzella-Nitti, Giuseppe. "The Two Books Prior to the Scientific Revolution." *Perspectives on Science and Christian Faith* 57 (2005) 235–48.

Universidad de Navarra. *Revelation*. 2nd ed. Navarre Bible. Dublin: Four Courts, 1998.

Vanhoozer, Kevin J. *Is There a Meaning in This Text? The Bible, the Reader, and the Morality of Literary Knowledge*. Grand Rapids: Zondervan, 1998.

Velde, Rudi A. te. *Aquinas on God: The "Divine Science" of the "Summa Theologiae."* Ashgate Studies in the History of Philosophical Theology. Surrey: Ashgate, 2006.

Vijgen, Jörgen. "Biblical Thomism: Past, Present and Future." *Ang* 95 (2018) 371–96.

Williamson, Peter S. *Catholic Principles for Interpreting Scripture: A Study of the Pontifical Biblical Commission's "The Interpretation of the Bible in the Church" (1993)*. Rome: Editrice Pontificio Istituto Biblico, 2001.

Wright, William M., IV, and Francis Martin. *Encountering the Living God in Scripture: Theological and Philosophical Principles for Interpretation*. Grand Rapids: Baker, 2019.

12

The Resurrection of the Body and the Future of Creation

ALENKA ARKO

INTRODUCTION

The resurrection is the most important theological assertion, which is why it must always be reaffirmed, perhaps even today. The *Catechism of the Catholic Church* states: "Belief in the resurrection of the dead has been an essential element of the Christian faith from its beginnings."[1] Nevertheless, a close examination of the history of theology has often given the impression that salvation was the exclusive prerogative of man's spiritual dimension. The final fate of the body was given little consideration and that of creation even less. Without a doubt, this is due to the complexity of the issue, as well as the paradoxical tendencies observed throughout history. It seems easier to credit the positive value to the soul or to the immaterial, spiritual dimension than to the material aspect, which undergoes continuous change and final dissolution.

Privileging or even reducing salvation to the spiritual dimension of life alone inevitably has serious consequences for preaching, catechesis, and, consequently, the spiritual life of Christians, who, in this way, do not correctly understand their true ultimate end, and, due to doctrinal ignorance, may fall prey to erroneous beliefs. In short, we observe an approach towards the body and the material world with a "gnostic" flavor, despite the fact—and here we can see a paradox—that we live in a culture marked by a cult of the body, though expressed in many ways. Furthermore, we live in a world where material goods are valued

---

1. *CCC* 991.

almost above all else, leading to the exploitation of natural resources, along with pollution, global warming, and various natural disasters, the consequences of which are felt by everyone, especially the poor.[2] It is important to emphasize that this tendency is also observed, even if in a veiled way, when theology prefers to speak about corporeity broadly as the visible dimension of human life rather than the material body, which in turn tends to "exclude" the material from salvation. Thus, a gap has been created between hope (the attainment of a spiritual perfection that does not consider the material as an integral aspect of life) and the reality of life, focused on sometimes excessive care for the body and the insatiable greed for material goods. For this reason, a proper understanding of the final, eschatological destiny of humanity and the world is crucial. It opens unprecedented horizons, although it retains its mysterious character, as the apostle reminds us: "For we walk by faith, not by sight" (2 Cor 5:7).

In theological literature, the resurrection is usually treated in two areas: the resurrection of Christ (christological sense) and the resurrection of the dead (anthropological sense). Here we focus on the second, though it is clear that we can only speak of the resurrection of the dead by starting from the resurrection of Christ (Col 1:18). Despite his resurrection having no analogy and no witnesses, he is the only one who has risen from the dead and will never die again. He is the first fruits of the new creation (1 Cor 15:20) that will reach its fullness in the resurrection of all and in the realization of "the new heavens and the new earth" (2 Pet 3:10–13; Rev 21:1–8).

SOME BIBLICAL DATA

The belief in the resurrection already began to develop in the Old Testament, albeit slowly and cautiously, until in its later books it reaches the formulation no longer of a collective experience, as evoked by the prophet Ezekiel in the passage on the revivification of the dry bones (Ezek 37:1–10), but rather the experience of the individual (Dan 12:2). Daniel's text does not state that after death "all will be awakened." He instead uses the expression "many of those who sleep in the region of the dust" (i.e., Sheol): the wise (those educated and able to discern and do good) to everlasting life, the others to shame and everlasting contempt. Nevertheless, one can think of a universal situation, as there is no reason why some would not partake in either salvation or in blame (see also 2 Macc 7:9–14).

---

2. Francis, *Laudato Si* §§48–52.

This belief is related to a holistic anthropology. The anthropological terminology of the Old Testament witnesses to this. Every anthropological term delineates the whole human being according to a particular aspect: *bāśār* (flesh) as a weak, perishable being; *nefeś* (usually translated as soul) as a being in need of help, and the seat of emotions; *rûah* (spirit) as a being open to God.[3] Sacred Scripture views man as a whole, not divisible into various parts, so that even in the late Old Testament texts influenced by Hellenism, it cannot conceive of eternal life as pertaining only to one dimension of humanity, namely, the soul. André Paul synthesizes this: in the later books of the Old Testament, resurrection is discussed not only as the resurrection of the body (the First Testament does not know a term equivalent to the Greek term *sōma*), but "in truth, much more than the body," resurrection "consists in the total metamorphosis of each of the human beings into their anthropological entirety . . . it is not just the body that is affected, but the person as such."[4] This "recreation" of human beings also extends to the world, which, like humanity, must first reach its end. If, in the texts on the end of history (e.g., Dan 2:31–45), we find visions of cosmic catastrophes that make the present world disappear, they are there precisely to prepare "space" for the novelty of transformed life.

> The solidarity of human beings (the microcosm) with the universe (the macrocosm) is confirmed, but is, so to speak, inverted: The human being is no longer the "scaled" reflection of the universe and the universe is reborn according to the sublimated image of human beings. The latter becomes immortal through its transformation, while the universe is discovered to be mortal, the condition of its re-creation akin to that of human beings.[5]

The New Testament knows of such a universal resurrection, which we might call "reanimation of the corpse," but it dedicates almost no interest to it (John 5:28–29; Acts 23:6–8). The authors of the New Testament consider the resurrection as the ultimate fulfillment of the life of humanity and the world, as the consummation of salvation history. For this reason, they speak of the resurrection as the gift of grace for those who have accepted Christ as Savior and conformed their lives to him. In this prospective, the resurrection is the fulfillment of the covenant that God made with humanity in the beginning, a fulfillment realized in the resurrection of Jesus, the Son of God made man. Likewise, it is the

---

3. Wolff, *Anthropologie des Alten Testaments*, 29–74.
4. Paul, *Immortalità o risurrezione*, 108.
5. Paul, *Immortalità o risurrezione*, 108.

revelation of the ultimate meaning of the earthly life of every person—the complete fulfillment of our identity as children of God, the definitive realization of our freedom enabled by grace (see Eph 1:5).

The Bible, therefore, on the one hand, maintains the conviction that the resurrection concerns absolutely all human beings. It strictly "defends" the holistic anthropology, while on the other hand, it makes it clear that the quality of their eternal life will depend on their moral life during their earthly existence. Furthermore, the New Testament emphasizes the specific nature of the Christian faith: resurrection in Christ, i.e., salvation that encompasses everything human and the entire cosmos, which is not just liberation from sin, but above all the free, gratuitous gift of God's love that grants us the dignity of being his children. With this, the New Testament does not deny the Old Testament assertion of a resurrection of all. It is true, however, that it does not concern itself much with the damned. In Jesus's dispute with the Sadducees, he describes the situation of the resurrected as follows: "those who are deemed worthy to attain to the coming age [*aiōnos ekeinou*] and to the resurrection of the dead.... They can no longer die, for they are like angels; and they are the children of God because they are the ones who will rise" (Luke 20:34–36).

Scripture also speaks about the renewal of the non-human world brought about by the paschal mystery of Christ (see Isa 43:19; 65:17; 66:22; Col 1:19–20; 2 Pet 3:10–13; 2 Cor 5:1; Rev 21:1–8). It consists of a transformation that will make creation capable of participating in the divine life in the endless first day of a new creation, of which the first creation was a prophetic anticipation. The apostle Paul in 1 Cor 15:24–28 speaks of the end as the victory over all enemy powers, including the cosmic powers explicitly named (v. 24). "This implies the liberation of creation, currently enslaved under the dominion of the powers that grip and disfigure it, to come under the authentic liberating dominion of the messianic sovereign."[6] In Rom 8:21 this liberation is interpreted as the participation of the whole creation in the "glorious freedom of the children of God." This, in fact, is the ancient Christian hope—not the dissolution, but the transformation of all creation, its sharing in the final destiny of humanity.

Alongside this, it is also important to note that Scripture does not use conceptual language in reference to the resurrection but rather figurative and metaphorical terms. It expresses the mystery of the eschaton in a provisional, i.e., incomplete way.[7] Therefore, to properly

---

6. Vidal, *Risurrezione dei morti*, 79.

7. Nitrola, *Trattato di escatologia*, 2:289.

and adequately understand biblical doctrine, it is very important to use right and careful hermeneutics that takes into account literary genre, its images and expressions, and the range of their possible meanings. Biblical eschatological images and metaphors are not photographs of eternal life, but they try to bring it closer to us, based on a careful reading of the life of Jesus and of our experience, which is always marked with the eschatological dimension of a tension between "already" and "not yet."

A HISTORICAL OVERVIEW

Patristic Period

The church fathers, in their confrontation with paganism, had to respond to the criticism that the resurrection is impossible. Therefore, it is not surprising that their focus was on the power of God, who alone is able to reunite the soul with the matter that once constituted the earthly body.[8] Gregory of Nyssa, for example, in *De anima et resurrectione*, integrates Christian teaching with the Stoic doctrine of the union of material realities, affirming that the soul knows the elements of its body and is somehow always in relation with them.[9] Moreover, the fathers realize that the resurrection of the body is necessary in order to do justice to the human being in its entirety, i.e., that belief in the immortality of the soul alone is insufficient.[10]

In addition to these objections, they also had to defend faith in the resurrection against Greek philosophers and against the various gnostic currents. The gnostics denied the goodness of the material world and the possibility of the body's salvation, as well as the possibility of the salvation of all humankind. According to them, only gnostics, as spiritual beings, will be saved (some currents allowed for the possibility that Christians, as psychic beings, might be saved), while material human beings, and matter in general, would ultimately be destroyed.[11] On the other hand, the Greek philosophers, particularly the Platonists (referring no longer to classical Platonism but a hellenized version known as Middle Platonism), saw matter as the cause of evil and conceived of it as a preexisting reality, co-eternal with God and inherently evil.[12] The body in their eyes was

---

8. Athenagoras, *Res.* 4–5 (*ANF* 2:151).
9. Gregory of Nyssa, *De anima et resurrectione* 18–20 (PG 46:41–48).
10. Athenagoras, *Res.* 22 (*ANF* 2:161).
11. Filoramo, *History of Gnosticism*.
12. Plato, *Tim.* 51a (*Complete Works*, 1254).

the prison, the tomb of the soul,[13] whereby the resurrection of the body would mean a deterioration of the condition of the soul liberated after death from carnal bonds, and once again definitively enclosed in the body. Therefore, resurrection is unworthy of the human being. The fathers in principle defended the goodness of everything created by God, the Supreme Good, who cannot call into life anything that is evil, and for that they defend also the goodness of the body and of the world, especially in the light of Christ's resurrection, his risen flesh,[14] and in the light of the sacramentality of creation. In the sacraments, especially the Eucharist, the material reality, in fact, becomes the very means for transmitting grace.[15]

Within the church itself, the open question was that of the identity between the earthly and the resurrected body. Some Christians believed in the resurrection of the body but held that the heavenly body had to differ from the earthly one.[16] This was a reaction to Stoic-type materialism, which considered everything that existed to be material. Origen reacted to this comprehension of the resurrected body, affirming that it could be only spiritual, though certainly not in the heretical way he was later accused of.[17] Origen "philosophically reflects on the human being, that is, on its soul, and starting from there—that is, considering the body as the body of the soul—he outlines the picture of the final events . . . and this is precisely what comes naturally to us even today."[18]

The identity of two bodies—earthly and resurrected—is a dogmatic truth based on New Testament revelation. The Risen One is the Crucified One ("It is I myself" [*egō eimi autos*] [Luke 24:39]). Grasping this revealed fact, the church's magisterium, when speaking of the resurrected body, emphasizes that we have to affirm a numerical identity, not merely a generic one, meaning that the risen body will not just be a human body, just "any" body, but "my" body: we will rise "in this flesh in which we now live";[19] neither do we believe "that we shall rise in ethereal or any other flesh [*carne*], (as some foolishly imagine), but in this very flesh in

---

13. Plato, *Phaed.* 62b4 (*Complete Works*, 54); *Phaedr.* 250c4–6 (*Complete Works*, 528); *Crat.* 400c (*Complete Works*, 118–19); *Gorg.* 493a3 (*Complete Works*, 836).

14. Tertullian, *Res.* 14.11 (ANF 3:554–55); 34 (ANF 3:569–70); *Apol.* 48.4 (ANF 3:54).

15. Irenaeus, *Haer.* 5.2.2–5.2.3 (ANF 1:528).

16. Origen, *Princ.* 2.10.1 (ANF 10:136–7). See also Plato, *Tim.* 41e, 44e (*Complete Works*, 1244, 1248); *Phaedr.* 247b (*Complete Works*, 525).

17. Synod of Constantinople, "Anathemas Against Origen" (DH 407).

18. Nitrola, *Trattato di escatologia*, 2:247.

19. *Fides Damasi* (DH 72).

which we live and exist and move."[20] Throughout history, however, we find various attempts and ways of interpreting this identity (in material, formal, or substantial ways) that are rather inadequate and unsuccessful.

Medieval Eschatology

In medieval theology we see two approaches to the resurrection of the flesh that recur later on: an excessively materialistic view of the resurrected body on the one hand and a spiritualization on the other. Both positions draw from philosophy: the first from Aristotle, the second from Plato.

Scholastic theology, under the influence of Aristotelian philosophy (never completely abandoning the Platonic perspective), placed significant emphasis on the unity of the human person and the universality of the resurrection. For Thomas Aquinas, the soul and the body are not two elements of a union that constitutes the human being, but two metaphysical principles: form and matter, act and potency. Now, the soul as the form of the body can only be immaterial and as such incorruptible and immortal, otherwise it would require another form, which would compromise man's substantial unity.[21] In death, in which the body separates from the soul, this unity is, however, compromised. For Thomas, this fact is so serious that it leads him to assert that the separated soul, in itself, is not a person. He emphasizes, however, that it retains the capacity for unibility (Lat. *unibilitas*).[22] Death is considered a defect of nature and the resurrection is the reunion of soul and body.[23]

The soul, after death, finds itself in a state contrary to nature, and for this reason, it is necessarily provisional, since "nothing unnatural can last forever."[24] In other words, the resurrection of the body is required by the very nature of the soul. Moreover, there are two more reasons why the body *must* rise. The first is the desire for happiness that can only be achieved when, in the resurrection, humanity once again attains the completeness of its nature. The second is the conviction that the reward or punishment must necessarily concern both soul and body.[25]

---

20. Council of Toledo, "Profession of the Faith" (DH 540).
21. Aquinas, SCG 2.5; Bertuzzi, "Immortalità dell'anima razionale."
22. Aquinas, ST I, q.29, a.1, ad 5 (Shapcote, 307).
23. Aquinas, SCG 4.79.
24. Aquinas, SCG 4.79: "Nihil autem quod est contra naturam, potest esse perpetuum."
25. Aquinas, SCG 4.79.

Thomas, in his doctrine on the resurrection, also reacted to the criticism of how this interpretation is coherent with the belief that the resurrection is the reward offered by Christ to the righteous. In reply, he stressed that, even though all will rise, "defect will not be repaired perfectly save in those who adhere to Christ, either by their own action in believing in him, or at least by the sacrament of faith,"[26] i.e., baptism. The resurrection will thus be a reality for all, but not for all will it reach the fullness of its effects.

Though he defends the unity of the human being, a crack nevertheless appears in the excessive detail of Aquinas's explanation of what the resurrected body will be like. He relates that the resurrected body will be incorruptible, i.e., rid of all that serves the corruptible life, namely food and sexuality. The body will not be spiritual, as some believe, but material. Defining the materiality of resurrected bodies, he affirms that they will not be *subtilia, et aeri et ventis similia*, but will have a determinate form, and although they will be celestial, this is not in the sense of nature, but in the sense of perfect power, like our body in youth.[27] While Tertullian, for example, avoids rough materialism when he says that the resurrected body will be *nec alius sed aliud*,[28] Thomas's desire to explain the reality of the resurrection in a descriptive, realistic way ultimately fails, especially because it goes against the logic to be observed in speaking of eschatological realities: continuity and discontinuity, the "already and not yet." It is precisely for the reason that not everything has been revealed to us yet, that we cannot claim to describe eschatological realities in detail. This problem will be particularly evident later in the treatises *De Novissimis*,[29] in which we see an "objectification" of the resurrection. Nitrola writes:

> Eschatology (and also theology in general) that followed and came after Thomas Aquinas has almost never been able to recognize this crack and therefore to grasp the metaphorical nature of

---

26. Aquinas, *SCG* 4.81.

27. Aquinas, *SCG* 4.81–4.89.

28. That is, not another body, but a different (i.e., transformed) earthly body (Tertullian, *Res.* 55 [*ANF* 3:588; Latin text: PL 2:876]).

29. The earliest example of such treatises is the work of Siuri, *Theologia de Novissimis* (1756), from which point until the mid-twentieth century treatises with this title followed one another abundantly. They considered the *novissima* (death, judgment, eternal life, and hell) as the ultimate, final realities, a series of events that can be treated separately from the rest of theological discourse. The eschatological future is not a promise, but an already given system, structured by the present (Giudici, "Escatologia," 399–400).

eschatological language. The result has been an eschatology that has synthesized the categories of the immortality of the soul and the resurrection of the body, without the slightest awareness of the different origins and their different grammar. Eschatology as the "history of the soul" has thus become definitively fixed in Aristotelian-Thomistic terms: the soul as form of the body, death as a separation of the soul from the body, the body dies, the soul does not, the soul lives after death as a reality separate from the body and will be reunited with the body on the last day.[30]

Spiritualization on the other hand is based on the emphasis on the immortality of the soul, which already in death obtains its reward or punishment: either salvation—the *visio beatifica*—or eternal damnation, as expressed in *Benedictus Deus*.[31] From this perspective, the resurrection seems secondary, unnecessary, and superfluous. It adds nothing to the soul that already enjoys eternal blessedness. It is not a surprise, then, that eschatology in the twentieth century has rejected this view of salvation as dualistic. For it is clear that the eternal destiny that human beings enjoy after death is the result of what they embodied during their earthly pilgrimage, the result of their history, so that the eternal life of the immortal soul and the shipwreck of the body in death cannot in any way constitute man's salvation.

The Twentieth Century

The attempt to address the open questions posed by Scholastic theology and supported by Christian spirituality (i.e., eschatological dualism and the attempt to go beyond it), find particular expression within twentieth-century Protestant theology. Of those who took up the subject, we mention two in particular. The first one is Carl Stange, who proposed a radical solution—the *thnetopsychism* of Tatian,[32] which affirms the death of both the soul and the body, a total death (Ger. *Ganztod*), and envisages a new creation in the resurrection of the whole person.[33] The second one is Oscar Cullmann, who also believed that death is the total destruction of life and that we can speak of life after death only on the condition of a new creative act of God. This creative act, which the author calls "the resurrection of the soul," does not itself bring about the fullness of life.

30. Nitrola, *Trattato di escatologia*, 2:289–90.
31. Benedict XII, *Benedictus Deus* (DH 1000–1002).
32. Tatian, *Or. Graec.* 13 (ANF 2:70–71).
33. Stange, *Unsterblichkeit der Seele*.

Instead, this will occur only at the end of history, when it will also extend over all creation. In fact, Cullmann, in his reflection, returns to Luther's idea of the sleep of the souls between death and resurrection. Such a sleep of the resurrected soul seemed to him a way to resolve the difficulty of the soul's life in the intermediate phase between the death of the individual and the resurrection at the end of history.[34]

In the Catholic Church, the position of radical death, which affects not only the body but also the soul, is found in the *New Dutch Catechism*,[35] which was later corrected. A variant of this thought was reproduced by Leonardo Boff, who believes that death is not the end of the body but the beginning "of another type of corporeality, more perfected and universal."[36] In this perspective, the resurrection is a new birth; it is not "the reanimation of a corpse, but the total realization of the capacities of the body-soul human being, the overcoming of all the alienations that mark existence."[37] In this way, the intermediate state is annulled, and the idea of resurrection in death begins to take shape, which in any case does not correspond to the final, total consummation, because it does not include the universe, which still awaits transformation.[38]

An initial outline of this doctrine can already be found in 1922 with the Protestant theologian Paul Althaus. It is built upon the notion of time being surrounded by eternity, whereby every moment in time is the ultimate time. Each individual, in death, enters this timeless reality; thus, the personal resurrection of each one is simultaneous with the resurrection of Christ. In this way, the intermediate state between the individual's death and the final resurrection is suppressed, since upon entering eternity, there is no longer any succession of moments, thus neither any waiting for the resurrection at the end of history.[39]

From the Catholic side we would like to point out the theology of Gisbert Greshake, who several times returns to the issue of the resurrection in death.[40] Greshake defends the timelessness of eternal life, and distinguishes between the material, physical body (Ger. *Körperlichkeit*) and corporeality (*Leiblichkeit*), which represents the ecstatic dimension in which the spirit, i.e., man's freedom in dialogue with God, is realized.

---

34. Cullmann, *Immortality of the Soul*, 24.
35. Hoger Katechetisch Instituut, *Nieuwe katechismus* §§569–74.
36. Boff, *Nostra resurrezione nella morte*, 113.
37. Boff, *Nostra resurrezione nella morte*, 122.
38. Boff, *Nostra resurrezione nella morte*, 130.
39. Althaus, *Letzten Dinge*, 141–59; "Retraktatzionen zur Eschatologie."
40. Nitrola, *Trattato di eschatologia*, 2:311.

Death, in this perspective, is the moment when *Körperlichkeit* reaches its end, dissolving into pure matter, while *Leiblichkeit* finally comes to fruition—is completed and fixed forever. Greshake writes: "The resurrection of the body does not mean the resurrection of the physical body or the corpse; resurrection rather means that in death, the whole human being, with each one's concrete world and history, receives a new future from God."[41]

The reception of Greshake's doctrine among Catholic theologians was mixed. One of the most persistent opponents was Joseph Ratzinger, who objects to both the timelessness of eternal life and the irrelevance of the material body, which obviously after death remains in time, i.e., in the grave where it disintegrates. A doctrine of this kind, according to Ratzinger, excludes the end of history, which coincides with the resurrection as a revealed fact and which places us in a relationship with all humanity—both those who have already died and those who have not yet been born. In addition, it nullifies the doctrine of purgatory, which no longer makes any sense, and ridicules and renders absurd the church's care for the burial of the human body. During the funeral rite, both the grave and the body are blessed, although, according to Greshake's proposal, the body has already been resurrected.[42] Moreover, the resurrection of *Leiblichkeit* seems to Ratzinger nothing more than the restoration of the doctrine of the immortality of the soul.[43] This discussion once again demonstrates how the question of the resurrection is complex and must be treated with care and great attention to the data of revelation.

Other authors have seen in Greshake's explanation of the resurrection an unacceptable exclusion of the collective dimension of man's eschatological fulfillment, implied by the faith that all the dead will together rise on the last day.[44] If everyone rises in the moment of his death, then the end of history becomes irrelevant and unnecessary. Such an eschatology means the relativization of the social dimension of human fulfillment, and persistence in the individual conception of salvation that the Council and theology after it struggled to overcome.[45]

The voice of the church's magisterium also made itself heard in this discussion with the "Letter on Certain Questions Regarding Eschatology" (*Recentiores Episcoporum Synodi*) (1979). The text has great dogmatic

41. Greshake, *Vita più forte*, 101.
42. Ratzinger, *Eschatology*, 108–9; 181–90.
43. Ratzinger, *Eschatology*, 108.
44. Ruiz de la Peña, *Altra dimensione*, 173–74.
45. Cozzi, "Linguaggio dogmatico," 148–49.

significance. Its introduction by Ratzinger, included in the Documenti e Studi series, states:

> This letter is limited to reaffirming what the Church teaches in the name of Christ and judges to belong to the essence of the faith. In this sense, although not having the authority of a dogmatic definition, the document considers *as dogmatic and unchangeable the substance of the teaching* contained in the seven points formulated, limiting itself to reiterating what is shown by other sources to belong to the faith of the Church.[46]

Regarding our topic, Ratzinger further explains that the document primarily emphasizes:

> The fundamental truth of the Christian faith concerning the resurrection of the dead, as affirmed in the Apostles' Creed (point 1) and teaches that this resurrection involves the whole person (point 2). This means it is more than just the mere survival of the "self"; it pertains to the entirety of the human being in order to unfold the final resurrection of humankind.[47]

Furthermore, the importance of Christ's resurrection is emphasized, since the resurrection of man "is nothing other than an extension of the reality of Christ's own resurrection."[48]

In this context, the existence of an intermediate state between the individual's death and the resurrection of the body is also firmly asserted. In this state, there exists "a spiritual element" that ensures the persistence of the conscious and free "self," that is, of the person. However, since the person is also material, this remaining spiritual dimension is now devoid of the materiality that has dissolved over time. This element is called the "soul," although the term in Scripture does not have a univocal meaning. It is said to be an *instrumentum verbale*. This means that it does not designate a philosophical or theological concept, but rather it is a necessary term to express the faith. "This does not mean it does not tell the truth, but only that it does so with provisional words,"[49] because "neither Scripture nor theology provides sufficient light for a proper picture of life after death."[50] To express it, we are compelled to use images

---

46. Ratzinger, introduction, 12; emphasis added.
47. Ratzinger, introduction, 13.
48. Ratzinger, introduction, 13.
49. Nitrola, *Trattato di escatologia*, 2:328.
50. Congregation for the Doctrine of the Faith, *Recentiores Episcoporum Synodi* (DH 4659).

and grasp their deep meaning without diluting them excessively, so as not to empty them of their significance.[51]

After considering the matter from the perspective of the history of doctrine, the question arises of how to speak today of the resurrection of the body, as defined by the various credos, which hold the highest dogmatic value for Christians. The suggestions provided by the text of the magisterium give us two indications: on the one hand, we do not have the right to renounce the materiality of the body. On the other, we must seek answers that are not overly physical, because the risen body is a transformed body!

WHAT DO WE MEAN BY "BODY"?

We have just seen that some modern theologians distinguish the term "body" (the physical, material reality) from corporeality. The latter generally denotes the human person, grasped in their connection with the world and in solidarity with others. It is therefore not "something" we can define and describe but the fundamental dimension of human existence. This very widespread distinction, used to make the complexity of the reality of the human being more intelligible, is not, however, without the danger of spiritualizing the body and thus excluding matter from salvation. The International Theological Commission even saw in such a distinction an "eschatological Docetism."[52] It is true that the salvation of the person means the fulfillment of relationships, without which there is no human life at all, but it is also true that relationships cannot be lived without the body, even less can we think of a human being without a body. The body is never an additional element to human existence. This is why the body is so important in our earthly existence as well as in our future life. In the eschatological perspective, it must therefore be emphasized that when we speak of the resurrection, we speak of the resurrection of the body, of the flesh, and with it also of the salvation of the entire material world.[53] Why?

"Body" is a dimension of the person that expresses their being in space and time, i.e., their historicity, torn between the past and the future. In this tension, the identity of a person is formed through their

---

51. Congregation for the Doctrine of the Faith, *Recentiores Episcoporum Synodi* (DH 4658).

52. International Theological Commission, *Current Questions in Eschatology* 2.1.

53. Congregation for the Doctrine of the Faith, "Translation of 'Carnis resurrectionem.'"

relationships with God, neighbor, and the world, though precisely as realized through their body. The body allows maturation, growth, conversion, as well as the possibility of an egotistical closing in on oneself before God and neighbor. That is why our life here and now carries a great responsibility.

Second, "body" is also a dimension that expresses mortality. As historical beings, we are called to embody during our lives our fundamental choice: to accept or reject God's invitation to live in communion with him, within the relations of the Holy Trinity, as *filii in Filio*. In other words, the body permits a human being to move from the possibility of a free choice to its finality, which is fulfilled precisely in death. In this light, mortality is not a consequence of sin, but of our being *in statu viae*. As affirmed by Karl Rahner:

> Death is not merely something that is "appropriate" to man in the sense that it is appropriate to a precious artefact not to be broken because to break it would be an outrage to its very nature and the purpose for which it was designed. On the contrary man is subject to death as a necessity of his innermost nature. It is on deeper grounds than merely biological ones that human nature inherently and inexorably tends towards death as its inevitable goal. The deepest and most ultimate reason for the connection with and orientation to death which is most intimately inherent in man, which makes him mortal and in virtue of this fact renders all men now and for ever subject to death in the truest sense, is the freedom of the spirit. It is this, ultimately speaking, that makes man mortal, and mortality in the biological sense is only the manifestation and the realisation in the concrete of this mortality, which has its origin and basis in the freedom with which man is endowed as spiritual.[54]

This means that in the resurrection, the relational structure will be both maintained and transformed: the relationship with others and with the world will not disappear, but at the same time, it will no longer be marked by historical limitations and precariousness.

With death, our identity, our history, and our free will reach their definitive state. This truth is applicable to every human being, including Jesus Christ. On the one hand, his death is the highest expression of his free will to reveal the Father's love for us in the total offering of his life; on the other hand, his resurrection is God's confirmation that such love is the fulfillment of his earthly life and also the promise of fulfillment of

---

54. Rahner, "On Christian Dying," 286–87.

our own. The Second Person of the Godhead, who became incarnate, did not wrap himself in flesh, but became flesh (John 1:14) to save our flesh.[55] After his resurrection and his return to the Father, he remains incarnate, as we too will remain. Pope Benedict XVI, in the final addition to his *Jesus of Nazareth* volumes, drawing on Karl Barth, states:

> There are two moments in the story of Jesus when God intervenes directly in the material world: the virgin birth and the resurrection from the tomb. . . . These two moments are a scandal to the modern spirit. God is "allowed" to act in ideas and thoughts, in the spiritual domain—but not in the material. That is shocking. He does not belong there. But that is precisely the point: . . . The question that they [the two moments] raise is: does matter also belong to him?[56]

Because of the mystery of Christ, we can hope and believe that our resurrection means the fulfillment of our earthly life and the beginning of a transformed, eternal one. Indeed, it is the flesh of Christ—something explicitly human, assumed by the Son of God for love's sake—that is the curtain through which it is necessary to enter in order to reach God[57] and achieve our identity without renouncing the flesh, but precisely within it. The risen Christ is the cause and model of our resurrection: we will rise *because* he rose and *in the way* that he rose. He is the firstborn of the dead (Col 1:5) and the first fruit of the resurrected (1 Cor 15:20).

Christ's resurrected body is thus the hermeneutical key to understanding our own resurrected body. Paul, in 1 Cor 15:44, speaks of it as a spiritual body (*sōma pneumatikon*), not in the sense of ceasing to be material, but transformed, penetrated by the Spirit. The apostle does not delve into the opposition between matter and spirit (in fact, it could be only moral, never anthropological). He does not speak of the material body, but of the difference between the psychical and the spiritual body. The *sōma psychikon* is the human being in its finitude and perishability, whereas the spiritual body is the human person fully animated by the Holy Spirit.[58] Ratzinger calls this Pauline perspective "pneumatological realism."[59] The relationship between the two bodies is understood as a succession between the first creation and the new, eschatological one. In vv. 39–41, there is an allusion to Gen 1, showing that, for Paul, the

---

55. Irenaeus, *Haer.* 5.14.1 (*ANF* 1:541).
56. Benedict XVI, *Infancy Narratives*, 56–57.
57. See Heb 10:19; Gioia, *Carne nell'eterno*, 77.
58. Collins, *First Corinthians*, 567.
59. Ratzinger, *Eschatology*, 170.

resurrection is the consummation of creation. He often uses the verb *zōopoiein* (to bring to life) for it (1 Cor 15:22, 45; Rom 4:17; 8:11).

> The history of humanity thus appears to be divided into two great phases: that of the first creation, dominated by the *psychē*, and that of the eschatological creation, dominated by the *pneuma*. Adam and the risen Christ are the original representatives of the two respective phases: the "psychic" and the "pneumatic" body are their concrete manifestations.[60]

Furthermore, there is an inner union between the two bodies: the spiritual one is transformed in relation to the psychical. The transfigured or risen body, therefore, is not a denial of mortal flesh or of one's history but rather an affirmation that it surpasses what is both provisional and subject to compromise with evil. The earthly body is not evil, but perishable. The world down here is not ugly, although it is also true that merely in its beauty, it cannot satisfy human desire. In the resurrection, it is not a matter of overcoming something imperfect, but of the fulfillment of God's promise, his faithfulness.[61] Ratzinger writes in his *Introduction to Christianity*: "The biological has been overtaken by the spirit, by love, which is stronger than death. The barrier of death has been broken through and a definitive future opened up for man and world."[62]

It also seems pertinent to observe that "the resurrection is not more credible the more one tries to go beyond the body and its creaturely limit, but rather the more one learns to inhabit the body, grasping its complexity of experience."[63] By contemplating this experience, we can understand something of the risen body, precisely its aspect of the "already," sensing perhaps something of the "not yet," especially what comes from the relationships of love. The apostle Paul, despite his efforts to understand and explain the resurrection, is very prudent, emphasizing that we are speaking of a mystery. In the range of his affirmations about the resurrection, the decisive one is that "we shall all be changed" (1 Cor 15:51).

---

60. Teani, "Contributo di Paolo," 179.
61. Cozzi, "Ripensare la resurrezione," 51–52.
62. Ratzinger, *Introduction to Christianity*, 259.
63. Cozzi, "Ripensare la resurrezione," 59.

THE QUESTION OF LANGUAGE

There is another dimension important for the reflection on the risen body and on eschatological realities in general: the issue of language and its hermeneutics. More precisely, it is necessary to reflect on the relationship between "linguistic expressive form, image, or mode of expression," on the one hand, and "the real content, the concept, or the thing," on the other.[64] The importance of this distinction was already emphasized by Karl Rahner in his famous essay *The Hermeneutics of Eschatological Assertions* (1960). In eschatology, the expressive form is very important because it allows us to say something about eschatology and helps us to overcome eschatological agnosticism. But not only that, the expressive form is also a source of realism in that it makes it clear that when it is used, not everything has yet been expressed; there remains something more to be said. In this way, the expressive form embodies the fundamental logic of eschatology, the tension between "already and not yet." This fact, however, does not discredit concepts, nor render them superfluous. Indeed, the circularity between images and concepts must always be preserved. Images are descriptive, alive, but can also be ambiguous; concepts, on the other hand, are abstract, less immediate, but more precise.

Expressive forms in eschatology are mainly images and metaphors. They indicate what is nonconceptual yet necessary for the concept, which is always a *conversio ad phantasma*. The sensible dimension of knowing, in fact, prevents access to the thing, separated from the image. This fact is very well observed in Scripture. The Bible offers us representative eschatological schemes that are different from reality. The last trumpet that will announce the end of the world denotes the solemnity of the coming of the eschaton (1 Cor 15:53; 1 Thess 4:16); the fire of hell is the image of the ultimate experience of sorrow for a life that has brought no fruits of love and communion with anyone and anything (Matt 25:41; Mark 9:48), and so on. Furthermore, in Scripture, different images are used to express the same reality, using, for example, heaven, paradise, wedding, banquet, and the new Jerusalem to describe eternal life.

This is even more true for metaphors, the figurative language that, rather than explaining, creates links and entire networks of meanings within which the content, including the eschatological one, can be understood. Today we can often find the conviction that the resurrection of the body is a metaphor. Not in the sense that it says nothing concrete

---

64. Ziegenaus, *Futuro della creazione*, 32.

or true about life beyond death, but because it is the "way of saying the truth non-descriptively. . . . The boundaries of metaphors are not clearly delineated, so that their message often overlaps or even becomes confused and difficult to systematize—or rather can be systematized in a *sui generis* framework, such as that of theology and particularly eschatology."[65]

The linguistic form of expression can be understood as much as one allows themself to be involved in the event inaugurated by Jesus Christ. Since full involvement will only be realized at the end of history, it is clear that in the historical dimension, it can never be exhausted. In the meantime, that is, until the eschatological consumption of the world, theology's task is to find the inner unity between representative schemes and reality.[66] And this is true above all when we are speaking about the resurrection.

THREE DIMENSIONS OF RESURRECTION

In the perspective we exposed, it seems reasonable to speak of three dimensions of the resurrection: the personal, the social or communal, and the cosmic.

On a *personal* level the resurrection of the body means that because of the resurrection, the personal history of the individual is not doomed to disappear in death, because in the resurrection God offers us a new life, which is not completely other, but different, transformed and yet, overall, my own life. Eternal life after the resurrection is thus a continuation of my history, of the relationships I have lived on earth, in my body, but now they no longer have the character of a "way," because in death we reach the goal of our earthly journey. The resurrection as salvation is no longer an offer that allows for a positive or negative response, but is the beginning of a new life for a person in all their dimensions, in which they have been striving to love their whole life, through the power of grace. The whole history of the individual is saved from death—in the moral sense from sin, in the personal sense from corruption—because he or she is received into communion with God in the power of the Holy Spirit.

One could say that the difference between the earthly and the resurrected body is the difference between historicity, in which decisions can be made, and definitiveness, in which decisions can no longer be made. Any attempt to define the resurrected body differently—in a biological or physical sense—seems unjustified. The resurrected body of

---

65. Nitrola, *Trattato di escatologia*, 2:330.
66. Nitrola, *Trattato di escatologia*, 1:246.

Jesus Christ again testifies to this. In his apparitions, the disciples did not recognize him immediately, but rather from his acts of love, that is, those acts which he had embodied in his earthly history. Therefore, it is legitimate to affirm that the dead and the risen are the same person, the guarantee of which is our immortal soul.[67]

The resurrection also has a *social* dimension. In dogmatics, we say that the resurrection will take place on the last day of history, i.e., it will take place for all people at the same time. The only exception is Christ, the firstborn of the resurrected (the Virgin Mary is said to have been "taken up body and soul to the glory of heaven").[68] The resurrection has a social character because our history is shaped in the tension between past and future, and in our relationships with our neighbors. Every human being is part of humanity, precisely through his or her corporeality. This is directly evident in the relationships with our parents, but in reality, since we belong to humanity, we are connected to everyone who lives, has lived, and will live, at any time and any place on earth.

But it is also true that our mortal, earthly body does not allow us to live relationships directly. On the one hand, the body is a mirror of the soul, reflecting our inner world—of course, to a certain extent, we can also conceal this inner world. We say that we put on masks; that we do not live authentically; that we define our attitudes according to situations and conditions; that we define their depth because we want to protect ourselves or manipulate our neighbors; and this is the consequence of our mortality. We could rightly say that the body, through mortality, is the last frontier in our relationships. In the resurrection, in a life that is no longer subject to death, this will no longer be necessary, but everyone will be in a deeply personal relationship with everyone else. Nothing will be hidden or unexpressed. The resurrected body will express fully our identity, which has been formed in the relationships with our neighbors, but also with all of humanity. Resurrection on the last day is not just a solemn last chord of history, which is shared by all, but is the consequence of our social nature. If we want to be exact, we cannot speak of the resurrection

---

67. Ruiz de la Peña, *Teologia dell'aldilà*, 213–27.

68. Pius XII, *Munificentissimus Deus* (DH 3902). The dogmatic definition of the assumption expressly refrained from affirming the death of Mary as a truth to be believed, which in the mid-twentieth century was a real theological controversy, despite the fact that tradition up to modern times as well as the liturgy have affirmed Mary's death, thereby guaranteeing both the full humanity of Mary and the truth of Christ's incarnation with all the consequences, including death. See also John of Damascus, *Hom. 2 in Dormitionem* (PG 96:743); Germanus of Constantinople, *Hom. 1 in Dormitionem* (PG 98:345C).

of each individual, but of one resurrection of humanity, which means the resurrection of each individual in relation to all.[69]

The last dimension of the resurrection is the *cosmic* one. The article of the creed about a new heaven and a new earth (2 Pet 3:13; Rev 21:1) is not a symbolic addition, but an expression of the truth that the rest of creation also shares in the resurrection, i.e., in its eschatological fulfillment. Obviously, when we are considering biblical texts, we have to take into account their literary genre (e.g., apocalypse) and what we have said about the figurative language that is one of its favorite tools. It means that trying to describe the future world in detail, to draw a map of it, would be to fall into the trap of apocalypticism, which has nothing to do with canonical biblical apocalypticism and our faith that the new creation will mean both the continuation of the first and its transformation by God. First, because apocalypticism does not connect the future to the present, the world to come is therefore a completely new reality; and second, because such an approach fails to take into account that the new creation is part of the infinite mystery of God, which we can only approach and can never fully grasp. *Gaudium et Spes* in fact soberly declares: "We do not know the time for the consummation of the earth and of humanity, nor do we know how all things will be transformed."[70]

Christian eschatology connects the fulfillment of the world to the fulfillment of the human being who himself is a part of the world. This anthropocentric view, under the influence of both the natural sciences (particularly astronomy and astrophysics) and modern culture, is today reformulated by some theologians. For them, it is partly true that the world finds its fulfillment in humanity as it is integrated into the process of human development. It does not, however, exhaustively account for the reality understood as the world. In their view, we cannot exclude the direct relationship between God and the world, which, therefore, it is not necessarily mediated by humanity.[71]

Today, such a view is presented as a way to overcome the anthropocentrism that is seen as the main cause for the current ecological crisis, brought about precisely by the understanding of the human being as the center and absolute owner of the rest of creation.[72] This view, which has been easy to take, nevertheless does not reflect the genuine sense of the biblical text on God's mandate to humanity (Gen 1:28). The human

---

69. Bordoni and Ciola, *Gesù nostra speranza*, 243–44.
70. Second Vatican Council, *Gaudium et Spes* §39.
71. Moltmann, *Coming of God*; "Cosmos and Theosis"; Russell, *Cosmology*.
72. White, "Roots of Ecological Crisis."

being is given a mission to govern the rest of creation as the image of God, i.e., as God governs it: caring for it and willing to bring it to its fulfillment. Human beings are in constant, active dialogue with the world in which they live, and this world, especially through work, also shapes the person's identity and likeness to God, who, in his creative activity, calls into being all things. If this is so, the resurrection of the body must also be linked to the transformation of all that is nonhuman, which has shaped the history of the individual and of humanity. This teaching is close to that of Paul in the Letter to the Romans: "Creation still retains the hope of being freed, like us, from its slavery to decadence, to enjoy the same freedom and glory as the children of God" (8:20–21).

Taking in account this fact, we must believe that it is absolutely necessary for the entire cosmic reality to partake in the renewal carried out by God in the new creation. Otherwise, a part of it would not be saved. Furthermore, the final renewal of the cosmos

> does not oblige us to deduce that the historical/salvific economy of humanity and the temporal history of the entire universe are marked by the same clock in terms of physical cosmology. Nor are we obliged to believe that the end of humanity's history on our planet should coincide with the general transfiguration of the whole cosmos, in the sense that the former is the cause of the latter.[73]

Our faith requires us to accept three facts.

First, our material, physical world is finite and not eternal. "The universe and life, as we know them, are not suitable to exist forever. The law of thermodynamic irreversibility applies at both the physical and biological levels. However rich the dynamisms of the physical cosmos may be, matter will tend anyway to exhaust its transformations."[74]

Science supposes two possible ends for the material world: freeze or fry. Both of these scenarios deny any idea of eternal life. They do not take into account the transformation of the material world; they only claim its inevitable end. According to scientific data, it also seems that humanity will come to an end before the cosmos, either through a self-destructive act or as a result of a process that will no longer allow humans to live on earth, followed by the end of the cosmos after the general exhaustion of energy of the physical cosmos, most probably due to its irreversible thermodynamic degradation.

---

73. Tanzella-Nitti, *Scientific Perspectives*, 417.
74. Tanzella-Nitti, *Scientific Perspectives*, 424.

Second fact: the Christian faith concerning the end of human life on earth, the cosmos, and history, however, asserts that all this will be caused by God when he wills it, which cannot and will not be predicted by scientific knowledge or based on cosmological data. The history of creation will come to an end not only by God's intervention but also when he wills it to be fulfilled (see Mark 13:32–36). Our future does not escape from the hands of him who created all things out of nothing, having established the origin and the end of time by his free will and power, for he is Lord of all history.

Third fact: the end of the history of creation will furthermore be not only the end caused by God's intervention but also its fulfillment (Mark 13:32–36). The fullness in which we believe, and which also includes the cosmos, is the extension of Christ's resurrection over the entire cosmos.[75] This happens inevitably through humanity, which is irrevocably and fatally connected with creation precisely through the body. It is subject to the same laws as the nonhuman world. In this light, we must believe that our body, like the entire material world, was created capable of transfiguration, which is neither an annihilation nor a substitution. "The physical universe seems to contain seeds that only the rain of grace can bring to fruition. The overall image, as we shall see, is one of a universe capable of pointing beyond itself; a universe that guards promises that only God can fulfil."[76]

Conclusion

This reflection has shown that "resurrection" means more than that suggested by the terminology used to express this reality: to stand up, to rise again, that is, to renew the state in which one was before death.[77] And even though we speak of the resurrection of the dead—and it is clear that what is mortal is only the body, the flesh—resurrection means much more than restoring to the human being the material dimension as it was prior to death. This is because, holding to a long theological tradition, it must be emphasized that the life of the immortal soul that survives after the death of the individual cannot be considered the fulfillment that God envisaged for man and the world even before creation (Eph 1:3–10). The Christian faith in the resurrection expresses the certainty in God's promised fulfillment that surpasses all our expectations—for ourselves,

---

75. Second Vatican Council, *Gaudium et Spes* §§38–39.
76. Tanzella-Nitti, *Scientific Perspectives*, 425.
77. Gr. *egeirō, anistemi, anastasis*.

for humanity, and for the world. This expectation is neither gnostic—it does not concern the spirit alone, but rather humanity, incarnate beings with flesh vivified by the Spirit—nor can it be explained only materially, because humanity cannot be reduced to matter, nor we do know how matter will be transformed by the Spirit of God.

We can only say that to rise from the dead means to attain the definitive state, the fullness that is, on the one hand, the reward for the commitment of our freedom in this life to respond to God and neighbor with love, and on the other hand, above all, the gift of grace, of the superabundant and transforming love of God the Father who wants everyone and everything to share in the destiny of the Risen Christ, in the transforming power of the Spirit. The resurrection of Christ is the fundamental datum that in every age gives the answer to the question: "What does it mean to rise from the dead?" (Mark 9:10). It testifies to vital communion, to the victory of love over every plague of division, sin, and corruption. It is, therefore, the answer to the deepest thirst of every human heart, namely, the thirst for meaning, security, peace, justice, and the love of one created in God's image, and which can only reach its ultimate goal in the communion of the Triune God, in which lives forever the humanity of the Second Person of the Trinity.

BIBLIOGRAPHY

Althaus, Paul. *Die letzten Dinge: Entwurf einer christlichen Eschatologie.* Gütersloh: Bertelsmann, 1922.

———. "Retraktatzionen zur Eschatologie." *TLZ* 75 (1950) 253–60.

Aquinas, Thomas. *Summa Contra Gentiles.* Aquinas Institute, n.d. https://aquinas.cc/la/en/~SCG1.

———. *Summa Theologiae: Prima Pars, 1–49.* Translated by Laurence Shapcote. 2nd ed. Latin-English Opera Omnia. Green Bay, WI: Aquinas Institute, 2017.

Benedict XVI. *The Infancy Narratives.* Translated by Philip J. Whitmore. Vol. 3 of *Jesus of Nazareth.* New York: Random House, 2012.

———. *See also* Ratzinger, Joseph.

Bertuzzi, Giovanni. "L'immortalità dell'anima razionale nella dottrina di san Tommaso." *DivThom* 95 (1992) 145–56.

Boff, Leonardo. *La nostra resurrezione nella morte.* 2nd ed. Assisi: Cittadella, 1984.

Bordoni, Marcello, and Nicola Ciola. *Gesù nostra speranza: Saggio di escatologia in prospettiva trinitaria.* Bologna: EDB, 2000.

Collins, Raymond F. *First Corinthians.* SP 7. Collegeville, MN: Liturgical, 1999.

Congregation for the Doctrine of the Faith. "Decisions Regarding the Translation of the Phrase 'Carnis resurrectionem' in the Apostles' Creed (December 14, 1983)." *Notitiae* 20 (1984) 180–81.

Cozzi, Alberto. "Il linguaggio dogmatico delle figure della speranza." In *Delle cose ultime: La grazia del presente e il compimento del tempo*, edited by Massimo Epis, 141–86. Milan: Glossa, 2020.

———. "Ripensare la risurrezione e/o annunciare il risorto? L'attuale teologia della resurrezione tra istanze di ripensamento del significato culturale ed esigenze di una nuova fondazione della fede e della speranza cristiane." In *Ripensare la risurrezione*, edited by Francesco Scanziani, 3–80. Associazione teologica italiana. Milan: Glossa, 2010.

Cullmann, Oscar. *Immortality of the Soul or Resurrection of the Dead? The Witness of the New Testament*. London: Epworth, 1958.

Filoramo, Giovanni. *The History of Gnosticism*. Oxford: Basil Blackwell, 1990.

Francis. *Laudato Si*. Vatican City: Vaticana, 2015.

Gioia, Michele de. *La carne nell'eterno: L'escatologia presente come dono antropologico*. Intellectus fidei 2. Rome: Viverein, 2020.

Giudici, Amilcare. "Escatologia." In *Nuovo dizionario di teologia*, edited by Giuseppe Barbaglio and Severino Dianich, 382–411. Cinisello Balsamo, It.: San Paolo, 2000.

Greshake, Gisbert. *Vita più forte della morte: Sulla speranza cristiana*. Brescia: Queriniana, 2009.

Hoger Katechetisch Instituut (Nijmegen). *De nieuwe katechismus: Geloofsverkondiging voor volwassenen; De geloofsleer van de Rooms Katholieke kerk*. Antwerp: Brand Hilversum, 1966.

International Theological Commission. *Some Current Questions in Eschatology*. Vatican City: Vaticana, 1992.

Moltmann, Jürgen. *The Coming of God: Christian Eschatology*. London: SCM, 1996.

———. "Cosmos and Theosis: Eschatological Perspectives in the Future of the Universe." In *The Far-Future Universe: Eschatology from the Cosmic Perspective*, edited by G. F. Ellis, 249–65. Radnor, PA: Templeton Foundation, 2002.

Nitrola, Antonio. *Trattato di escatologia*. 2 vols. Cinisello Balsamo, It.: San Paolo, 2001, 2010.

Paul, André. *Immortalità o risurrezione: Affacciarsi oggi sull'oltrevita, fra utopia e fede*. Brescia: Queriniana, 2019.

Plato. *Complete Works*. Edited by John M. Cooper. Indianapolis: Hackett, 1997.

Rahner, Karl. "On Christian Dying." In *Further Theology of the Spiritual Life 1*, translated by David Bourke, 285–93. Theological Investigations 7. New York: Herder and Herder, 1971.

Ratzinger, Joseph. *Eschatology: Death and Eternal Life*. Translated by Michael Waldstein. Dogmatic Theology 9. Washington, DC: Catholic University of America Press, 1988.

———. *Introduction to Christianity*. Translated by J. R. Foster. Communio. New York: Herder and Herder, 1970.

———. Introduction to *Temi attuali di escatologia: Documenti, commenti e studi*, by Congregazione per la dottrina della fede, 9–17. Documenti e Studi 5. Vatican City: Vaticana, 2000.

———. See also Benedict XVI.

Ruiz de la Peña, Juan Luis. *L'altra dimensione. Escatologia cristiana*. 2nd ed. Torino: Borla, 1981.

———. *Teologia dell'aldilà: Escatologia cristiana*. Rome: Borla, 1988.

Russell, Robert John. *Cosmology: From Alpha to Omega; The Creative Mutual Interaction of Theology and Science*. Theology and the Sciences. Minneapolis: Fortress, 2008.

Second Vatican Council. "*Gaudium et Spes*: On the Church in the Modern World." Vatican, Dec. 7, 1965. https://www.vatican.va/archive/hist_councils/ii_vatican_council/documents/vat-ii_const_19651207_gaudium-et-spes_en.html.

Stange, Carl. *Die Unsterblichkeit der Seele*. Güterlsoh: Bertelsmann, 1925.

Tanzella-Nitti, Giuseppe. *Scientific Perspectives in Fundamental Theology: Understanding Christian Faith in the Age of Scientific Reason*. Claremont Studies in Science & Religion. Claremont, CA: Claremont, 2022.

Teani, Maurizio. "Il contributo di Paolo per ripensare corporeità e risurrezione." In *Ripensare la risurrezione*, edited by Francesco Scanziani, 163–93. Associazione teologica italiana. Milan: Glossa, 2010.

Vidal, Senén. *La risurrezione dei morti: Testimonianze bibliche*. Bologna: EDB, 2017.

White, Lynn, Jr. "The Historical Roots of Our Ecological Crisis." *Science*, n.s., 155 (1967) 1203–7.

Wolff, Hans Walter. *Die Anthropologie des Alten Testaments*. Munich: Gütersloher, 2010.

Ziegenaus, Antonio. *Il futuro della creazione: Eschatologia*. Vatican City: Lateran University Press, 2015.

www.ingramcontent.com/pod-product-compliance
Lightning Source LLC
Chambersburg PA
CBHW071246230426
43668CB00011B/1610